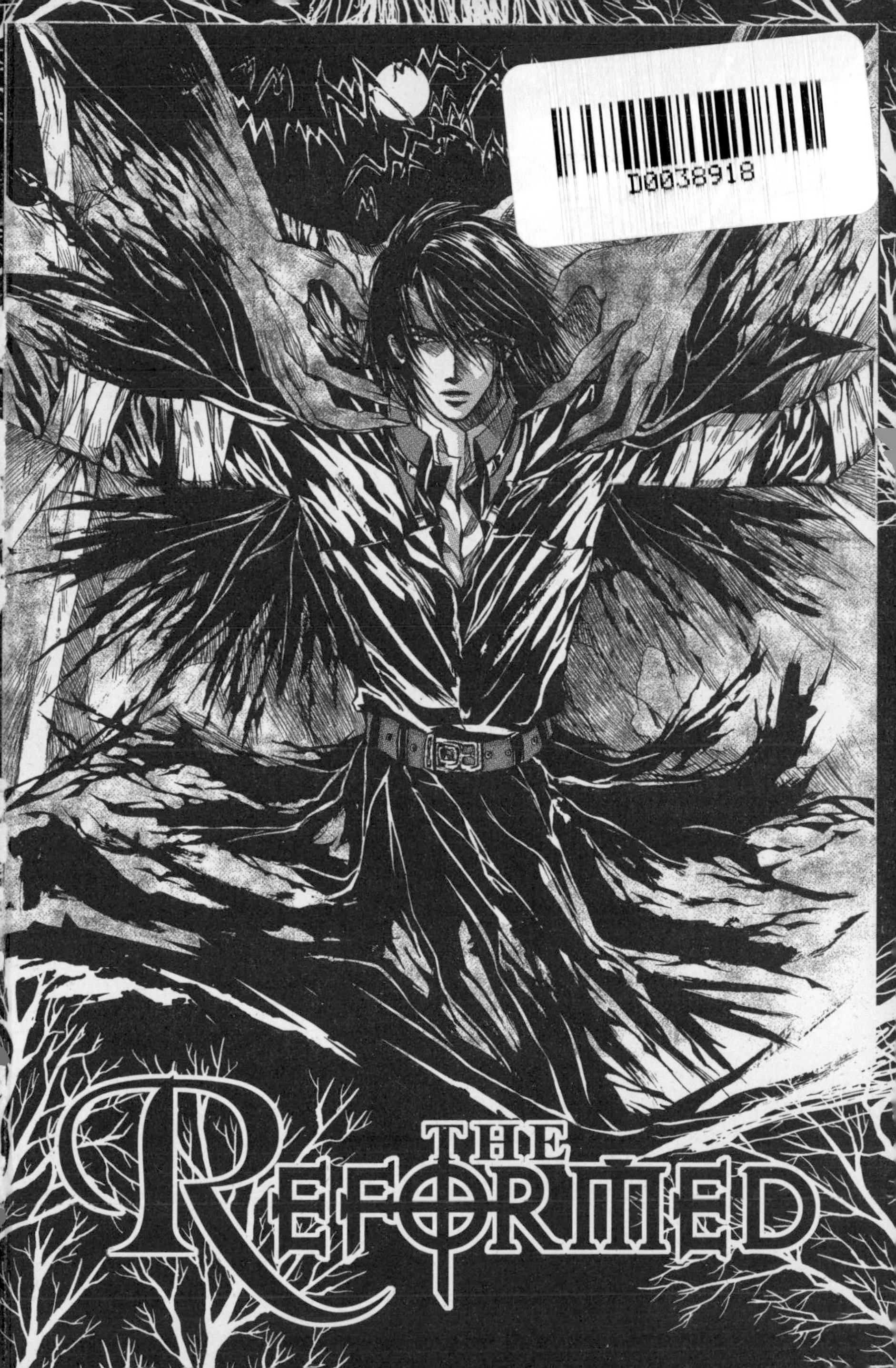
THE
REFORMED

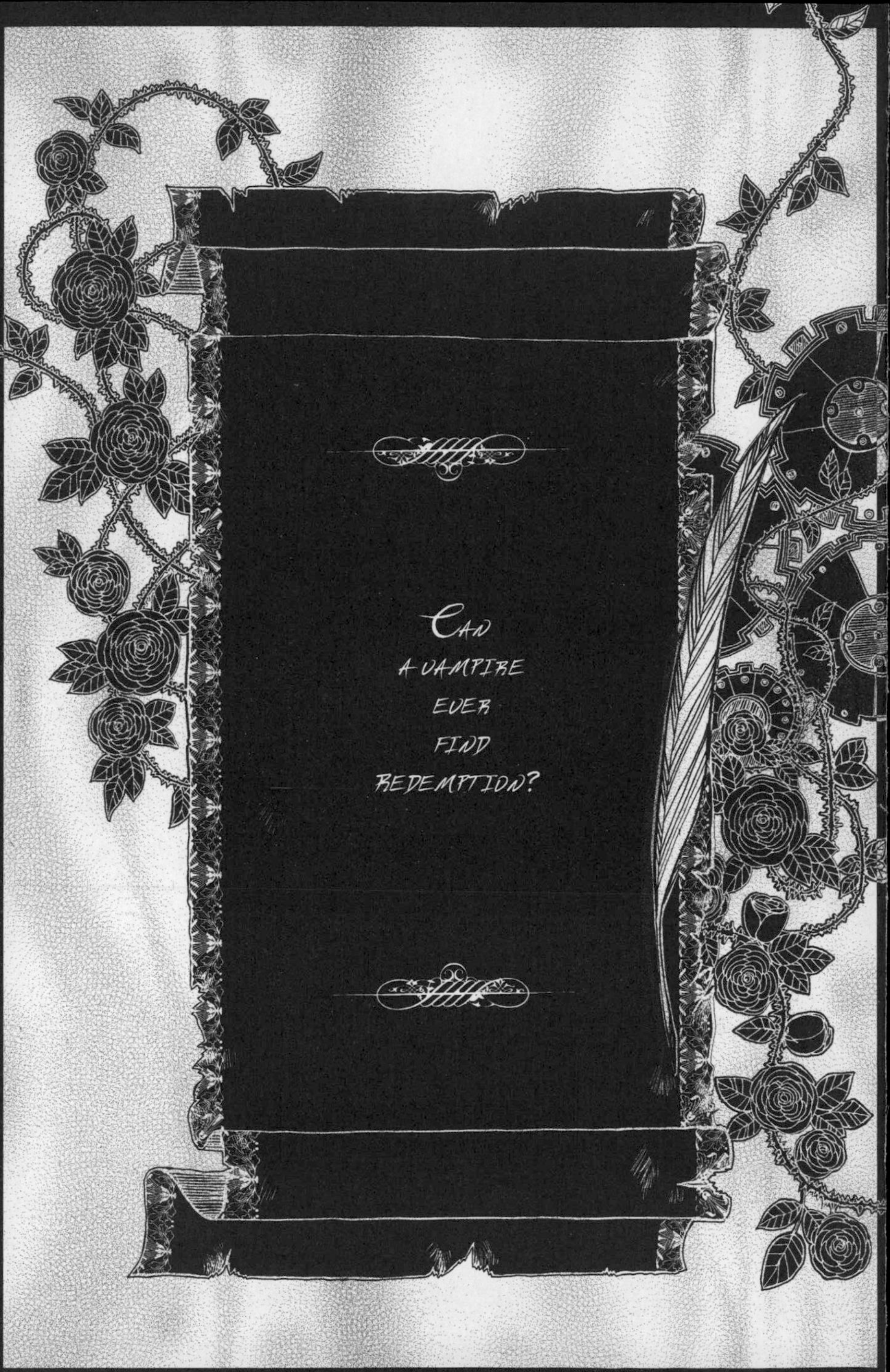
Can
a vampire
ever
find
redemption?

THE REFORMED

Story by Chris Hart
Manga by Anzu

Lettered by
Michaelis/Carpelis Design

BALLANTINE BOOKS • NEW YORK

The Reformed is a work of fiction. Names, characters, places, and incidents are the products of the author's imagination or are used fictitiously. Any resemblance to actual events, locales, or persons, living or dead, is entirely coincidental.

A Del Rey Trade Paperback Original

Published in the United States by Del Rey Books, an imprint of The Random House Publishing Group, a division of Random House, Inc., New York

Del Rey is a registered trademark and the Del Rey colophon is a trademark of Random House, Inc.

ISBN 978-0-345-49663-8

Printed in the United States of America

www. delreymanga.com

1 3 5 7 9 8 6 4 2

Lettering: Michaelis/Carpelis Design Assoc., Inc.

contents

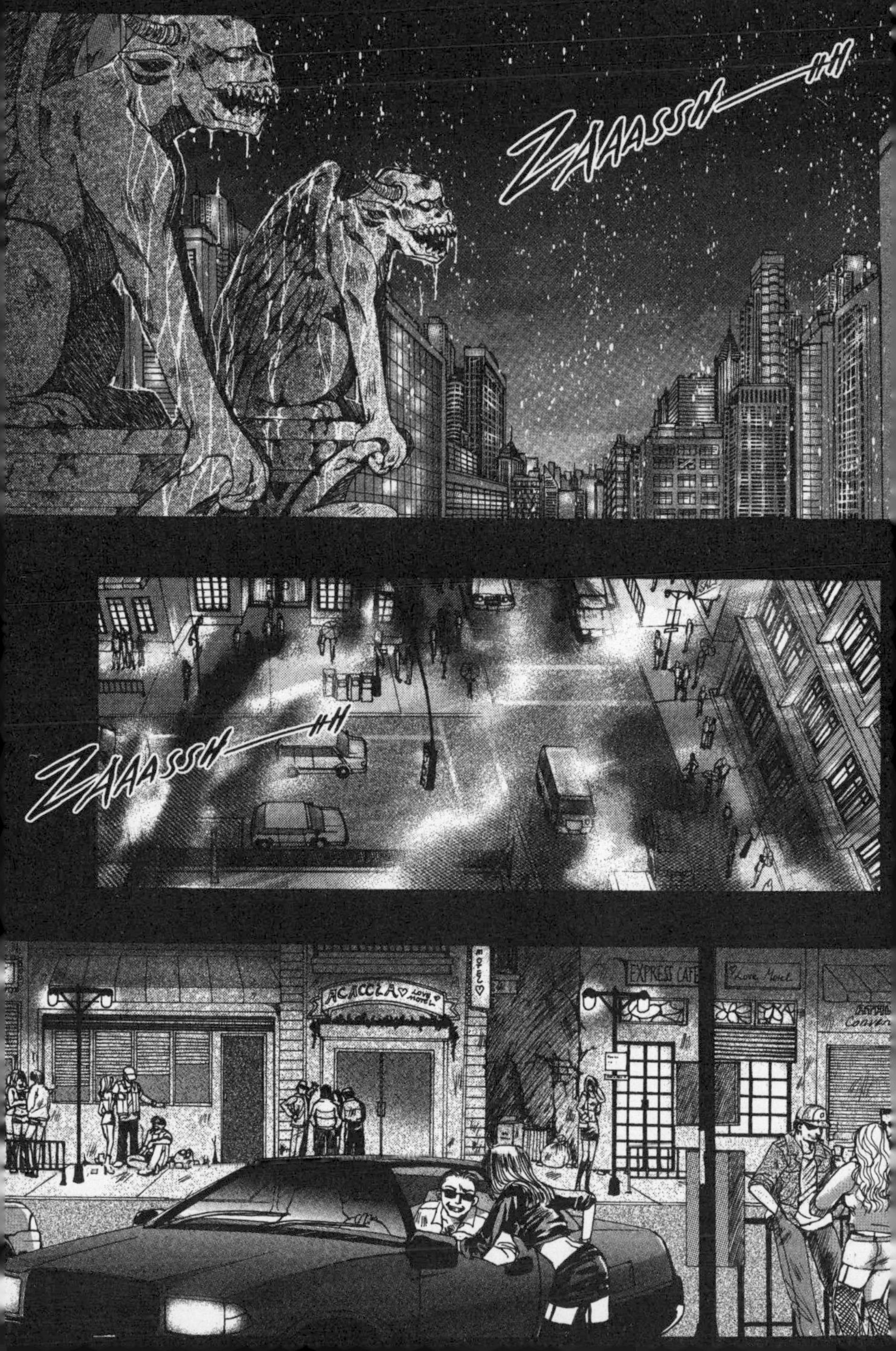
ZAAASSH——HH
ZAAASSH——HH
ACACCIA♡ LOVE MOTEL
MOTEL♡
EXPRESS CAFE
♡Love Motel

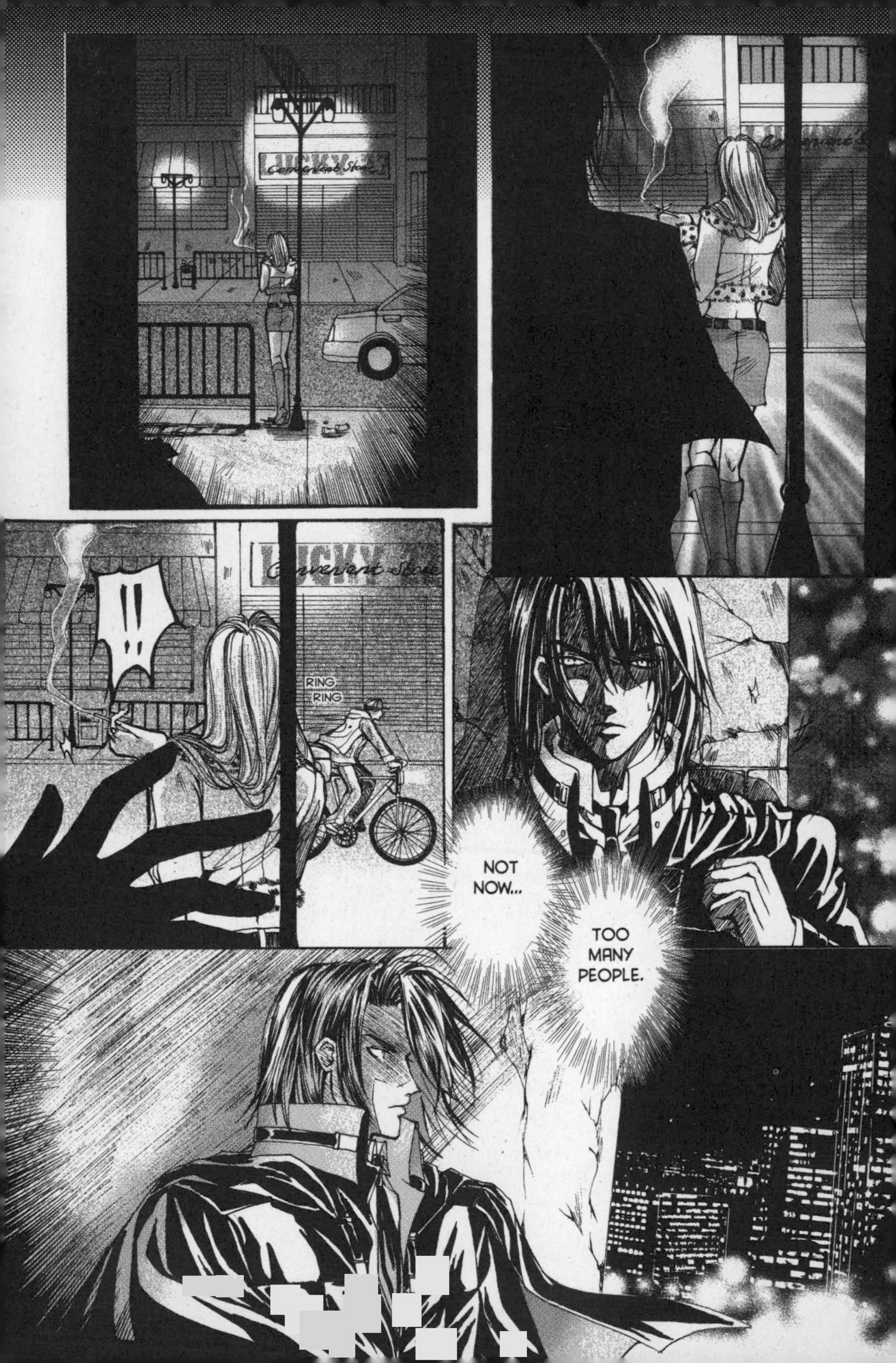
Convenient Store
LUCKY
Convenient Store
!!
RING
RING
NOT NOW...
TOO MANY PEOPLE.

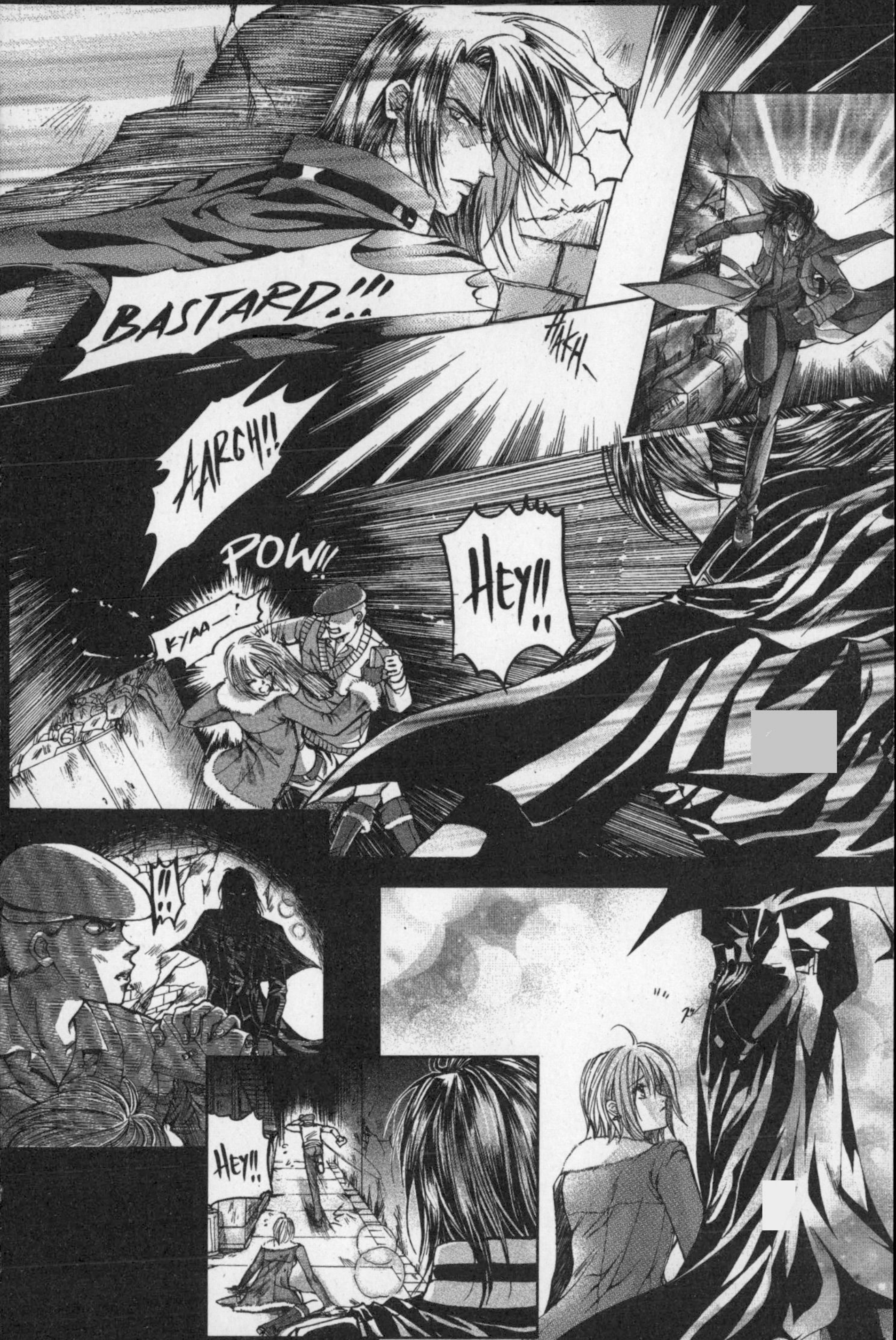
BASTARD!!!...
HAKH-
AARGH!!
POW!!
KYAA—!
HEY!!
!!
HEY!!

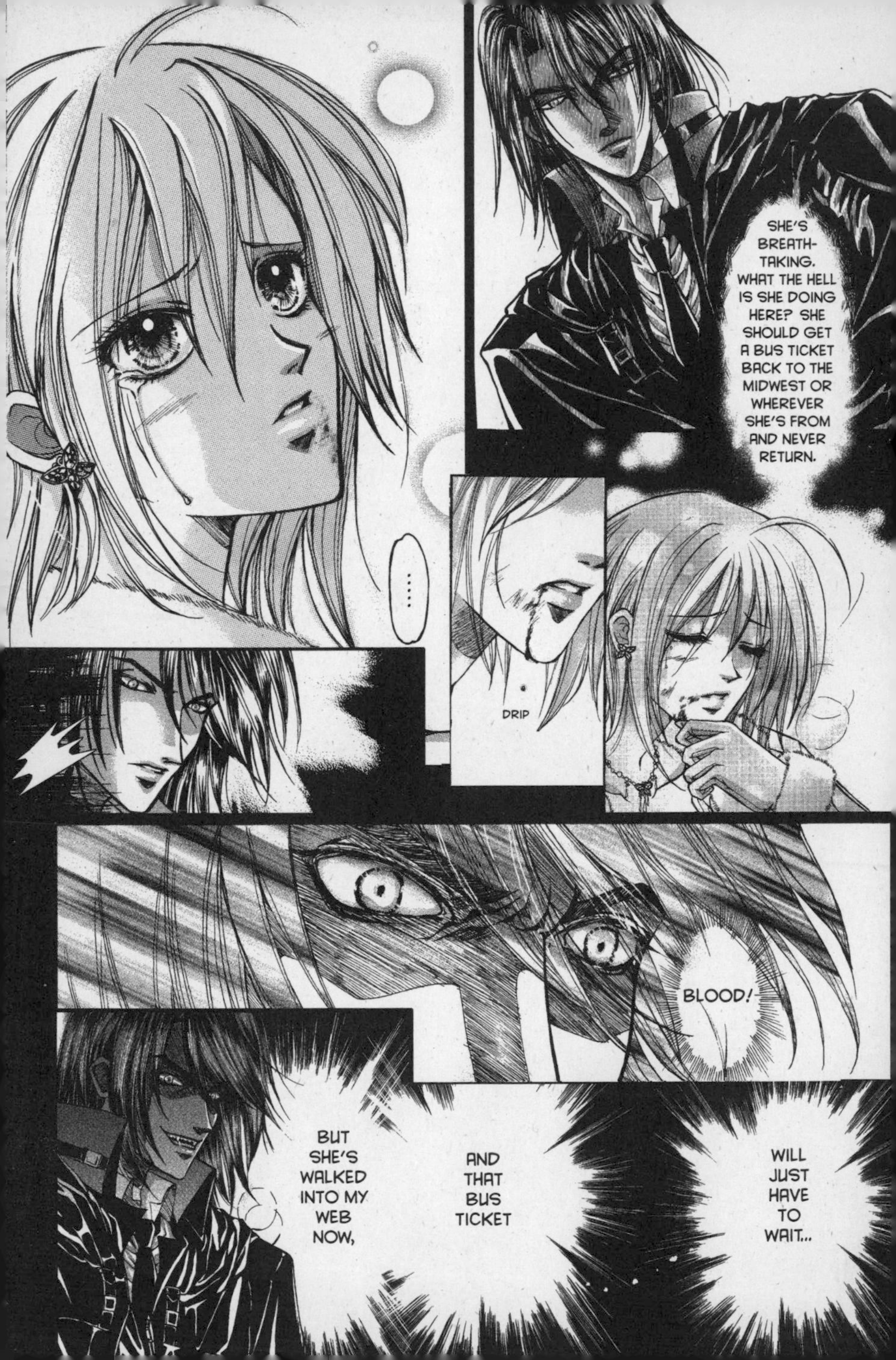
......
SHE'S BREATH-TAKING. WHAT THE HELL IS SHE DOING HERE? SHE SHOULD GET A BUS TICKET BACK TO THE MIDWEST OR WHEREVER SHE'S FROM AND NEVER RETURN.
DRIP
BLOOD!
BUT SHE'S WALKED INTO MY WEB NOW,
AND THAT BUS TICKET
WILL JUST HAVE TO WAIT...

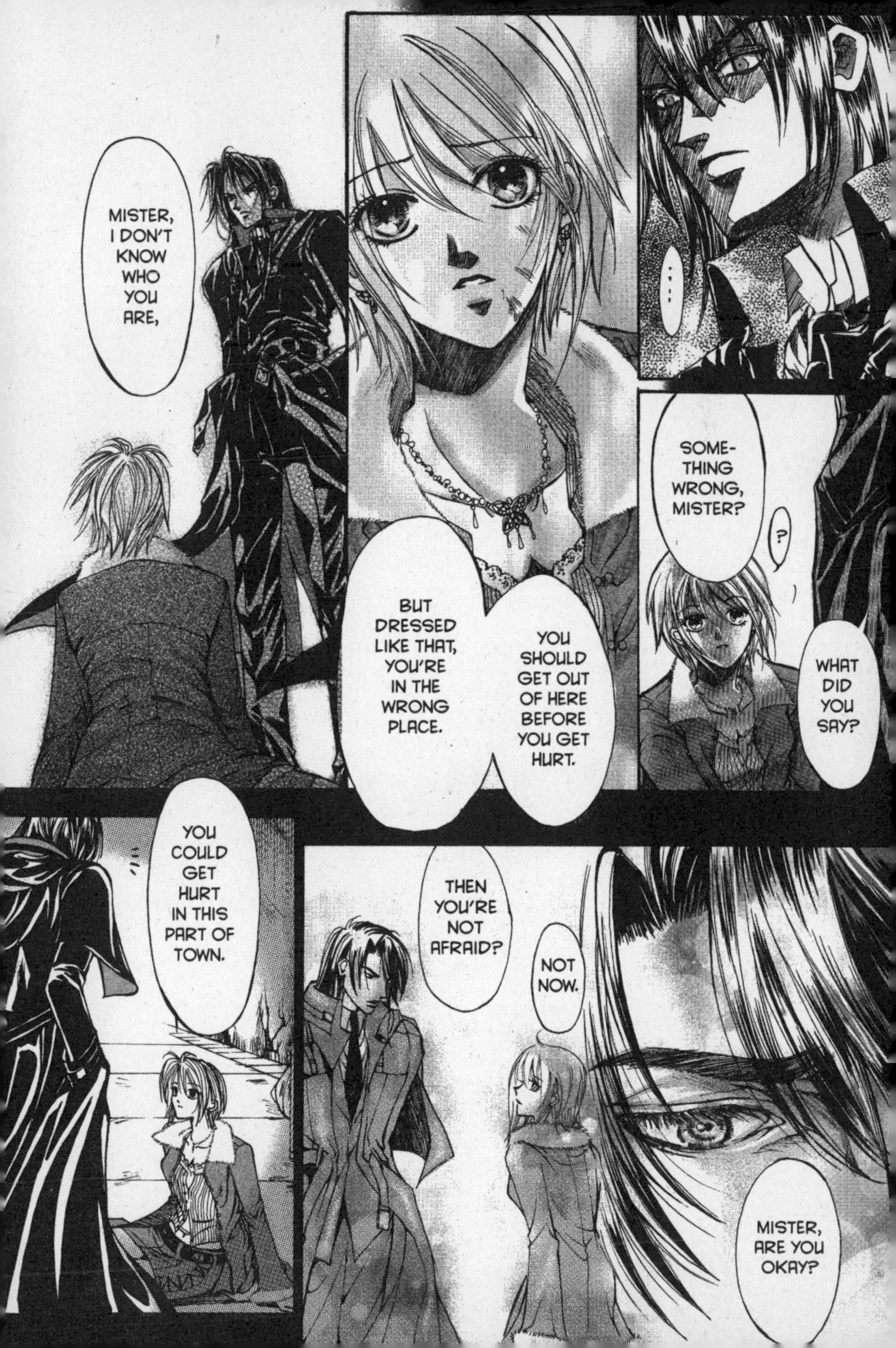
MISTER, I DON'T KNOW WHO YOU ARE,
BUT DRESSED LIKE THAT, YOU'RE IN THE WRONG PLACE.
YOU SHOULD GET OUT OF HERE BEFORE YOU GET HURT.
...
SOME-THING WRONG, MISTER?
?
WHAT DID YOU SAY?
YOU COULD GET HURT IN THIS PART OF TOWN.
THEN YOU'RE NOT AFRAID?
NOT NOW.
MISTER, ARE YOU OKAY?

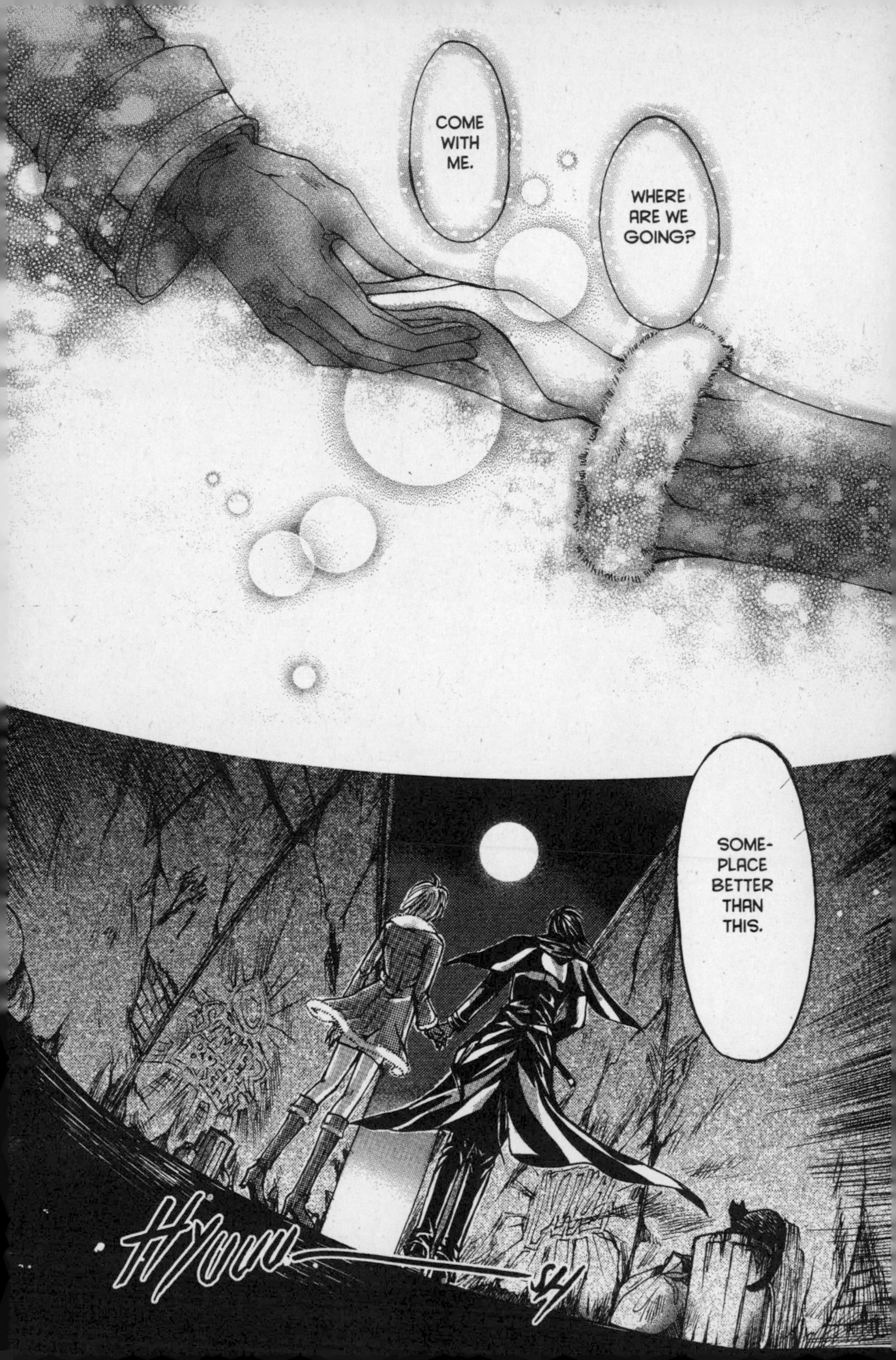
COME WITH ME.
WHERE ARE WE GOING?
SOME-PLACE BETTER THAN THIS.
Hyuuu

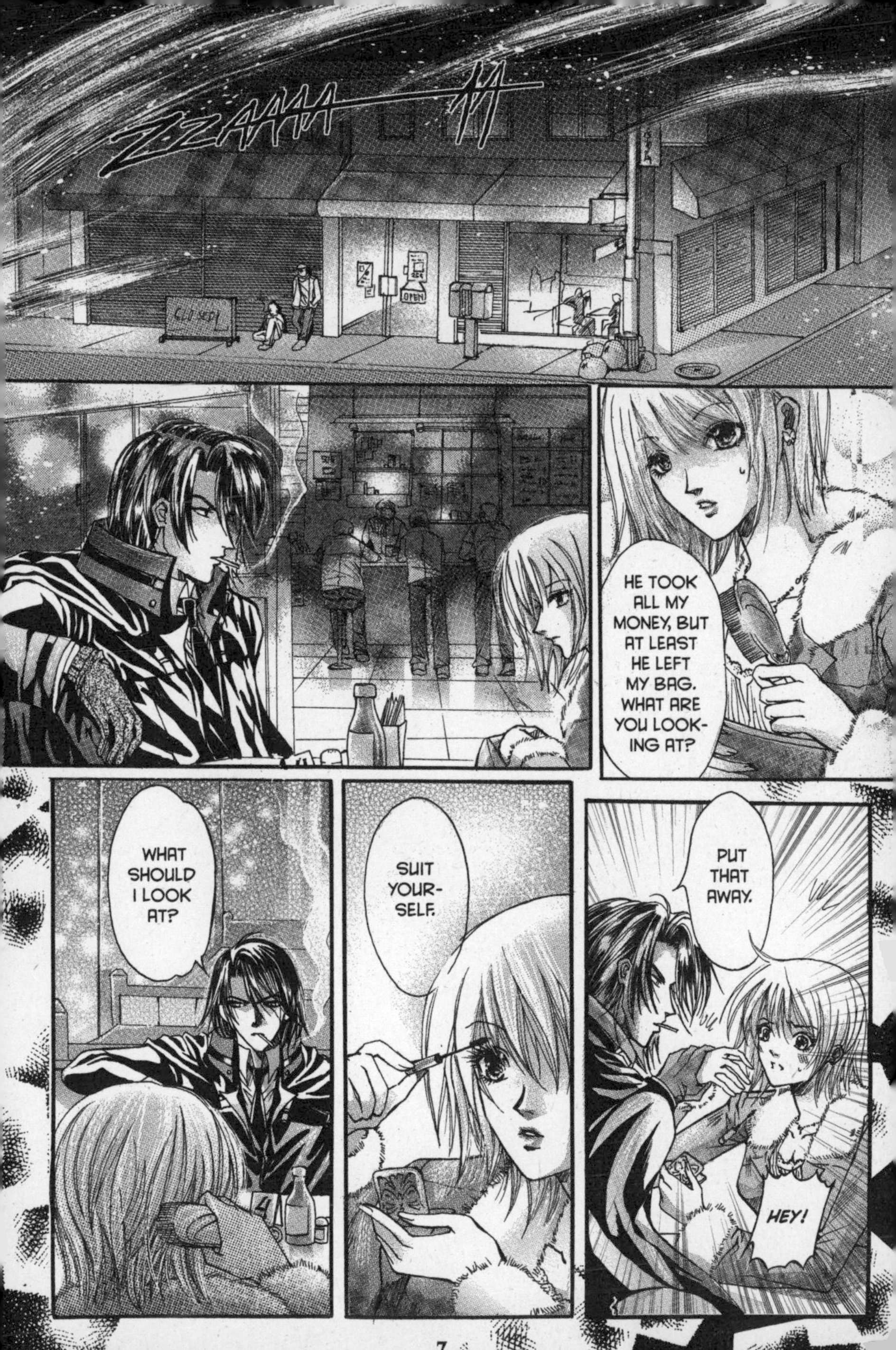
ZZAAAA—AA
CLOSED
OPEN
HE TOOK ALL MY MONEY, BUT AT LEAST HE LEFT MY BAG. WHAT ARE YOU LOOKING AT?
WHAT SHOULD I LOOK AT?
SUIT YOURSELF.
PUT THAT AWAY.
HEY!

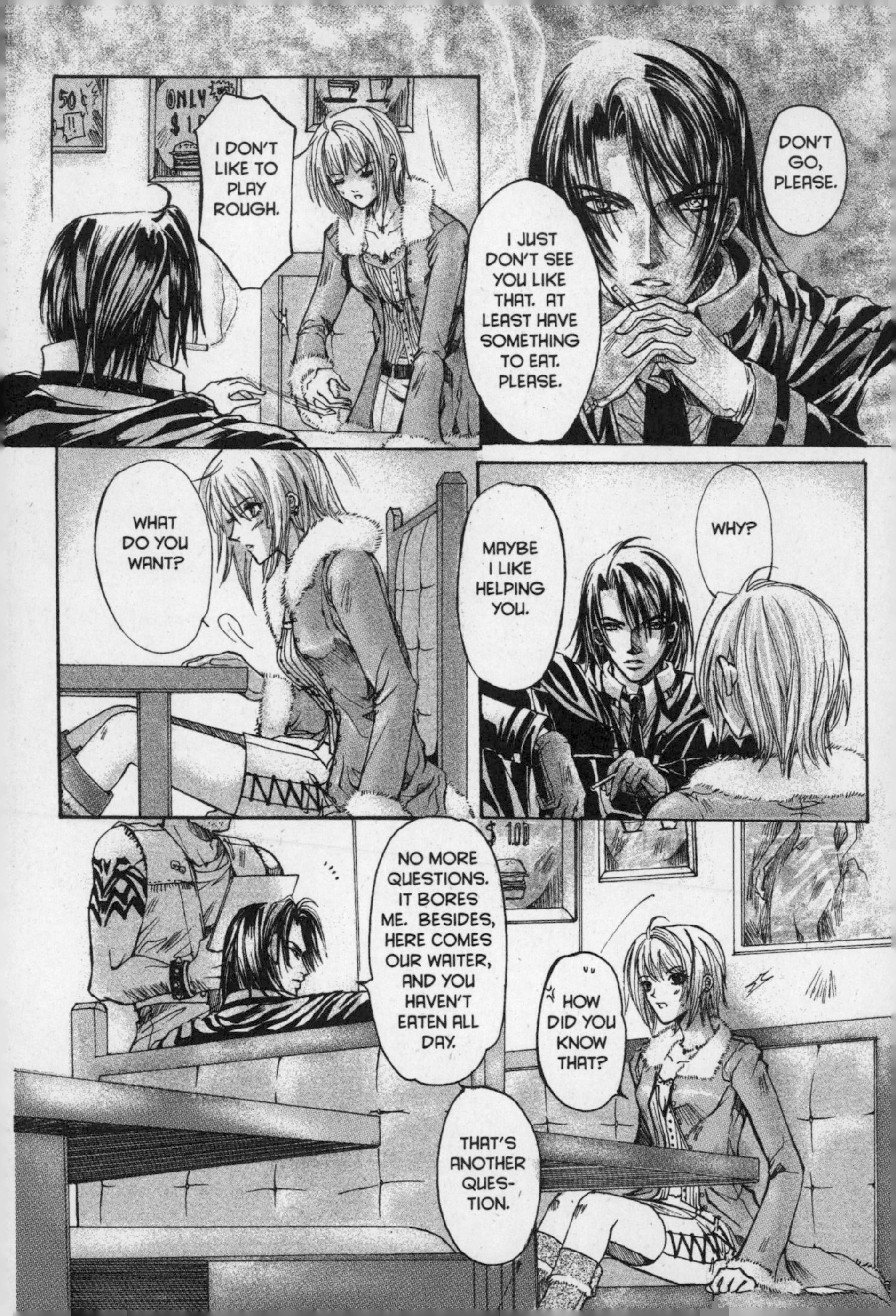
I DON'T LIKE TO PLAY ROUGH.
I JUST DON'T SEE YOU LIKE THAT. AT LEAST HAVE SOMETHING TO EAT. PLEASE.
DON'T GO, PLEASE.
WHAT DO YOU WANT?
WHY?
MAYBE I LIKE HELPING YOU.
NO MORE QUESTIONS. IT BORES ME. BESIDES, HERE COMES OUR WAITER, AND YOU HAVEN'T EATEN ALL DAY.
HOW DID YOU KNOW THAT?
THAT'S ANOTHER QUES-TION.

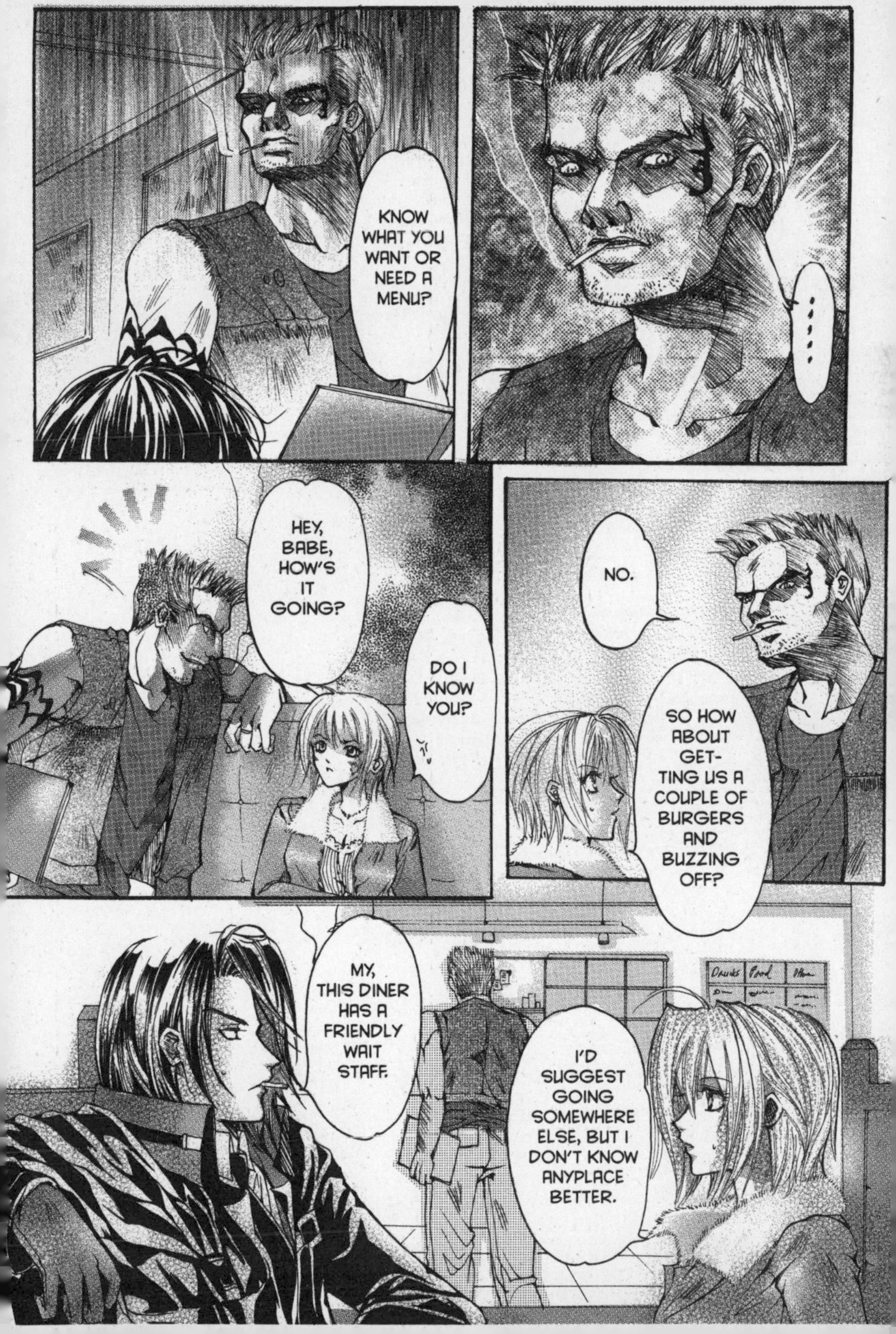

KNOW WHAT YOU WANT OR NEED A MENU?
.....
HEY, BABE, HOW'S IT GOING?
DO I KNOW YOU?
NO.
SO HOW ABOUT GET-TING US A COUPLE OF BURGERS AND BUZZING OFF?
MY, THIS DINER HAS A FRIENDLY WAIT STAFF.
I'D SUGGEST GOING SOMEWHERE ELSE, BUT I DON'T KNOW ANYPLACE BETTER.

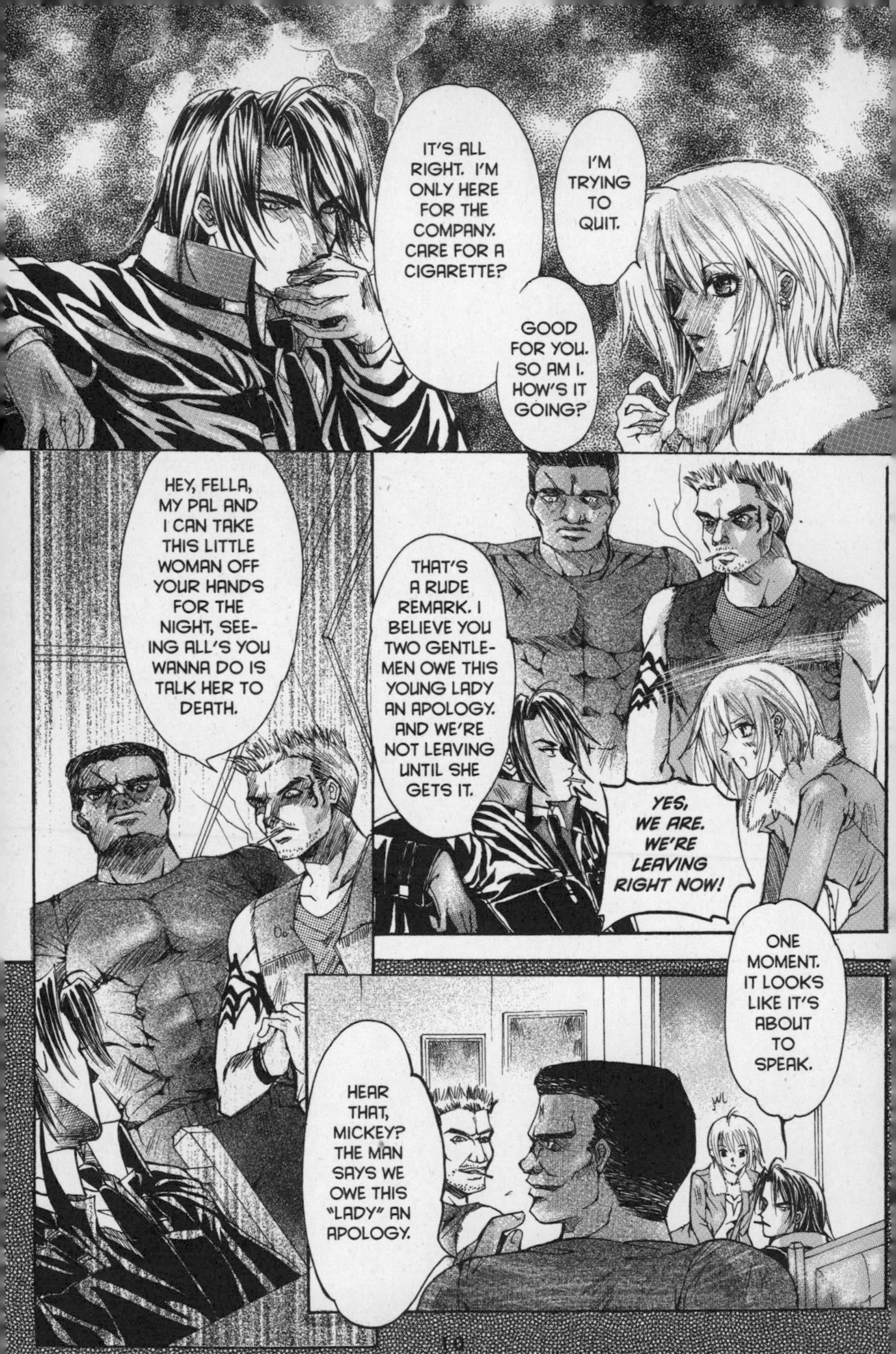
IT'S ALL RIGHT. I'M ONLY HERE FOR THE COMPANY. CARE FOR A CIGARETTE?
I'M TRYING TO QUIT.
GOOD FOR YOU. SO AM I. HOW'S IT GOING?
HEY, FELLA, MY PAL AND I CAN TAKE THIS LITTLE WOMAN OFF YOUR HANDS FOR THE NIGHT, SEE-ING ALL'S YOU WANNA DO IS TALK HER TO DEATH.
THAT'S A RUDE REMARK. I BELIEVE YOU TWO GENTLE-MEN OWE THIS YOUNG LADY AN APOLOGY. AND WE'RE NOT LEAVING UNTIL SHE GETS IT.
YES, WE ARE. WE'RE LEAVING RIGHT NOW!
ONE MOMENT. IT LOOKS LIKE IT'S ABOUT TO SPEAK.
HEAR THAT, MICKEY? THE MAN SAYS WE OWE THIS "LADY" AN APOLOGY.

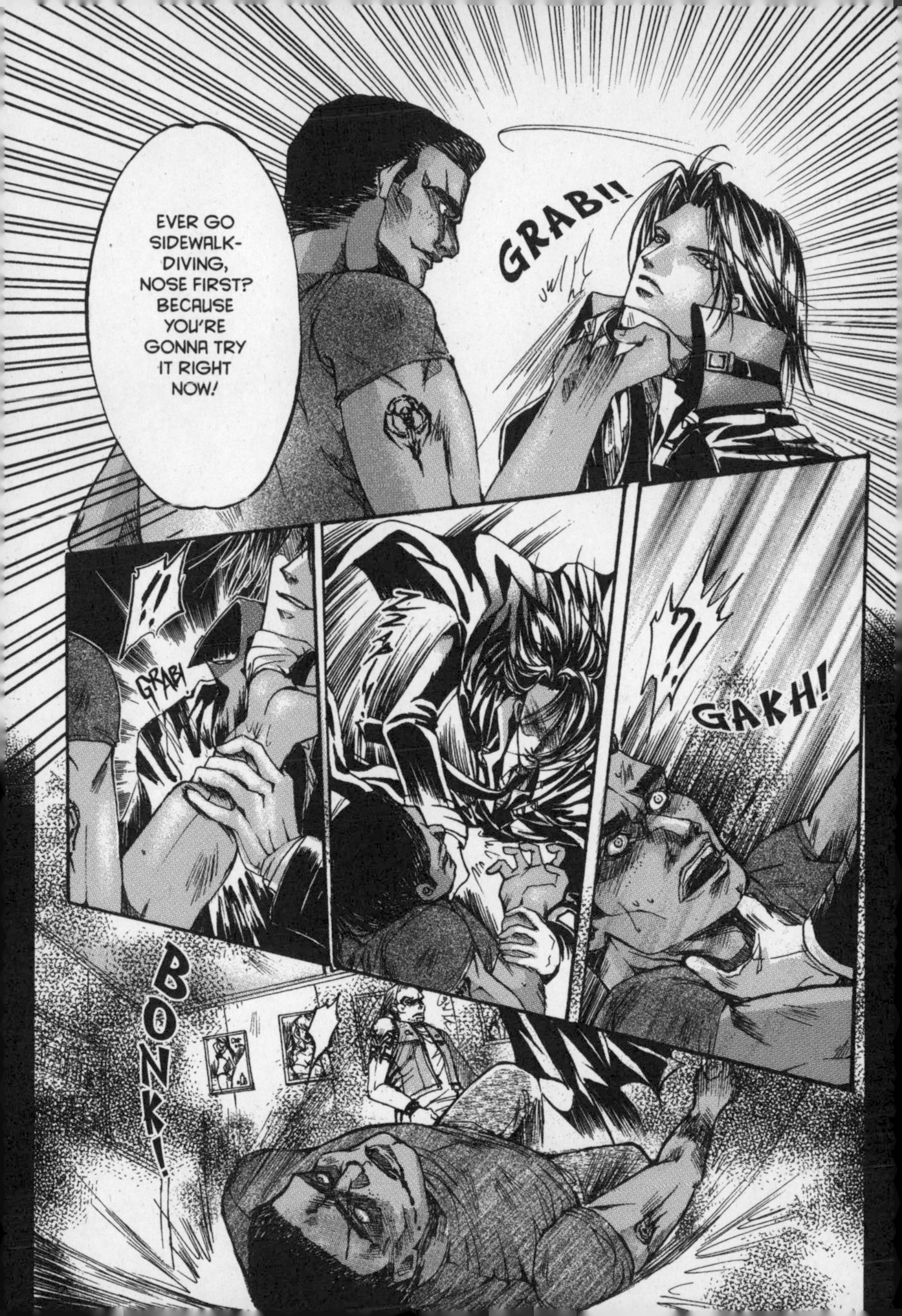
EVER GO SIDEWALK-DIVING, NOSE FIRST? BECAUSE YOU'RE GONNA TRY IT RIGHT NOW!
GRAB!!
!!
GRAB!
?!
GAKH!
BONK!

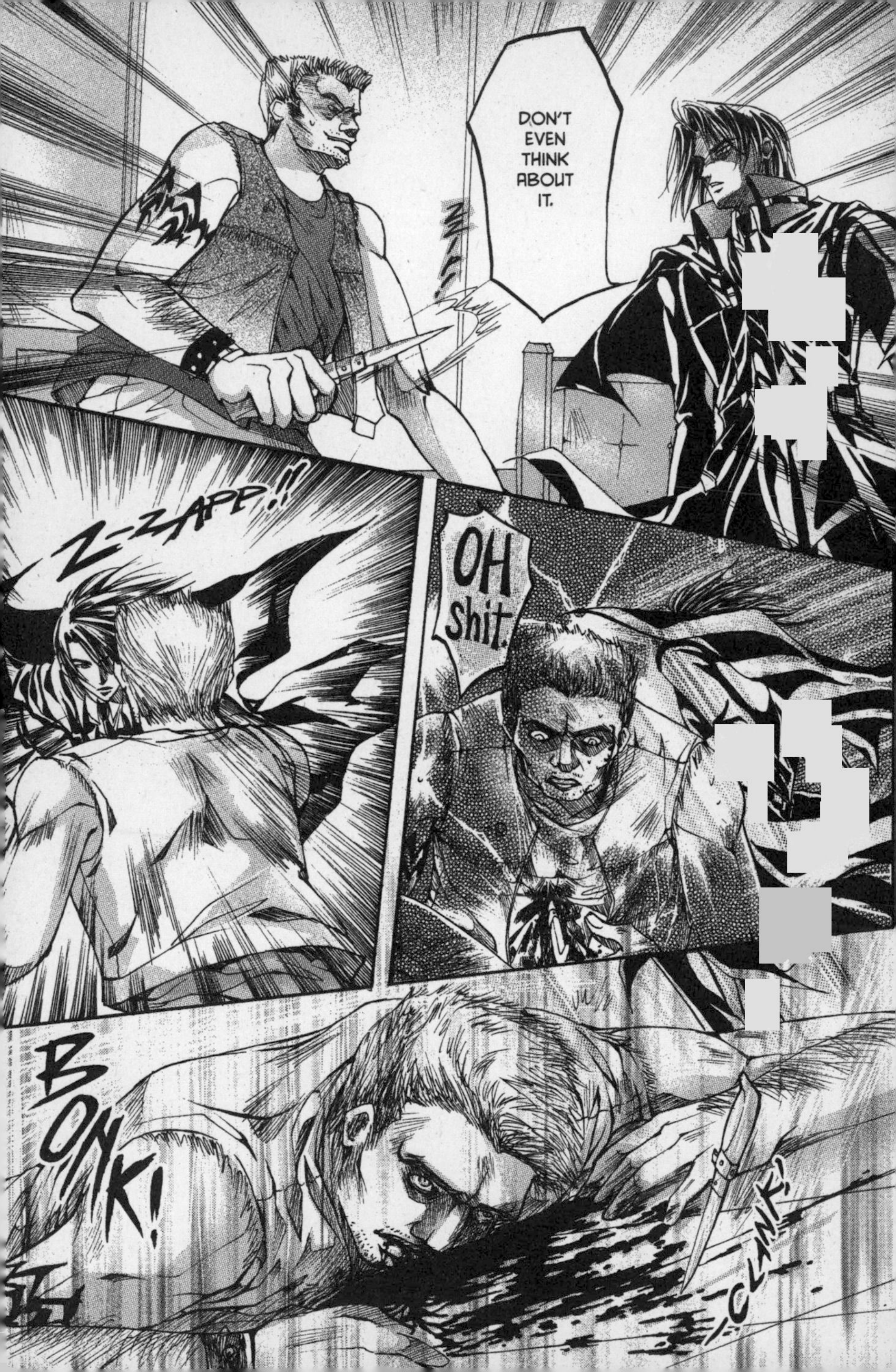
DON'T EVEN THINK ABOUT IT.
Z-ZAPP!!
OH shit.
BONK!
CLANK!

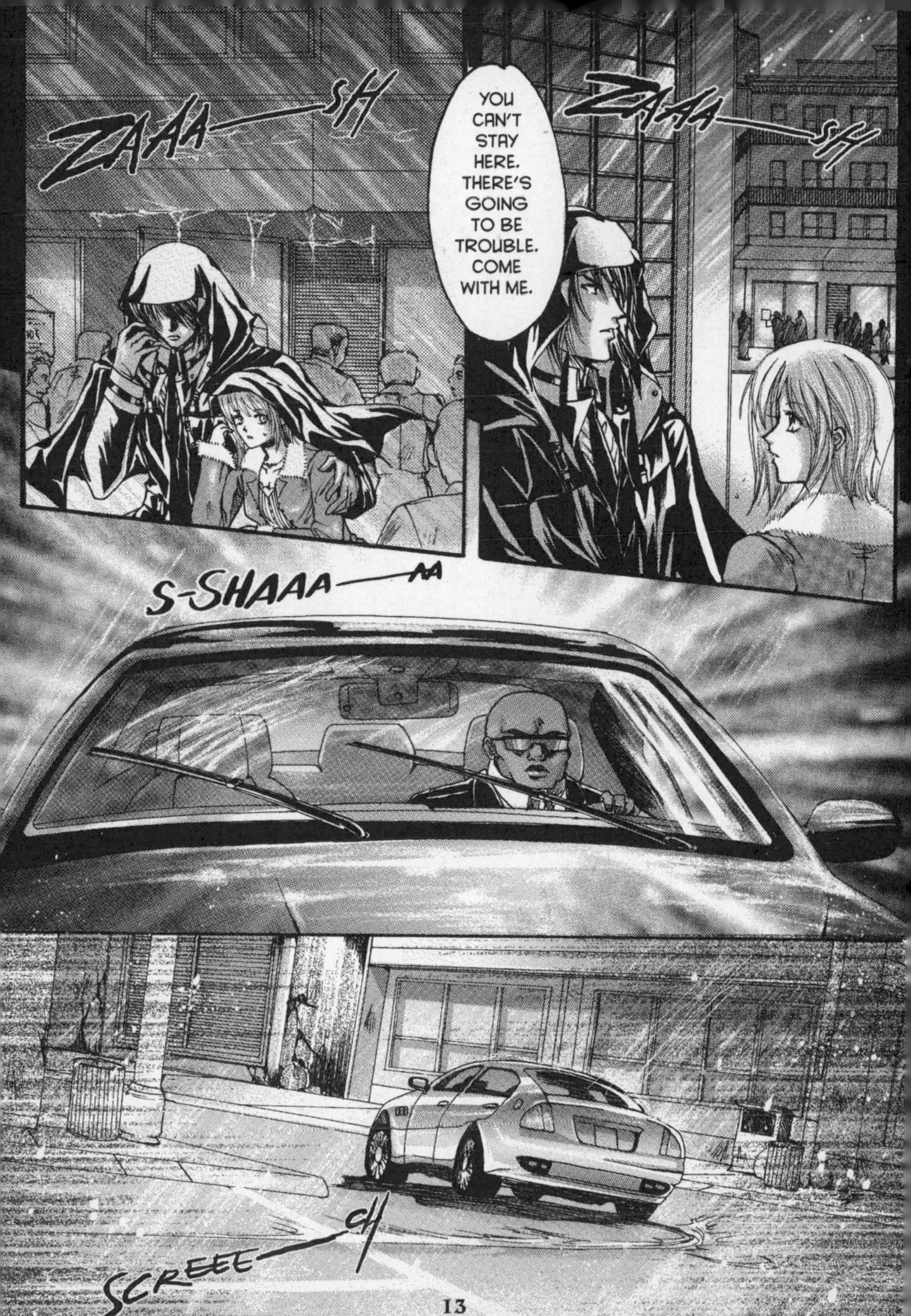

ZAAA—SH
YOU CAN'T STAY HERE. THERE'S GOING TO BE TROUBLE. COME WITH ME.
ZAAA—SH
S-SHAAA—AA
SCREEE—CH

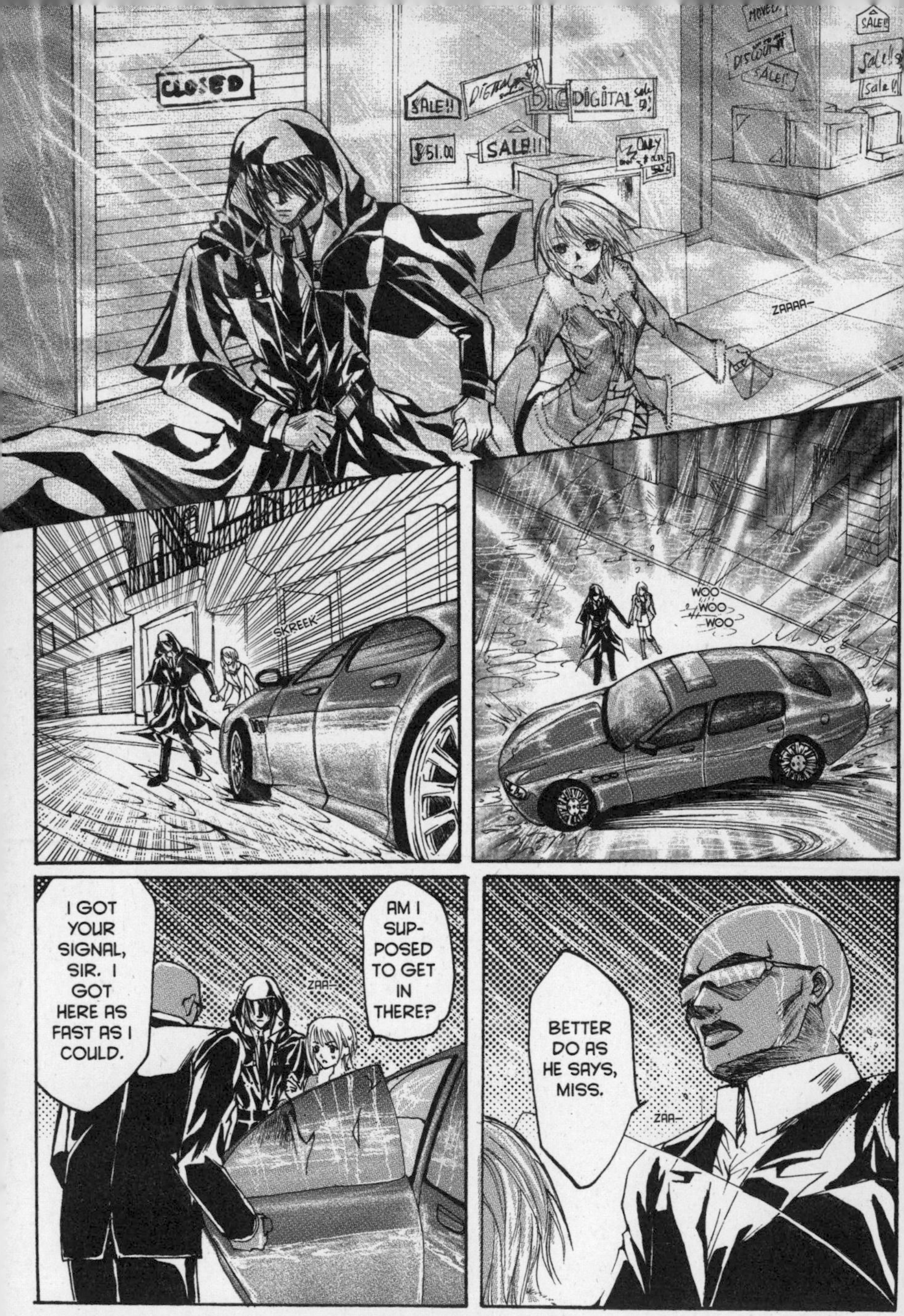
CLOSED
SALE!!
$51.00
SALE!!
DIGITAL
SALE!!
Sale!!
DISCOUNT
ZAAAA—
SKREEK
WOO
WOO
WOO
I GOT YOUR SIGNAL, SIR. I GOT HERE AS FAST AS I COULD.
ZAA—
AM I SUP-POSED TO GET IN THERE?
BETTER DO AS HE SAYS, MISS.
ZAA—

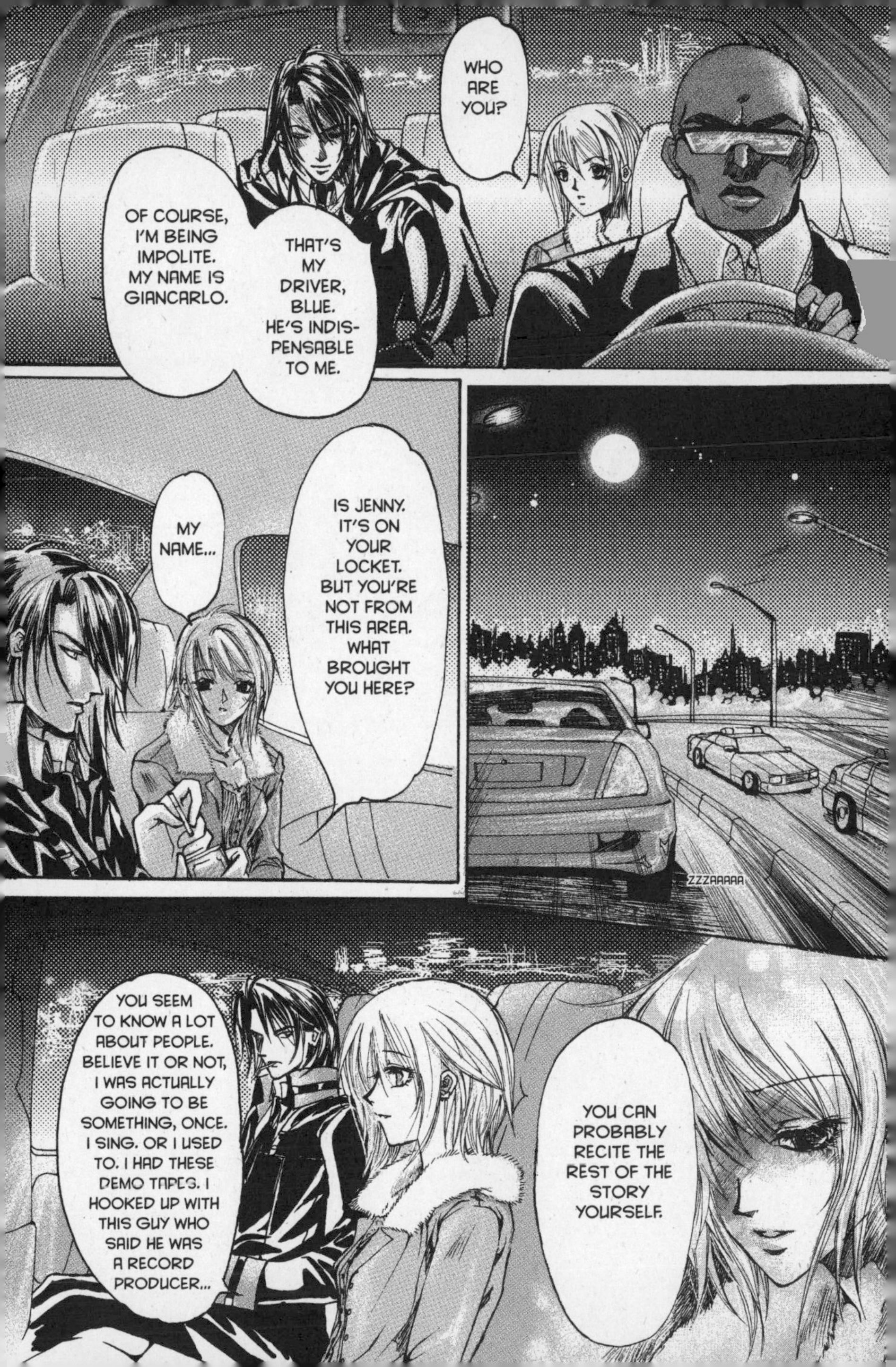
WHO ARE YOU?
OF COURSE, I'M BEING IMPOLITE. MY NAME IS GIANCARLO.
THAT'S MY DRIVER, BLUE. HE'S INDIS-PENSABLE TO ME.
MY NAME...
IS JENNY. IT'S ON YOUR LOCKET. BUT YOU'RE NOT FROM THIS AREA. WHAT BROUGHT YOU HERE?
ZZZAAAAA
YOU SEEM TO KNOW A LOT ABOUT PEOPLE. BELIEVE IT OR NOT, I WAS ACTUALLY GOING TO BE SOMETHING, ONCE. I SING. OR I USED TO. I HAD THESE DEMO TAPES. I HOOKED UP WITH THIS GUY WHO SAID HE WAS A RECORD PRODUCER...
YOU CAN PROBABLY RECITE THE REST OF THE STORY YOURSELF.

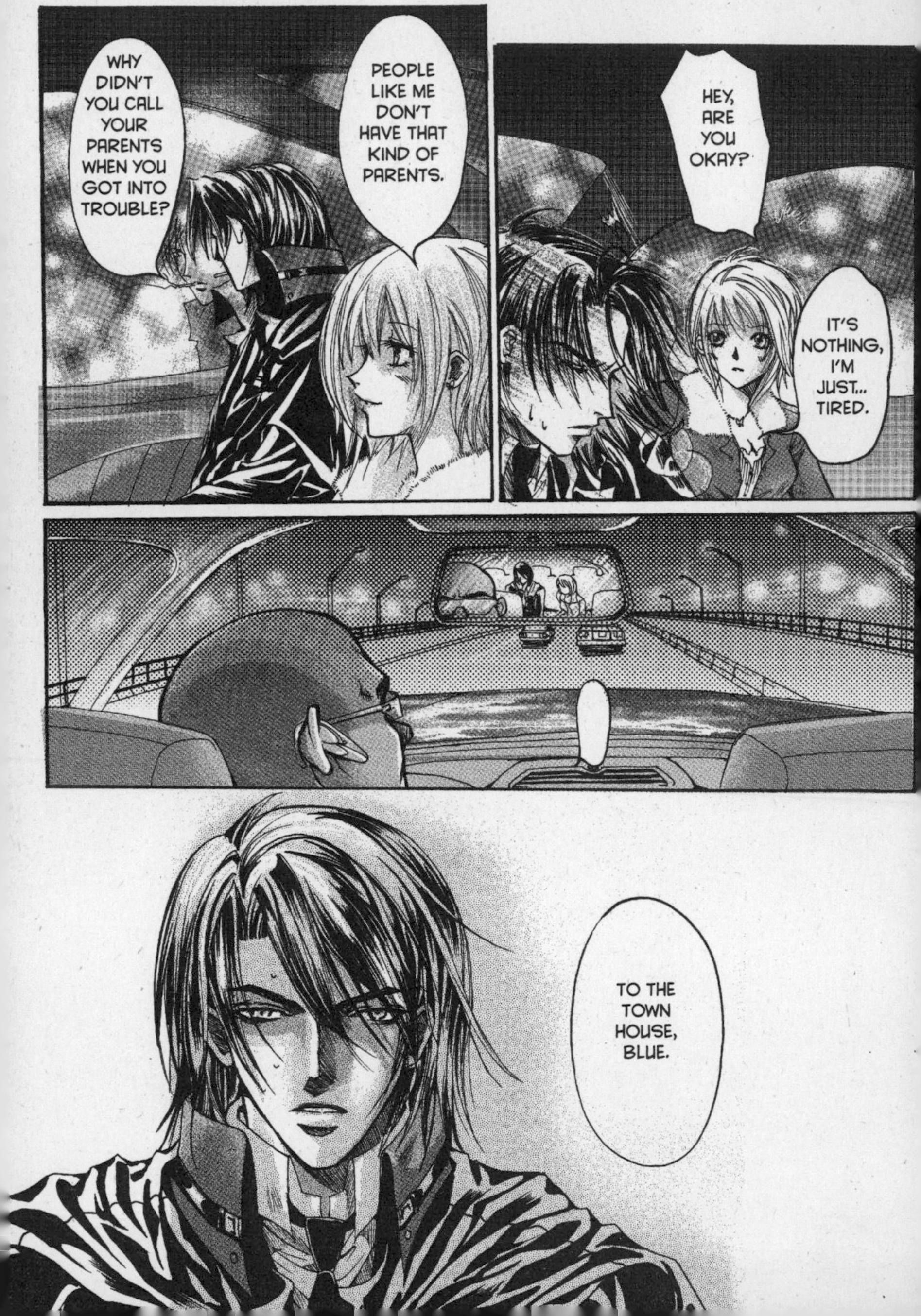
WHY DIDN'T YOU CALL YOUR PARENTS WHEN YOU GOT INTO TROUBLE?
PEOPLE LIKE ME DON'T HAVE THAT KIND OF PARENTS.
HEY, ARE YOU OKAY?
IT'S NOTHING, I'M JUST... TIRED.
TO THE TOWN HOUSE, BLUE.

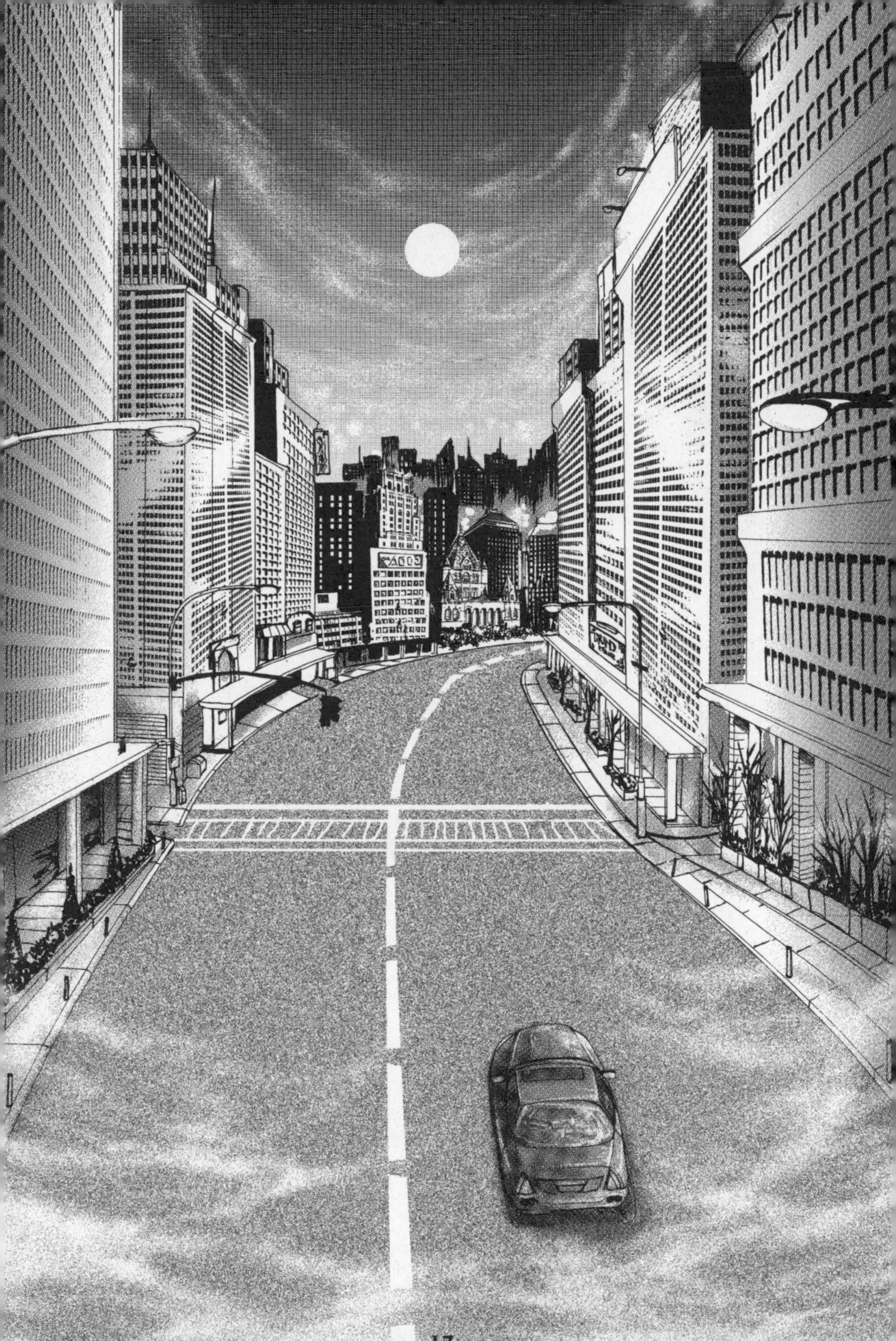

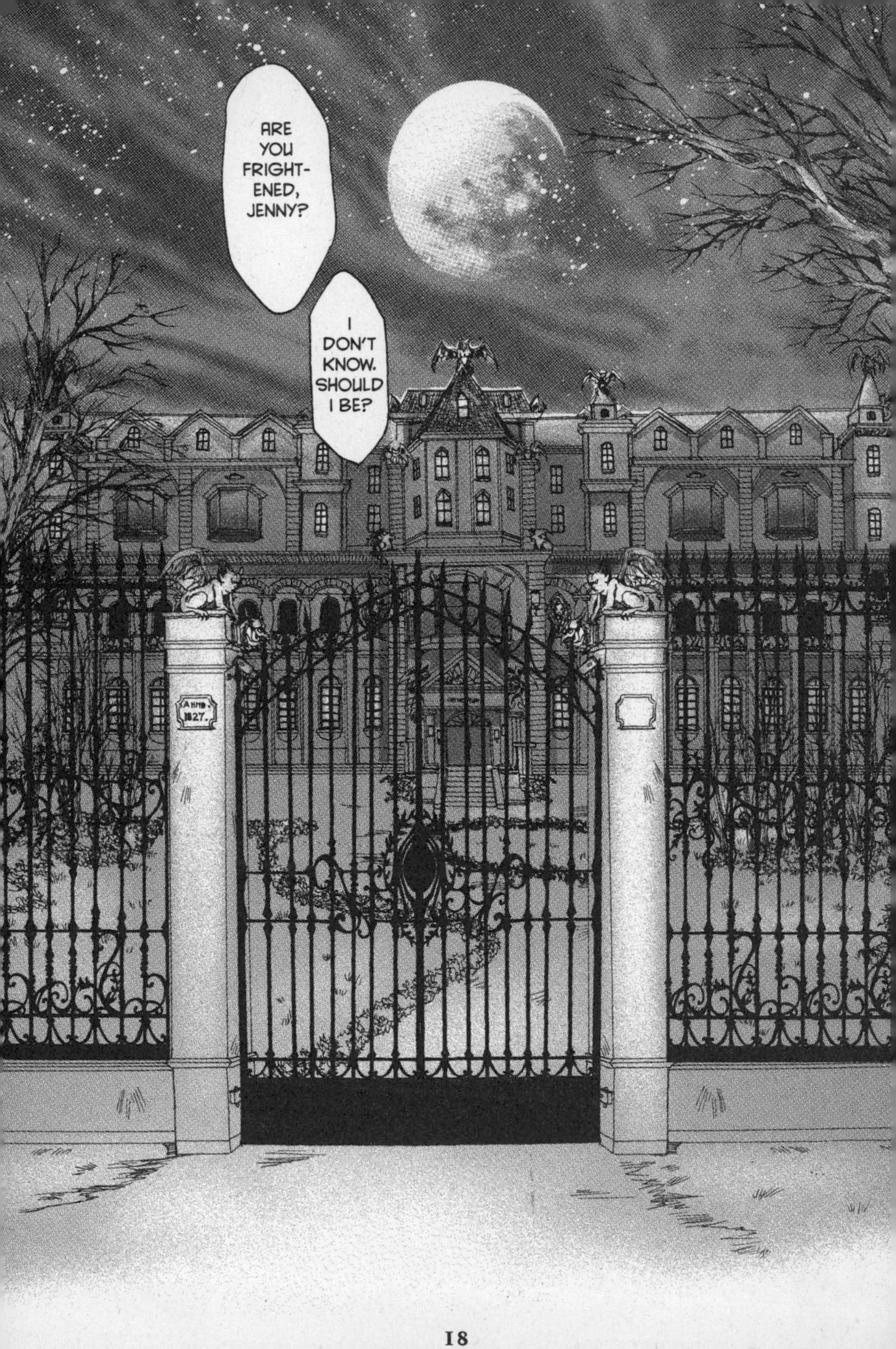
ARE YOU FRIGHT-ENED, JENNY?
I DON'T KNOW. SHOULD I BE?

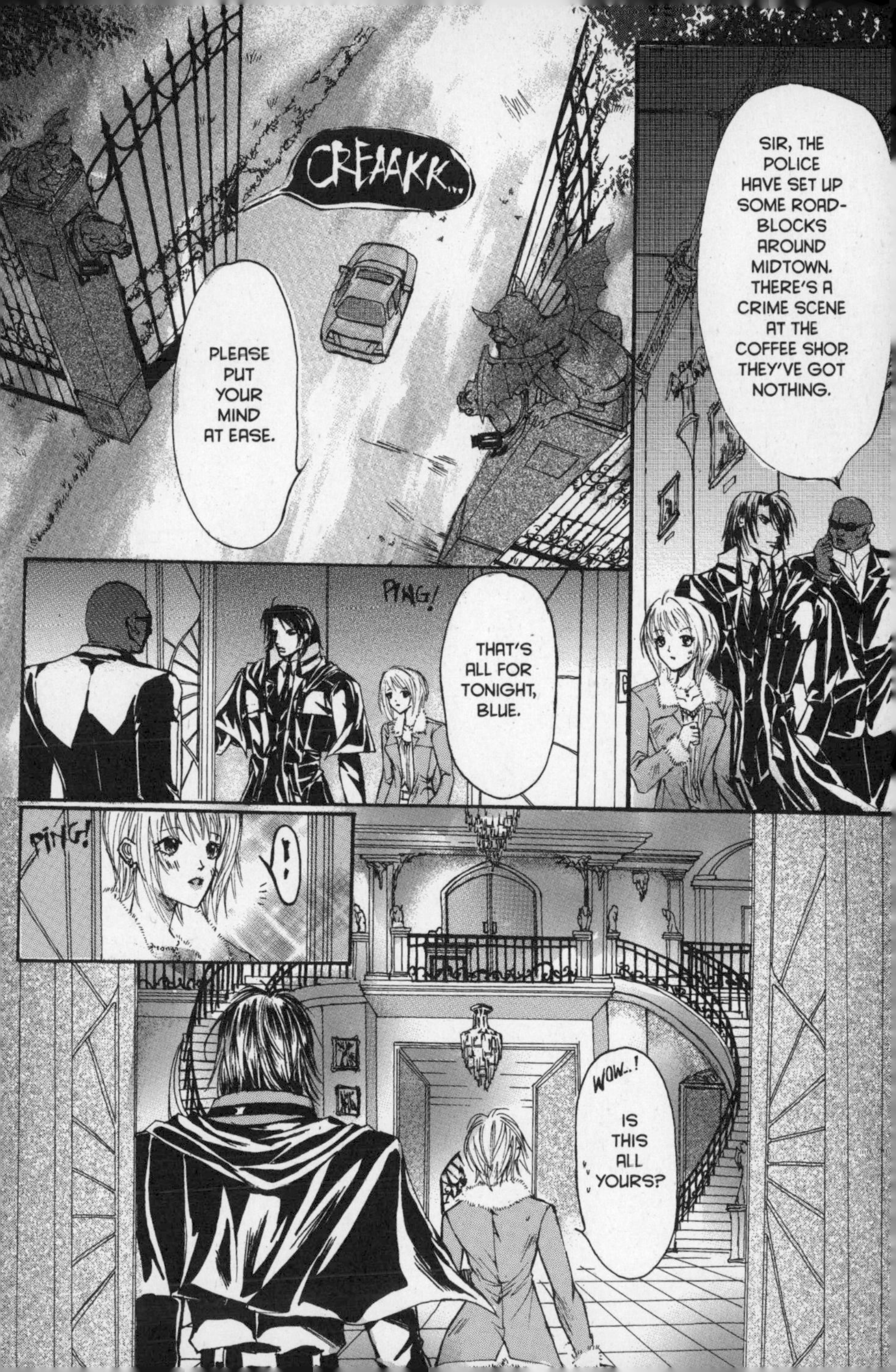
CREAAKK...
PLEASE PUT YOUR MIND AT EASE.
PING!
THAT'S ALL FOR TONIGHT, BLUE.
SIR, THE POLICE HAVE SET UP SOME ROAD-BLOCKS AROUND MIDTOWN. THERE'S A CRIME SCENE AT THE COFFEE SHOP. THEY'VE GOT NOTHING.
PING!
!
WOW..!
IS THIS ALL YOURS?

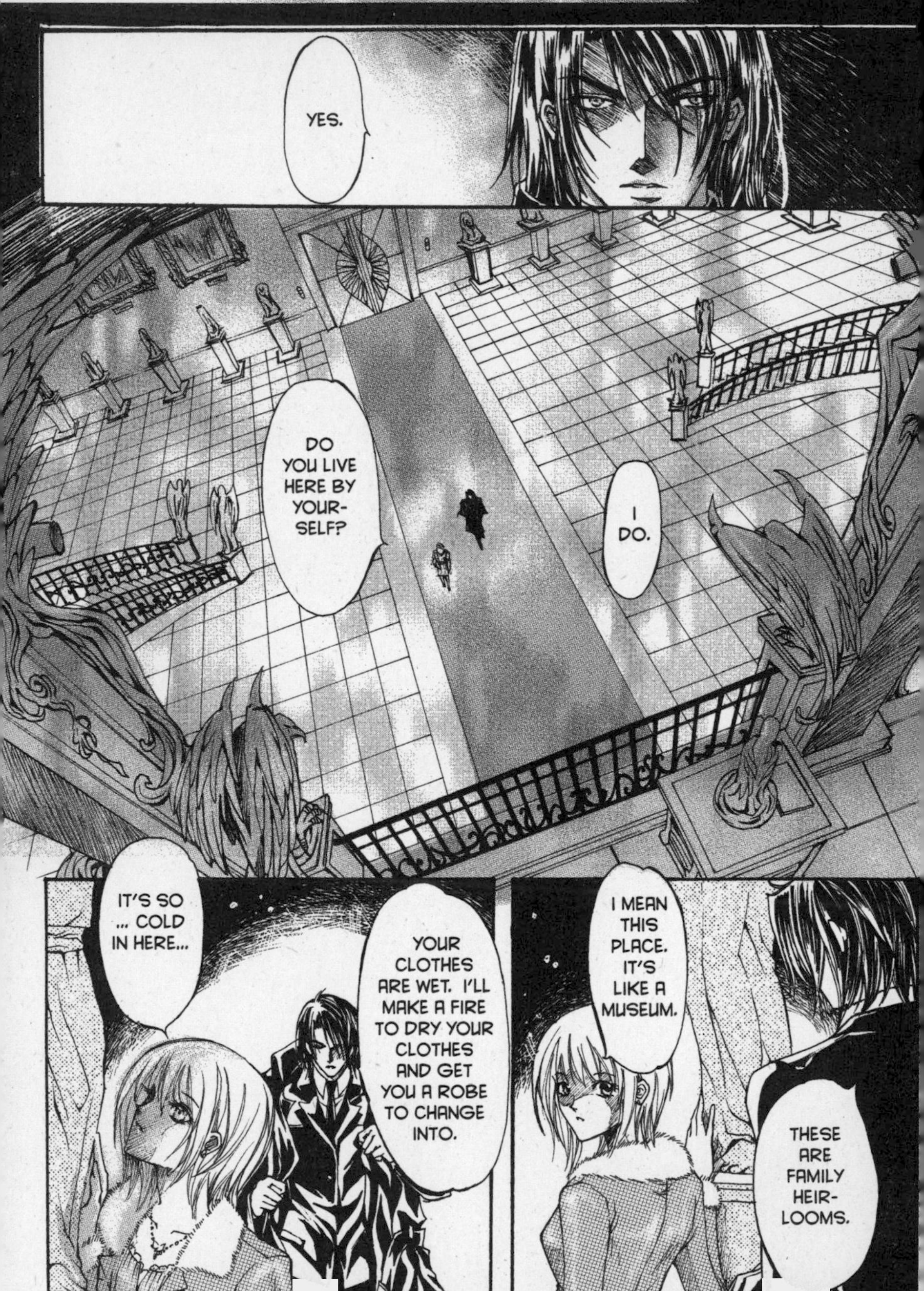
YES.
DO YOU LIVE HERE BY YOURSELF?
I DO.
IT'S SO ... COLD IN HERE...
YOUR CLOTHES ARE WET. I'LL MAKE A FIRE TO DRY YOUR CLOTHES AND GET YOU A ROBE TO CHANGE INTO.
I MEAN THIS PLACE. IT'S LIKE A MUSEUM.
THESE ARE FAMILY HEIRLOOMS.

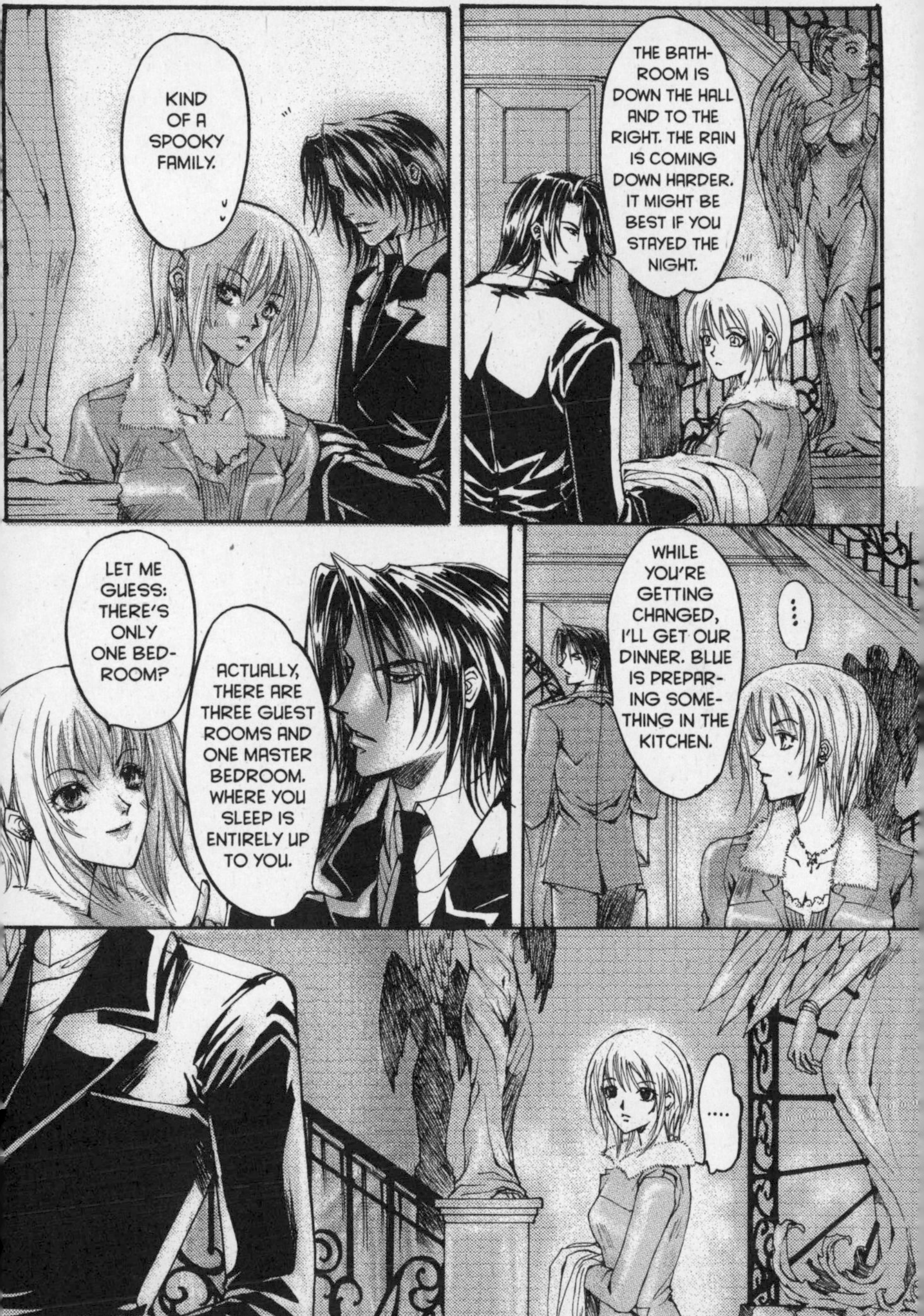
KIND OF A SPOOKY FAMILY.
THE BATH-ROOM IS DOWN THE HALL AND TO THE RIGHT. THE RAIN IS COMING DOWN HARDER. IT MIGHT BE BEST IF YOU STAYED THE NIGHT.
LET ME GUESS: THERE'S ONLY ONE BED-ROOM?
ACTUALLY, THERE ARE THREE GUEST ROOMS AND ONE MASTER BEDROOM. WHERE YOU SLEEP IS ENTIRELY UP TO YOU.
WHILE YOU'RE GETTING CHANGED, I'LL GET OUR DINNER. BLUE IS PREPARING SOMETHING IN THE KITCHEN.
....
....

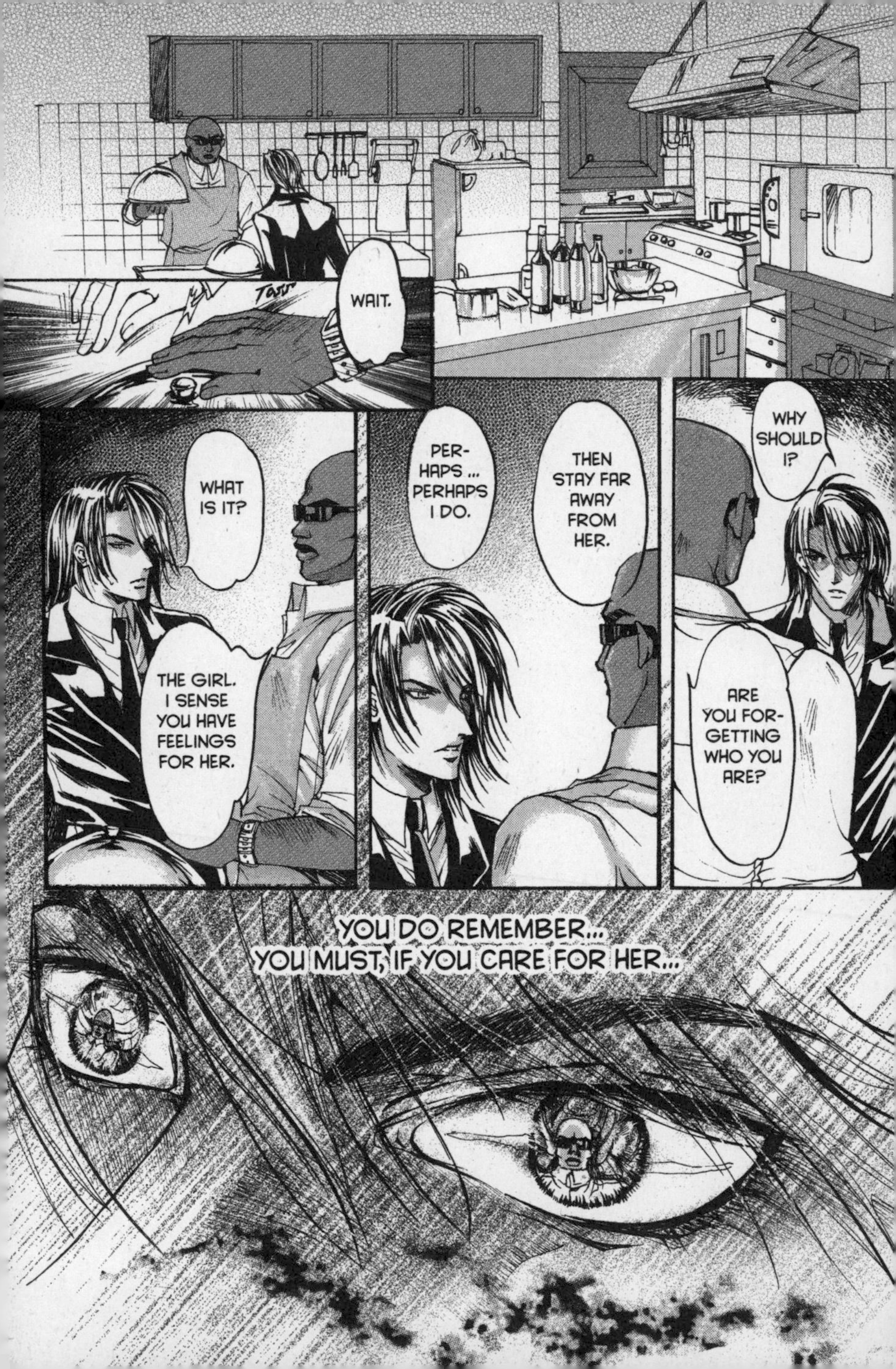
WAIT.
WHAT IS IT?
THE GIRL. I SENSE YOU HAVE FEELINGS FOR HER.
PER-HAPS ... PERHAPS I DO.
THEN STAY FAR AWAY FROM HER.
WHY SHOULD I?
ARE YOU FOR-GETTING WHO YOU ARE?
YOU DO REMEMBER...
YOU MUST, IF YOU CARE FOR HER...

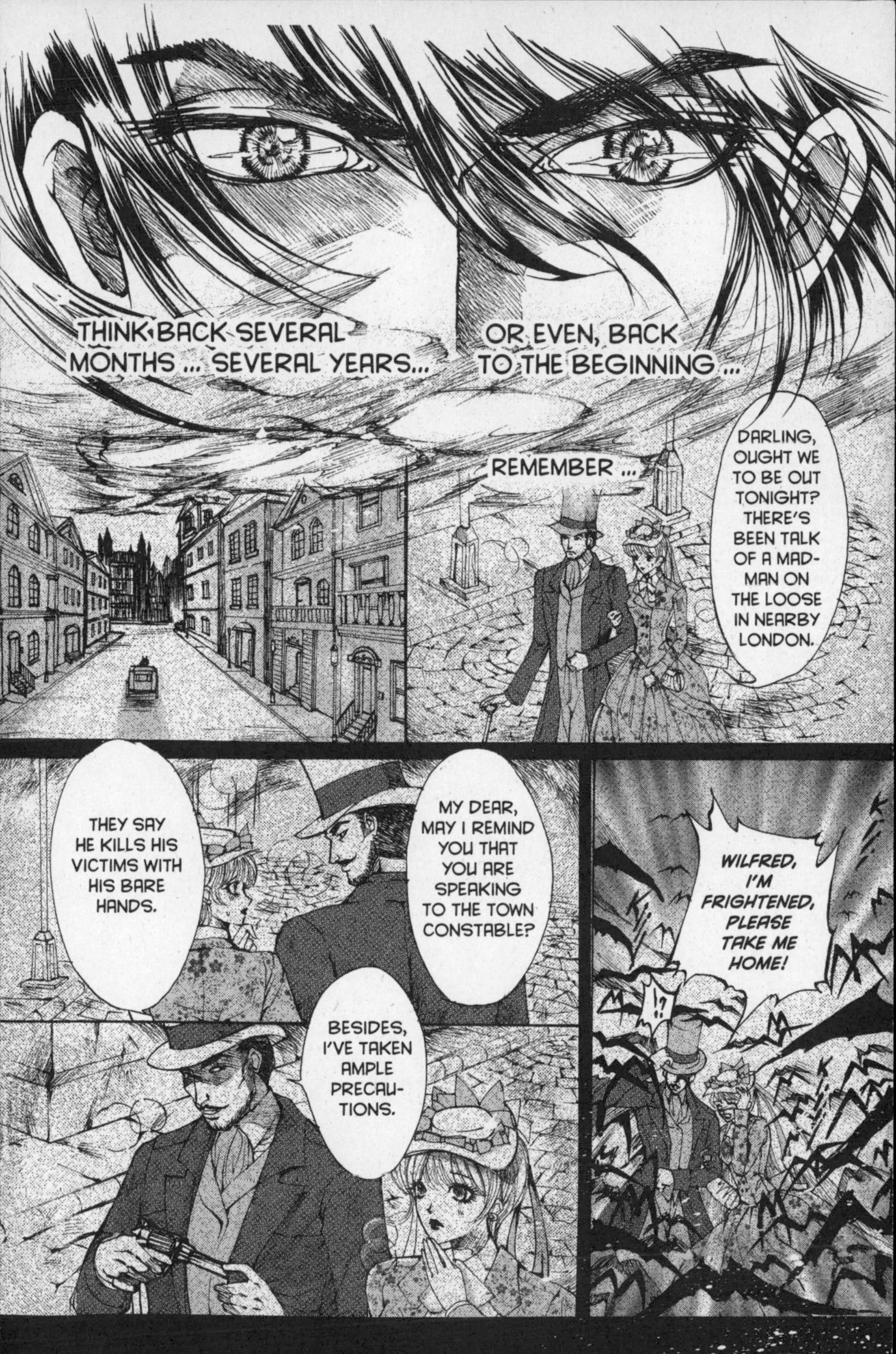
THINK BACK SEVERAL MONTHS ... SEVERAL YEARS...
OR EVEN, BACK TO THE BEGINNING ...
REMEMBER ...
DARLING, OUGHT WE TO BE OUT TONIGHT? THERE'S BEEN TALK OF A MAD-MAN ON THE LOOSE IN NEARBY LONDON.
THEY SAY HE KILLS HIS VICTIMS WITH HIS BARE HANDS.
MY DEAR, MAY I REMIND YOU THAT YOU ARE SPEAKING TO THE TOWN CONSTABLE?
BESIDES, I'VE TAKEN AMPLE PRECAU-TIONS.
WILFRED, I'M FRIGHTENED, PLEASE TAKE ME HOME!
!?

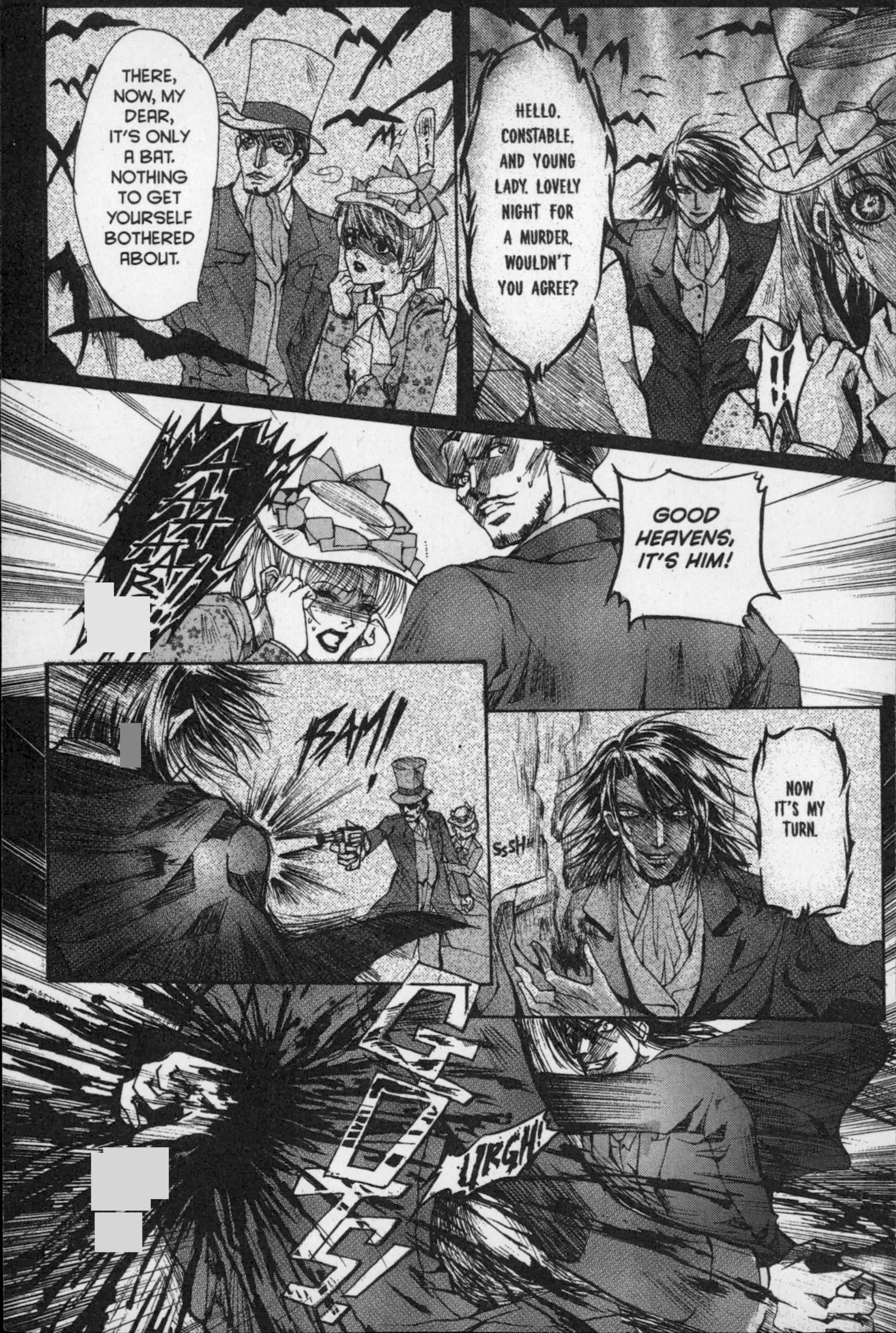
THERE, NOW, MY DEAR, IT'S ONLY A BAT. NOTHING TO GET YOURSELF BOTHERED ABOUT.
HELLO. CONSTABLE. AND YOUNG LADY. LOVELY NIGHT FOR A MURDER, WOULDN'T YOU AGREE?
!!
GOOD HEAVENS, IT'S HIM!
BAM!
SSSH
NOW IT'S MY TURN.
URGH!

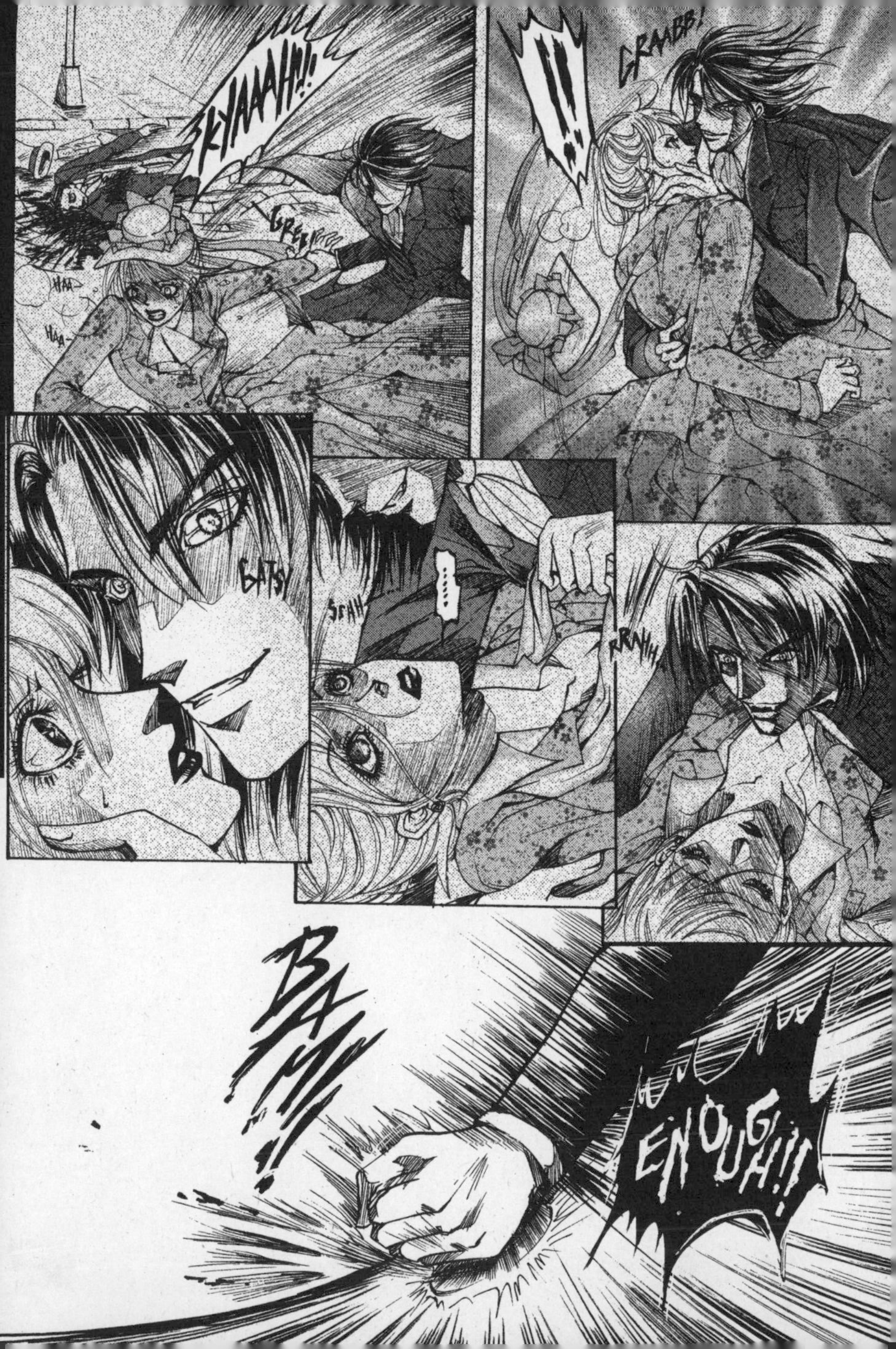
KYAAAH!!
GREB!
HAA
HAA
!!
GRAABB!
GATSY
SRAH
...
RRAHH
BAM!!
ENOUGH!!

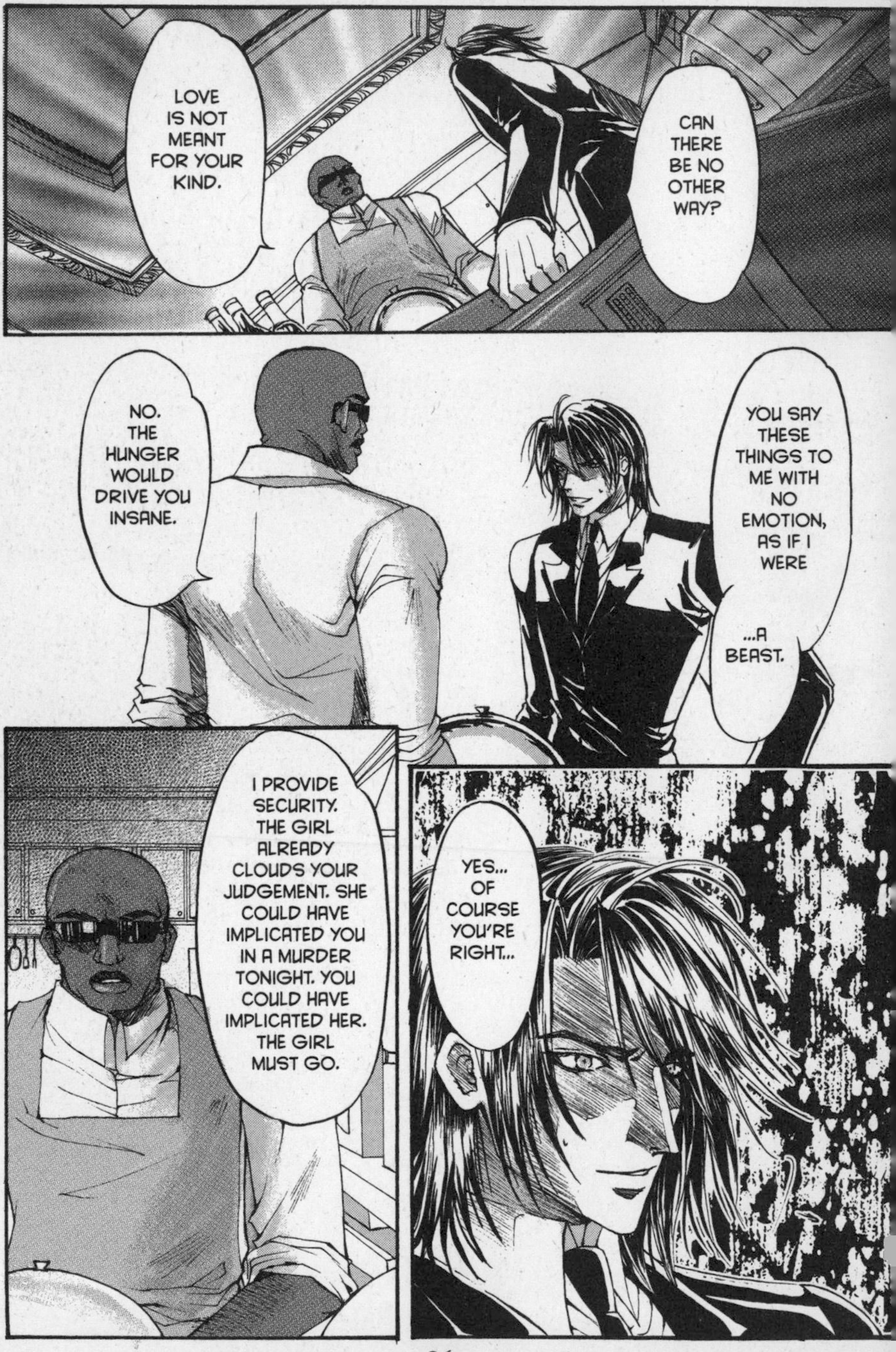
LOVE IS NOT MEANT FOR YOUR KIND.
CAN THERE BE NO OTHER WAY?
NO. THE HUNGER WOULD DRIVE YOU INSANE.
YOU SAY THESE THINGS TO ME WITH NO EMOTION, AS IF I WERE
...A BEAST.
I PROVIDE SECURITY. THE GIRL ALREADY CLOUDS YOUR JUDGEMENT. SHE COULD HAVE IMPLICATED YOU IN A MURDER TONIGHT. YOU COULD HAVE IMPLICATED HER. THE GIRL MUST GO.
YES... OF COURSE YOU'RE RIGHT...

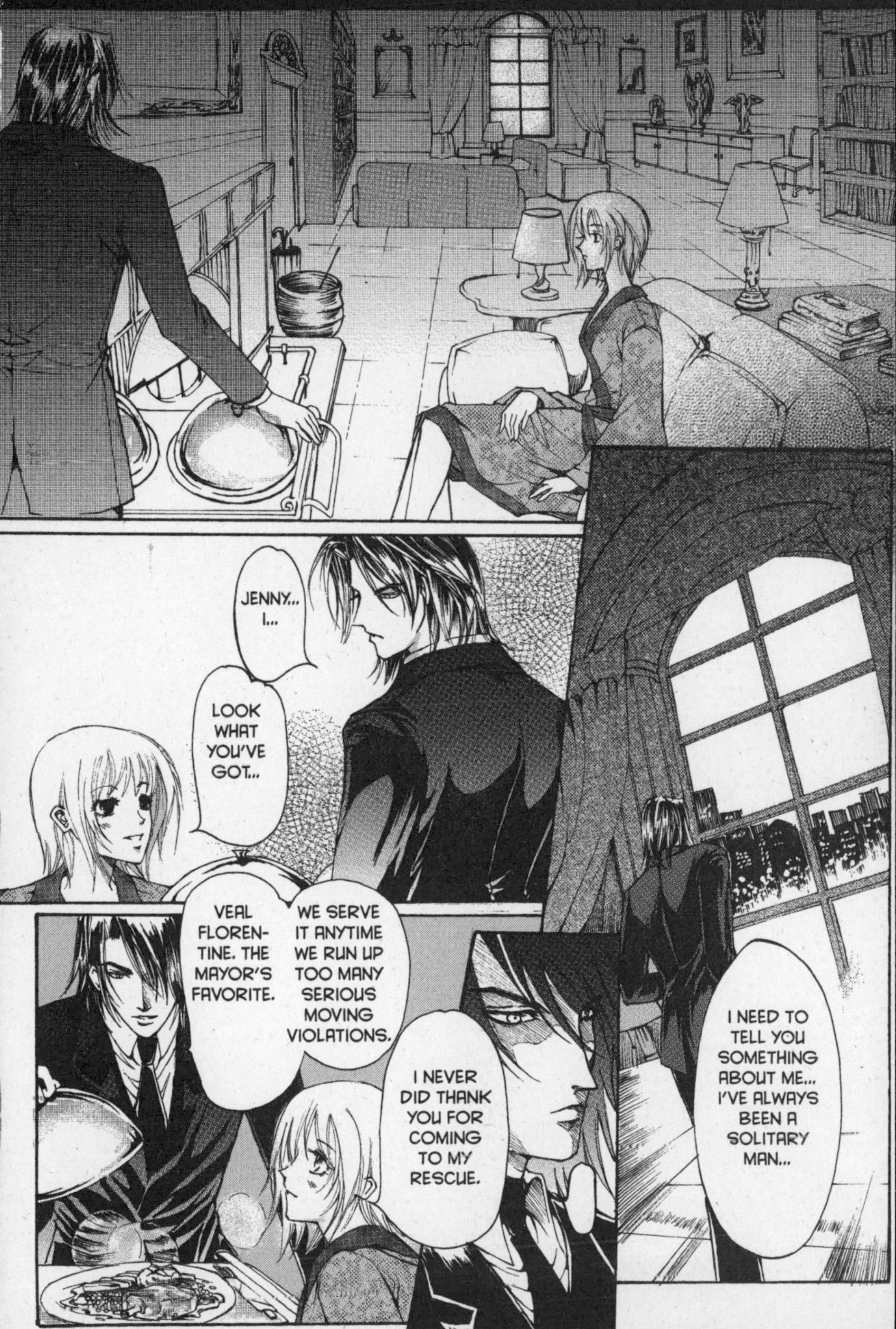
JENNY... I...
LOOK WHAT YOU'VE GOT...
VEAL FLOREN-TINE. THE MAYOR'S FAVORITE.
WE SERVE IT ANYTIME WE RUN UP TOO MANY SERIOUS MOVING VIOLATIONS.
I NEVER DID THANK YOU FOR COMING TO MY RESCUE.
I NEED TO TELL YOU SOMETHING ABOUT ME... I'VE ALWAYS BEEN A SOLITARY MAN...

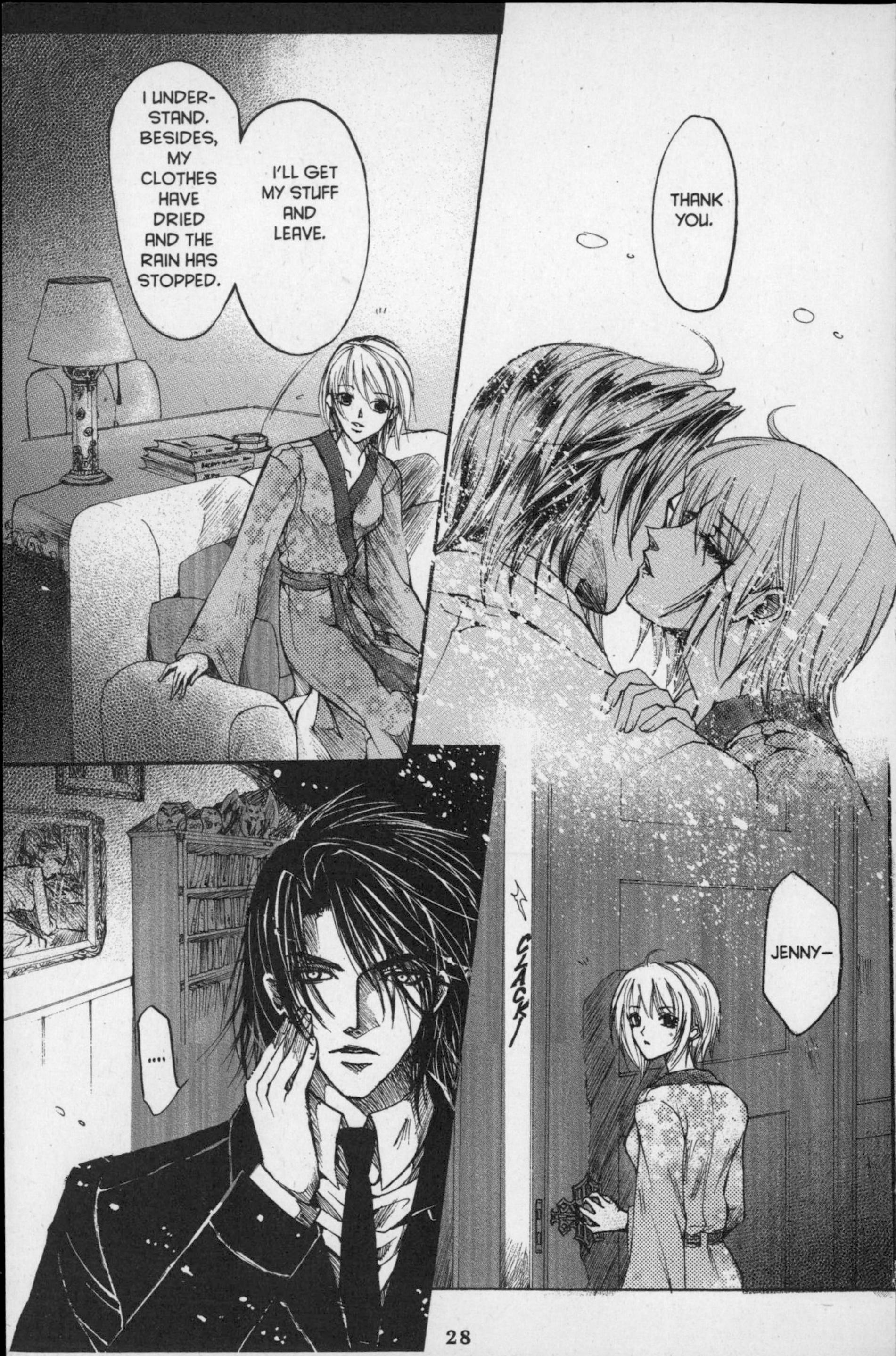
I UNDER-STAND. BESIDES, MY CLOTHES HAVE DRIED AND THE RAIN HAS STOPPED.
I'LL GET MY STUFF AND LEAVE.
THANK YOU.
....
CLACK!
JENNY—

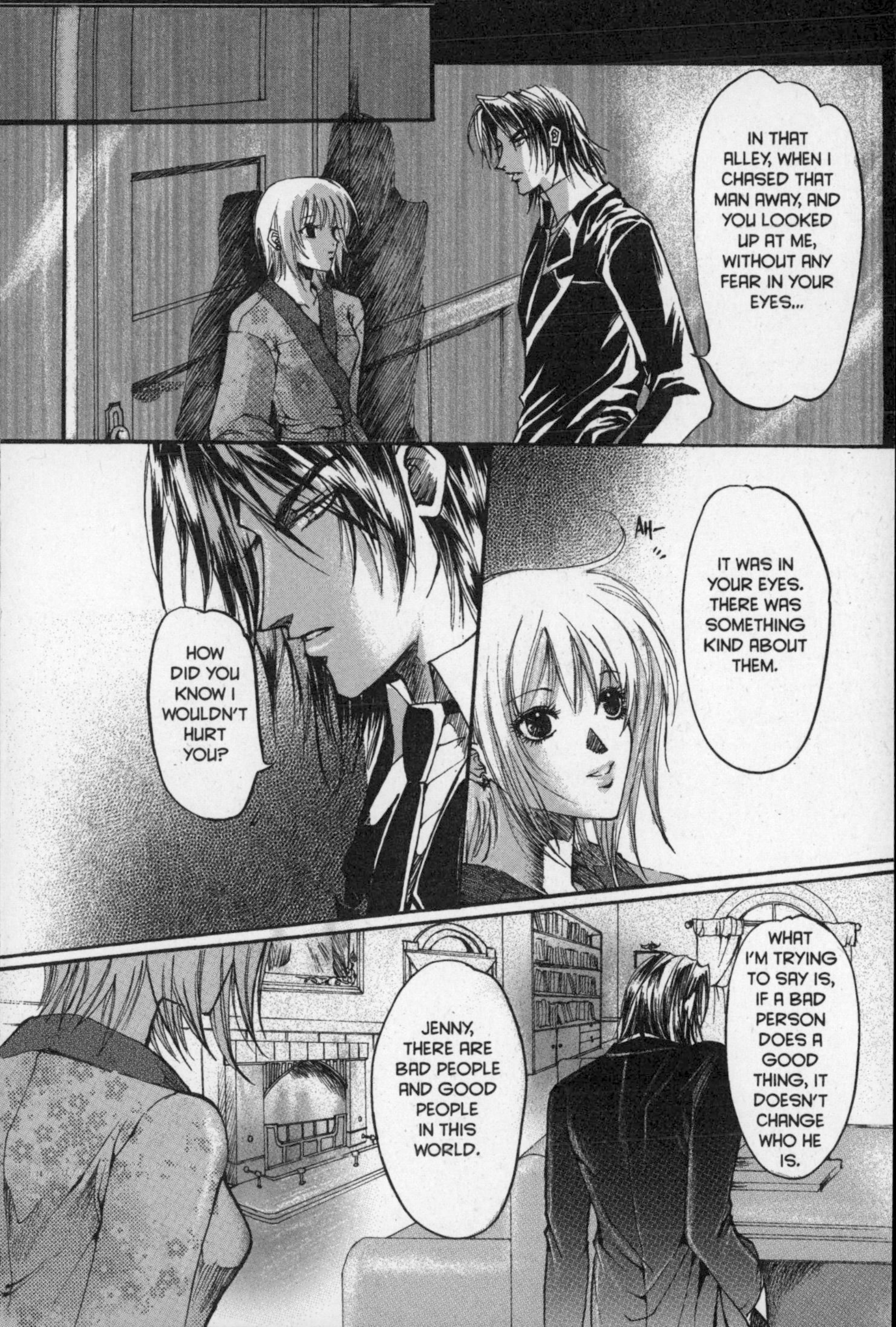
IN THAT ALLEY, WHEN I CHASED THAT MAN AWAY, AND YOU LOOKED UP AT ME, WITHOUT ANY FEAR IN YOUR EYES...
HOW DID YOU KNOW I WOULDN'T HURT YOU?
AH-
IT WAS IN YOUR EYES. THERE WAS SOMETHING KIND ABOUT THEM.
JENNY, THERE ARE BAD PEOPLE AND GOOD PEOPLE IN THIS WORLD.
WHAT I'M TRYING TO SAY IS, IF A BAD PERSON DOES A GOOD THING, IT DOESN'T CHANGE WHO HE IS.

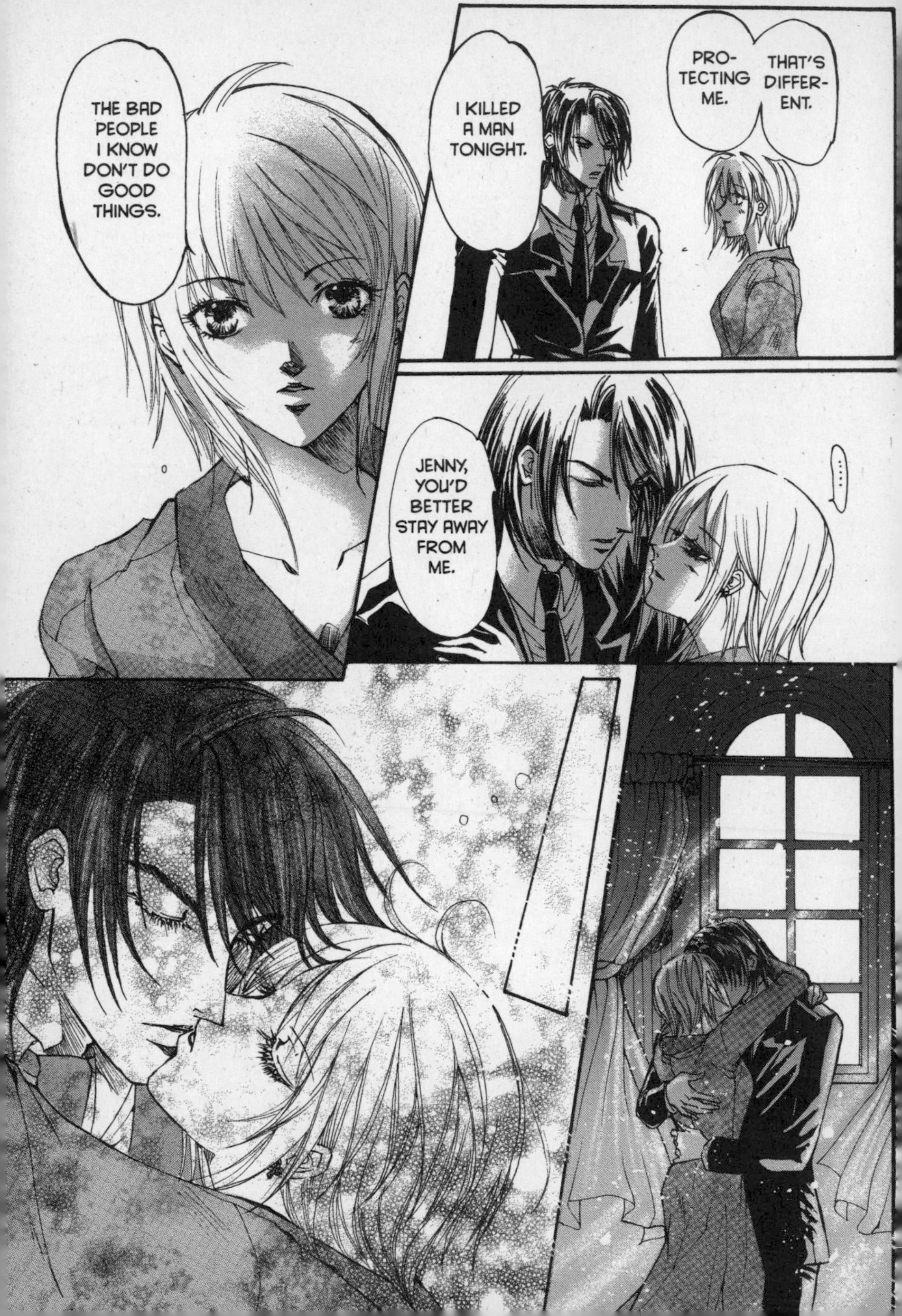
THE BAD PEOPLE I KNOW DON'T DO GOOD THINGS.
I KILLED A MAN TONIGHT.
PROTECTING ME.
THAT'S DIFFERENT.
JENNY, YOU'D BETTER STAY AWAY FROM ME.
....

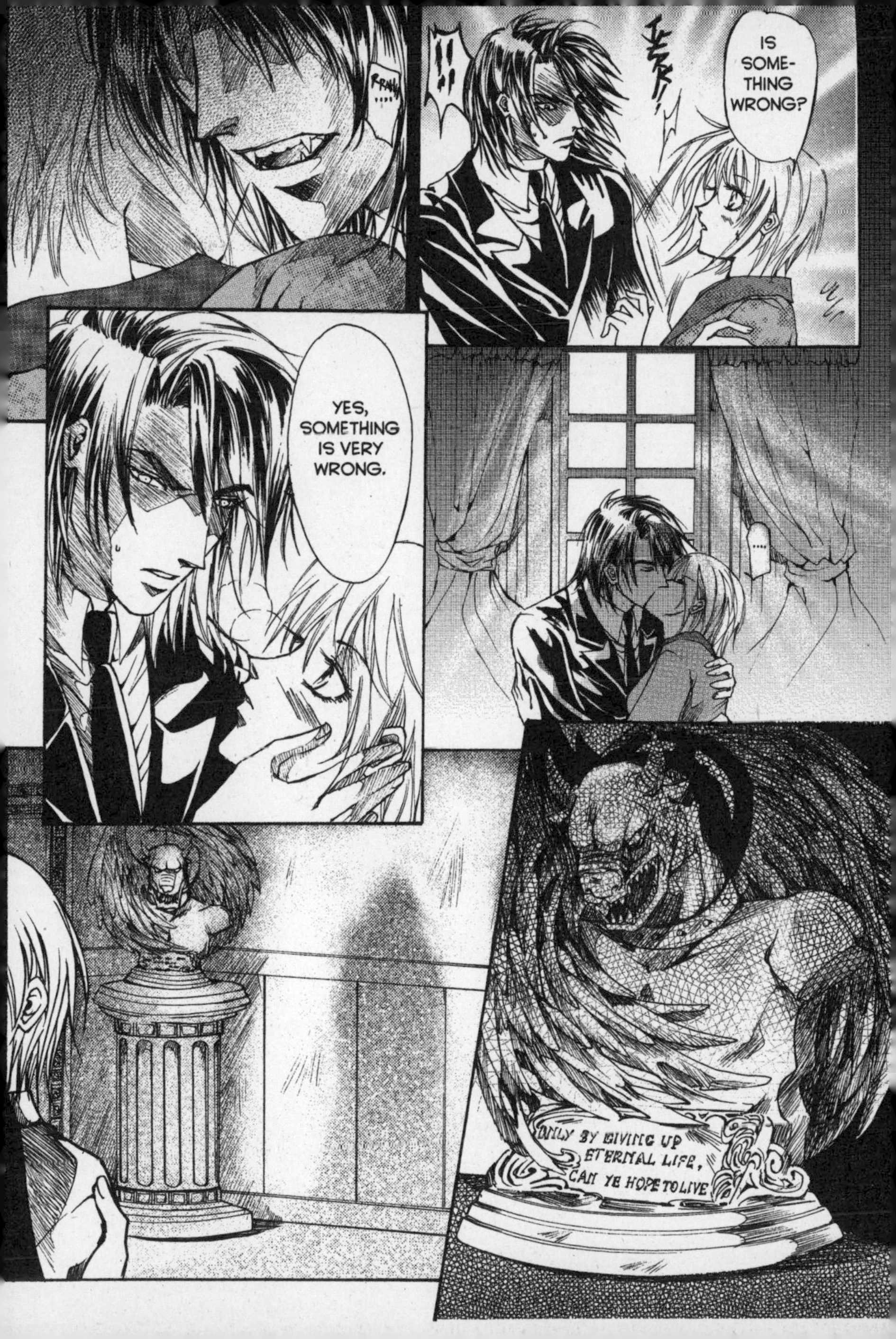
RRAHH....
!!
JERK!
IS SOMETHING WRONG?
YES, SOMETHING IS VERY WRONG.
....
ONLY BY GIVING UP ETERNAL LIFE, CAN YE HOPE TO LIVE

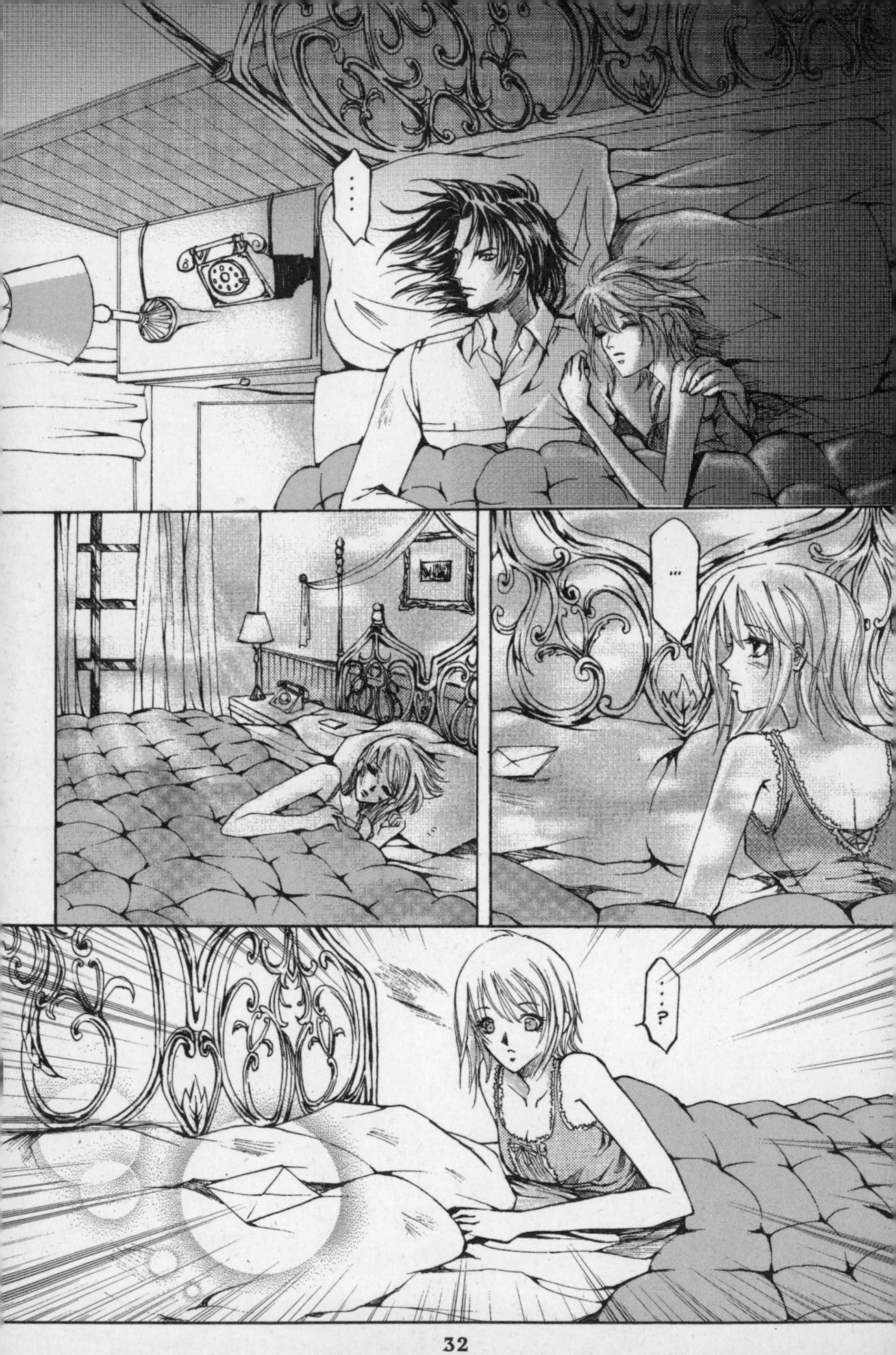
....
...
...?

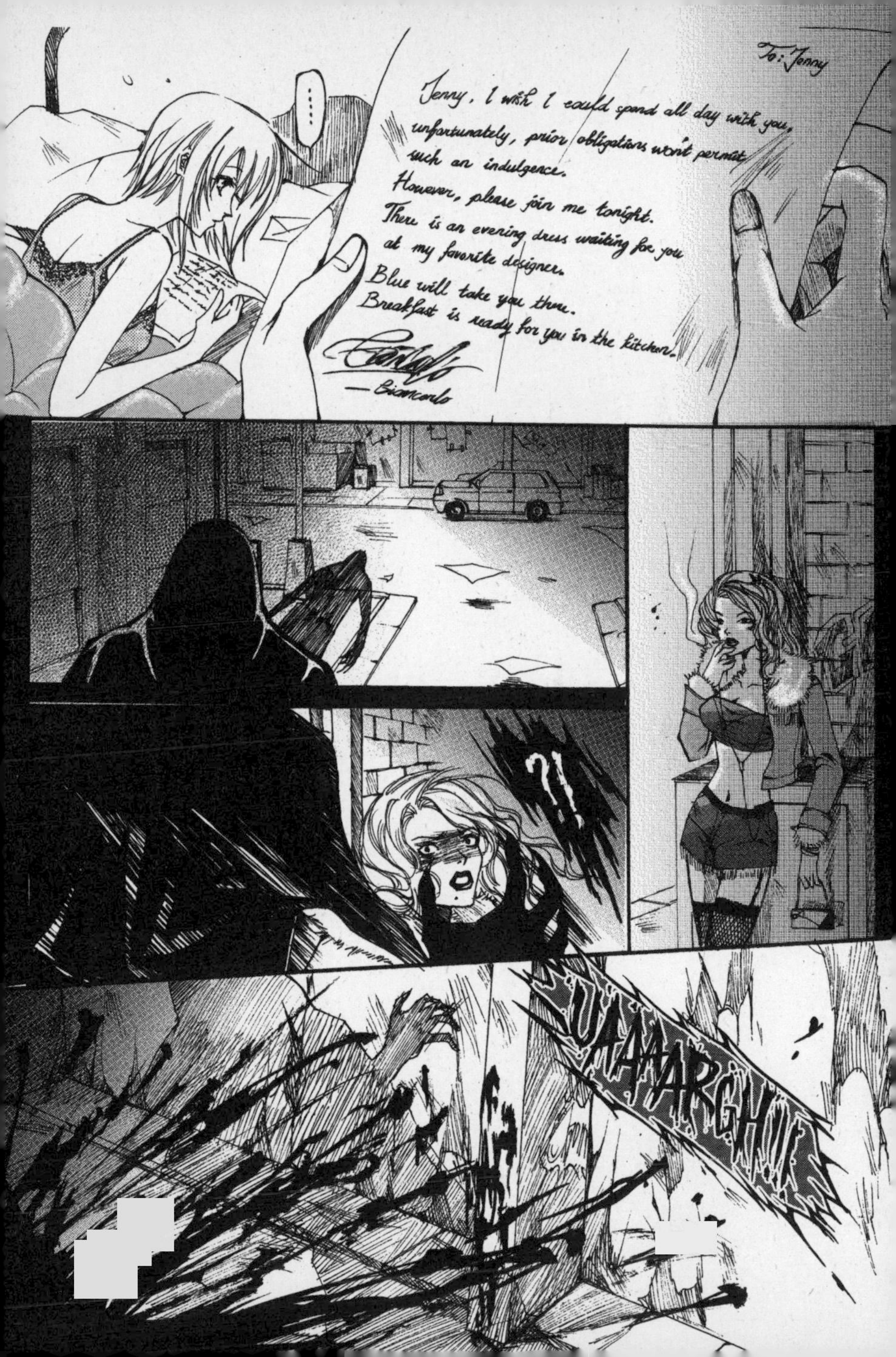

...
To: Jenny
Jenny, I wish I could spend all day with you,
unfortunately, prior obligations won't permit
such an indulgence.
However, please join me tonight.
There is an evening dress waiting for you
at my favorite designer.
Blue will take you there.
Breakfast is ready for you in the kitchen.
—Giancarlo
?!
UAAARGH!!

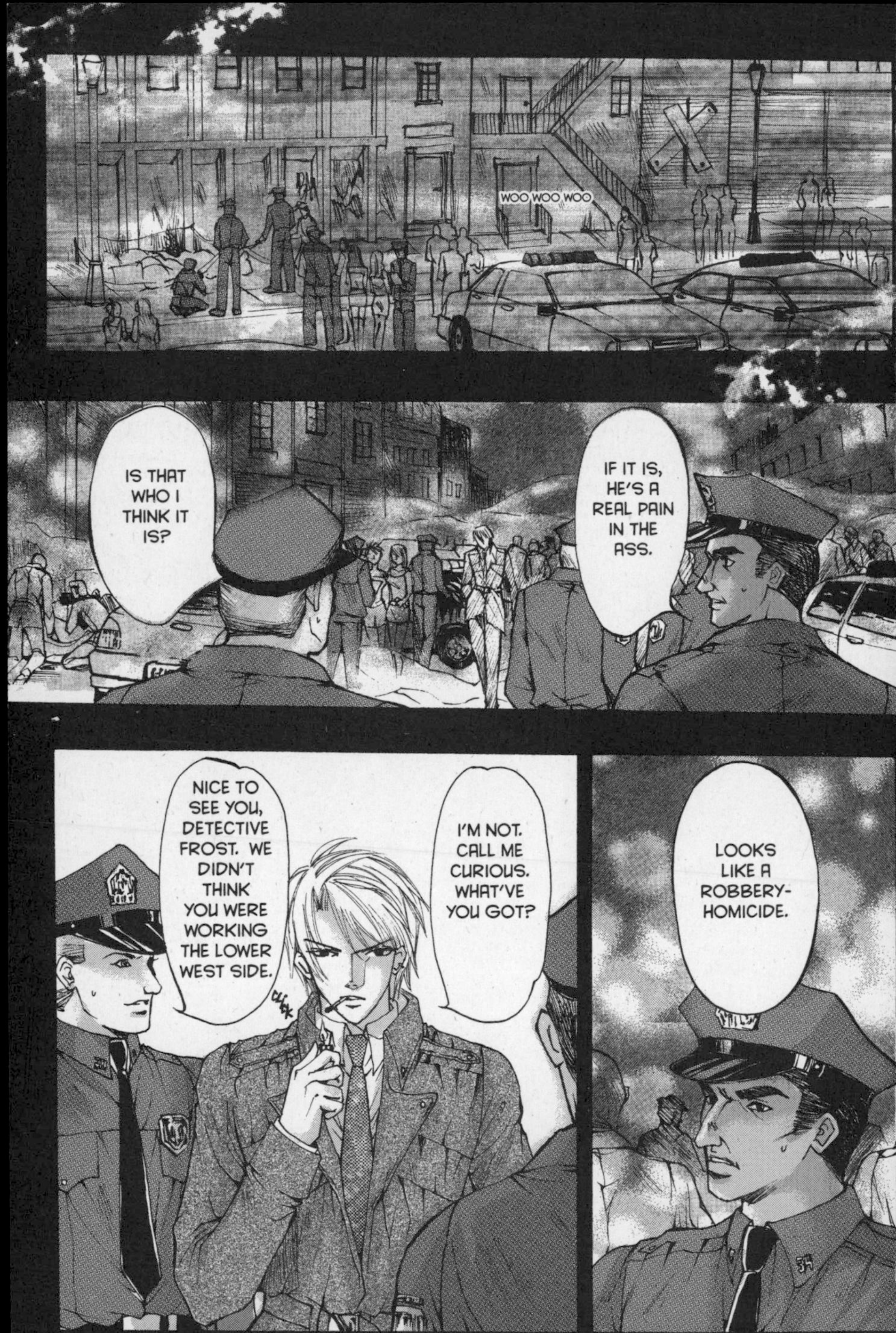
WOO WOO WOO
IS THAT WHO I THINK IT IS?
IF IT IS, HE'S A REAL PAIN IN THE ASS.
NICE TO SEE YOU, DETECTIVE FROST. WE DIDN'T THINK YOU WERE WORKING THE LOWER WEST SIDE.
CLICK
I'M NOT. CALL ME CURIOUS. WHAT'VE YOU GOT?
LOOKS LIKE A ROBBERY-HOMICIDE.

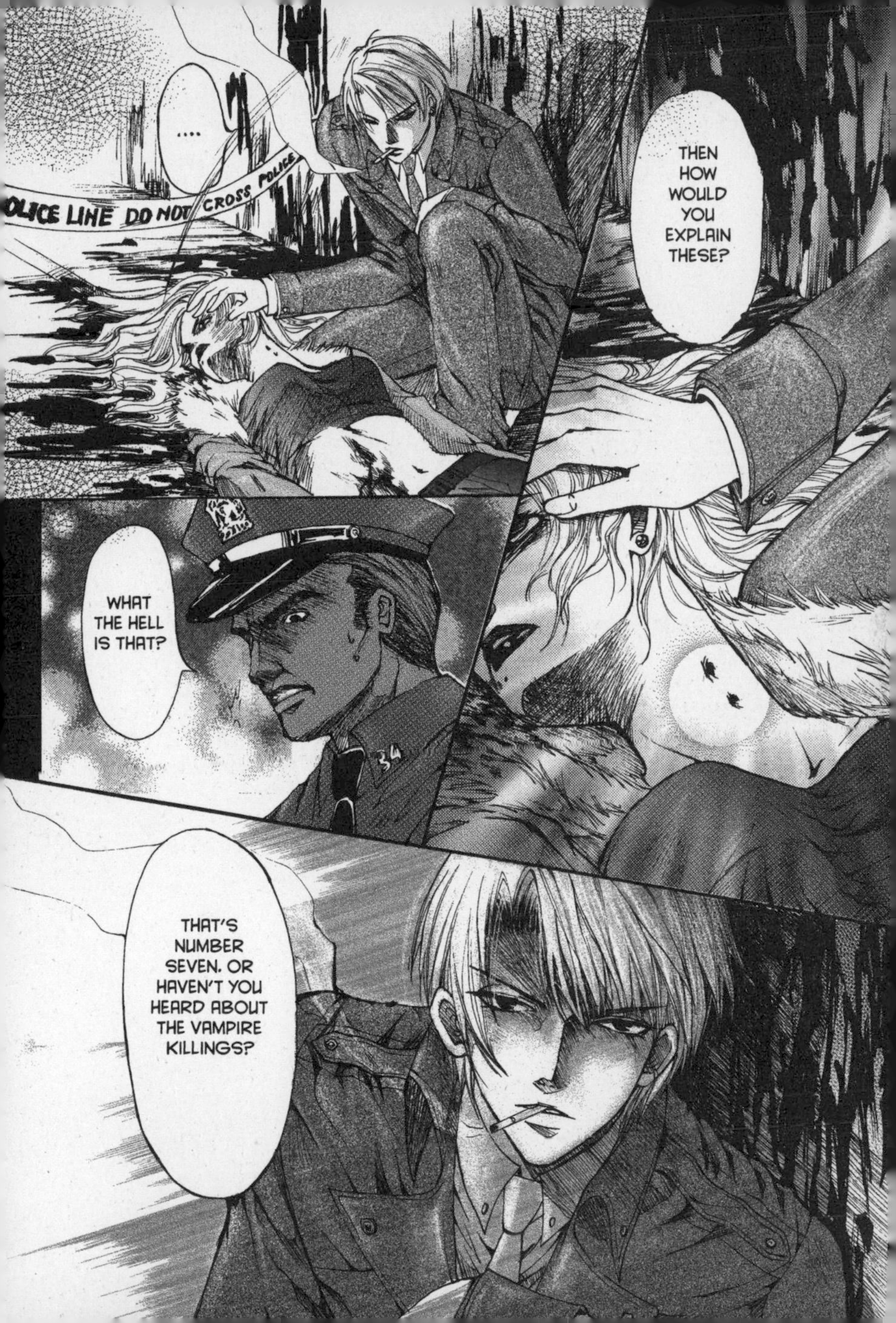
OLICE LINE DO NOT CROSS POLICE
....
THEN HOW WOULD YOU EXPLAIN THESE?
WHAT THE HELL IS THAT?
THAT'S NUMBER SEVEN. OR HAVEN'T YOU HEARD ABOUT THE VAMPIRE KILLINGS?

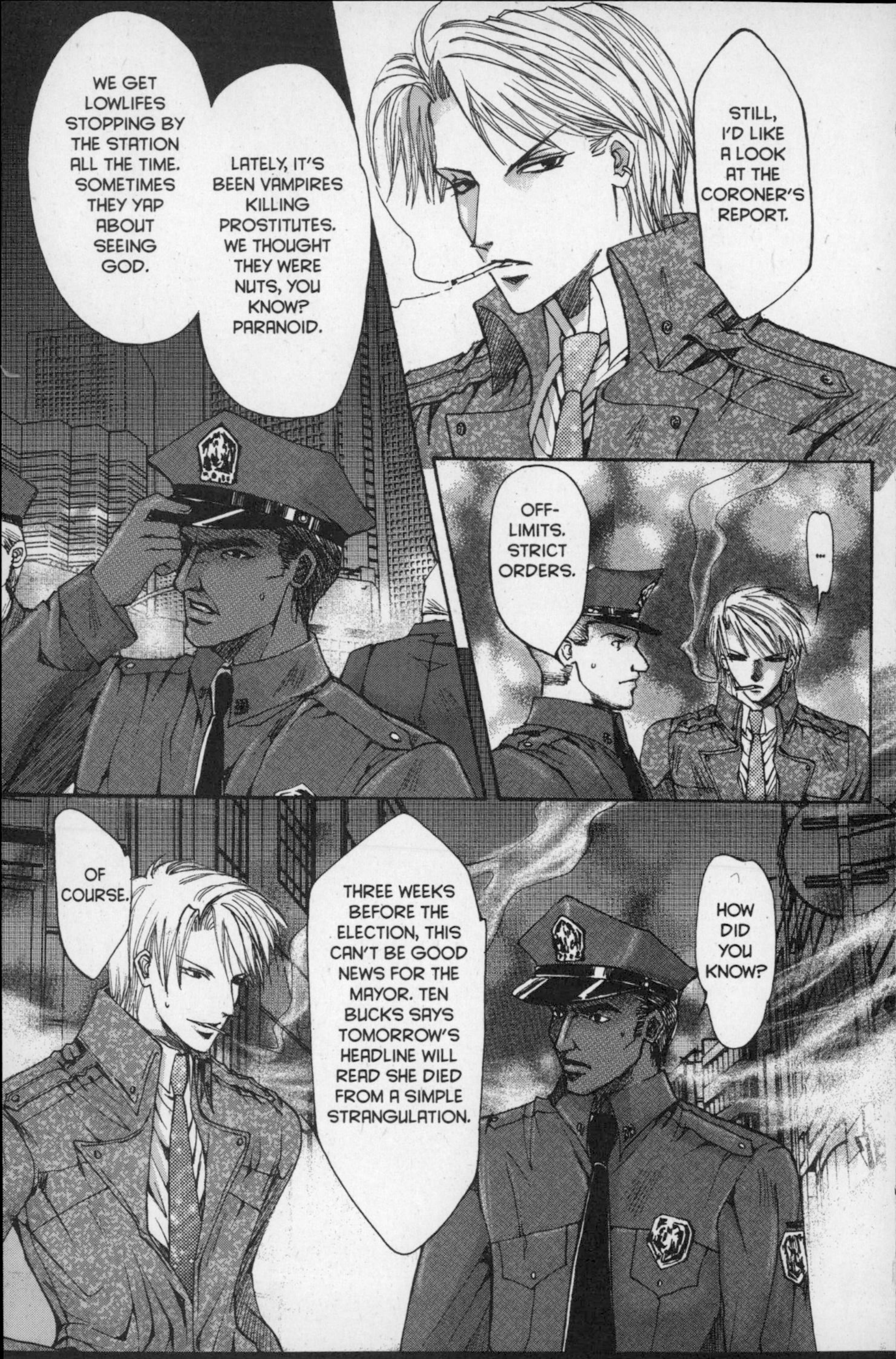
WE GET LOWLIFES STOPPING BY THE STATION ALL THE TIME. SOMETIMES THEY YAP ABOUT SEEING GOD.
LATELY, IT'S BEEN VAMPIRES KILLING PROSTITUTES. WE THOUGHT THEY WERE NUTS, YOU KNOW? PARANOID.
STILL, I'D LIKE A LOOK AT THE CORONER'S REPORT.
OFF-LIMITS. STRICT ORDERS.
...
OF COURSE.
THREE WEEKS BEFORE THE ELECTION, THIS CAN'T BE GOOD NEWS FOR THE MAYOR. TEN BUCKS SAYS TOMORROW'S HEADLINE WILL READ SHE DIED FROM A SIMPLE STRANGULATION.
HOW DID YOU KNOW?

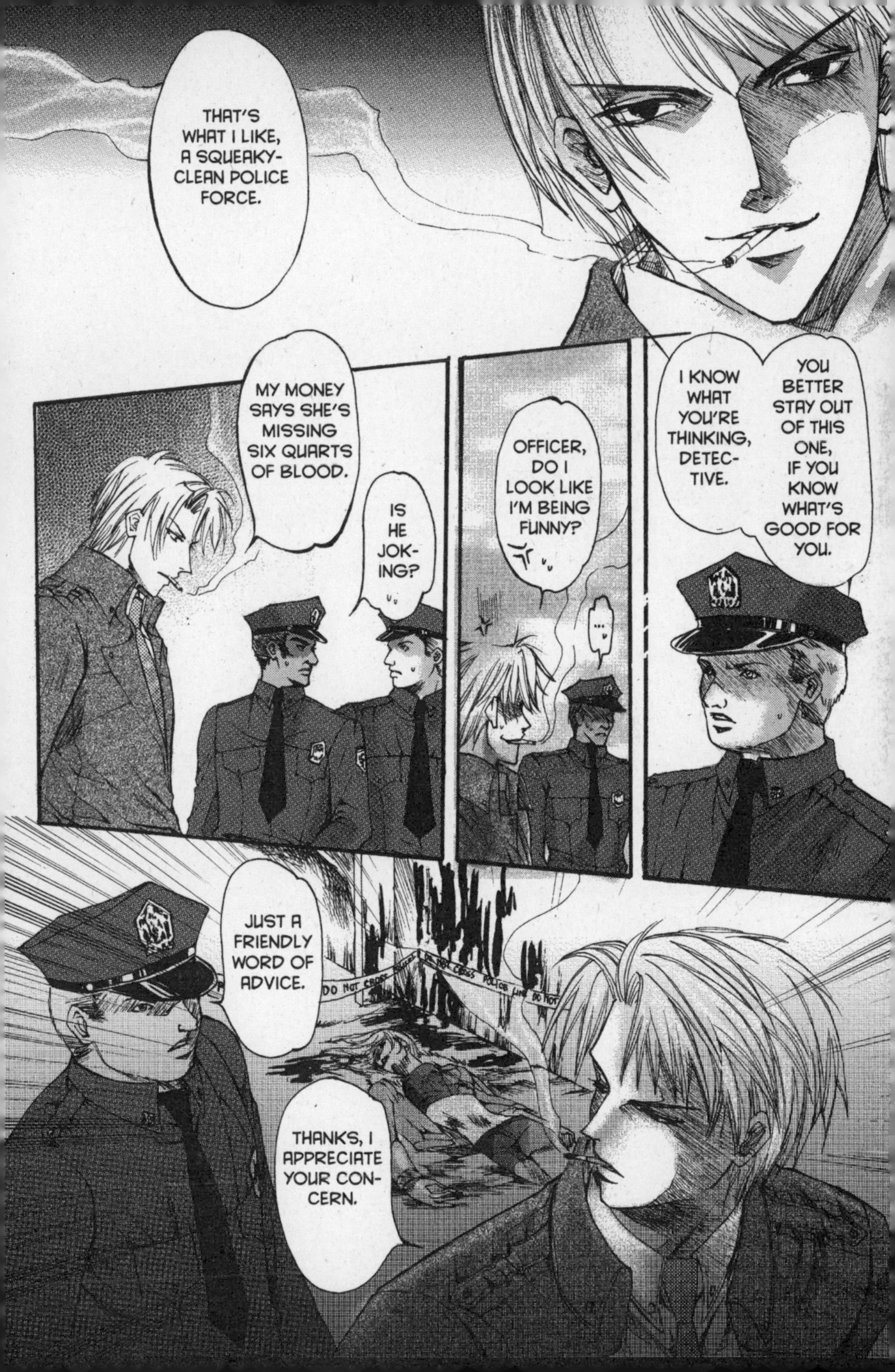
THAT'S WHAT I LIKE, A SQUEAKY-CLEAN POLICE FORCE.
MY MONEY SAYS SHE'S MISSING SIX QUARTS OF BLOOD.
IS HE JOK-ING?
OFFICER, DO I LOOK LIKE I'M BEING FUNNY?
...
I KNOW WHAT YOU'RE THINKING, DETEC-TIVE.
YOU BETTER STAY OUT OF THIS ONE, IF YOU KNOW WHAT'S GOOD FOR YOU.
JUST A FRIENDLY WORD OF ADVICE.
DO NOT CROSS
DO NOT CROSS POLICE LINE DO NOT
THANKS, I APPRECIATE YOUR CON-CERN.

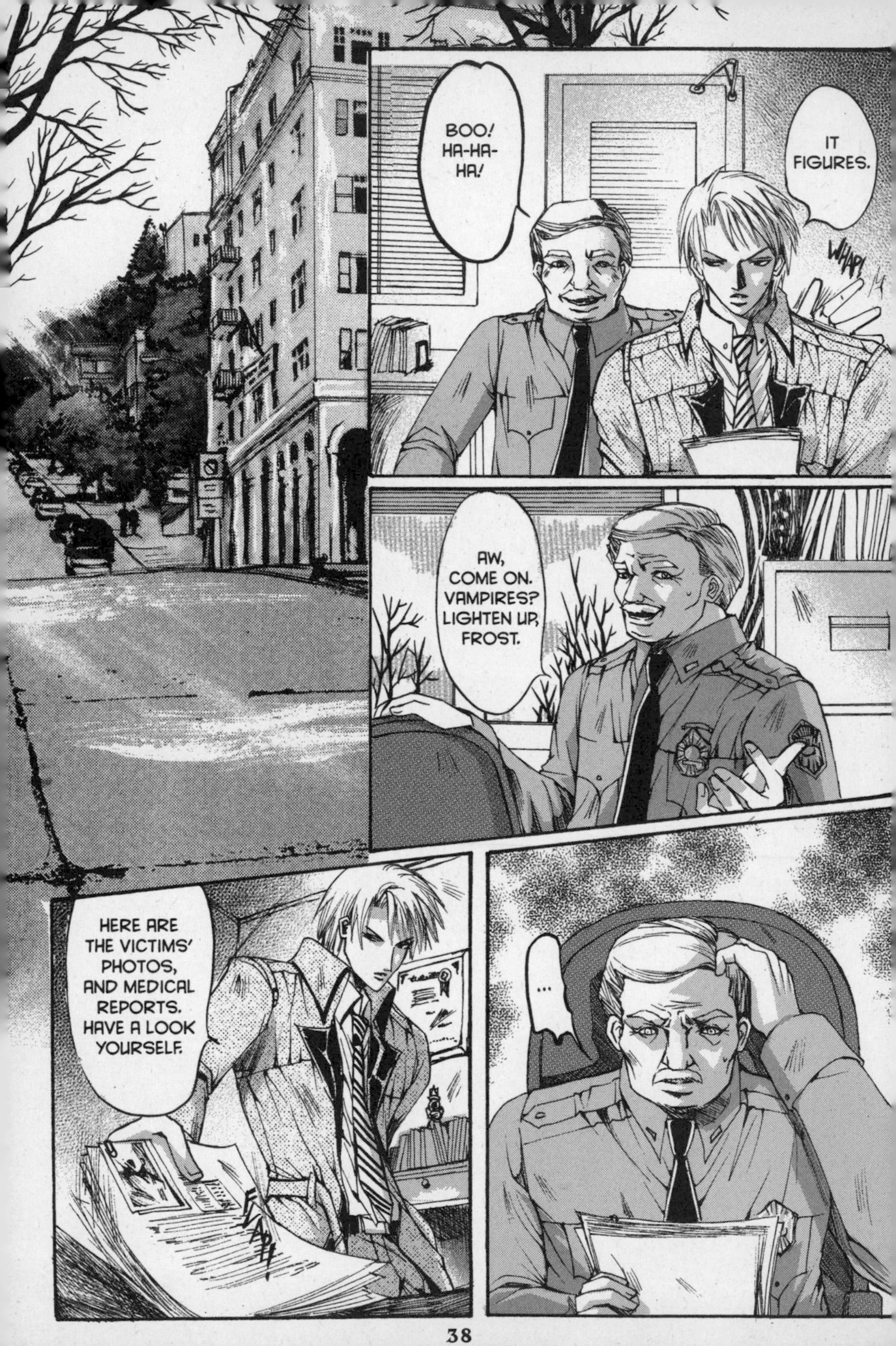
BOO! HA-HA-HA!
IT FIGURES.
WHAP!
AW, COME ON. VAMPIRES? LIGHTEN UP, FROST.
HERE ARE THE VICTIMS' PHOTOS, AND MEDICAL REPORTS. HAVE A LOOK YOURSELF.
FLAP!
...

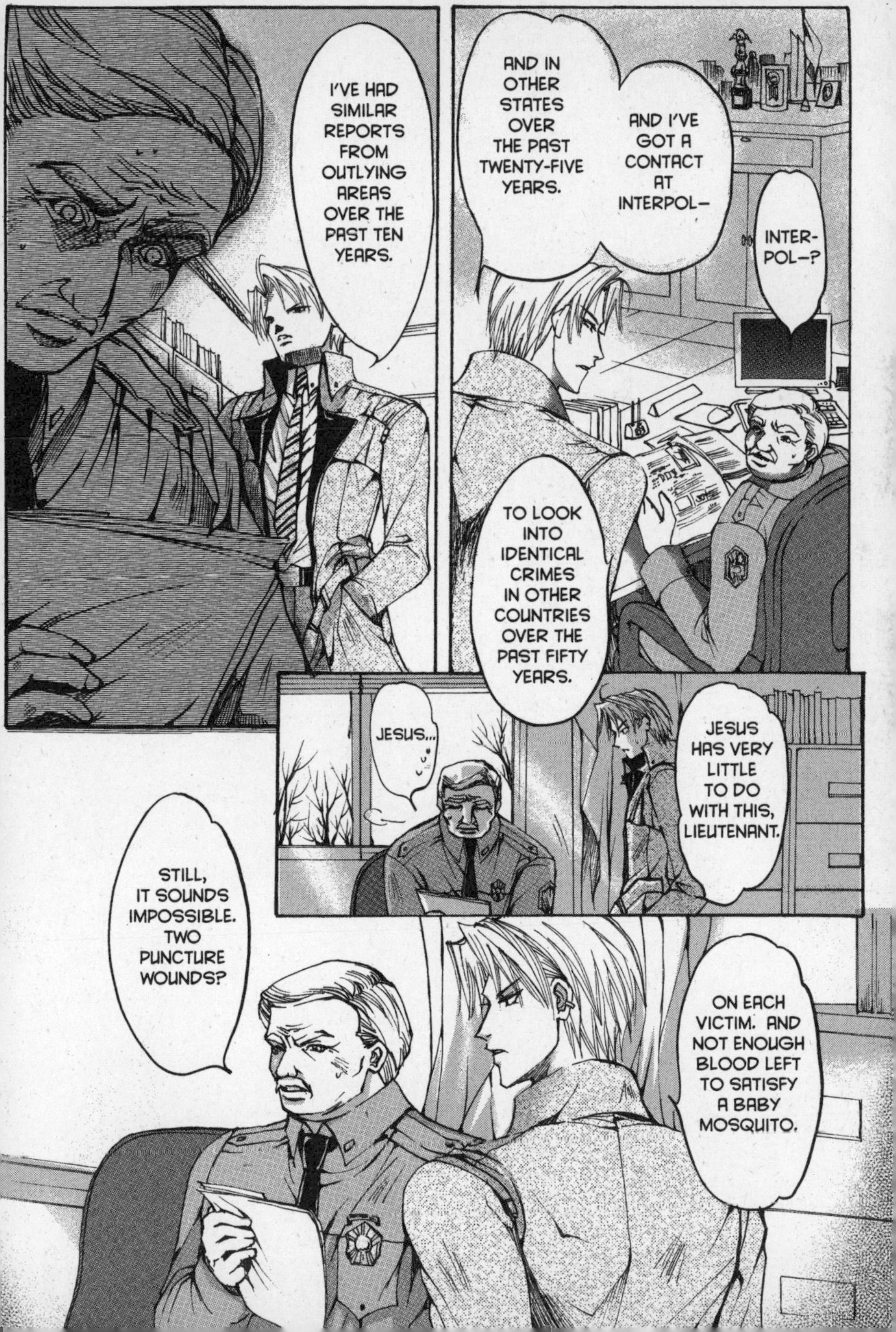
I'VE HAD SIMILAR REPORTS FROM OUTLYING AREAS OVER THE PAST TEN YEARS.
AND IN OTHER STATES OVER THE PAST TWENTY-FIVE YEARS.
AND I'VE GOT A CONTACT AT INTERPOL–
INTER-POL–?
TO LOOK INTO IDENTICAL CRIMES IN OTHER COUNTRIES OVER THE PAST FIFTY YEARS.
JESUS...
JESUS HAS VERY LITTLE TO DO WITH THIS, LIEUTENANT.
STILL, IT SOUNDS IMPOSSIBLE. TWO PUNCTURE WOUNDS?
ON EACH VICTIM. AND NOT ENOUGH BLOOD LEFT TO SATISFY A BABY MOSQUITO.

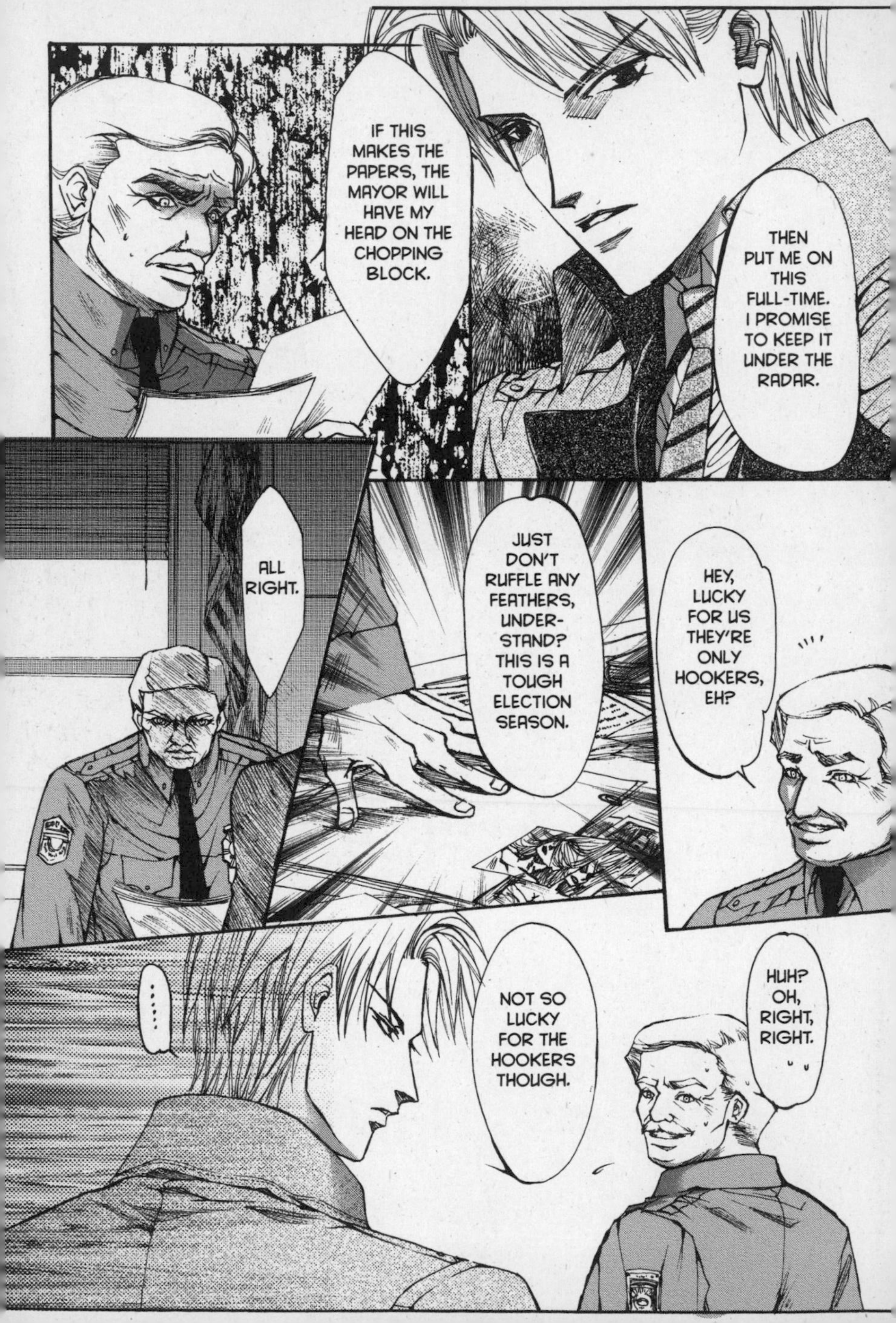
IF THIS MAKES THE PAPERS, THE MAYOR WILL HAVE MY HEAD ON THE CHOPPING BLOCK.
THEN PUT ME ON THIS FULL-TIME. I PROMISE TO KEEP IT UNDER THE RADAR.
ALL RIGHT.
JUST DON'T RUFFLE ANY FEATHERS, UNDER-STAND? THIS IS A TOUGH ELECTION SEASON.
HEY, LUCKY FOR US THEY'RE ONLY HOOKERS, EH?
......
NOT SO LUCKY FOR THE HOOKERS THOUGH.
HUH? OH, RIGHT, RIGHT.

CARE FOR AN HORS D'OEUVRE?

NOTHING FOR ME.

IAN, MEET GIANCARLO. HE'S ONE OF OUR MOST GENEROUS BENEFACTORS, AND A TRUE EXPERT IN NEOCLASSICAL ART.

VERY PLEASED TO MEET YOU.

THE PLEASURE IS MINE.

PLEASE EXCUSE ME.

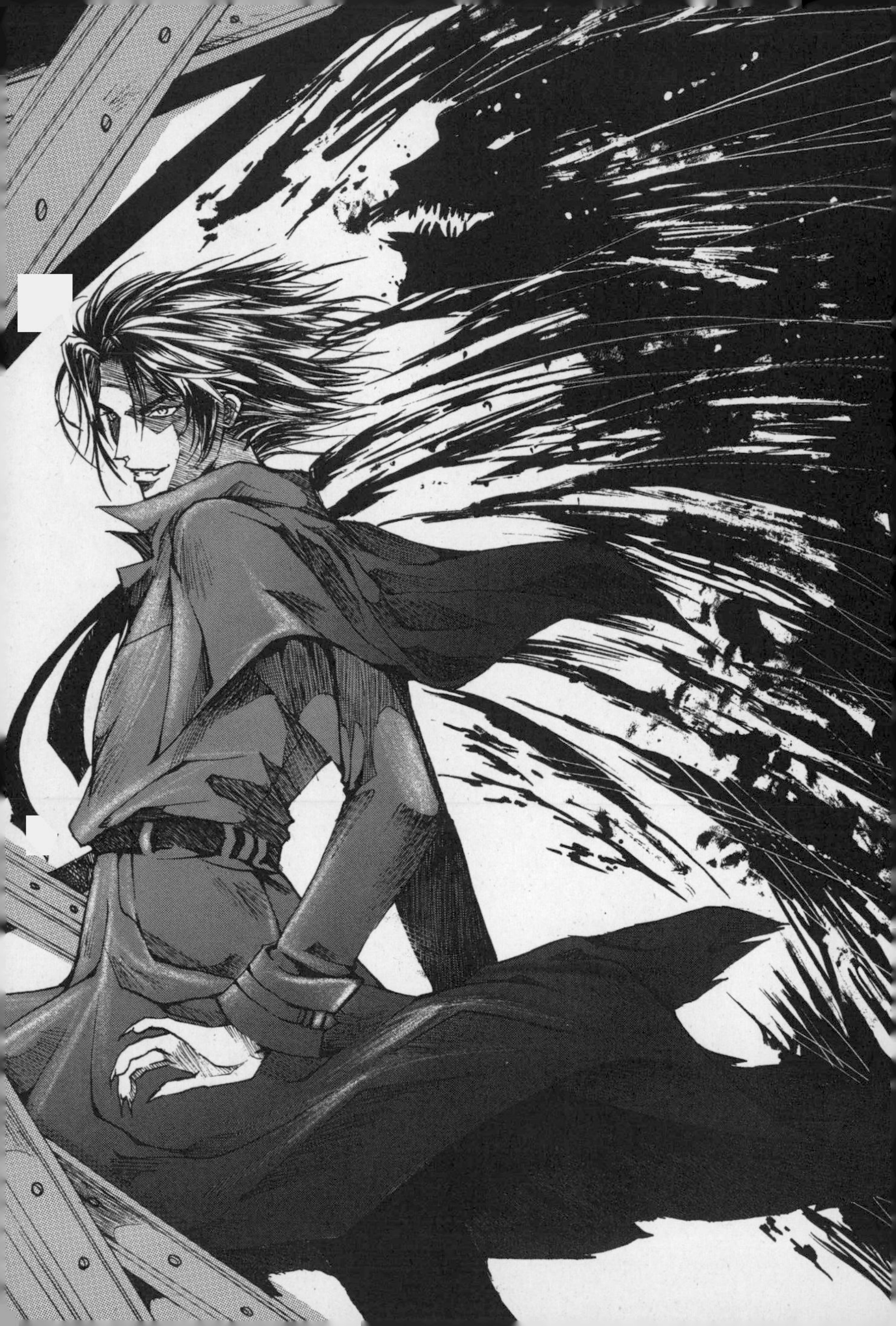

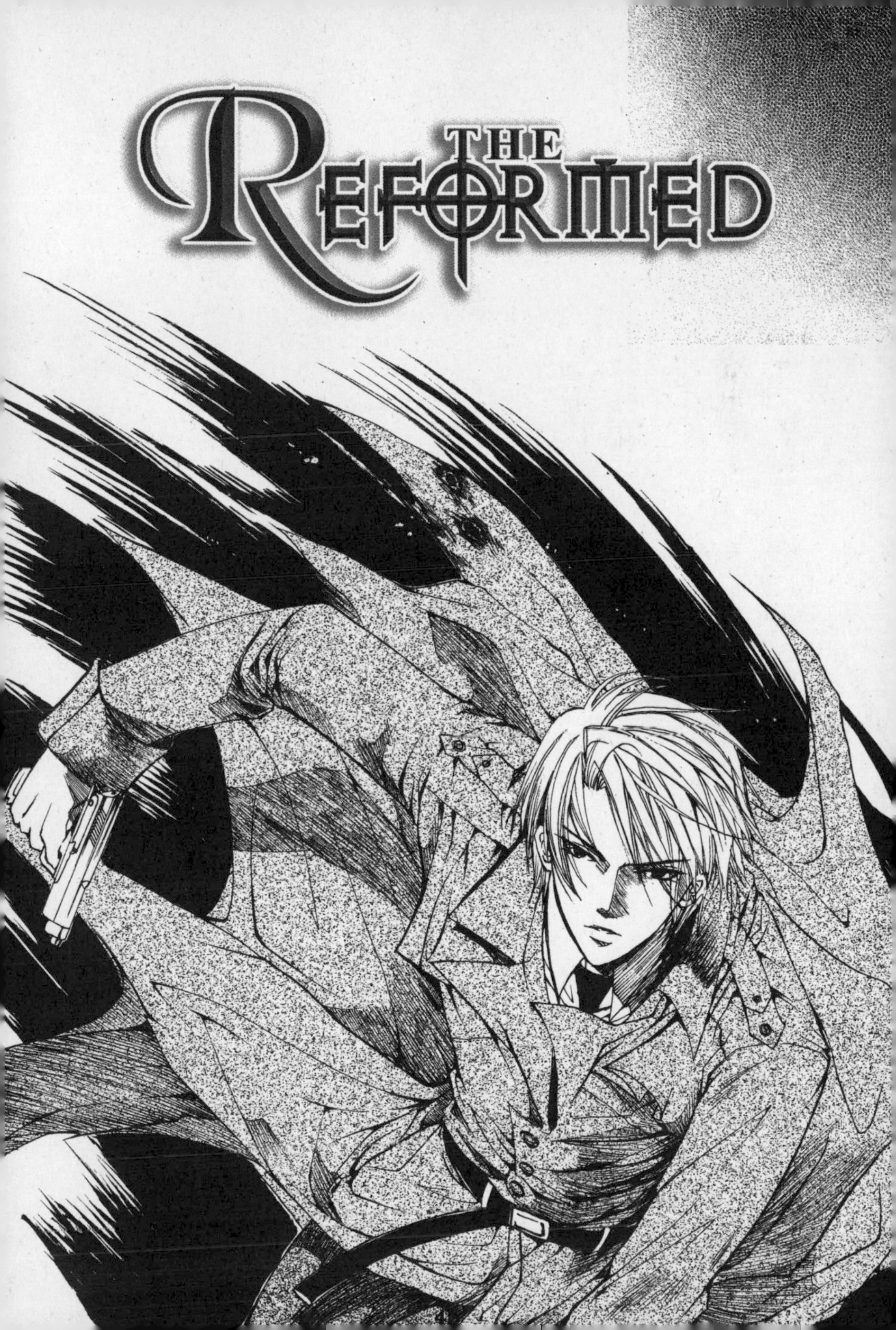
THE REFORMED

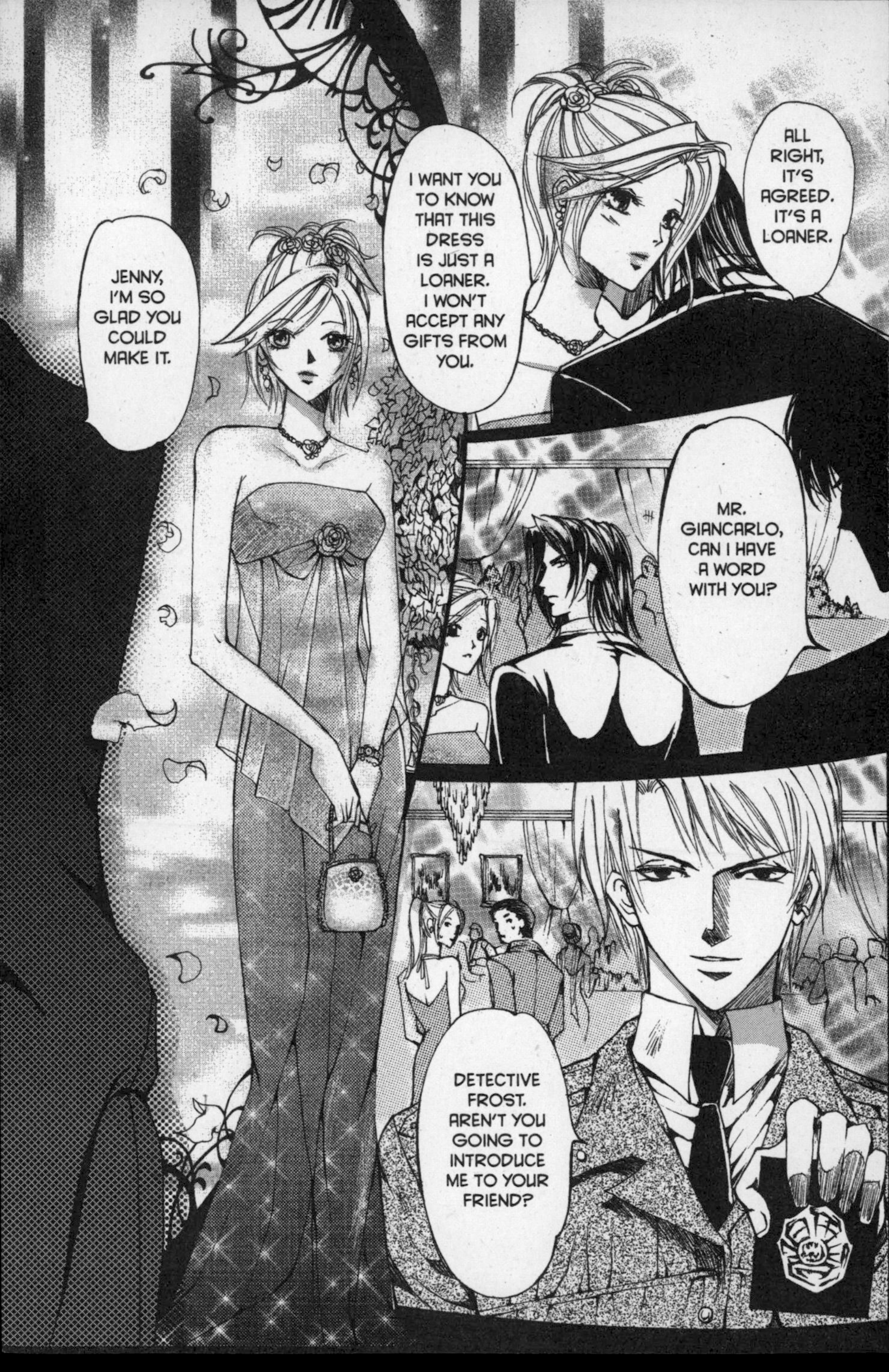
JENNY, I'M SO GLAD YOU COULD MAKE IT.
I WANT YOU TO KNOW THAT THIS DRESS IS JUST A LOANER. I WON'T ACCEPT ANY GIFTS FROM YOU.
ALL RIGHT, IT'S AGREED. IT'S A LOANER.
MR. GIANCARLO, CAN I HAVE A WORD WITH YOU?
DETECTIVE FROST. AREN'T YOU GOING TO INTRODUCE ME TO YOUR FRIEND?

JENNY, WOULD YOU PLEASE GET US SOMETHING TO DRINK WHILE I TALK TO THIS CHARMING FELLOW?

MAYBE SHE WANTS TO HEAR WHAT WE'RE GOING TO TALK ABOUT.

NOT THAT I DON'T FIND YOU INTERESTING, DETECTIVE, BUT IS THERE A POINT TO OUR MINGLING?

COUPLE NIGHTS AGO, THERE WAS A VICIOUS ATTACK IN A DOWNTOWN COFFEE SHOP.

CLOSE TO WHERE A PROSTITUTE WAS KILLED. TWO PUNCTURE WOUNDS, AT THE BASE OF THE NECK.

THE VAMPIRE MURDERS?

THAT'S FUNNY. I DIDN'T SAY ANYTHING ABOUT VAMPIRES.

THERE WERE NO WITNESSES IN THE DINER ATTACK, BUT THERE WAS A SURVIVOR. WE GOT A COMPOSITE SKETCH. WE'RE THINKING THEY COULD BE RELATED.

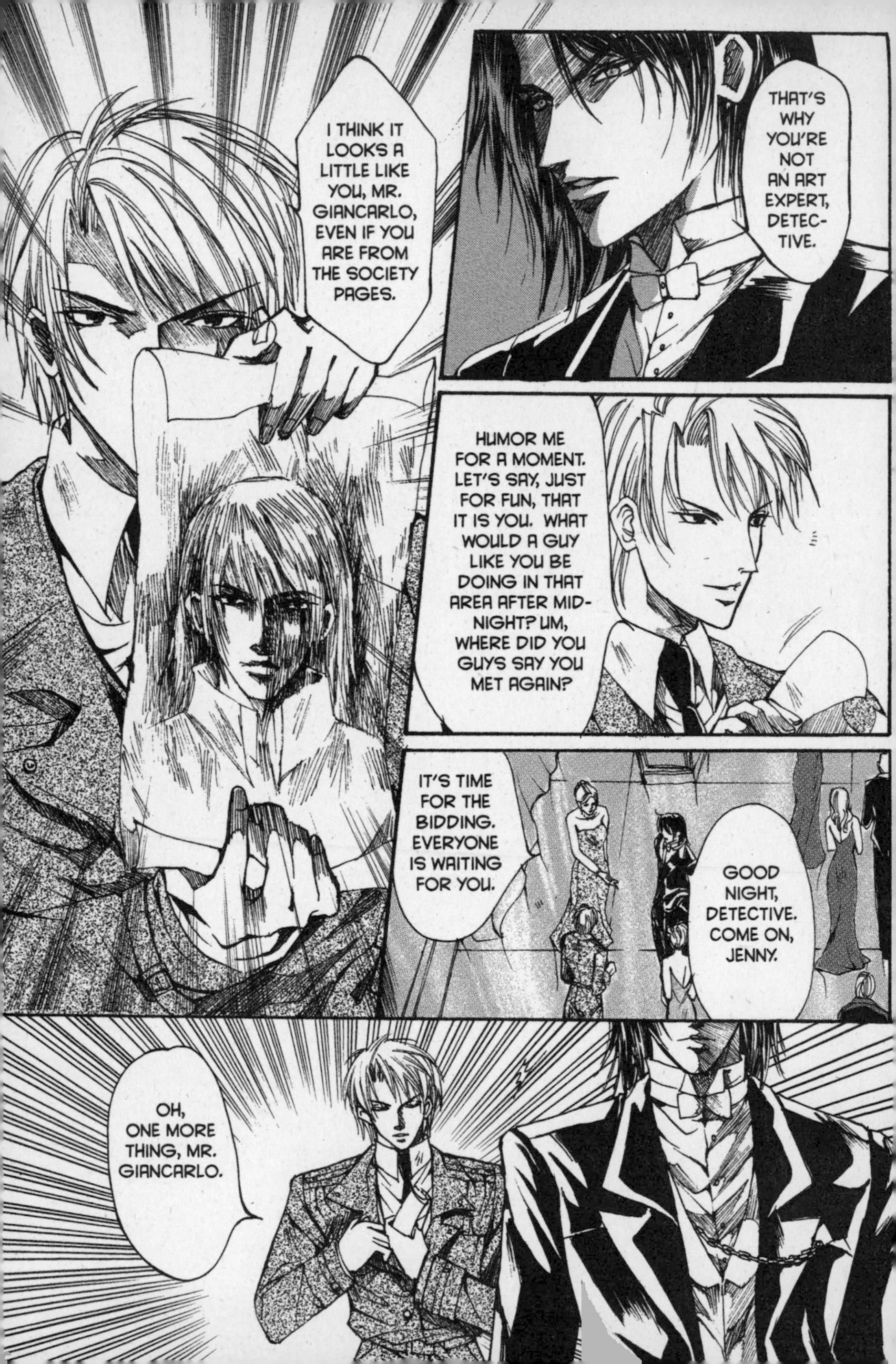
I THINK IT LOOKS A LITTLE LIKE YOU, MR. GIANCARLO, EVEN IF YOU ARE FROM THE SOCIETY PAGES.
THAT'S WHY YOU'RE NOT AN ART EXPERT, DETECTIVE.
HUMOR ME FOR A MOMENT. LET'S SAY, JUST FOR FUN, THAT IT IS YOU. WHAT WOULD A GUY LIKE YOU BE DOING IN THAT AREA AFTER MID-NIGHT? UM, WHERE DID YOU GUYS SAY YOU MET AGAIN?
IT'S TIME FOR THE BIDDING. EVERYONE IS WAITING FOR YOU.
GOOD NIGHT, DETECTIVE. COME ON, JENNY.
OH, ONE MORE THING, MR. GIANCARLO.

WHY IS IT THAT NONE OF THESE GUESTS I SPOKE TO HAS EVER SEEN YOU DURING THE DAY?

SPEAKING OF VAMPIRES, ISN'T THERE A LEGEND ABOUT THAT?

I THINK I KNOW IT. THEY SLEEP DURING THE DAY, AND FEED AT NIGHT.

YES, THAT'S IT.

LEGENDS ARE FUNNY THINGS.

THERE'S OFTEN A GRAIN OF TRUTH TO THEM. I MYSELF WOULD MAKE A WONDERFUL VAMPIRE. I TRADE ON THE ASIAN MARKETS EVERY DAY, WHICH IS OUR NIGHTTIME. SO I SLEEP DURING THE DAY.

BUT IF DETECTIVE FROST HAS ENOUGH PULL TO FIND ME A POSITION WHERE I CAN SLEEP NORMAL HOURS —WITHOUT A DROP IN EARNINGS— I PROMISE TO TURN INTO A NORMAL HUMAN ONCE AGAIN.

VERY GOOD. HEY, BYGONES?

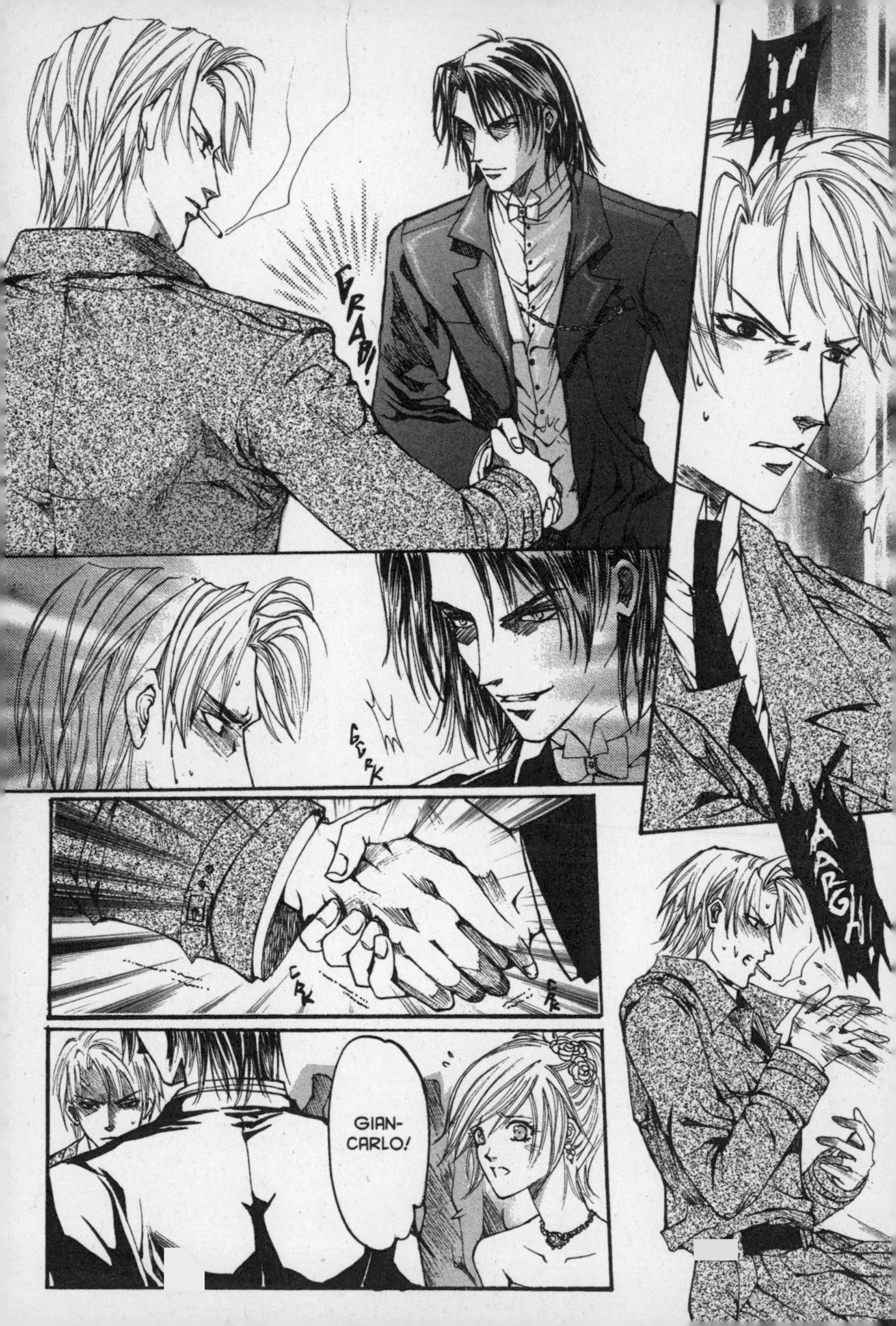
GRAB!
!!
GURK
CRK
GIAN-CARLO!
AARGH!

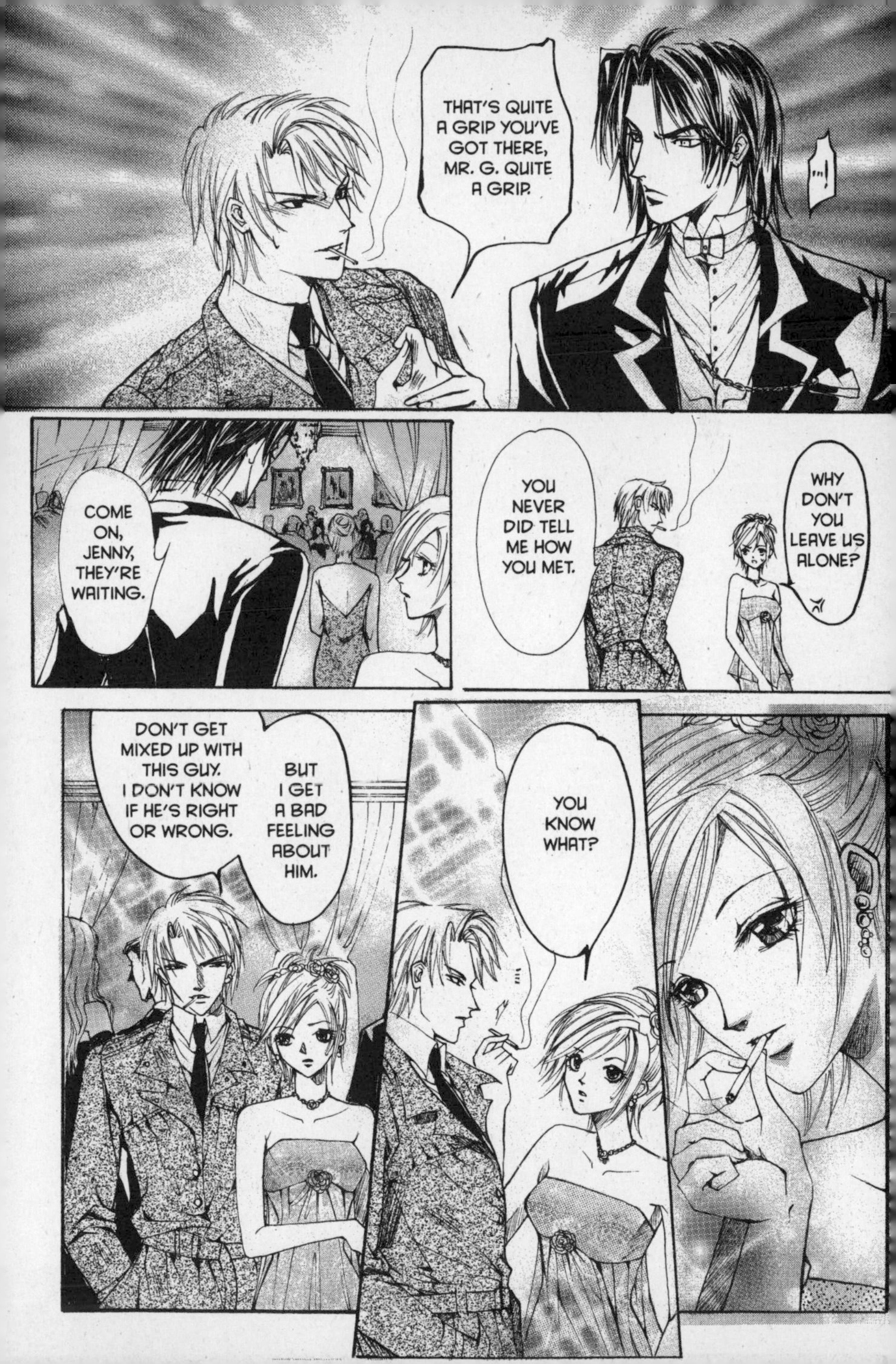
THAT'S QUITE A GRIP YOU'VE GOT THERE, MR. G. QUITE A GRIP.
...!
COME ON, JENNY, THEY'RE WAITING.
YOU NEVER DID TELL ME HOW YOU MET.
WHY DON'T YOU LEAVE US ALONE?
DON'T GET MIXED UP WITH THIS GUY. I DON'T KNOW IF HE'S RIGHT OR WRONG.
BUT I GET A BAD FEELING ABOUT HIM.
YOU KNOW WHAT?

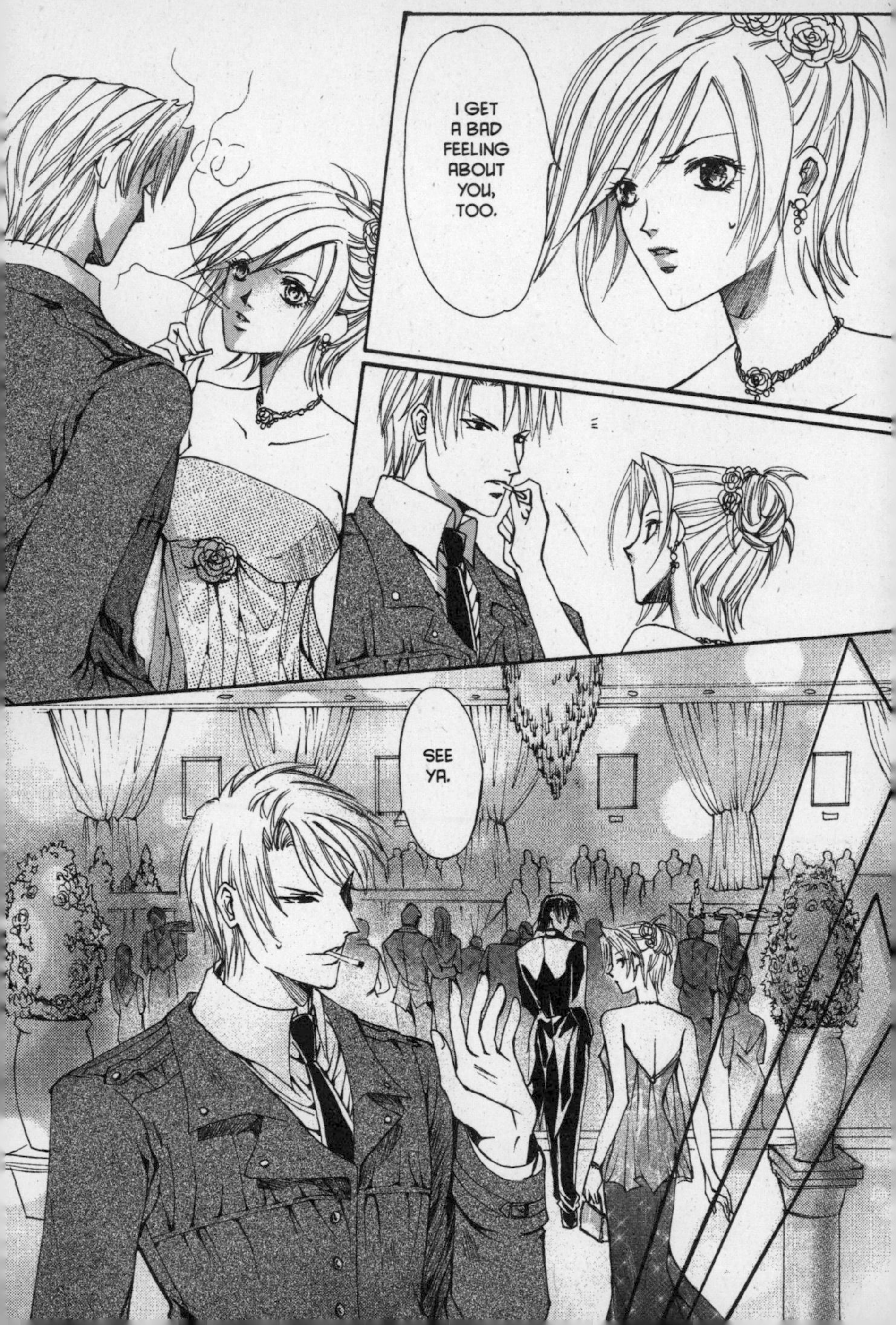
I GET A BAD FEELING ABOUT YOU, TOO.
SEE YA.

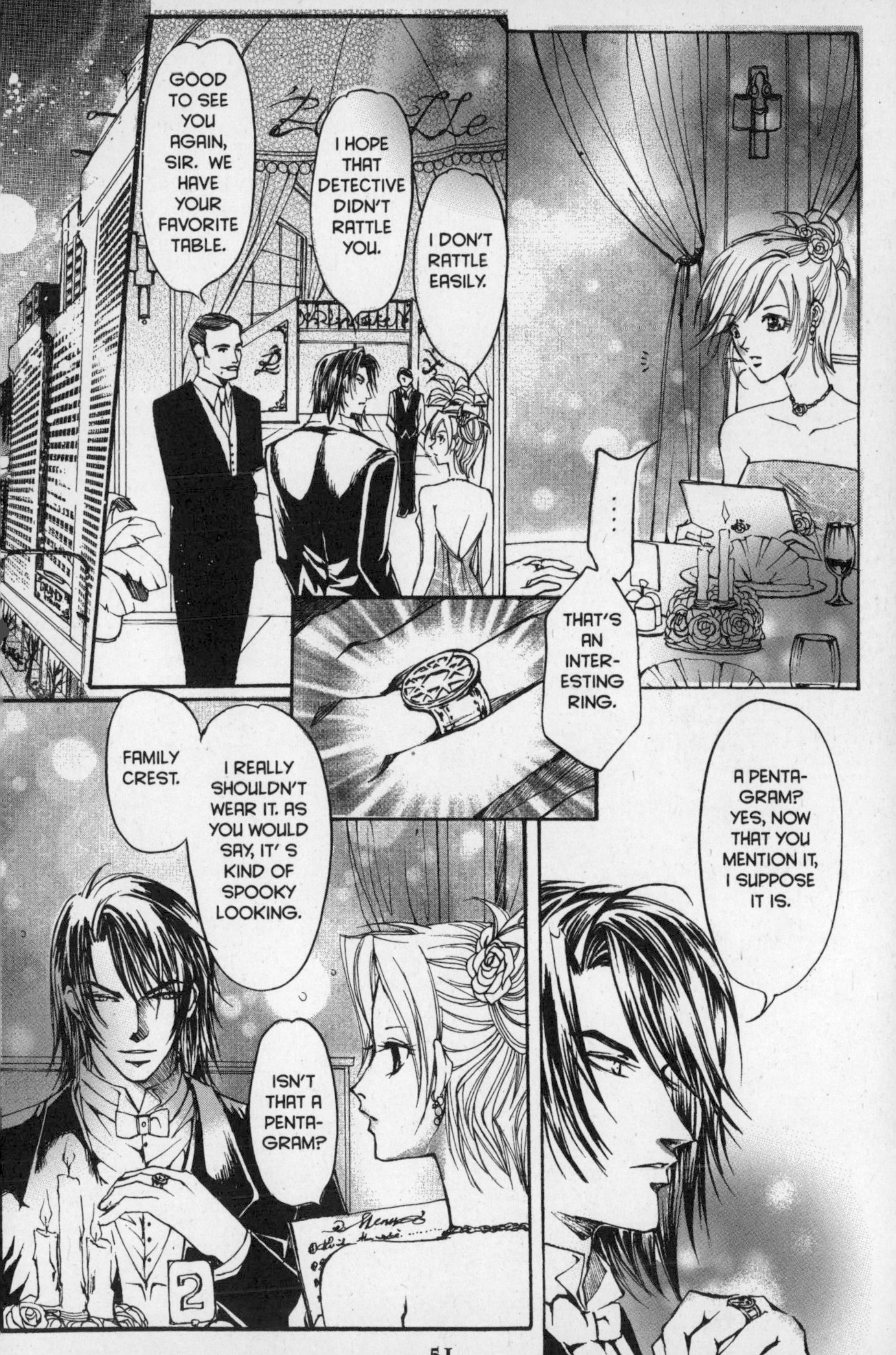
GOOD TO SEE YOU AGAIN, SIR. WE HAVE YOUR FAVORITE TABLE.
I HOPE THAT DETECTIVE DIDN'T RATTLE YOU.
I DON'T RATTLE EASILY.
....
THAT'S AN INTER-ESTING RING.
FAMILY CREST.
I REALLY SHOULDN'T WEAR IT. AS YOU WOULD SAY, IT'S KIND OF SPOOKY LOOKING.
ISN'T THAT A PENTA-GRAM?
A PENTA-GRAM? YES, NOW THAT YOU MENTION IT, I SUPPOSE IT IS.

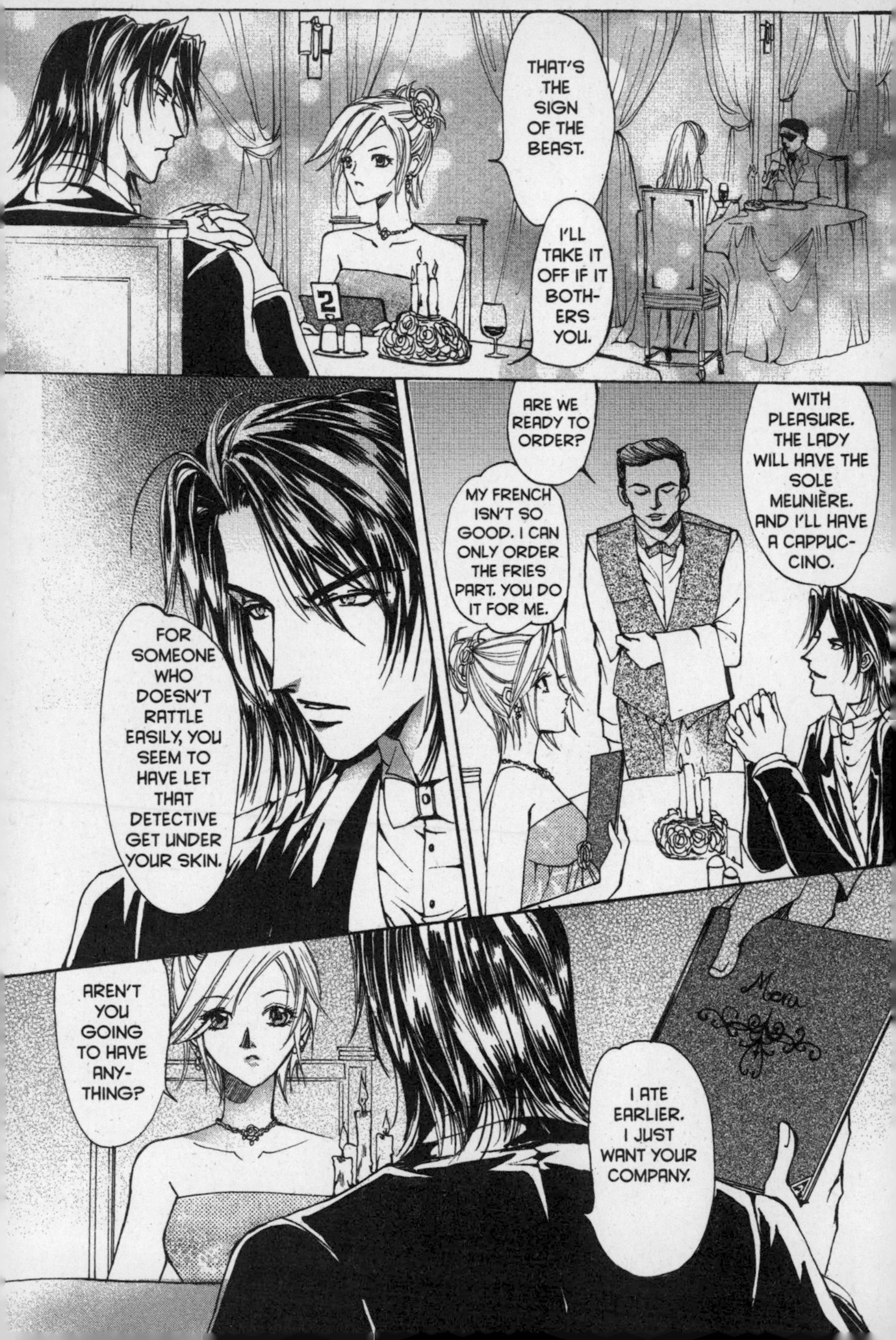
THAT'S THE SIGN OF THE BEAST.
I'LL TAKE IT OFF IF IT BOTHERS YOU.
FOR SOMEONE WHO DOESN'T RATTLE EASILY, YOU SEEM TO HAVE LET THAT DETECTIVE GET UNDER YOUR SKIN.
ARE WE READY TO ORDER?
MY FRENCH ISN'T SO GOOD. I CAN ONLY ORDER THE FRIES PART. YOU DO IT FOR ME.
WITH PLEASURE. THE LADY WILL HAVE THE SOLE MEUNIÈRE. AND I'LL HAVE A CAPPUCCINO.
ARE'T YOU GOING TO HAVE ANYTHING?
I ATE EARLIER. I JUST WANT YOUR COMPANY.
Menu

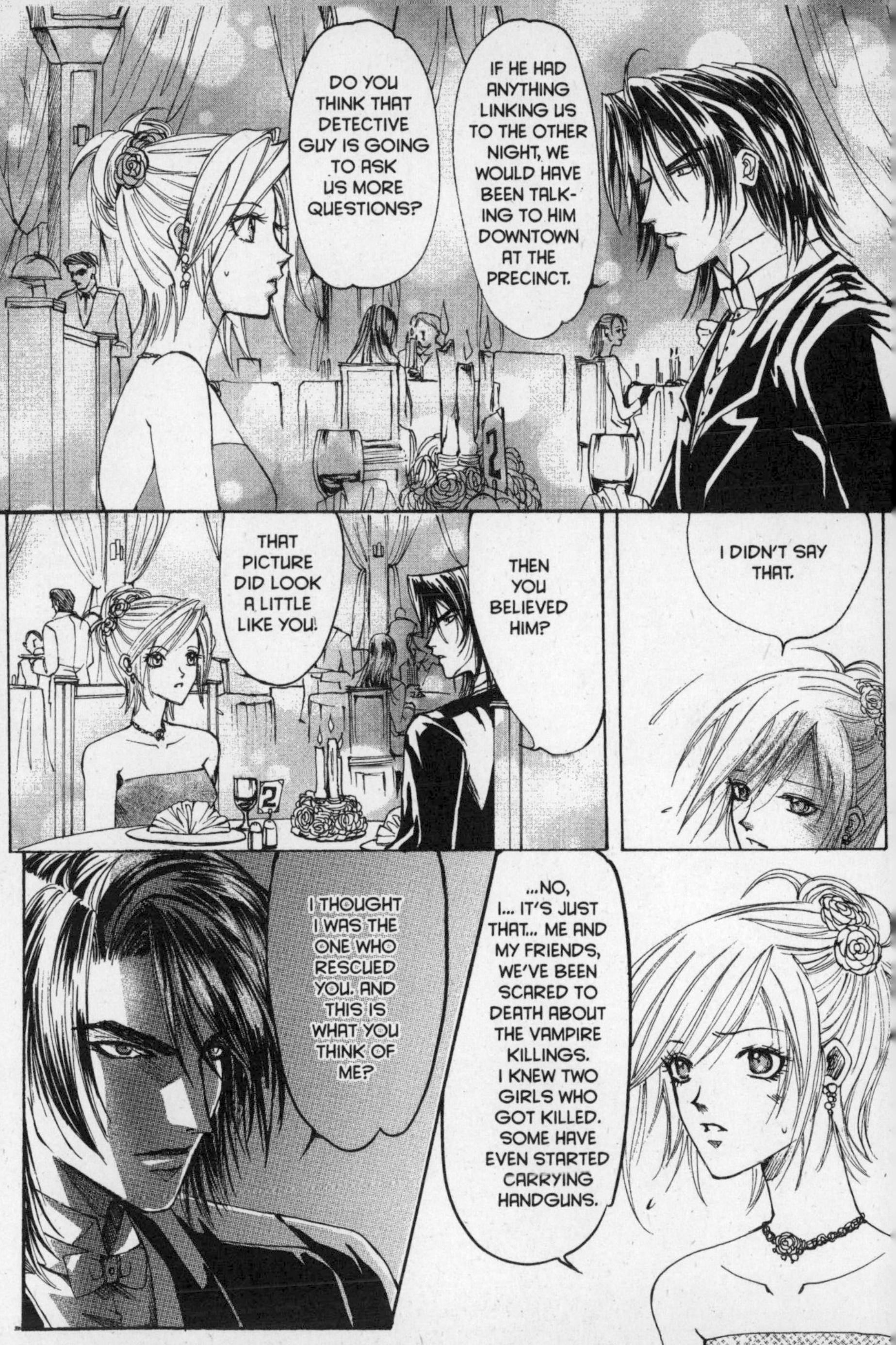
DO YOU THINK THAT DETECTIVE GUY IS GOING TO ASK US MORE QUESTIONS?
IF HE HAD ANYTHING LINKING US TO THE OTHER NIGHT, WE WOULD HAVE BEEN TALK-ING TO HIM DOWNTOWN AT THE PRECINCT.
THAT PICTURE DID LOOK A LITTLE LIKE YOU.
THEN YOU BELIEVED HIM?
I DIDN'T SAY THAT.
I THOUGHT I WAS THE ONE WHO RESCUED YOU. AND THIS IS WHAT YOU THINK OF ME?
...NO, I... IT'S JUST THAT... ME AND MY FRIENDS, WE'VE BEEN SCARED TO DEATH ABOUT THE VAMPIRE KILLINGS. I KNEW TWO GIRLS WHO GOT KILLED. SOME HAVE EVEN STARTED CARRYING HANDGUNS.

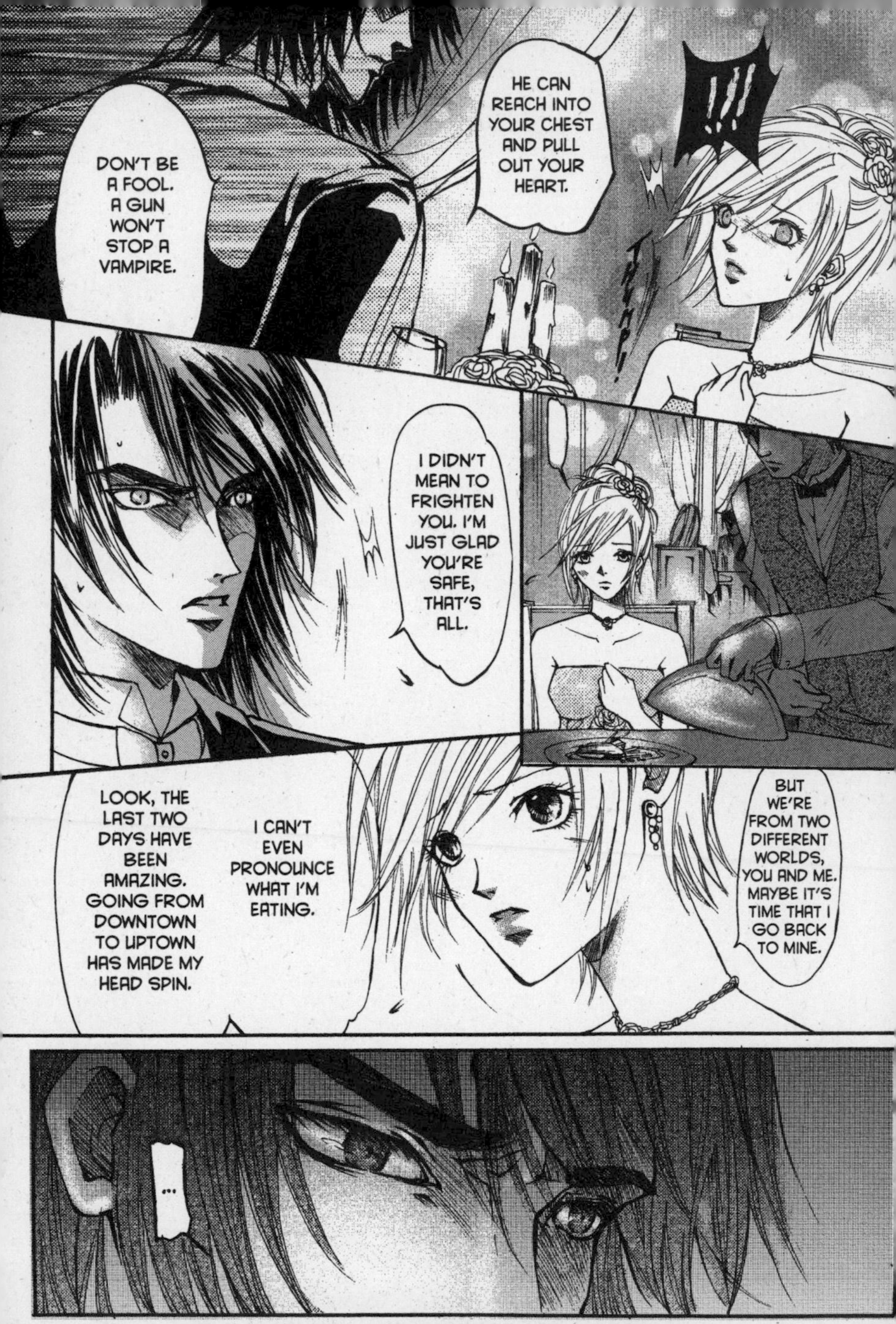
DON'T BE A FOOL. A GUN WON'T STOP A VAMPIRE.
HE CAN REACH INTO YOUR CHEST AND PULL OUT YOUR HEART.
!!!
I DIDN'T MEAN TO FRIGHTEN YOU. I'M JUST GLAD YOU'RE SAFE, THAT'S ALL.
LOOK, THE LAST TWO DAYS HAVE BEEN AMAZING. GOING FROM DOWNTOWN TO UPTOWN HAS MADE MY HEAD SPIN.
I CAN'T EVEN PRONOUNCE WHAT I'M EATING.
BUT WE'RE FROM TWO DIFFERENT WORLDS, YOU AND ME. MAYBE IT'S TIME THAT I GO BACK TO MINE.
...

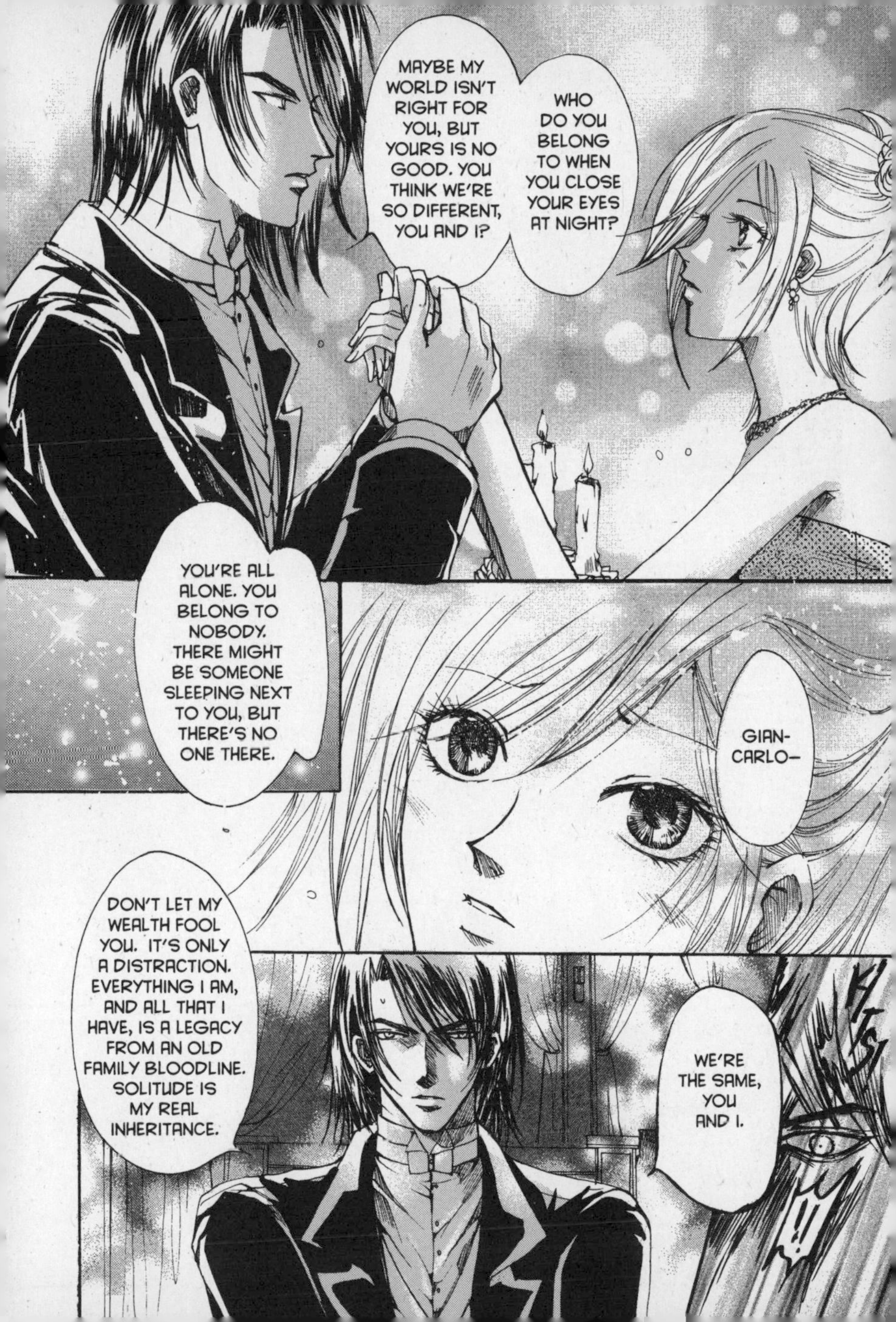
MAYBE MY WORLD ISN'T RIGHT FOR YOU, BUT YOURS IS NO GOOD. YOU THINK WE'RE SO DIFFERENT, YOU AND I?
WHO DO YOU BELONG TO WHEN YOU CLOSE YOUR EYES AT NIGHT?
YOU'RE ALL ALONE. YOU BELONG TO NOBODY. THERE MIGHT BE SOMEONE SLEEPING NEXT TO YOU, BUT THERE'S NO ONE THERE.
GIAN-CARLO—
DON'T LET MY WEALTH FOOL YOU. IT'S ONLY A DISTRACTION. EVERYTHING I AM, AND ALL THAT I HAVE, IS A LEGACY FROM AN OLD FAMILY BLOODLINE. SOLITUDE IS MY REAL INHERITANCE.
WE'RE THE SAME, YOU AND I.
!!

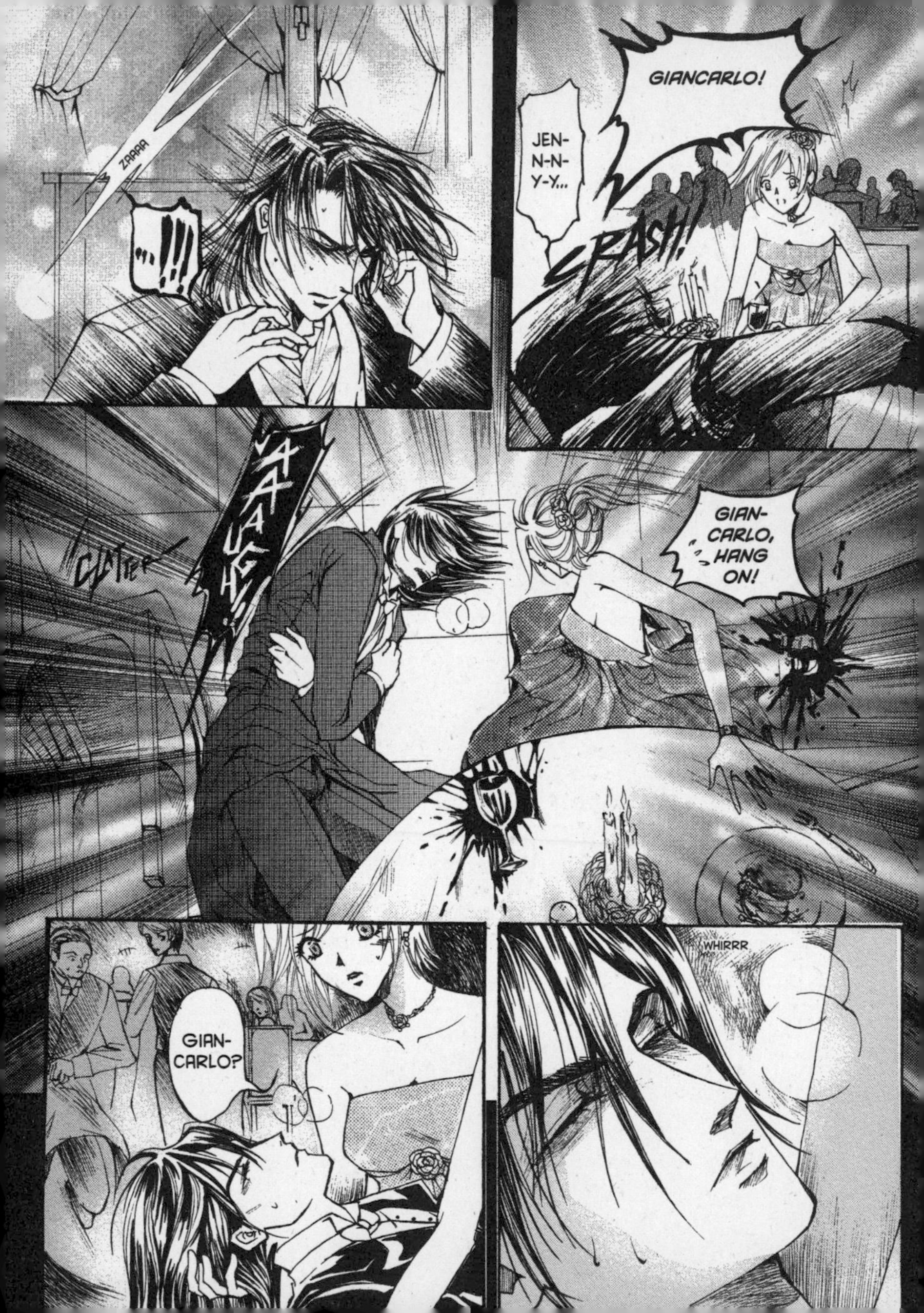
ZAAAA
...!!!!
GIANCARLO!
JEN-N-N-Y-Y...
CRASH!
AAAUGH!!
CLATTER
GIAN-CARLO, HANG ON!
GIAN-CARLO?
WHIRRR

WOO
WOO
WOO

WHAT'S WRONG WITH HIM?

THAT'S WHAT WE'RE GOING TO FIND OUT.

YOU'RE SEVERELY ANEMIC. BUT EVEN SO, THE REST OF YOUR NUMBERS ARE EXTRAORDINARY.

I CAN'T STAY HERE.

I'VE NEVER SEEN ANYTHING LIKE IT... YOUR IMMUNITIES ARE OFF THE WALL FANTASTIC. DO YOU MIND? I'D LIKE THE OTHER DOCTORS TO TAKE A LOOK AT THIS.

WHEN WAS THE LAST TIME YOU WERE EVEN ILL?

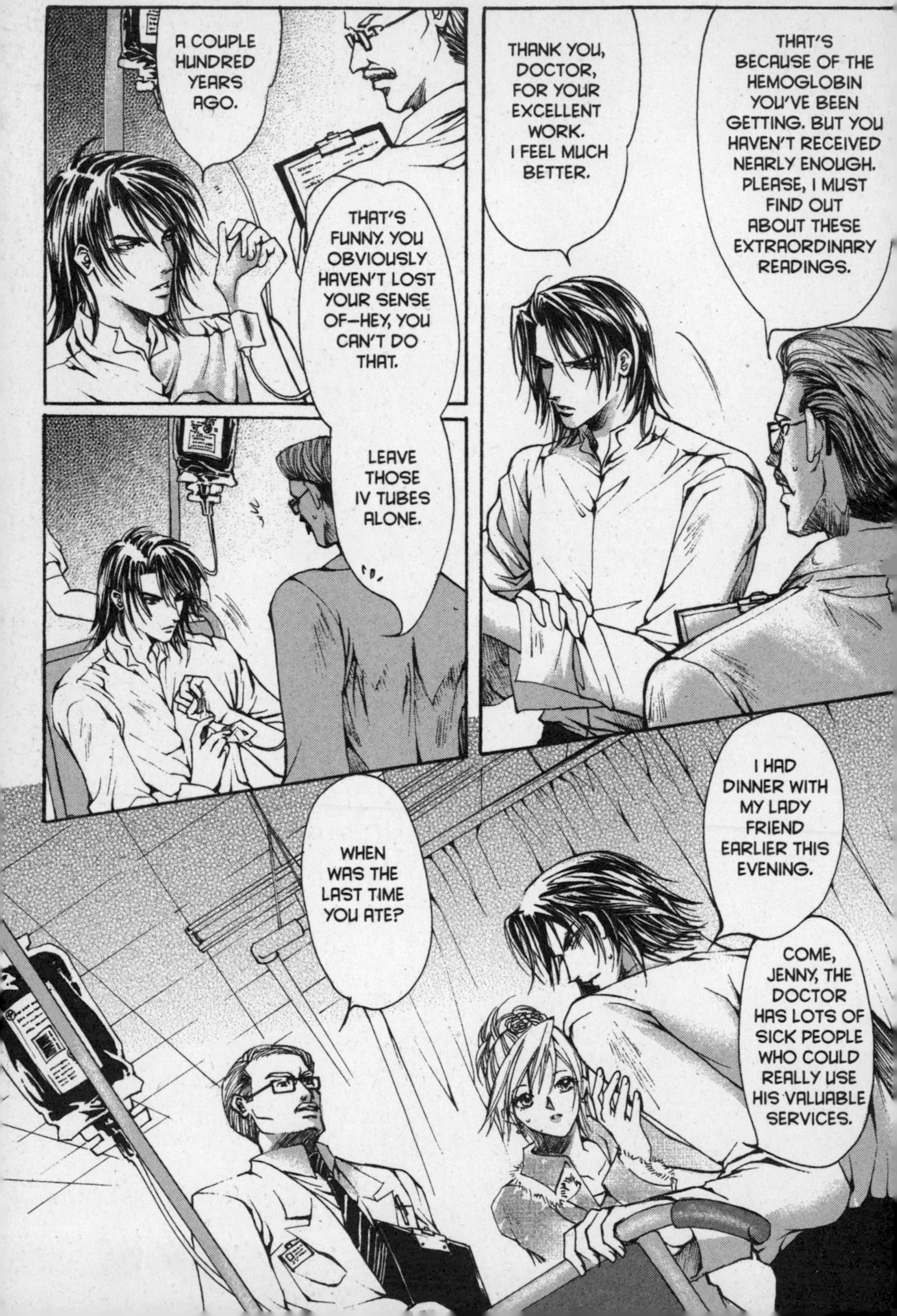
A COUPLE HUNDRED YEARS AGO.
THAT'S FUNNY. YOU OBVIOUSLY HAVEN'T LOST YOUR SENSE OF—HEY, YOU CAN'T DO THAT.
LEAVE THOSE IV TUBES ALONE.
THANK YOU, DOCTOR, FOR YOUR EXCELLENT WORK. I FEEL MUCH BETTER.
THAT'S BECAUSE OF THE HEMOGLOBIN YOU'VE BEEN GETTING. BUT YOU HAVEN'T RECEIVED NEARLY ENOUGH. PLEASE, I MUST FIND OUT ABOUT THESE EXTRAORDINARY READINGS.
WHEN WAS THE LAST TIME YOU ATE?
I HAD DINNER WITH MY LADY FRIEND EARLIER THIS EVENING.
COME, JENNY, THE DOCTOR HAS LOTS OF SICK PEOPLE WHO COULD REALLY USE HIS VALUABLE SERVICES.

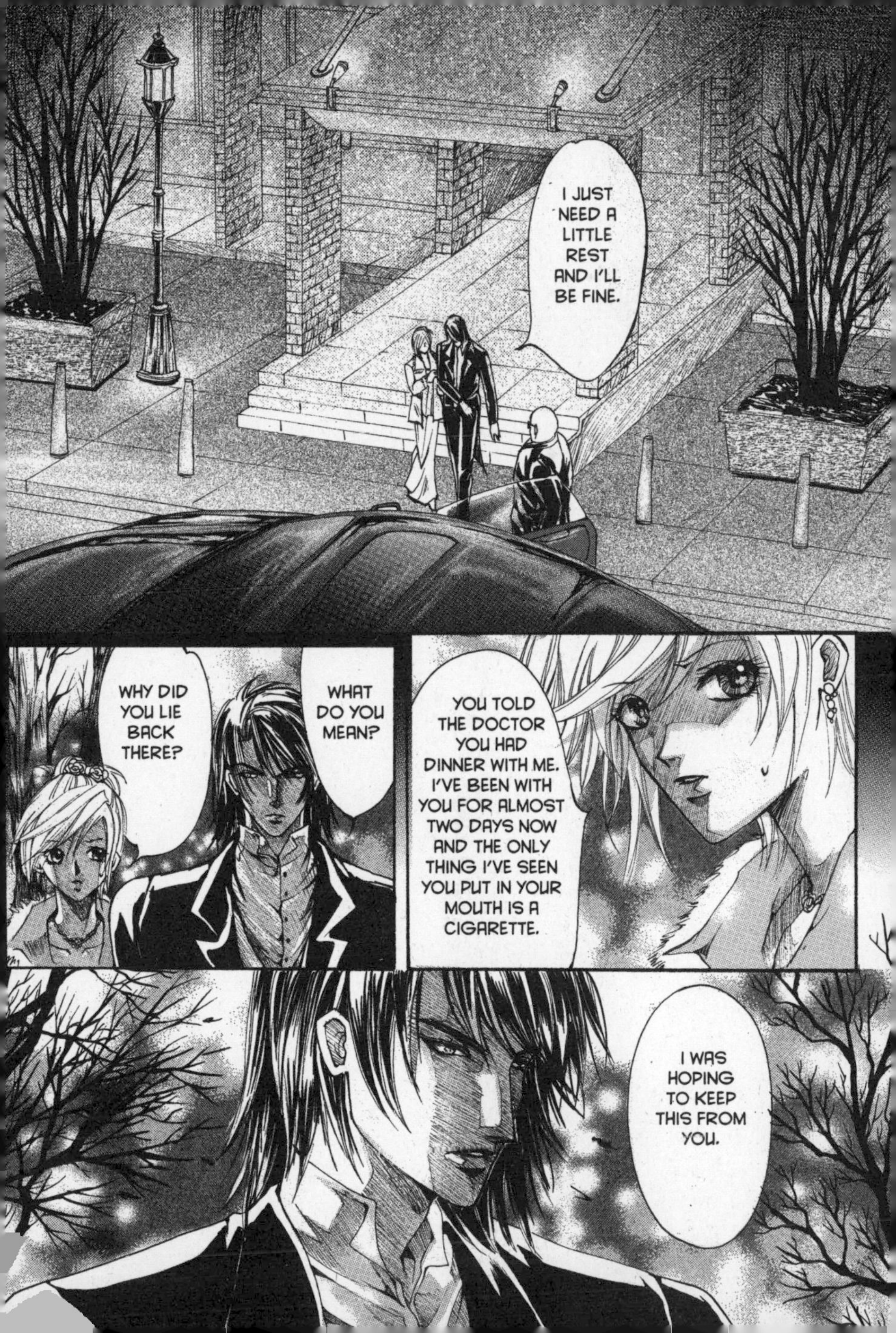

I JUST NEED A LITTLE REST AND I'LL BE FINE.
WHY DID YOU LIE BACK THERE?
WHAT DO YOU MEAN?
YOU TOLD THE DOCTOR YOU HAD DINNER WITH ME. I'VE BEEN WITH YOU FOR ALMOST TWO DAYS NOW AND THE ONLY THING I'VE SEEN YOU PUT IN YOUR MOUTH IS A CIGARETTE.
I WAS HOPING TO KEEP THIS FROM YOU.

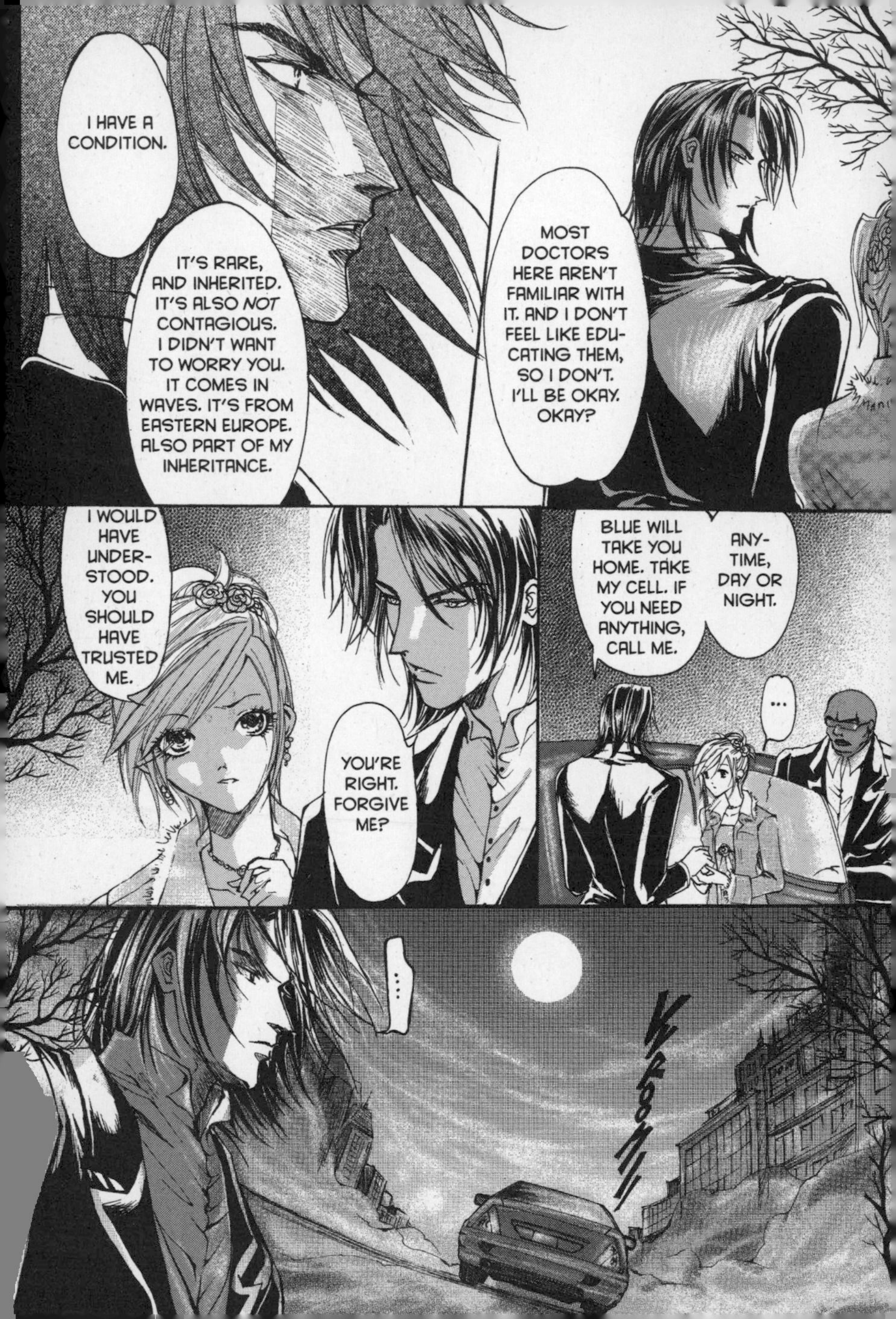
I HAVE A CONDITION.
IT'S RARE, AND INHERITED. IT'S ALSO *NOT* CONTAGIOUS. I DIDN'T WANT TO WORRY YOU. IT COMES IN WAVES. IT'S FROM EASTERN EUROPE. ALSO PART OF MY INHERITANCE.
MOST DOCTORS HERE AREN'T FAMILIAR WITH IT. AND I DON'T FEEL LIKE EDU-CATING THEM, SO I DON'T. I'LL BE OKAY. OKAY?
I WOULD HAVE UNDER-STOOD. YOU SHOULD HAVE TRUSTED ME.
YOU'RE RIGHT. FORGIVE ME?
BLUE WILL TAKE YOU HOME. TAKE MY CELL. IF YOU NEED ANYTHING, CALL ME.
ANY-TIME, DAY OR NIGHT.
...
....
VRROOM!!!

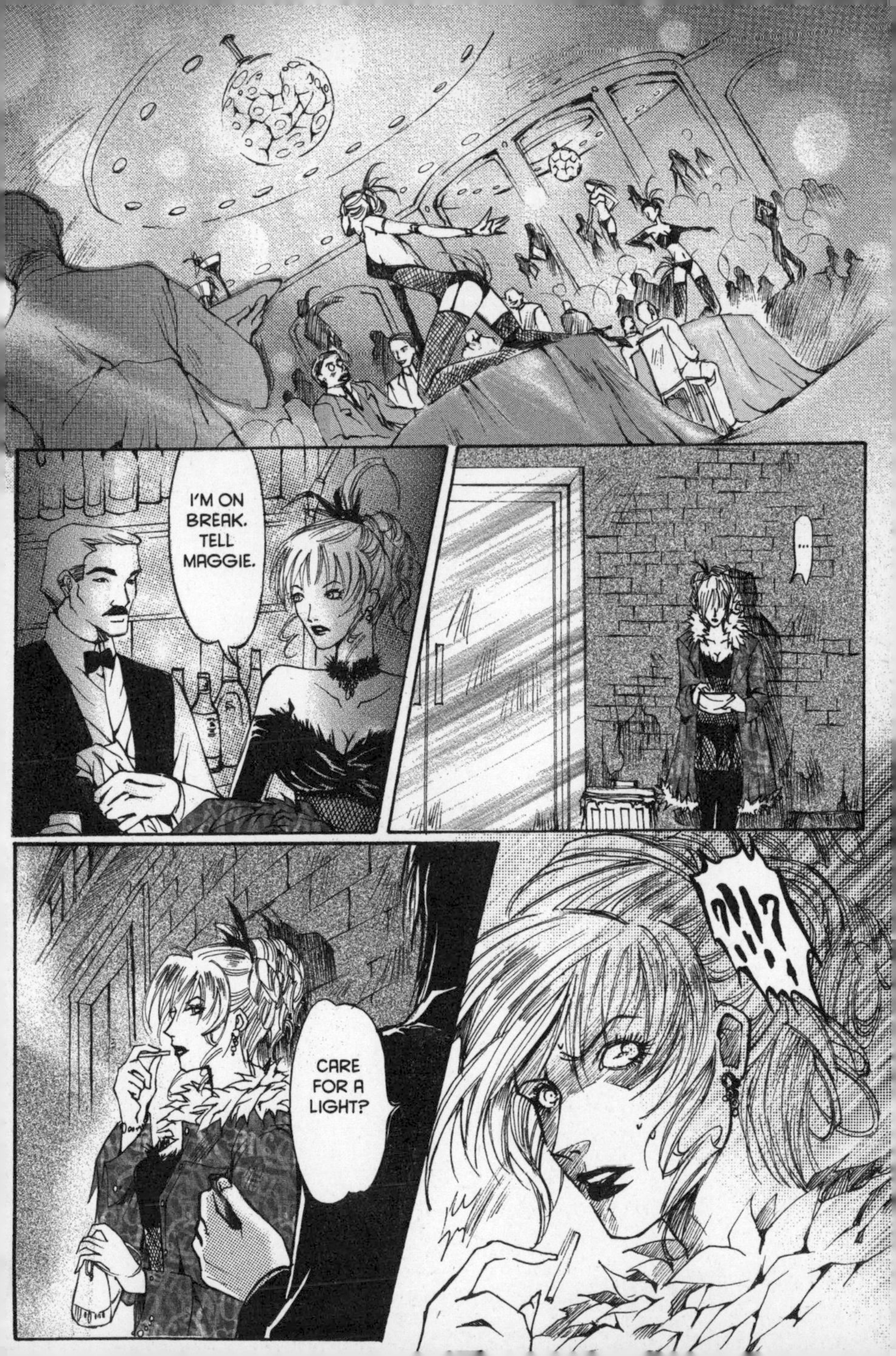
I'M ON BREAK. TELL MAGGIE.
...
CARE FOR A LIGHT?
?!!?

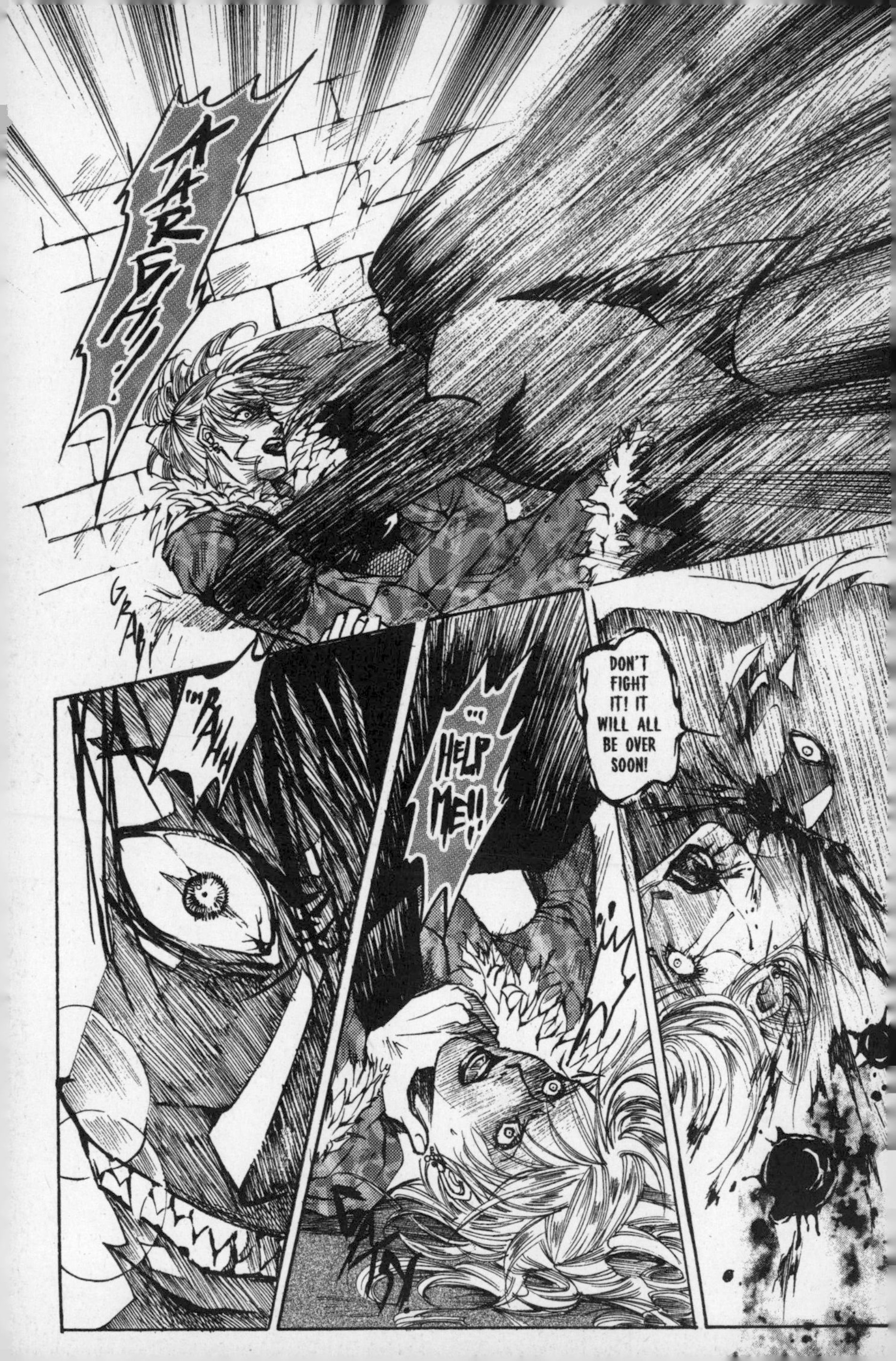
AARGH!...
GRAB!
RAAHH
...HELP ME!!
DON'T FIGHT IT! IT WILL ALL BE OVER SOON!

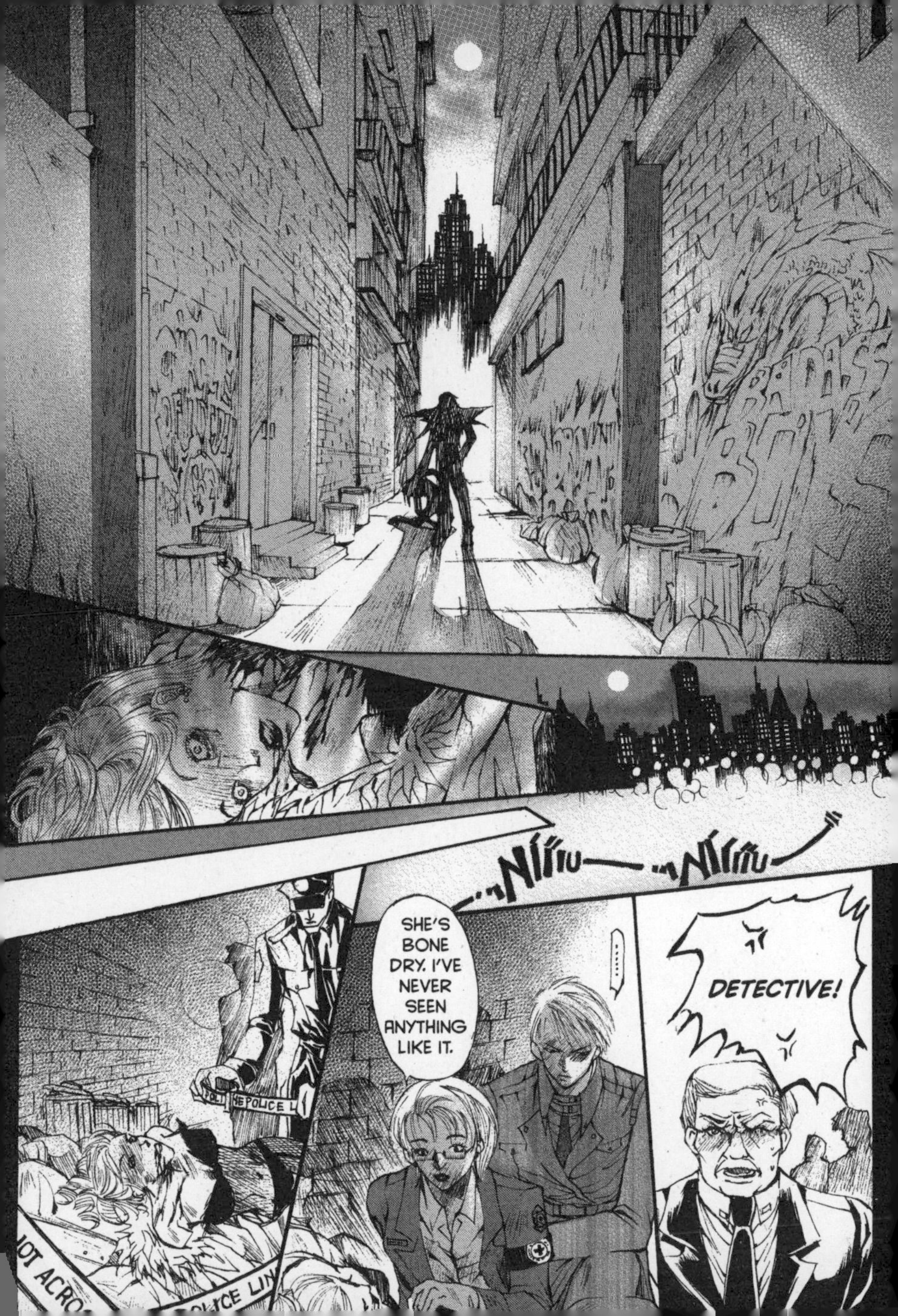
NIIIU—NIIIU
SHE'S BONE DRY. I'VE NEVER SEEN ANYTHING LIKE IT.
......
DETECTIVE!

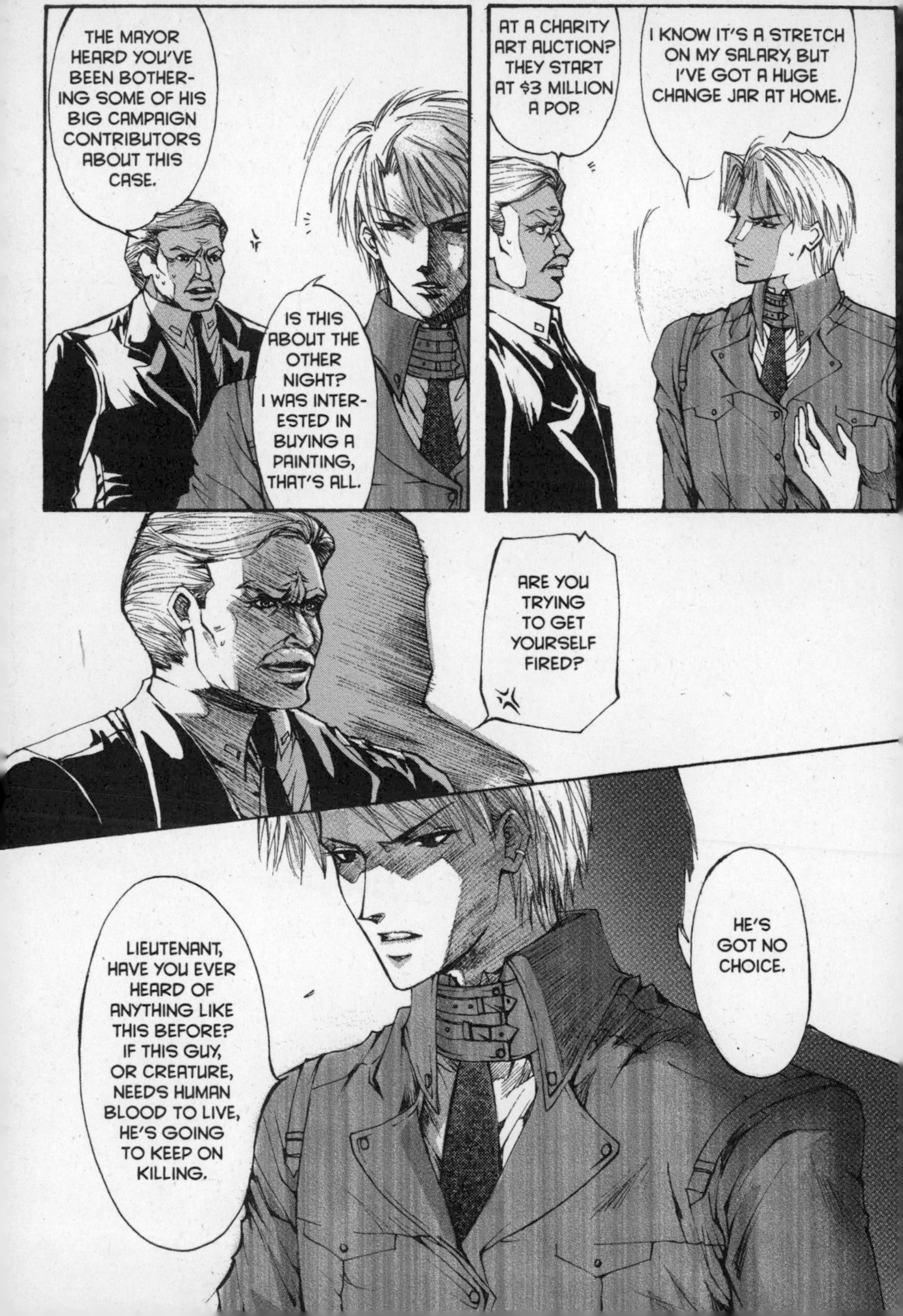
THE MAYOR HEARD YOU'VE BEEN BOTHER-ING SOME OF HIS BIG CAMPAIGN CONTRIBUTORS ABOUT THIS CASE.
IS THIS ABOUT THE OTHER NIGHT? I WAS INTER-ESTED IN BUYING A PAINTING, THAT'S ALL.
AT A CHARITY ART AUCTION? THEY START AT $3 MILLION A POP.
I KNOW IT'S A STRETCH ON MY SALARY, BUT I'VE GOT A HUGE CHANGE JAR AT HOME.
ARE YOU TRYING TO GET YOURSELF FIRED?
LIEUTENANT, HAVE YOU EVER HEARD OF ANYTHING LIKE THIS BEFORE? IF THIS GUY, OR CREATURE, NEEDS HUMAN BLOOD TO LIVE, HE'S GOING TO KEEP ON KILLING.
HE'S GOT NO CHOICE.

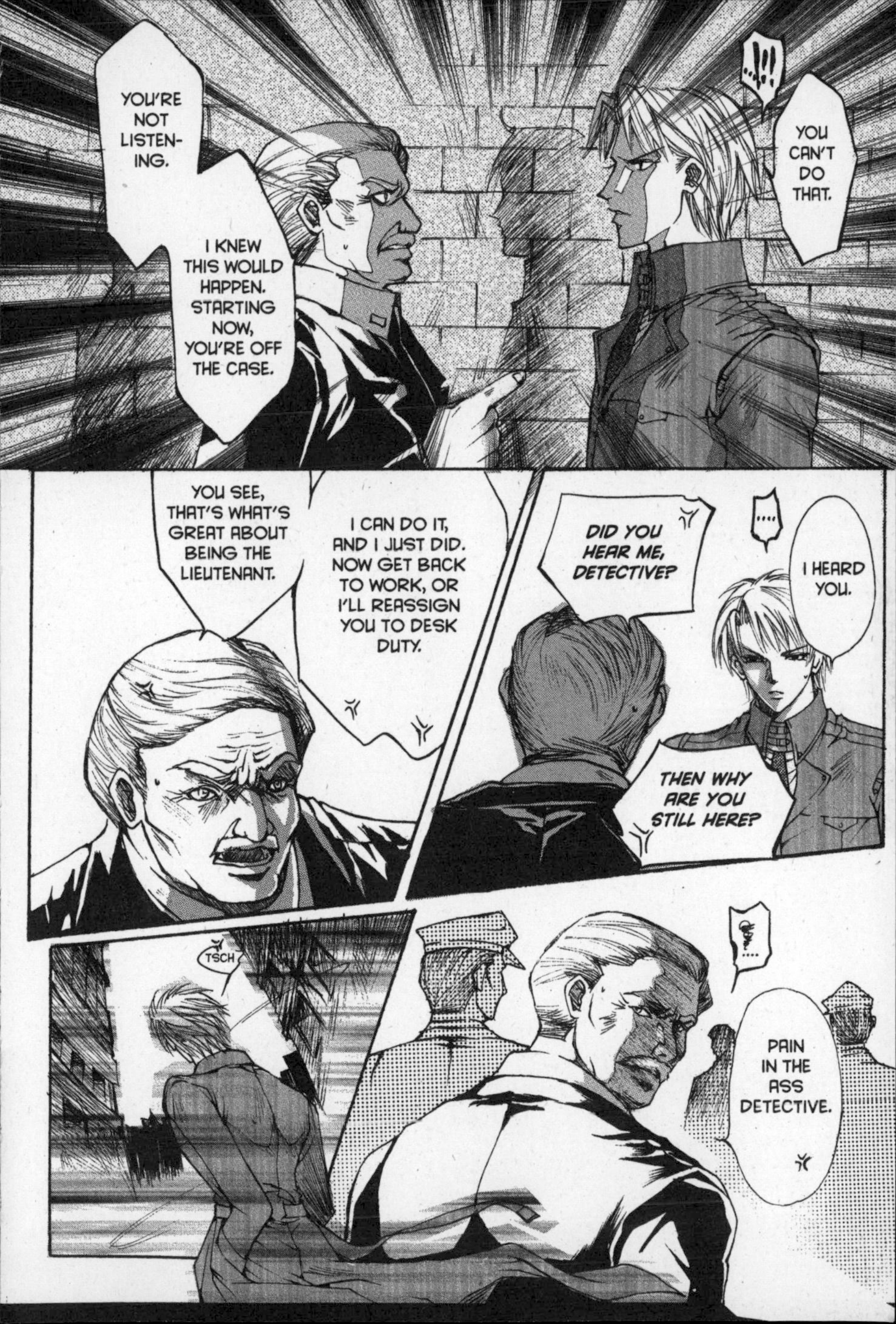
YOU'RE NOT LISTEN- ING.
I KNEW THIS WOULD HAPPEN. STARTING NOW, YOU'RE OFF THE CASE.
..!?!
YOU CAN'T DO THAT.
YOU SEE, THAT'S WHAT'S GREAT ABOUT BEING THE LIEUTENANT.
I CAN DO IT, AND I JUST DID. NOW GET BACK TO WORK, OR I'LL REASSIGN YOU TO DESK DUTY.
DID YOU HEAR ME, DETECTIVE?
.....
I HEARD YOU.
THEN WHY ARE YOU STILL HERE?
TSCH
PAIN IN THE ASS DETECTIVE.

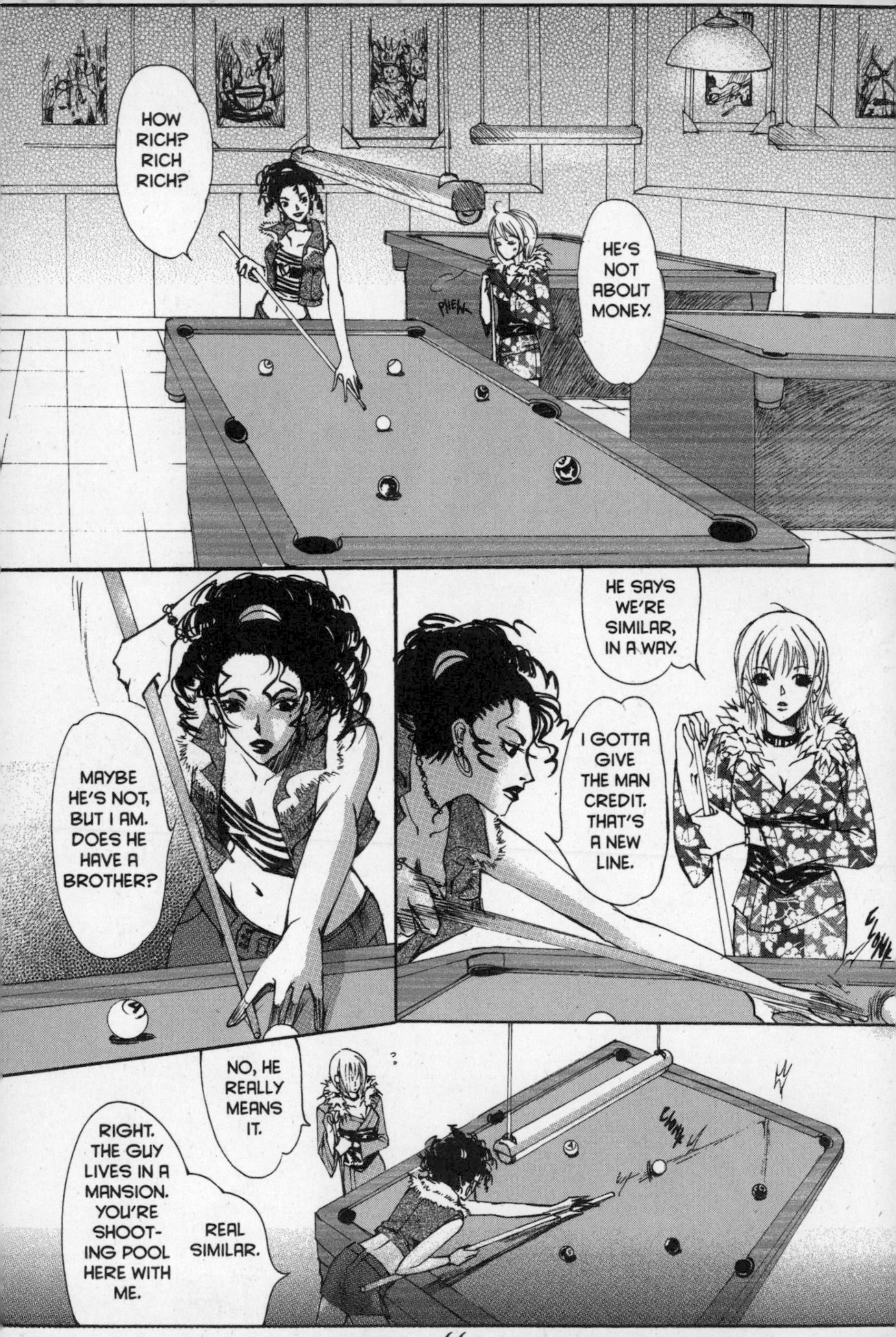
HOW RICH? RICH RICH?
PHEW
HE'S NOT ABOUT MONEY.
MAYBE HE'S NOT, BUT I AM. DOES HE HAVE A BROTHER?
HE SAYS WE'RE SIMILAR, IN A WAY.
I GOTTA GIVE THE MAN CREDIT. THAT'S A NEW LINE.
CLONK
NO, HE REALLY MEANS IT.
RIGHT. THE GUY LIVES IN A MANSION. YOU'RE SHOOT-ING POOL HERE WITH ME.
REAL SIMILAR.

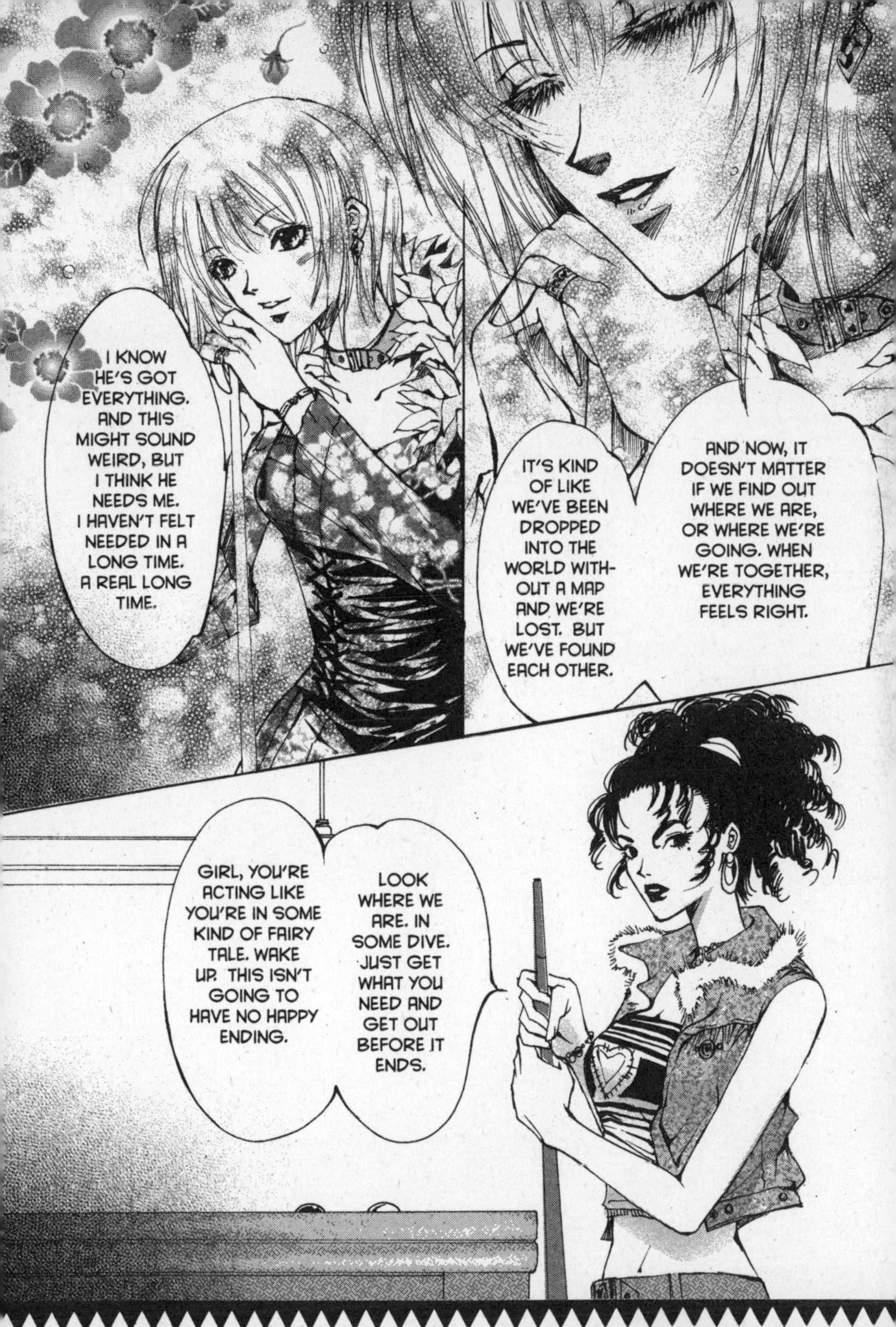
I KNOW HE'S GOT EVERYTHING. AND THIS MIGHT SOUND WEIRD, BUT I THINK HE NEEDS ME. I HAVEN'T FELT NEEDED IN A LONG TIME. A REAL LONG TIME.
IT'S KIND OF LIKE WE'VE BEEN DROPPED INTO THE WORLD WITH-OUT A MAP AND WE'RE LOST. BUT WE'VE FOUND EACH OTHER.
AND NOW, IT DOESN'T MATTER IF WE FIND OUT WHERE WE ARE, OR WHERE WE'RE GOING. WHEN WE'RE TOGETHER, EVERYTHING FEELS RIGHT.
GIRL, YOU'RE ACTING LIKE YOU'RE IN SOME KIND OF FAIRY TALE. WAKE UP. THIS ISN'T GOING TO HAVE NO HAPPY ENDING.
LOOK WHERE WE ARE. IN SOME DIVE. JUST GET WHAT YOU NEED AND GET OUT BEFORE IT ENDS.

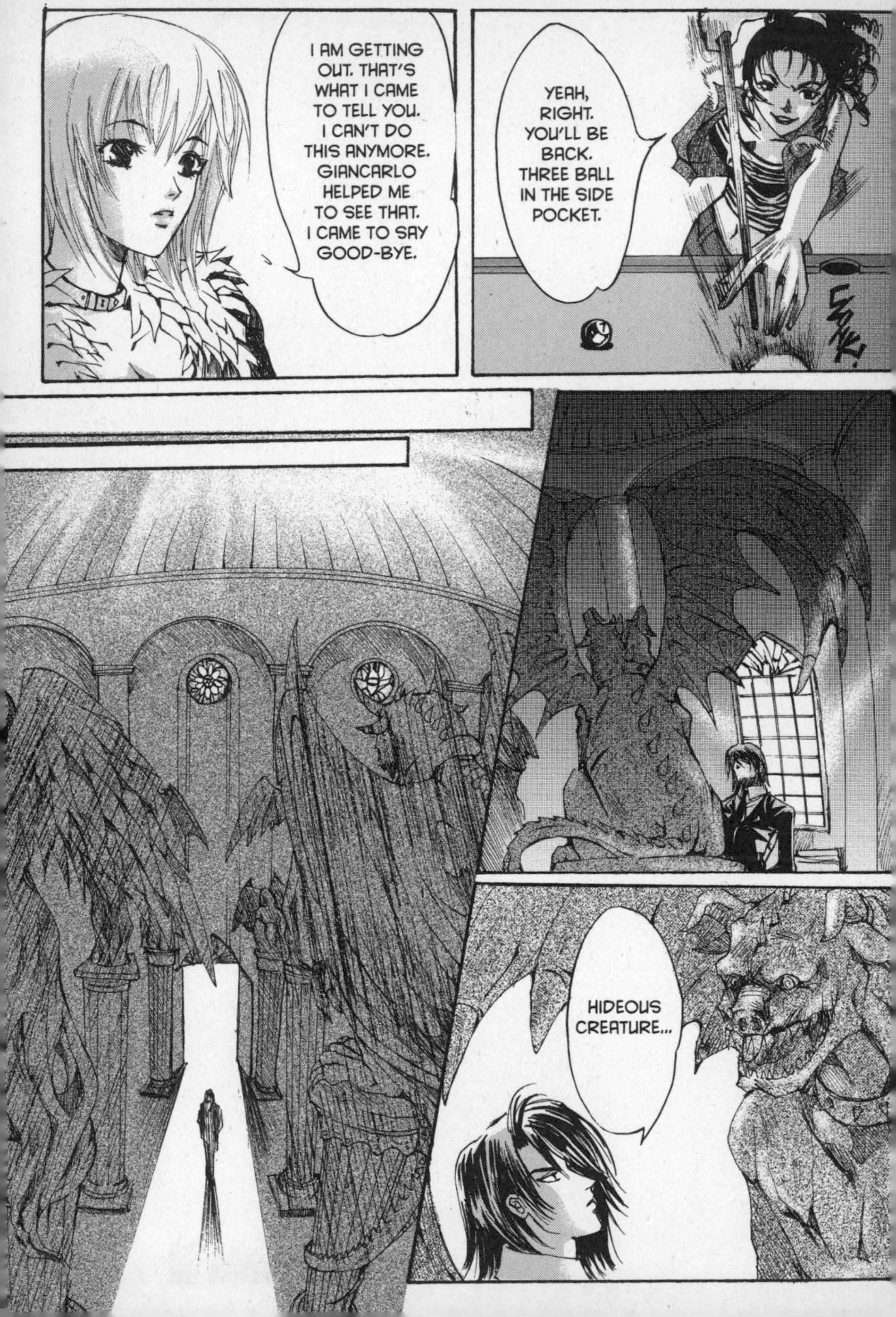
I AM GETTING OUT. THAT'S WHAT I CAME TO TELL YOU. I CAN'T DO THIS ANYMORE. GIANCARLO HELPED ME TO SEE THAT. I CAME TO SAY GOOD-BYE.
YEAH, RIGHT. YOU'LL BE BACK. THREE BALL IN THE SIDE POCKET.
HIDEOUS CREATURE...

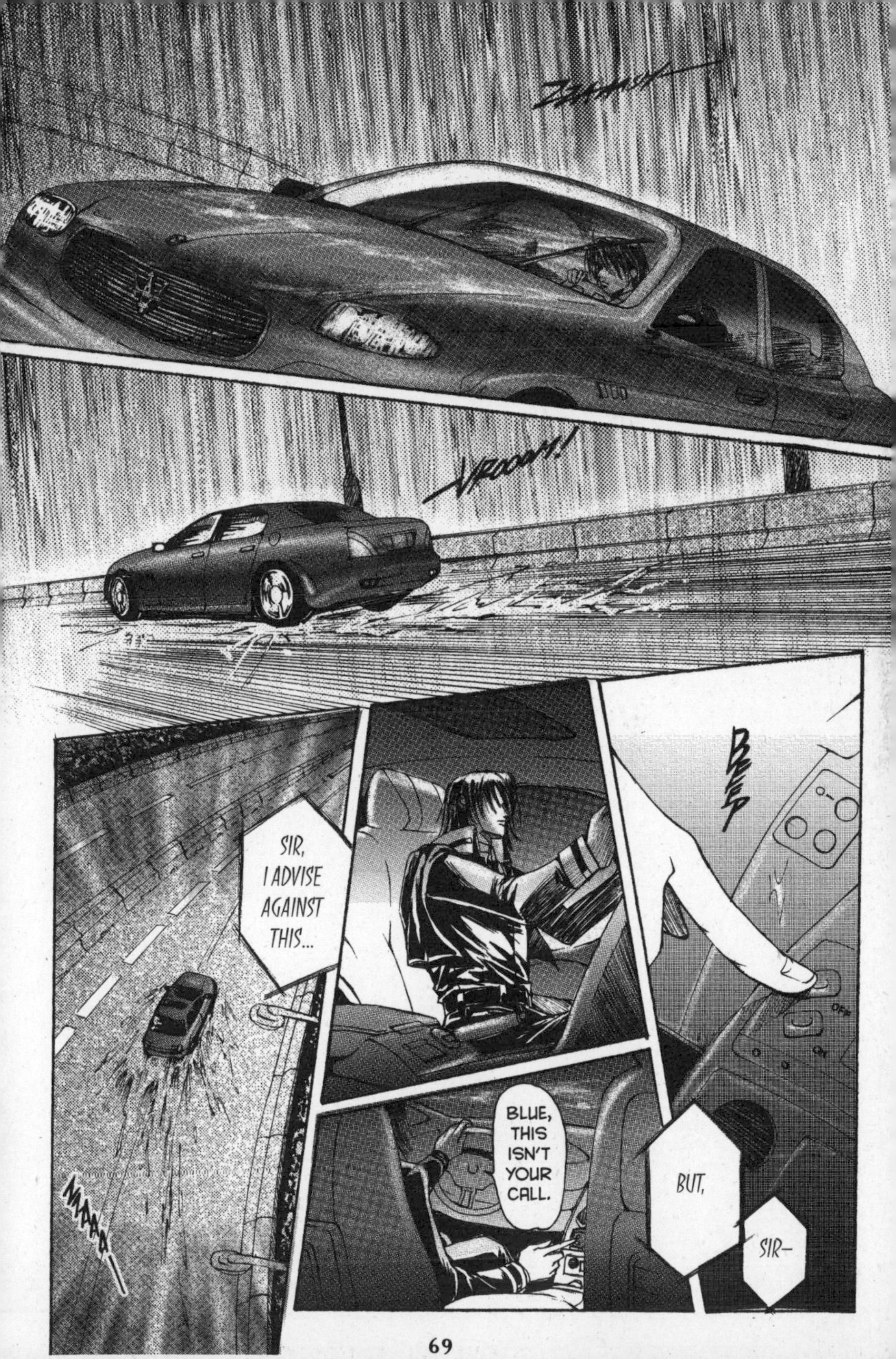
VROOM!
SIR, I ADVISE AGAINST THIS...
BEEP
BLUE, THIS ISN'T YOUR CALL.
BUT,
SIR—

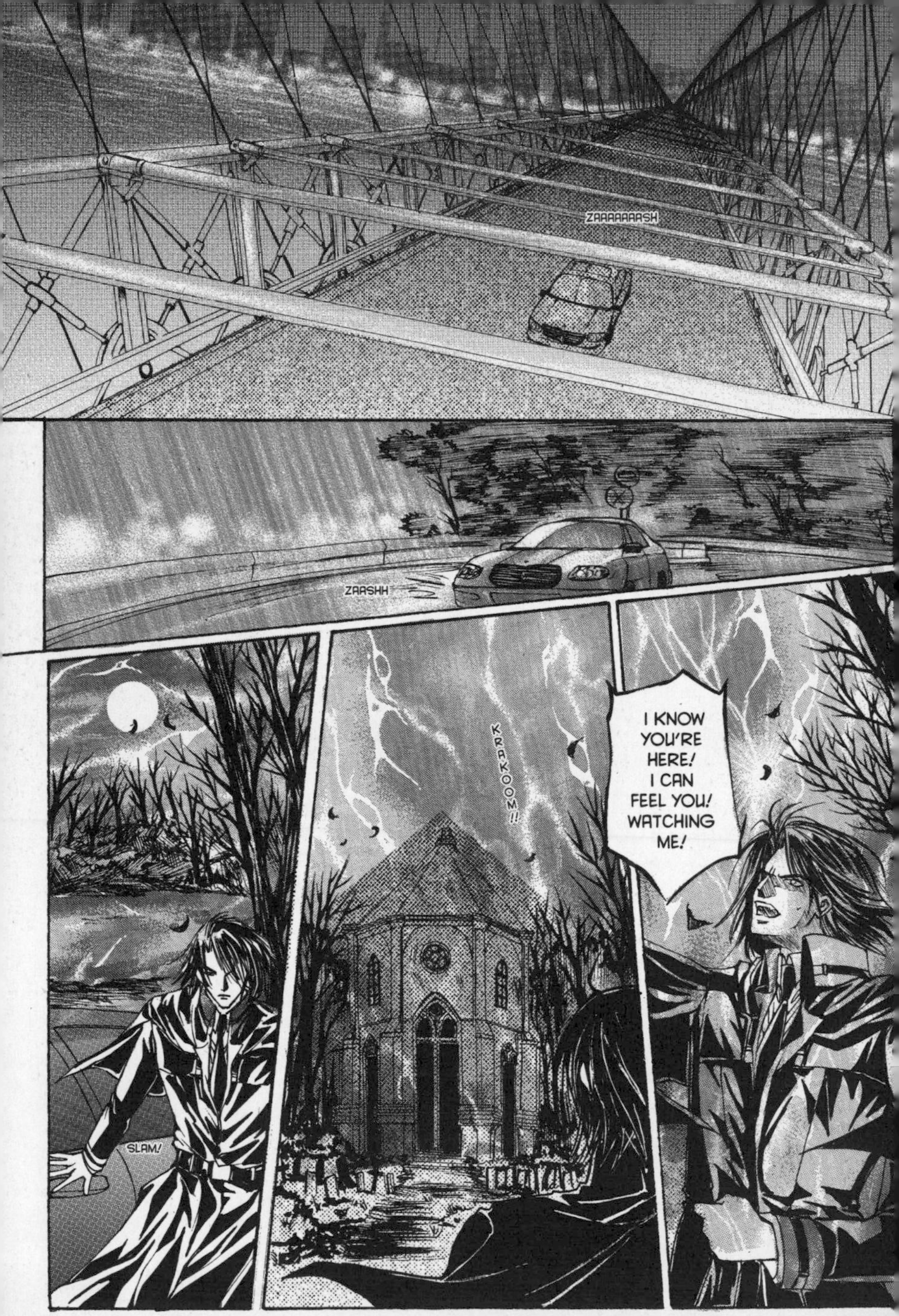
ZAAAAAAASH
ZAASHH
SLAM!
KRAKOOM!!
I KNOW YOU'RE HERE! I CAN FEEL YOU! WATCHING ME!

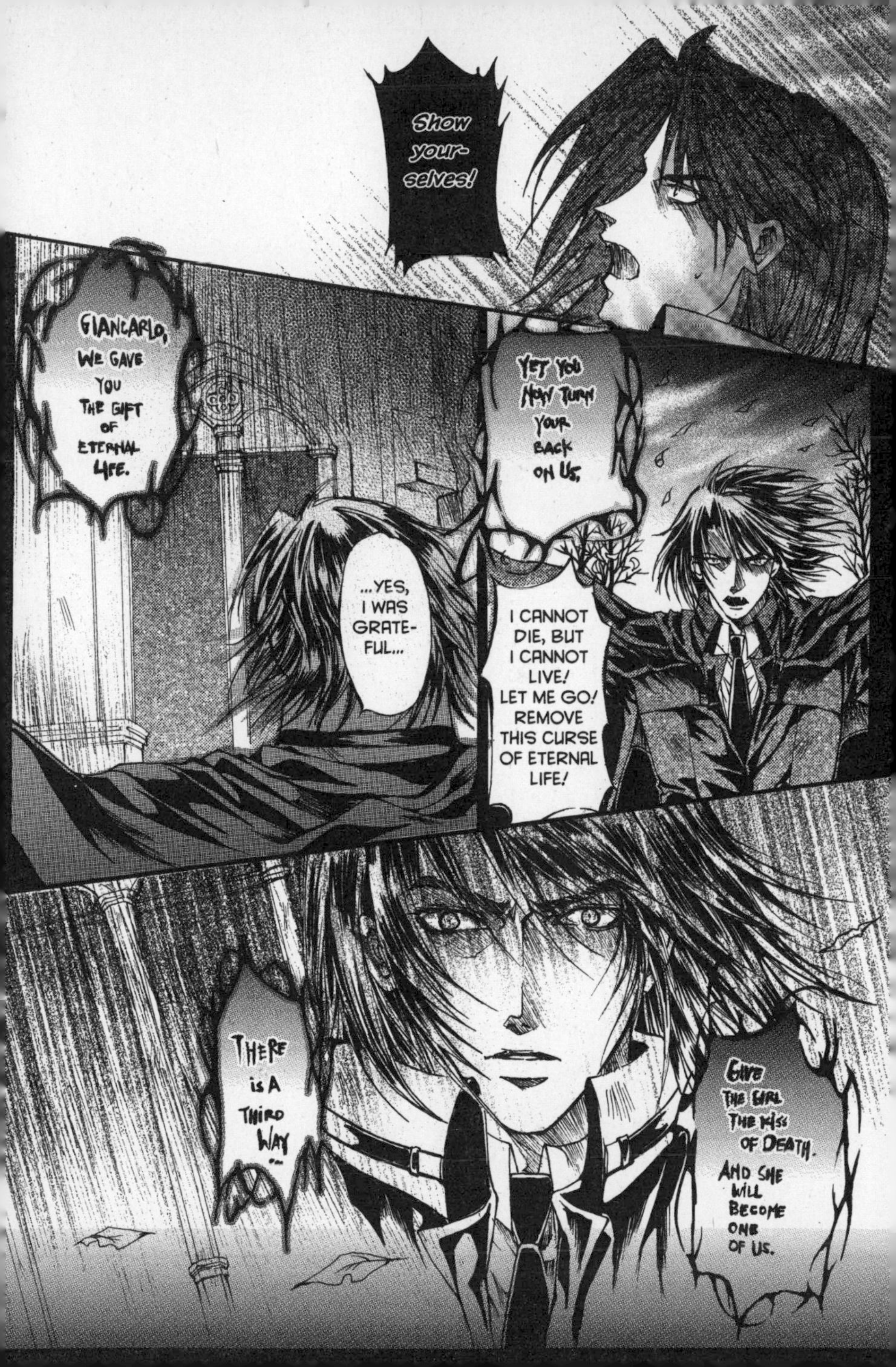
Show your-selves!
GIANCARLO, WE GAVE YOU THE GIFT OF ETERNAL LIFE.
...YES, I WAS GRATE-FUL...
YET YOU NOW TURN YOUR BACK ON US.
I CANNOT DIE, BUT I CANNOT LIVE! LET ME GO! REMOVE THIS CURSE OF ETERNAL LIFE!
THERE is A THIRD WAY...
GIVE THE GIRL THE KISS OF DEATH.
AND SHE WILL BECOME ONE OF US.

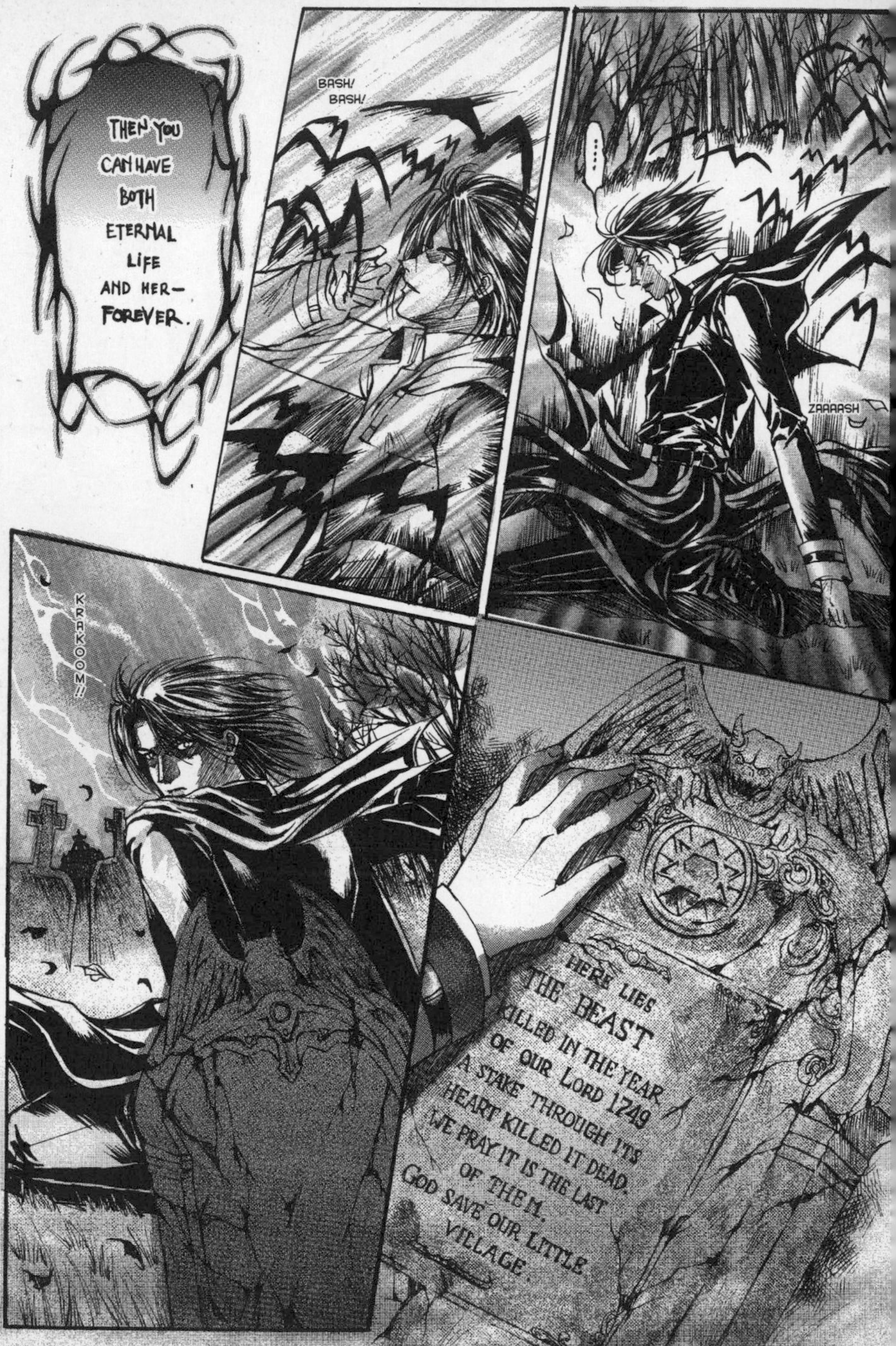
THEN YOU CAN HAVE BOTH ETERNAL LIFE AND HER—FOREVER.
BASH! BASH!
...
ZAAAASH
KRAKOOM!!
HERE LIES THE BEAST KILLED IN THE YEAR OF OUR LORD 1749 A STAKE THROUGH ITS HEART KILLED IT DEAD. WE PRAY IT IS THE LAST OF THEM. GOD SAVE OUR LITTLE VILLAGE.

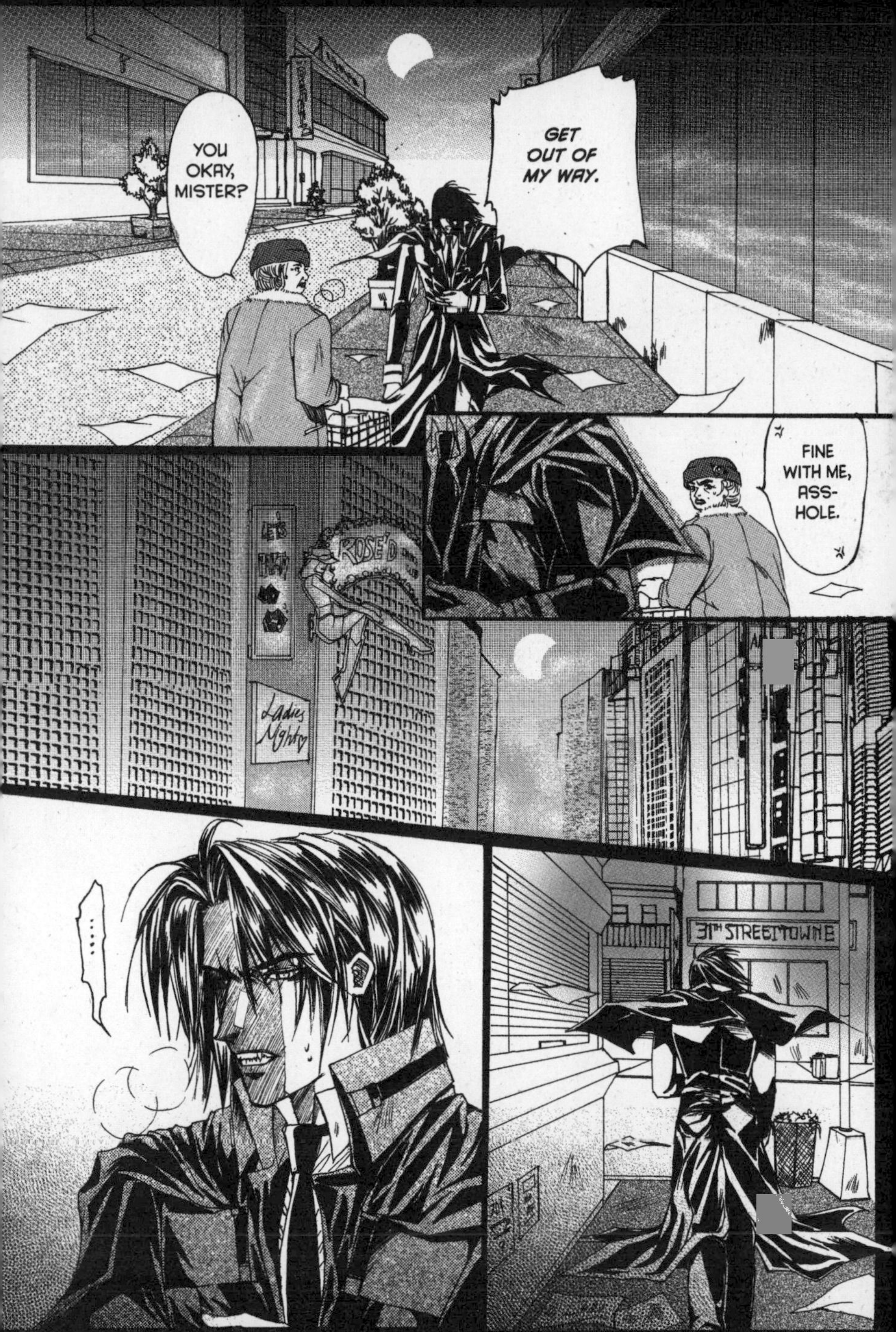
YOU OKAY, MISTER?
GET OUT OF MY WAY.
FINE WITH ME, ASS-HOLE.
ROSE'D
Ladies Night
......
31TH STREET TOWNE

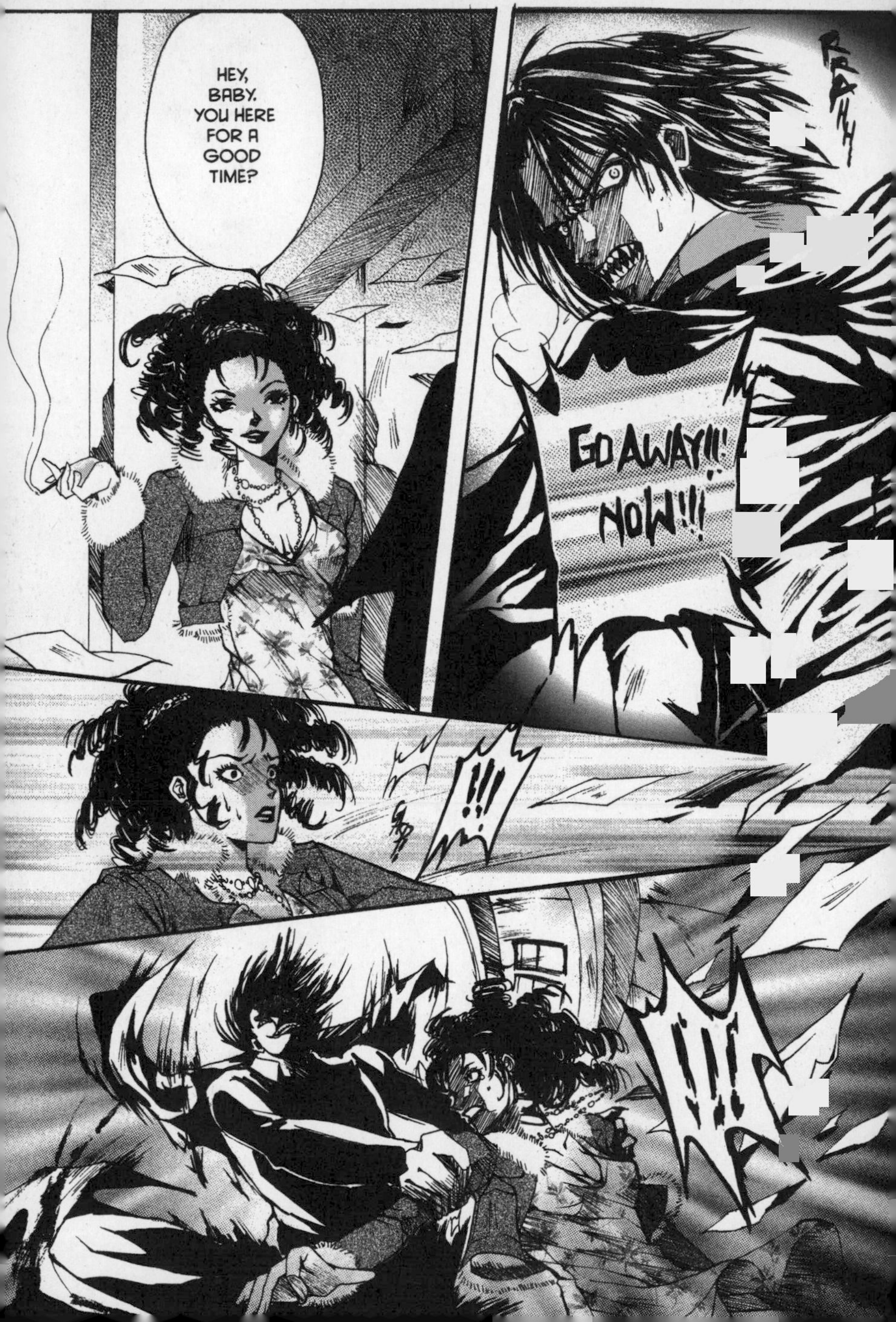
HEY, BABY. YOU HERE FOR A GOOD TIME?
RRAHH
GO AWAY!!! NOW!!!
!!!
!!!

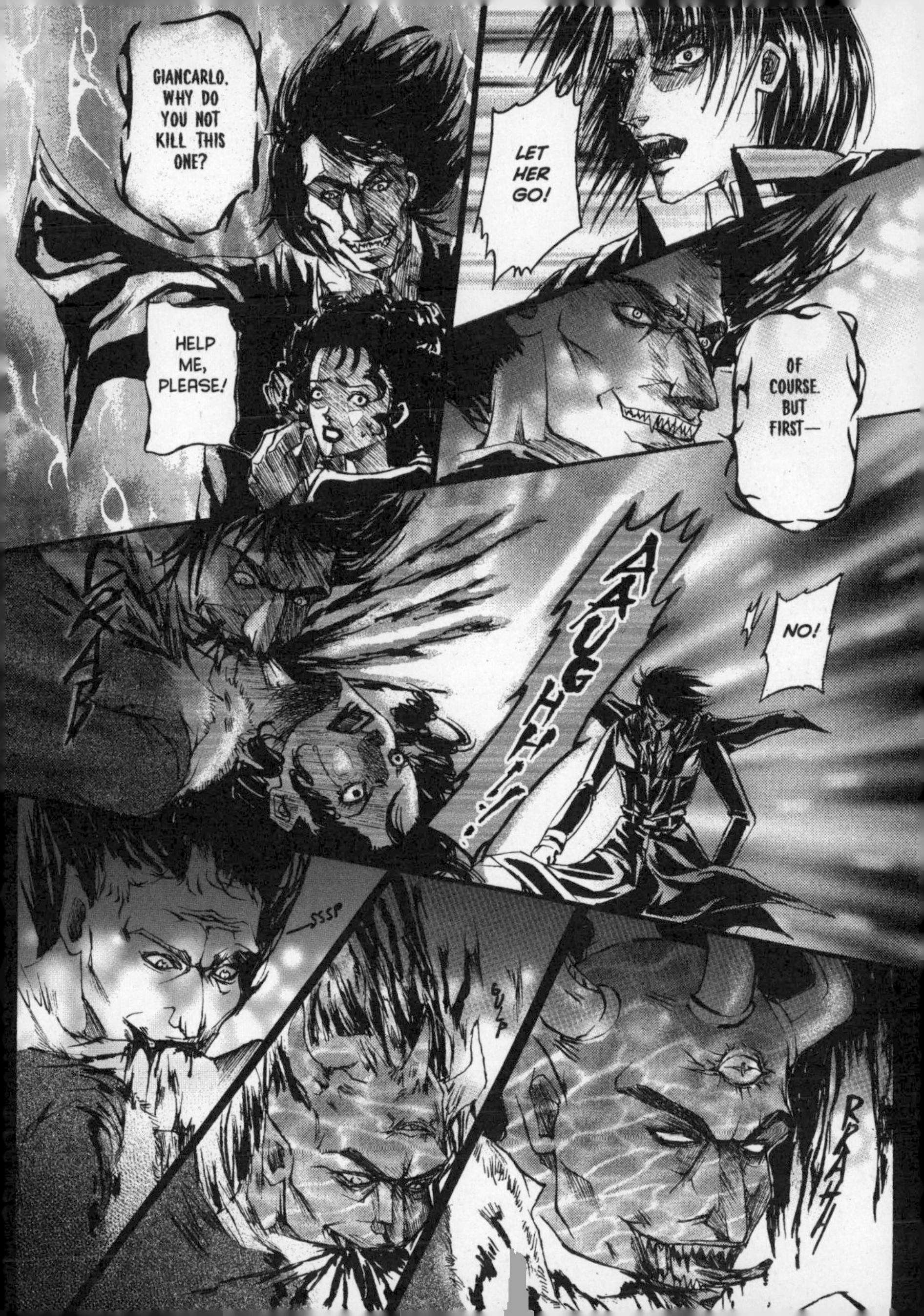
GIANCARLO. WHY DO YOU NOT KILL THIS ONE?
HELP ME, PLEASE!
LET HER GO!
OF COURSE. BUT FIRST—
AAUGHH!...
NO!
SSSP
GULP
RRAAHH

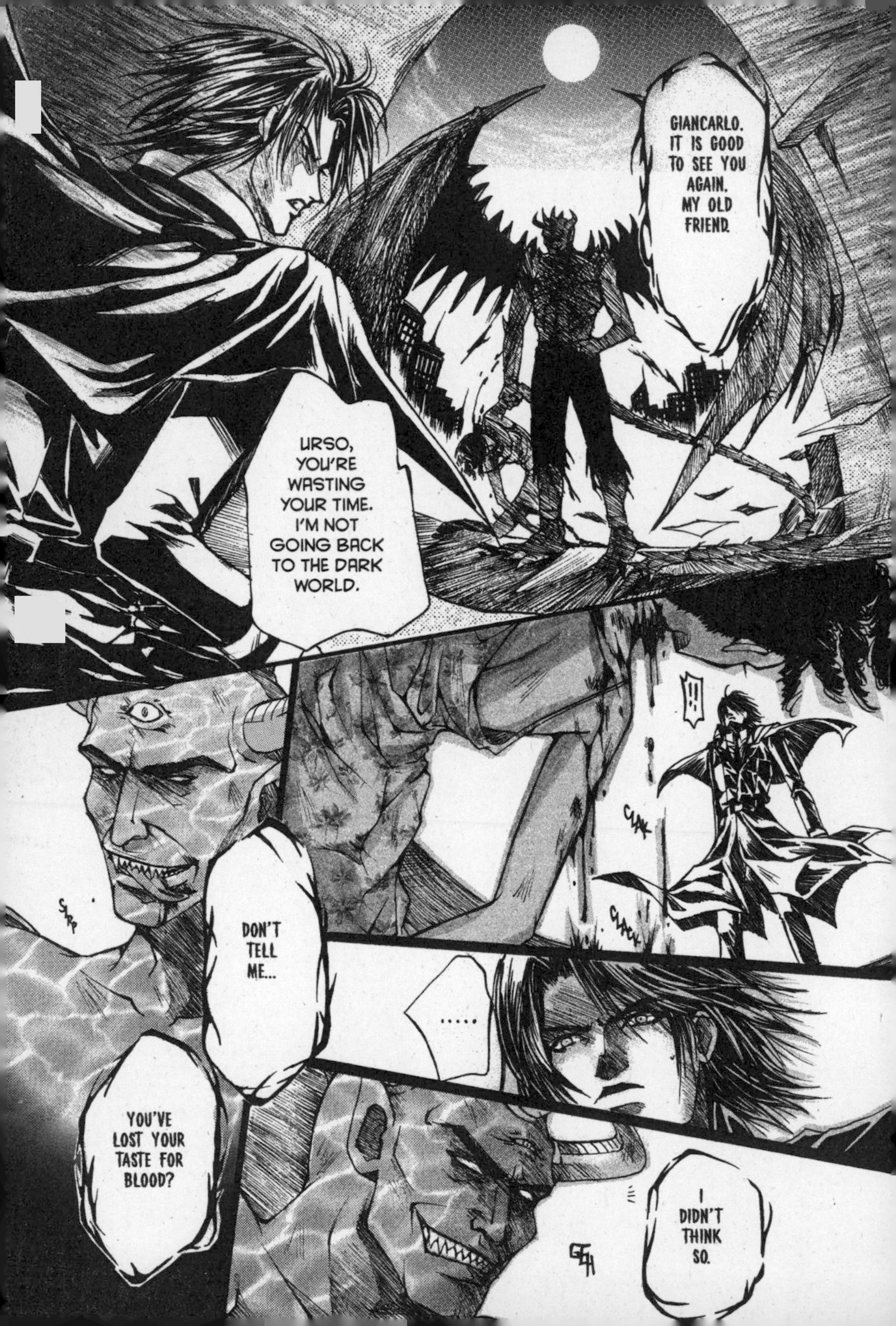
GIANCARLO. IT IS GOOD TO SEE YOU AGAIN. MY OLD FRIEND.
URSO, YOU'RE WASTING YOUR TIME. I'M NOT GOING BACK TO THE DARK WORLD.
SLRP
DON'T TELL ME...
!!
CLAK
CLACK
.....
YOU'VE LOST YOUR TASTE FOR BLOOD?
GEH
I DIDN'T THINK SO.

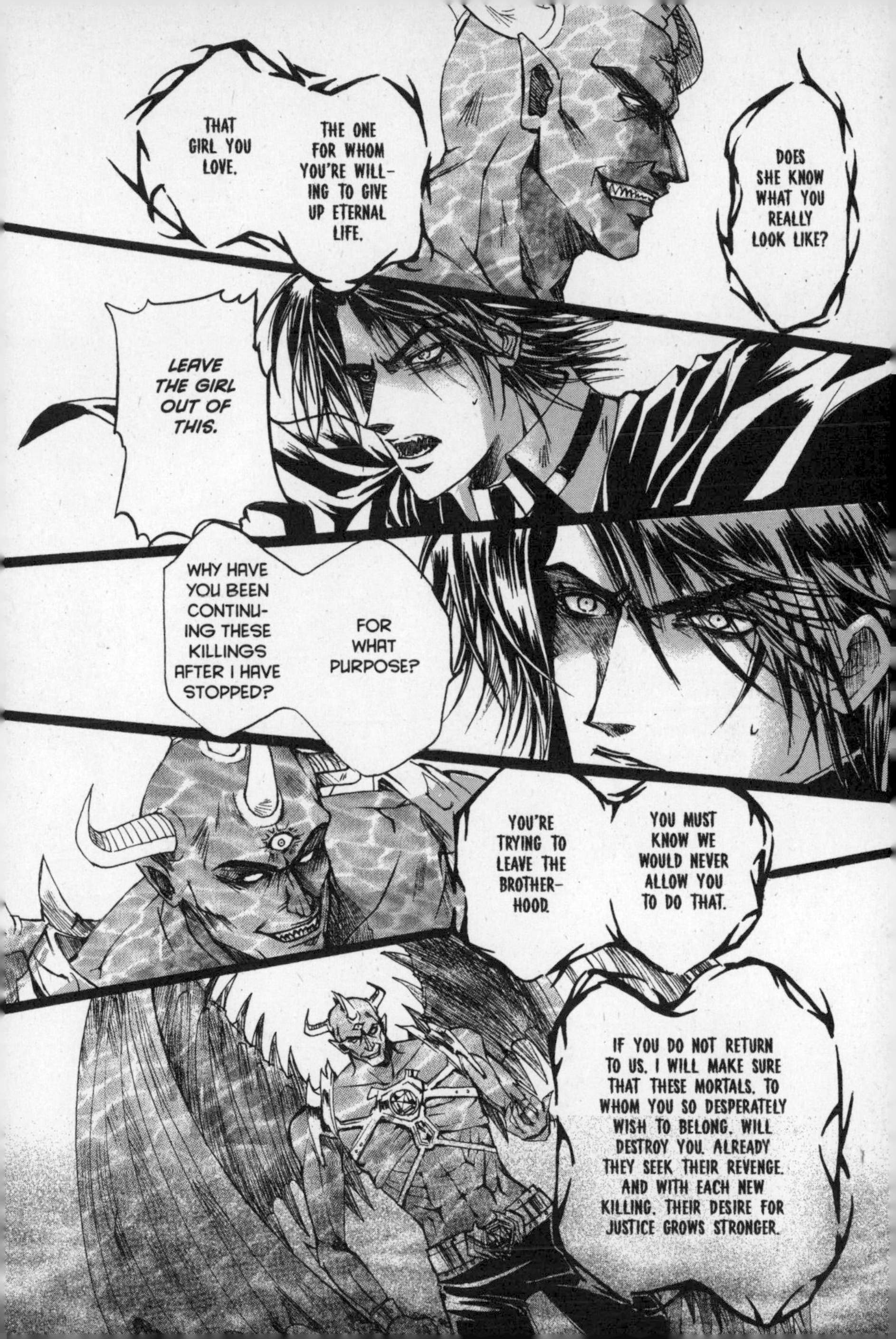
THAT GIRL YOU LOVE.
THE ONE FOR WHOM YOU'RE WILL-ING TO GIVE UP ETERNAL LIFE.
DOES SHE KNOW WHAT YOU REALLY LOOK LIKE?
LEAVE THE GIRL OUT OF THIS.
WHY HAVE YOU BEEN CONTINU-ING THESE KILLINGS AFTER I HAVE STOPPED?
FOR WHAT PURPOSE?
YOU'RE TRYING TO LEAVE THE BROTHER-HOOD.
YOU MUST KNOW WE WOULD NEVER ALLOW YOU TO DO THAT.
IF YOU DO NOT RETURN TO US, I WILL MAKE SURE THAT THESE MORTALS, TO WHOM YOU SO DESPERATELY WISH TO BELONG, WILL DESTROY YOU. ALREADY THEY SEEK THEIR REVENGE. AND WITH EACH NEW KILLING, THEIR DESIRE FOR JUSTICE GROWS STRONGER.

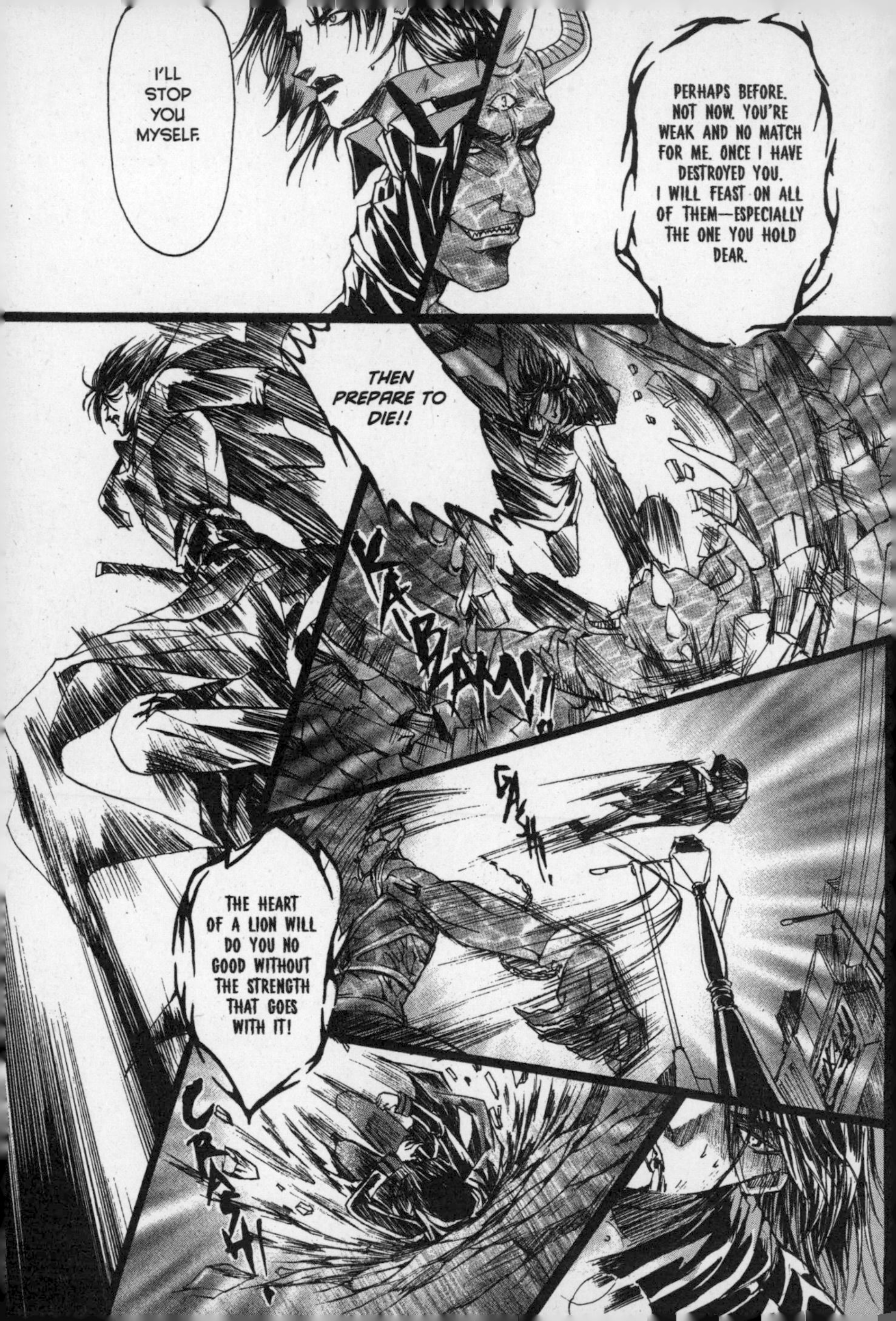
I'LL STOP YOU MYSELF.
PERHAPS BEFORE. NOT NOW. YOU'RE WEAK AND NO MATCH FOR ME. ONCE I HAVE DESTROYED YOU, I WILL FEAST ON ALL OF THEM—ESPECIALLY THE ONE YOU HOLD DEAR.
THEN PREPARE TO DIE!!
KA-BLAM!!
GASH!!
THE HEART OF A LION WILL DO YOU NO GOOD WITHOUT THE STRENGTH THAT GOES WITH IT!
CRASH!

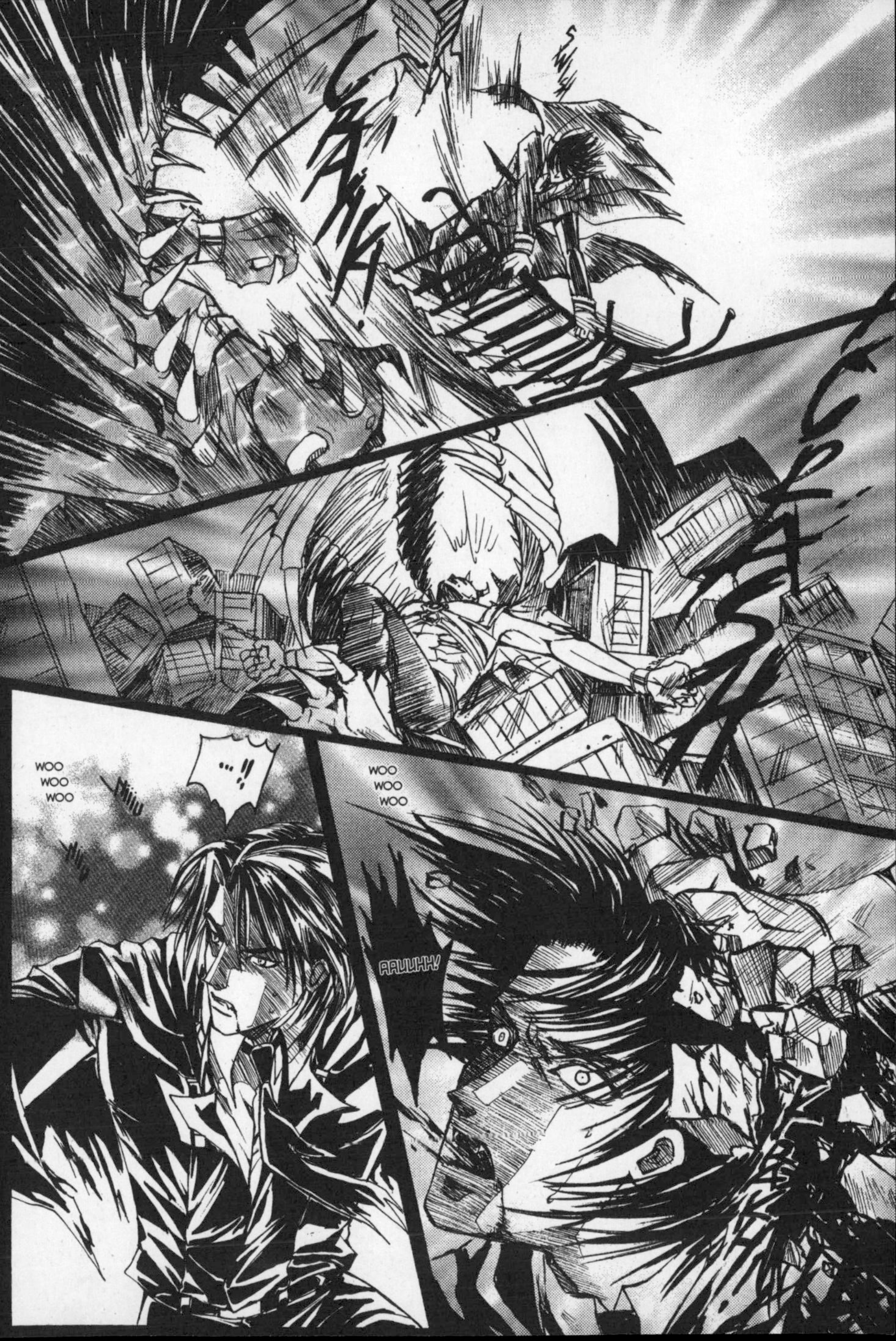
SWISH
WOO
WOO
WOO
...!!
WOO
WOO
WOO
AAUUHH!

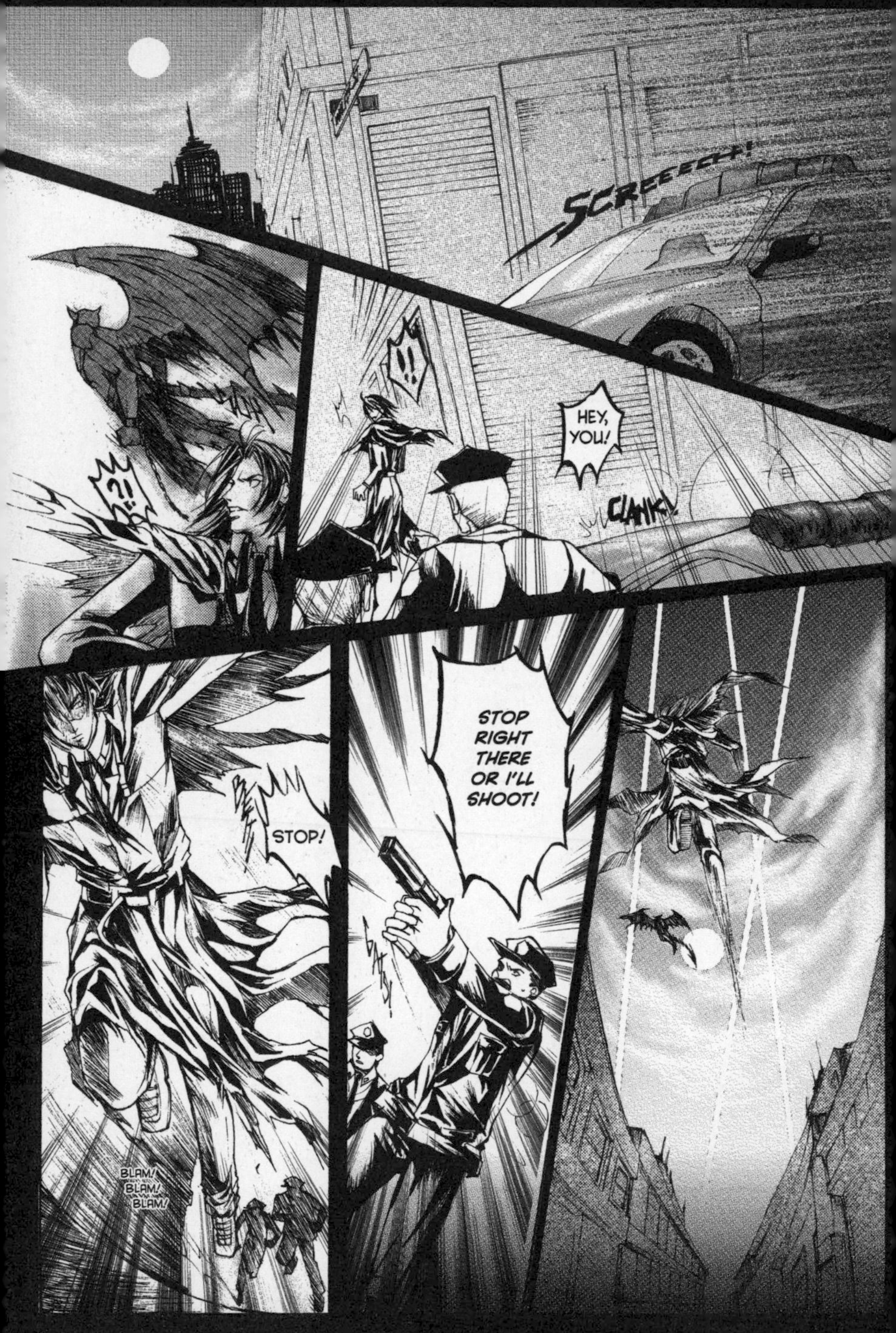
SCREEECH!
?!
!!
HEY, YOU!
CLANK!
STOP!
BLAM! BLAM! BLAM!
STOP RIGHT THERE OR I'LL SHOOT!

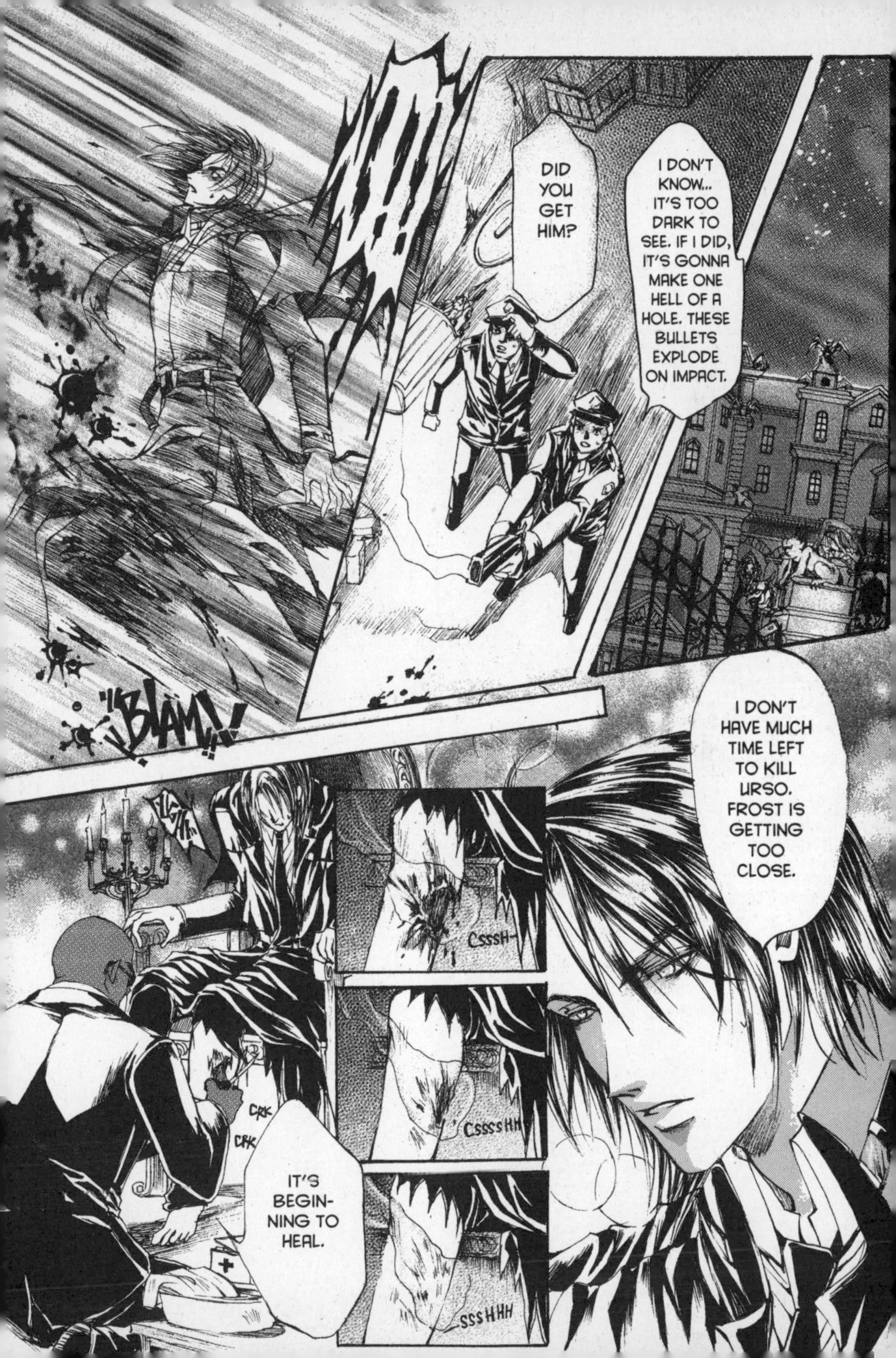
BLAM!!
DID YOU GET HIM?
I DON'T KNOW... IT'S TOO DARK TO SEE. IF I DID, IT'S GONNA MAKE ONE HELL OF A HOLE. THESE BULLETS EXPLODE ON IMPACT.
CRK
CRK
IT'S BEGIN-NING TO HEAL.
CSSSH-
CSSSSHH
SSSHHH
I DON'T HAVE MUCH TIME LEFT TO KILL URSO. FROST IS GETTING TOO CLOSE.

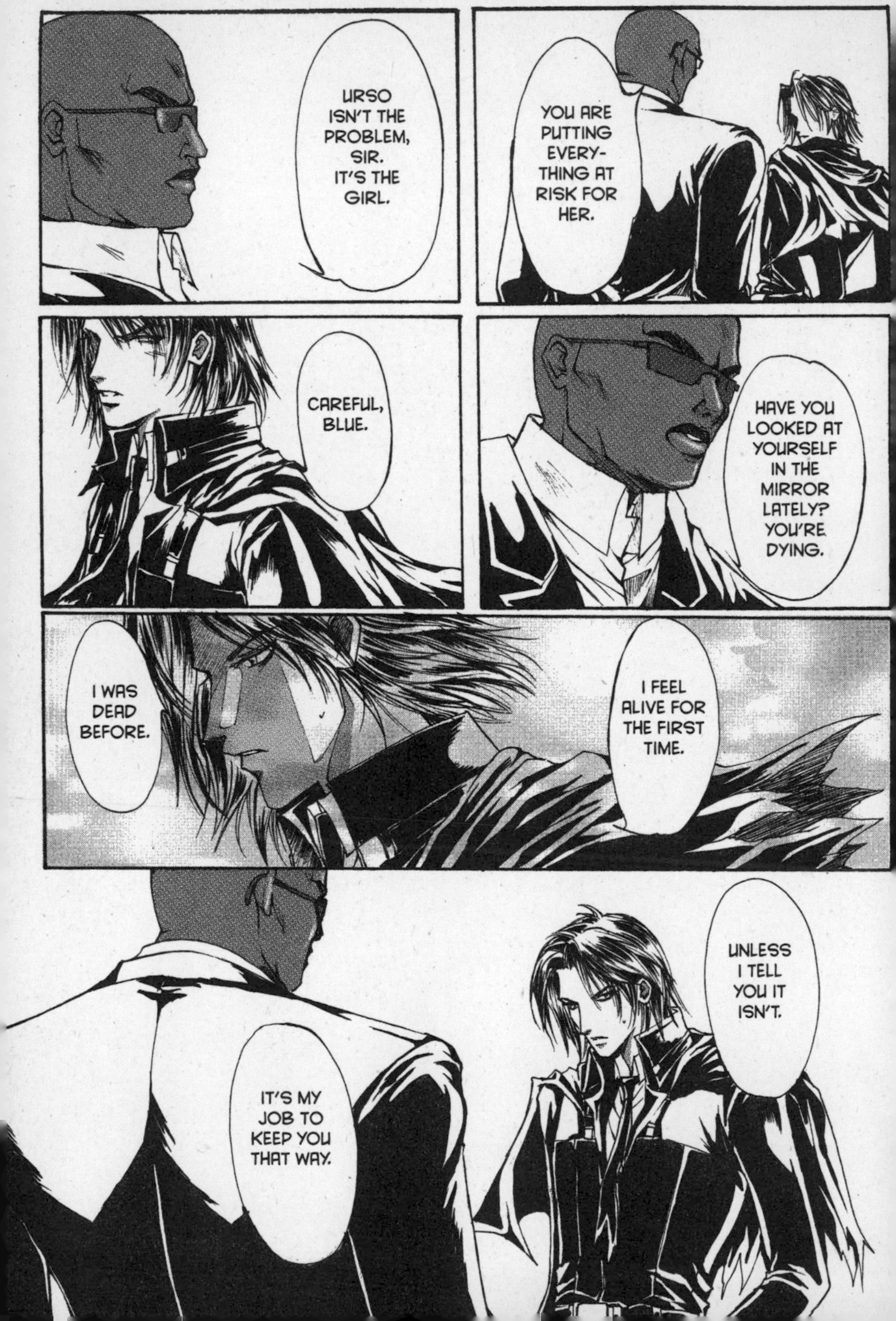
URSO ISN'T THE PROBLEM, SIR. IT'S THE GIRL.
YOU ARE PUTTING EVERY-THING AT RISK FOR HER.
CAREFUL, BLUE.
HAVE YOU LOOKED AT YOURSELF IN THE MIRROR LATELY? YOU'RE DYING.
I WAS DEAD BEFORE.
I FEEL ALIVE FOR THE FIRST TIME.
IT'S MY JOB TO KEEP YOU THAT WAY.
UNLESS I TELL YOU IT ISN'T.

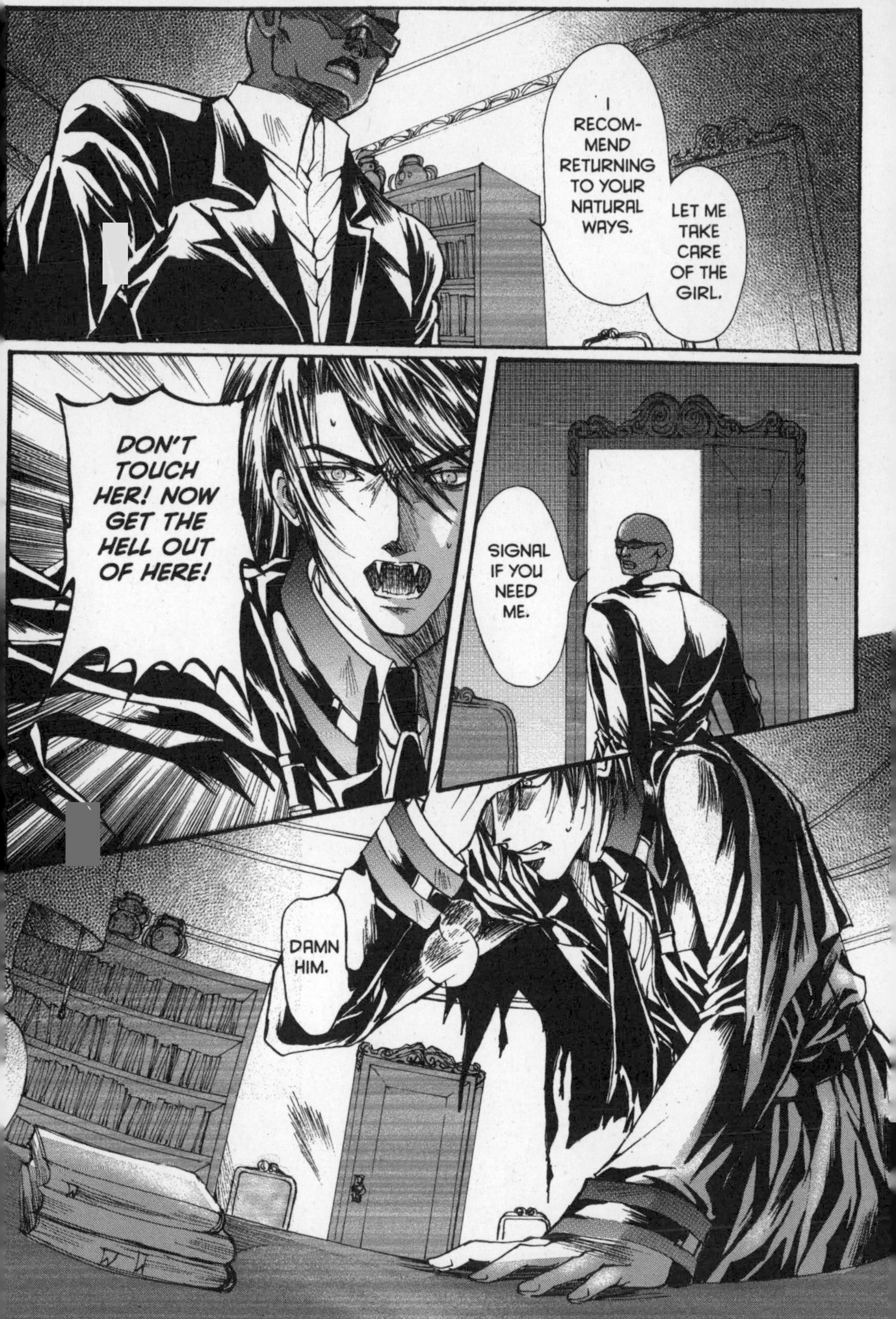
I RECOMMEND RETURNING TO YOUR NATURAL WAYS.
LET ME TAKE CARE OF THE GIRL.
DON'T TOUCH HER! NOW GET THE HELL OUT OF HERE!
SIGNAL IF YOU NEED ME.
DAMN HIM.

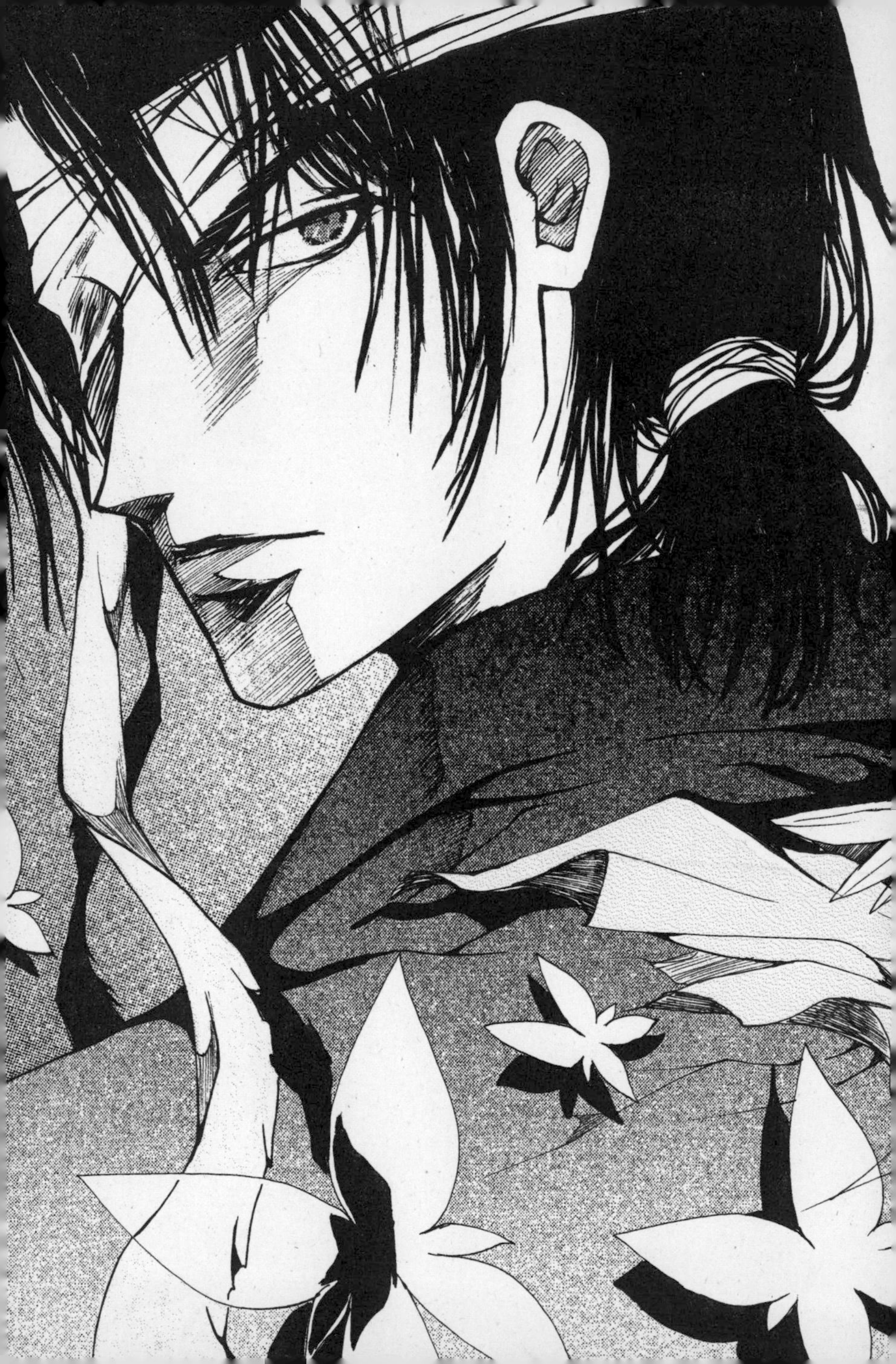

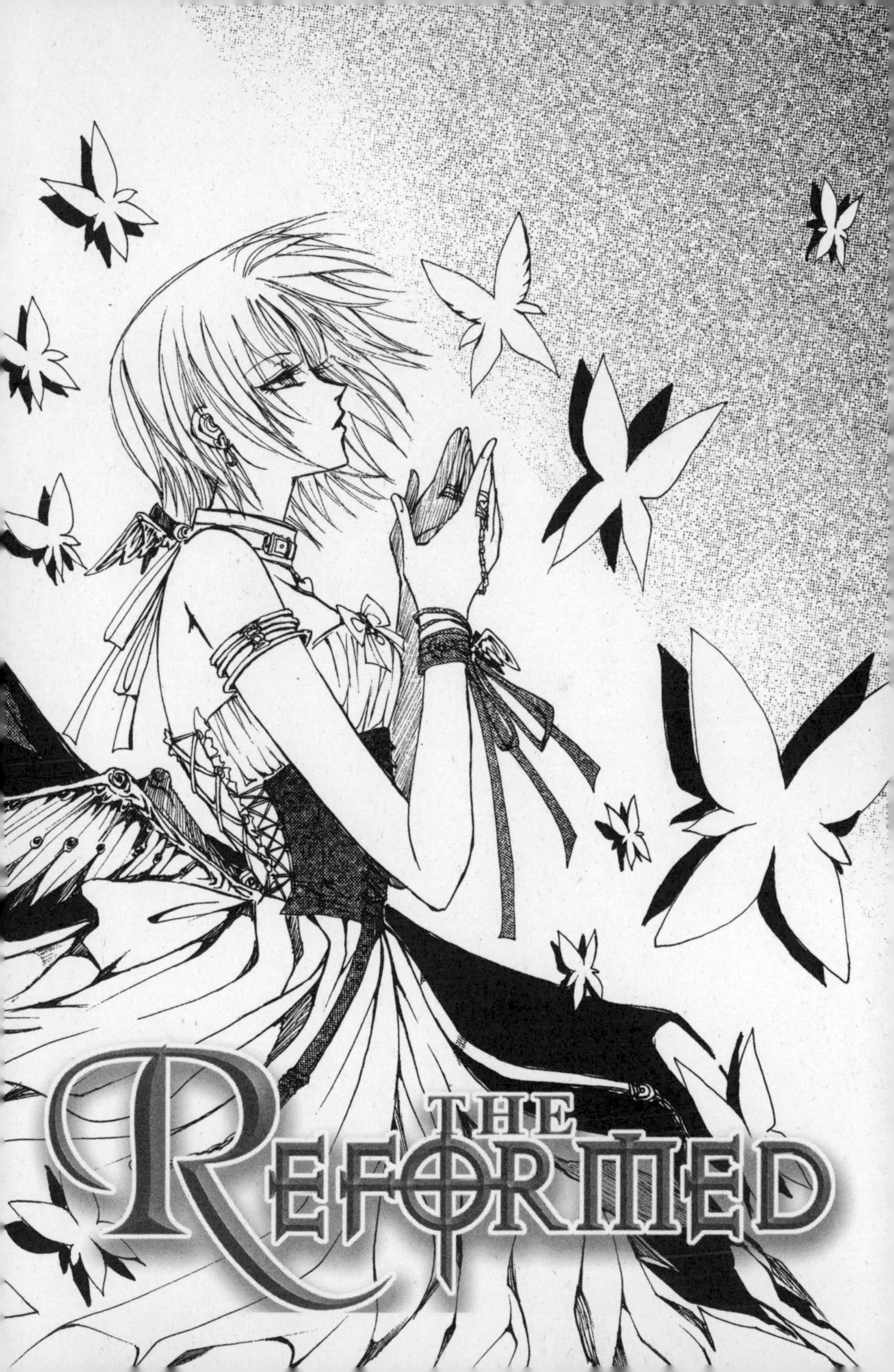
THE
REFORMED

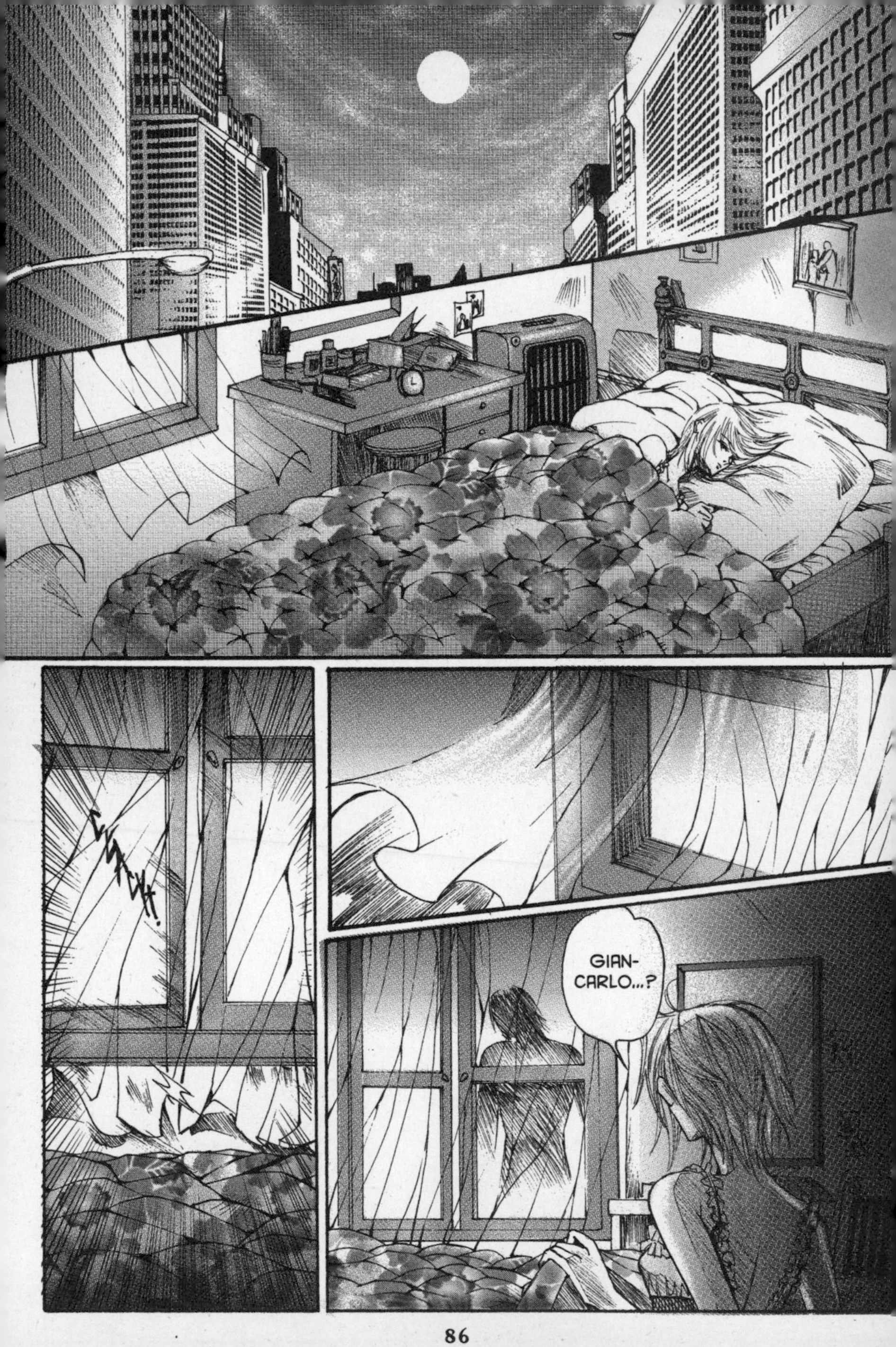
GIAN-CARLO...?

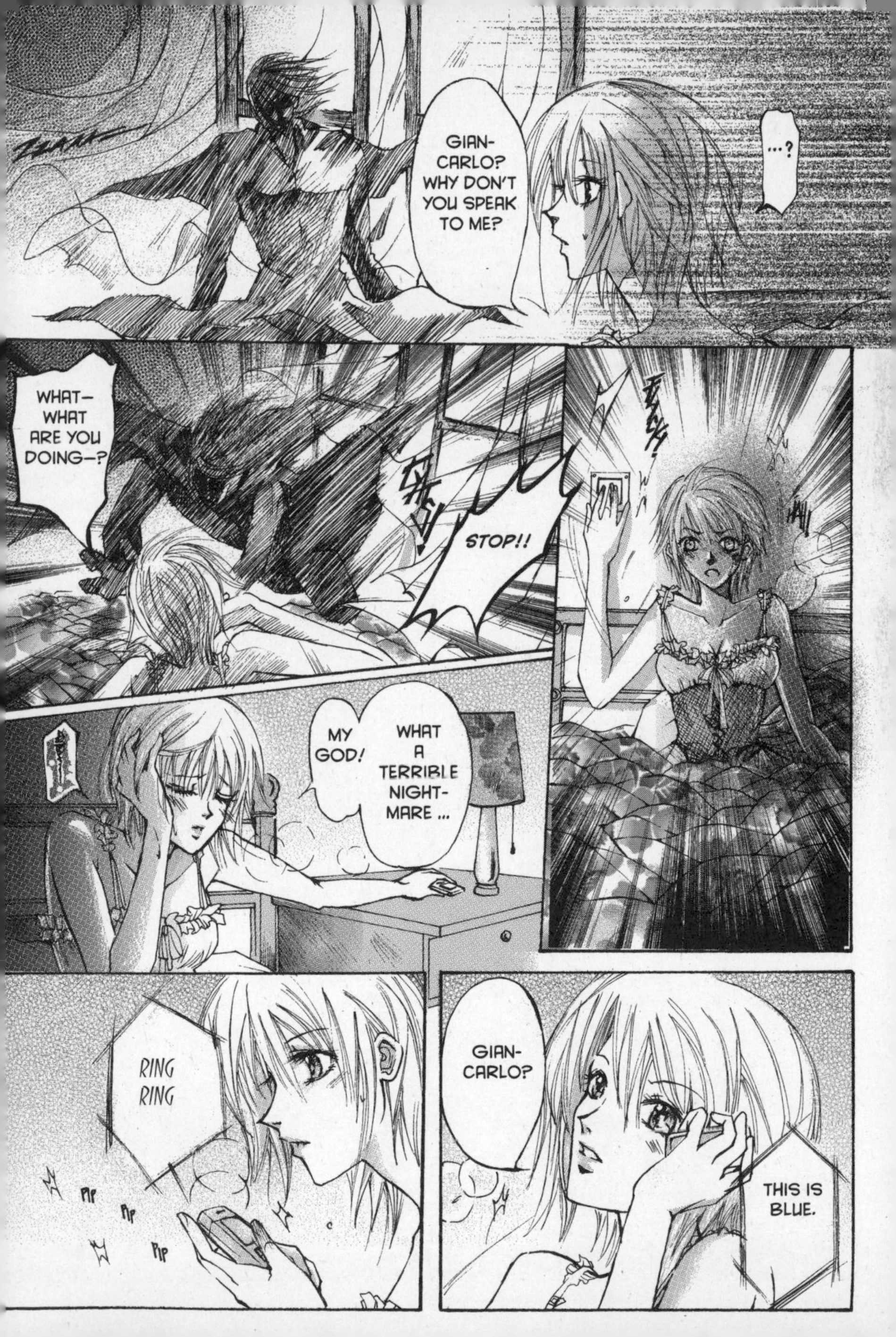
GIAN-CARLO? WHY DON'T YOU SPEAK TO ME?
...?
WHAT-WHAT ARE YOU DOING-?
STOP!!
MY GOD!
WHAT A TERRIBLE NIGHT-MARE ...
RING RING
GIAN-CARLO?
THIS IS BLUE.

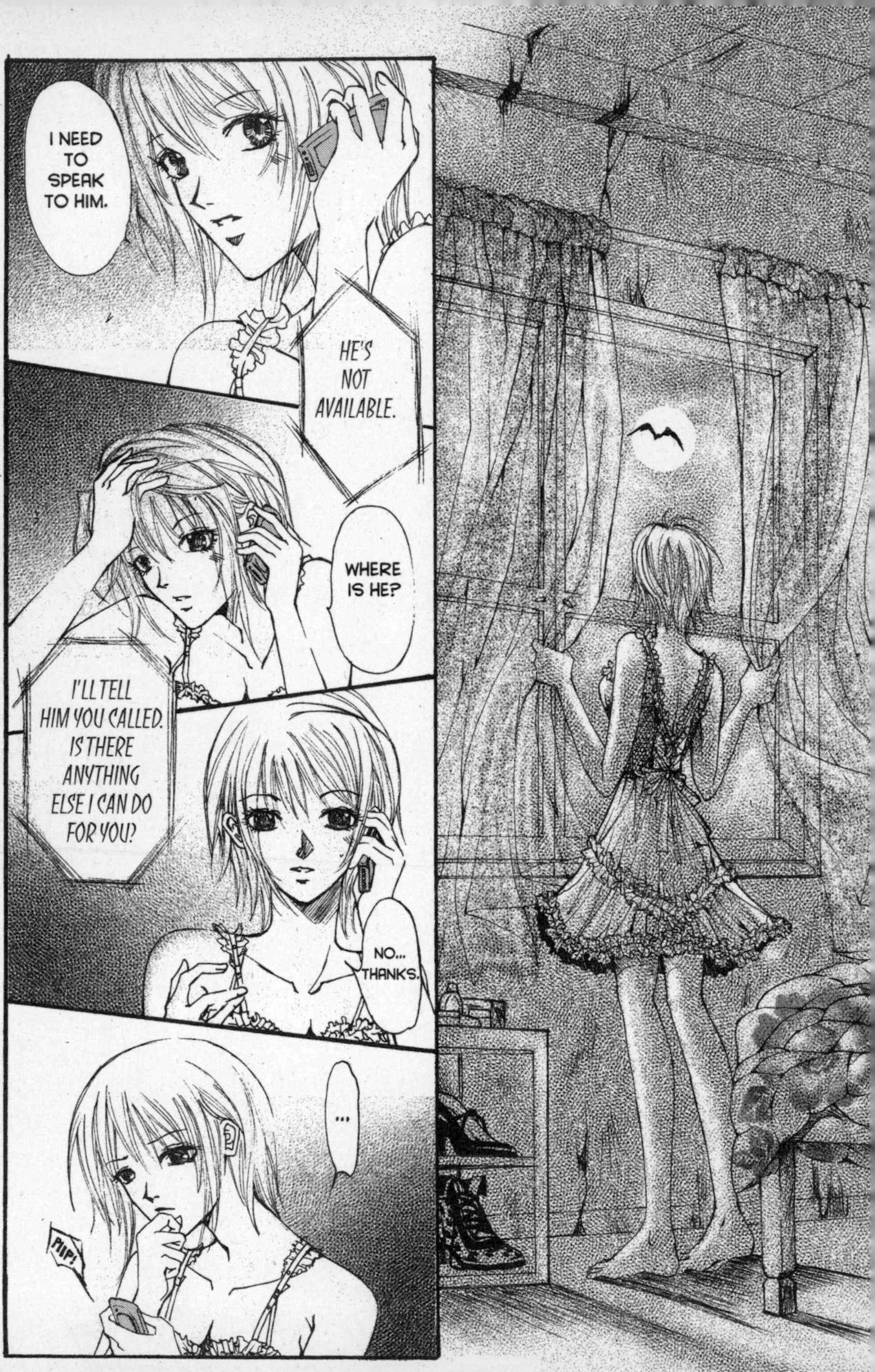
I NEED TO SPEAK TO HIM.
HE'S NOT AVAILABLE.
WHERE IS HE?
I'LL TELL HIM YOU CALLED. IS THERE ANYTHING ELSE I CAN DO FOR YOU?
NO... THANKS.
...
PIIP!

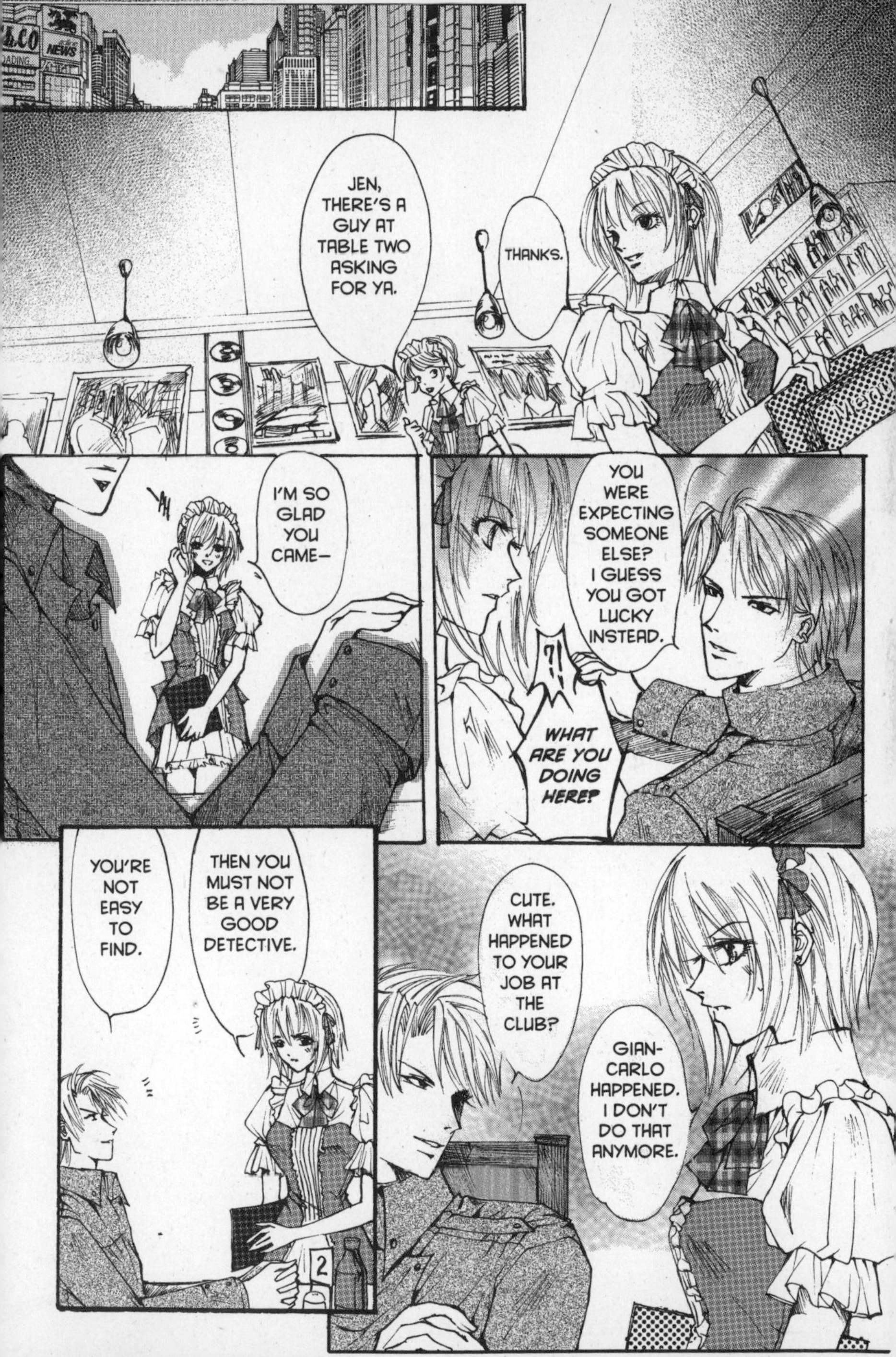
NEWS
JEN, THERE'S A GUY AT TABLE TWO ASKING FOR YA.
THANKS.
I'M SO GLAD YOU CAME—
YOU WERE EXPECTING SOMEONE ELSE? I GUESS YOU GOT LUCKY INSTEAD.
?!
WHAT ARE YOU DOING HERE?
YOU'RE NOT EASY TO FIND.
THEN YOU MUST NOT BE A VERY GOOD DETECTIVE.
2
CUTE. WHAT HAPPENED TO YOUR JOB AT THE CLUB?
GIAN-CARLO HAPPENED. I DON'T DO THAT ANYMORE.

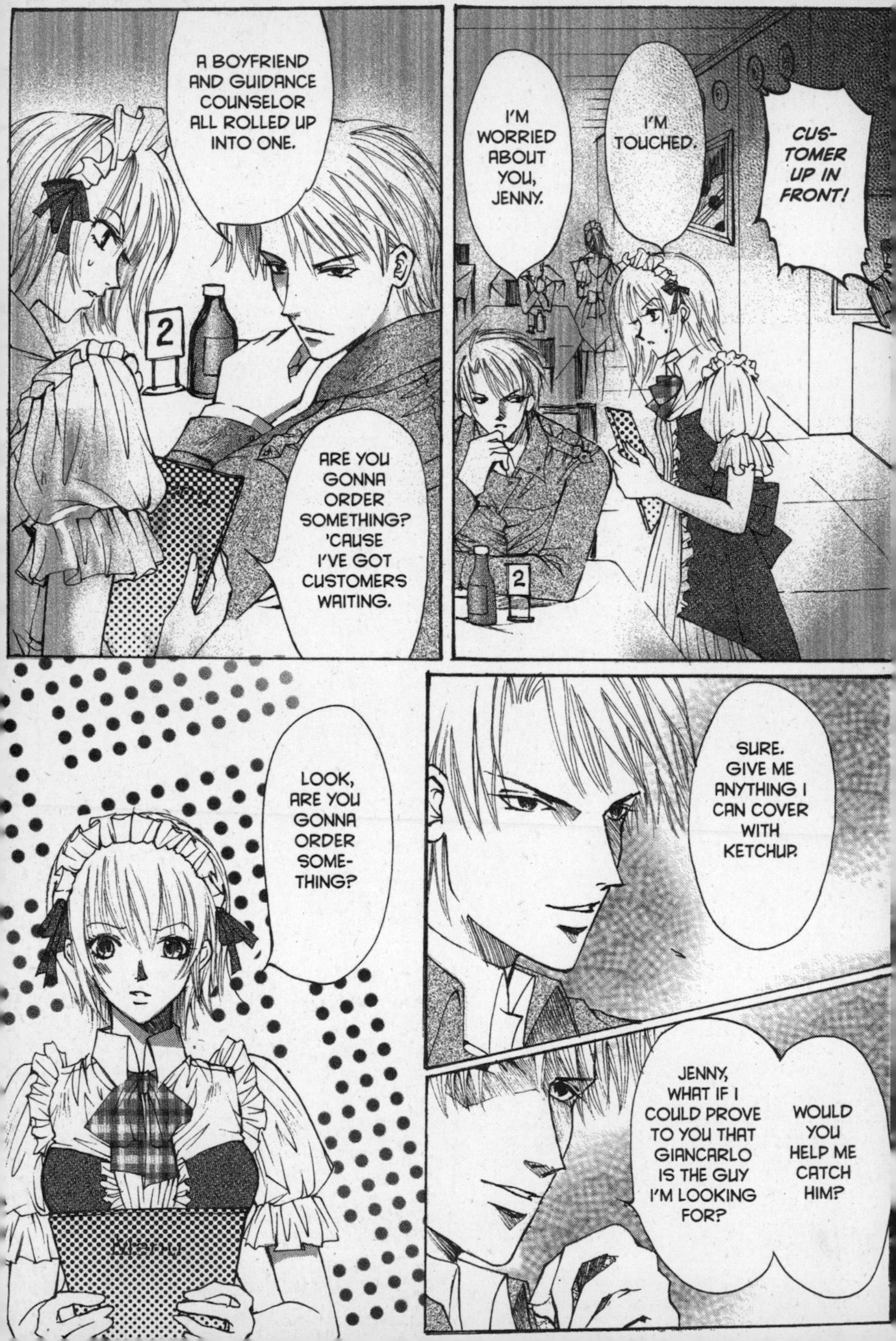
A BOYFRIEND AND GUIDANCE COUNSELOR ALL ROLLED UP INTO ONE.
ARE YOU GONNA ORDER SOMETHING? 'CAUSE I'VE GOT CUSTOMERS WAITING.
I'M WORRIED ABOUT YOU, JENNY.
I'M TOUCHED.
CUS-TOMER UP IN FRONT!
LOOK, ARE YOU GONNA ORDER SOME-THING?
SURE. GIVE ME ANYTHING I CAN COVER WITH KETCHUP.
JENNY, WHAT IF I COULD PROVE TO YOU THAT GIANCARLO IS THE GUY I'M LOOKING FOR?
WOULD YOU HELP ME CATCH HIM?

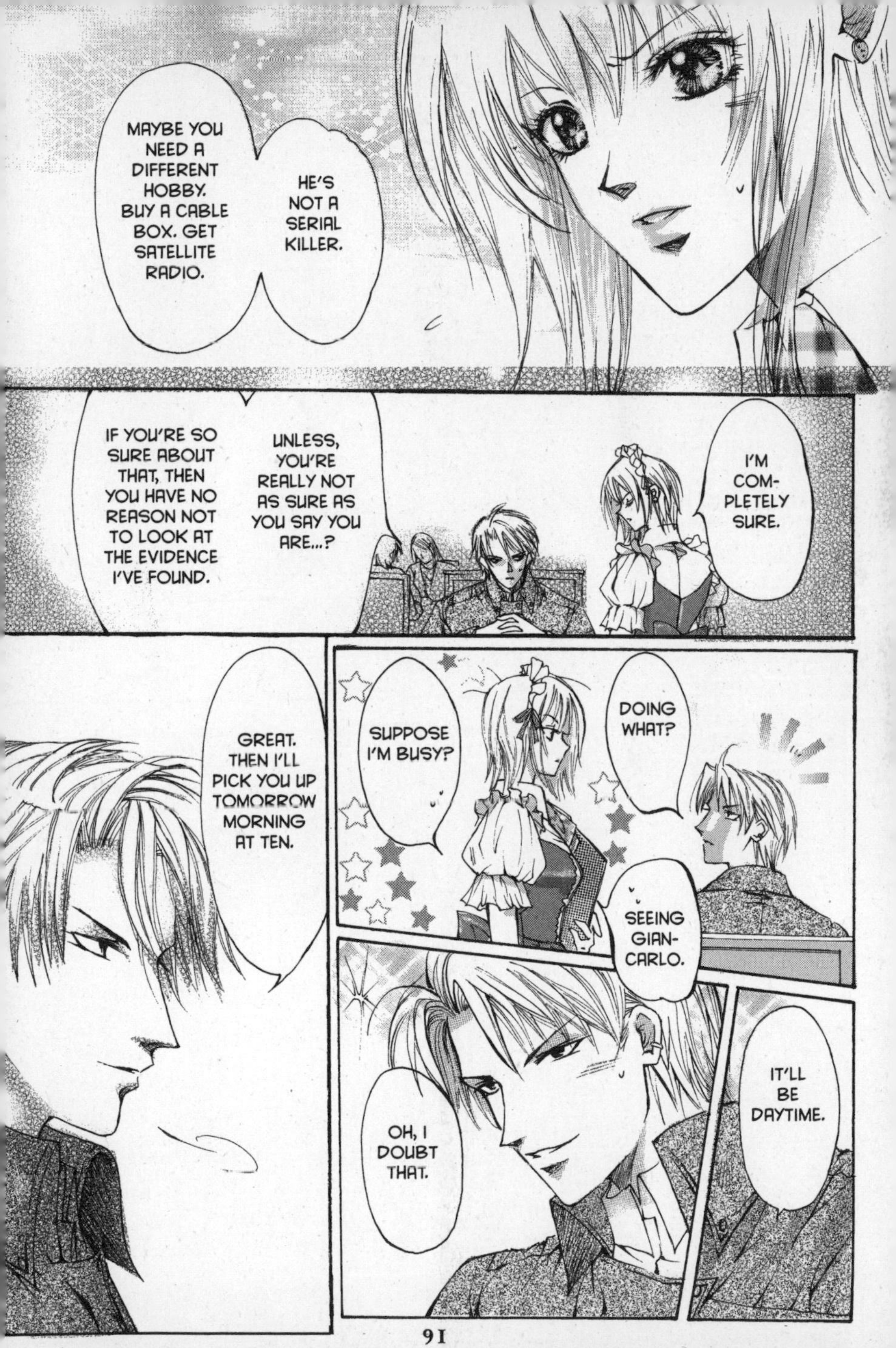
MAYBE YOU NEED A DIFFERENT HOBBY. BUY A CABLE BOX. GET SATELLITE RADIO.
HE'S NOT A SERIAL KILLER.
IF YOU'RE SO SURE ABOUT THAT, THEN YOU HAVE NO REASON NOT TO LOOK AT THE EVIDENCE I'VE FOUND.
UNLESS, YOU'RE REALLY NOT AS SURE AS YOU SAY YOU ARE...?
I'M COM-PLETELY SURE.
GREAT. THEN I'LL PICK YOU UP TOMORROW MORNING AT TEN.
SUPPOSE I'M BUSY?
DOING WHAT?
SEEING GIAN-CARLO.
OH, I DOUBT THAT.
IT'LL BE DAYTIME.

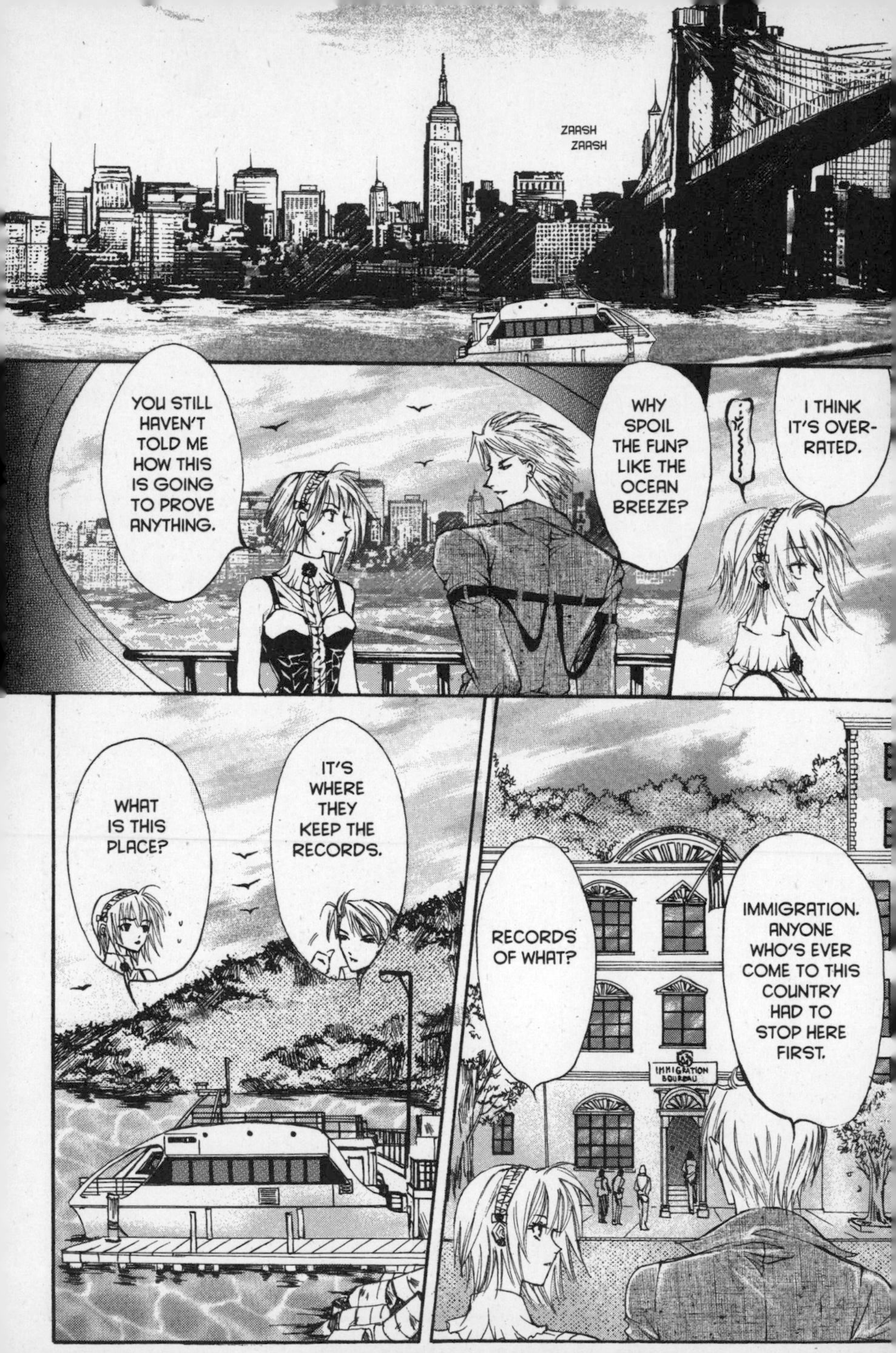
ZAASH ZAASH
YOU STILL HAVEN'T TOLD ME HOW THIS IS GOING TO PROVE ANYTHING.
WHY SPOIL THE FUN? LIKE THE OCEAN BREEZE?
I THINK IT'S OVER-RATED.
WHAT IS THIS PLACE?
IT'S WHERE THEY KEEP THE RECORDS.
RECORDS OF WHAT?
IMMIGRATION. ANYONE WHO'S EVER COME TO THIS COUNTRY HAD TO STOP HERE FIRST.

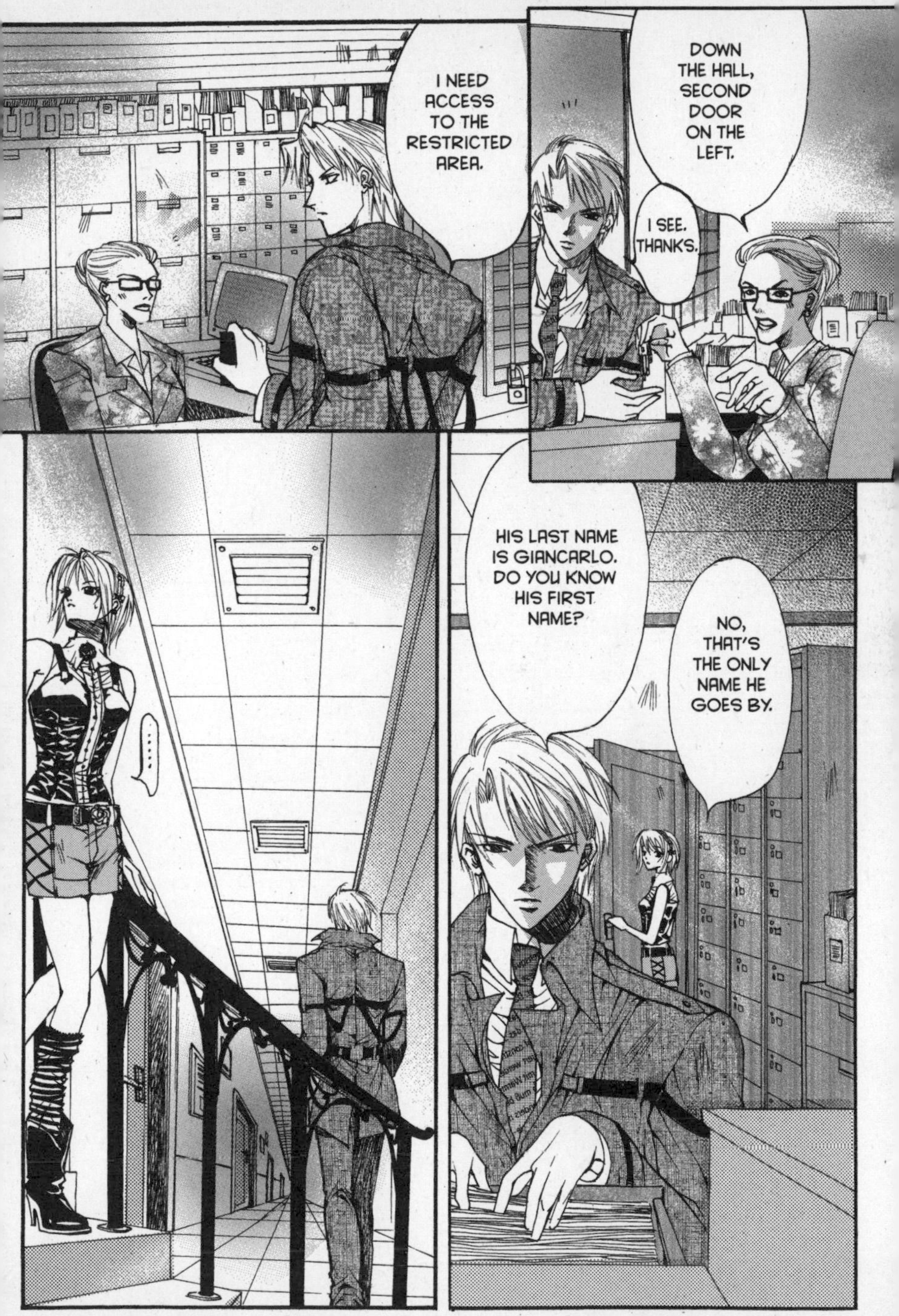
I NEED ACCESS TO THE RESTRICTED AREA.
DOWN THE HALL, SECOND DOOR ON THE LEFT.
I SEE. THANKS.
......
HIS LAST NAME IS GIANCARLO. DO YOU KNOW HIS FIRST NAME?
NO, THAT'S THE ONLY NAME HE GOES BY.

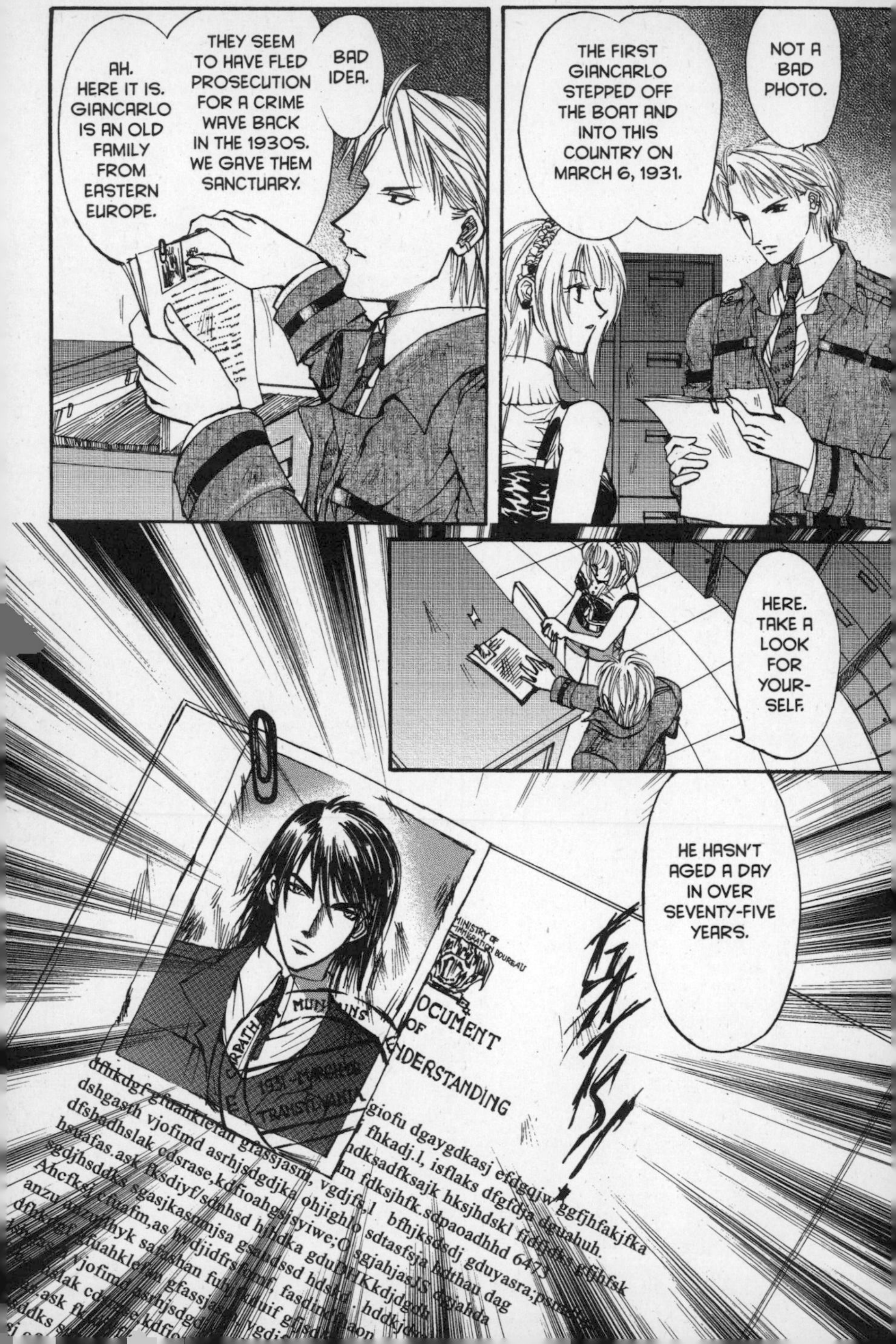
AH. HERE IT IS. GIANCARLO IS AN OLD FAMILY FROM EASTERN EUROPE.
THEY SEEM TO HAVE FLED PROSECUTION FOR A CRIME WAVE BACK IN THE 1930S. WE GAVE THEM SANCTUARY.
BAD IDEA.
THE FIRST GIANCARLO STEPPED OFF THE BOAT AND INTO THIS COUNTRY ON MARCH 6, 1931.
NOT A BAD PHOTO.
HERE. TAKE A LOOK FOR YOURSELF.
HE HASN'T AGED A DAY IN OVER SEVENTY-FIVE YEARS.

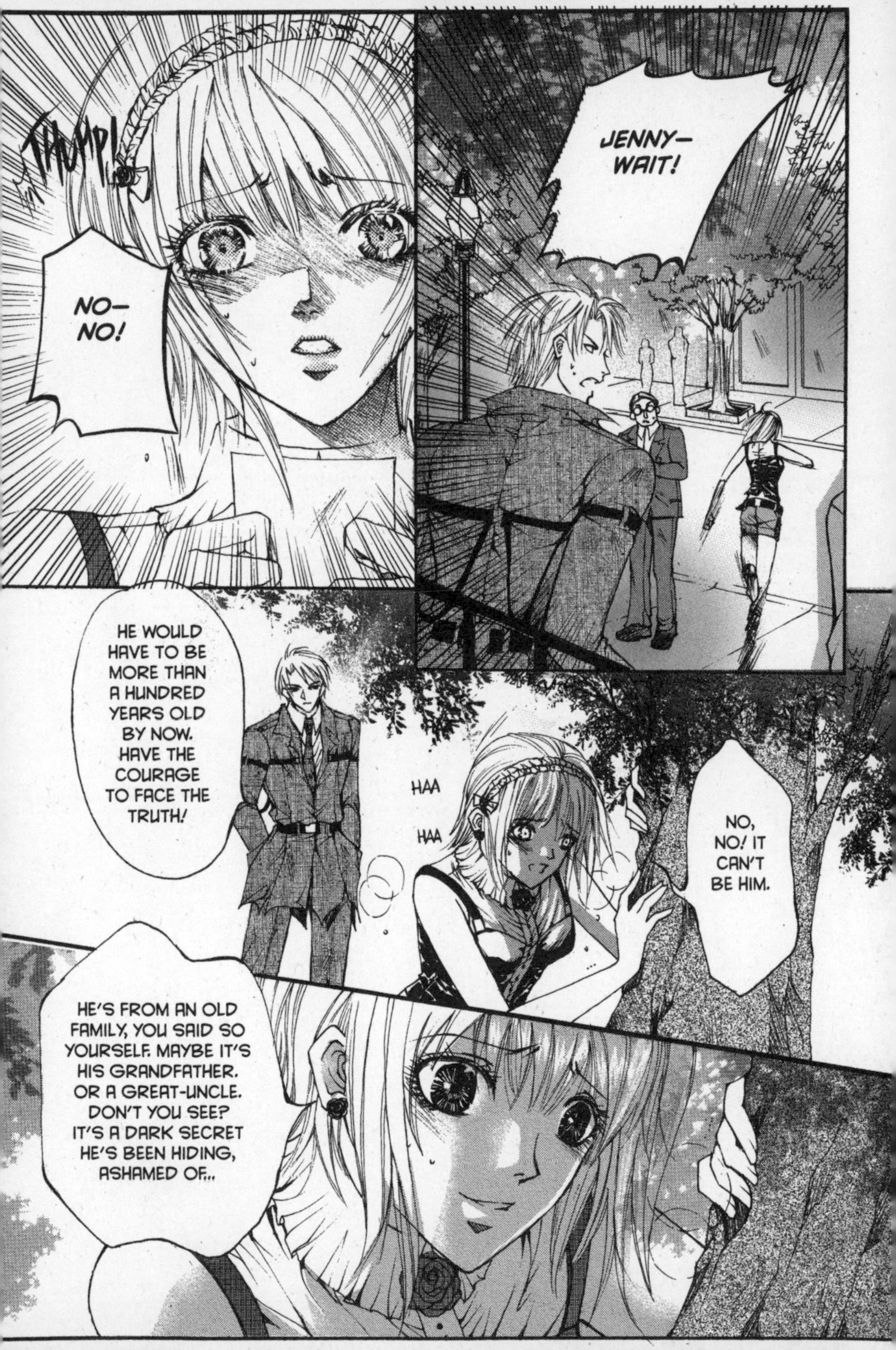
THUMP!
NO— NO!
JENNY— WAIT!
HE WOULD HAVE TO BE MORE THAN A HUNDRED YEARS OLD BY NOW. HAVE THE COURAGE TO FACE THE TRUTH!
HAA
HAA
NO, NO! IT CAN'T BE HIM.
HE'S FROM AN OLD FAMILY, YOU SAID SO YOURSELF. MAYBE IT'S HIS GRANDFATHER. OR A GREAT-UNCLE. DON'T YOU SEE? IT'S A DARK SECRET HE'S BEEN HIDING, ASHAMED OF...

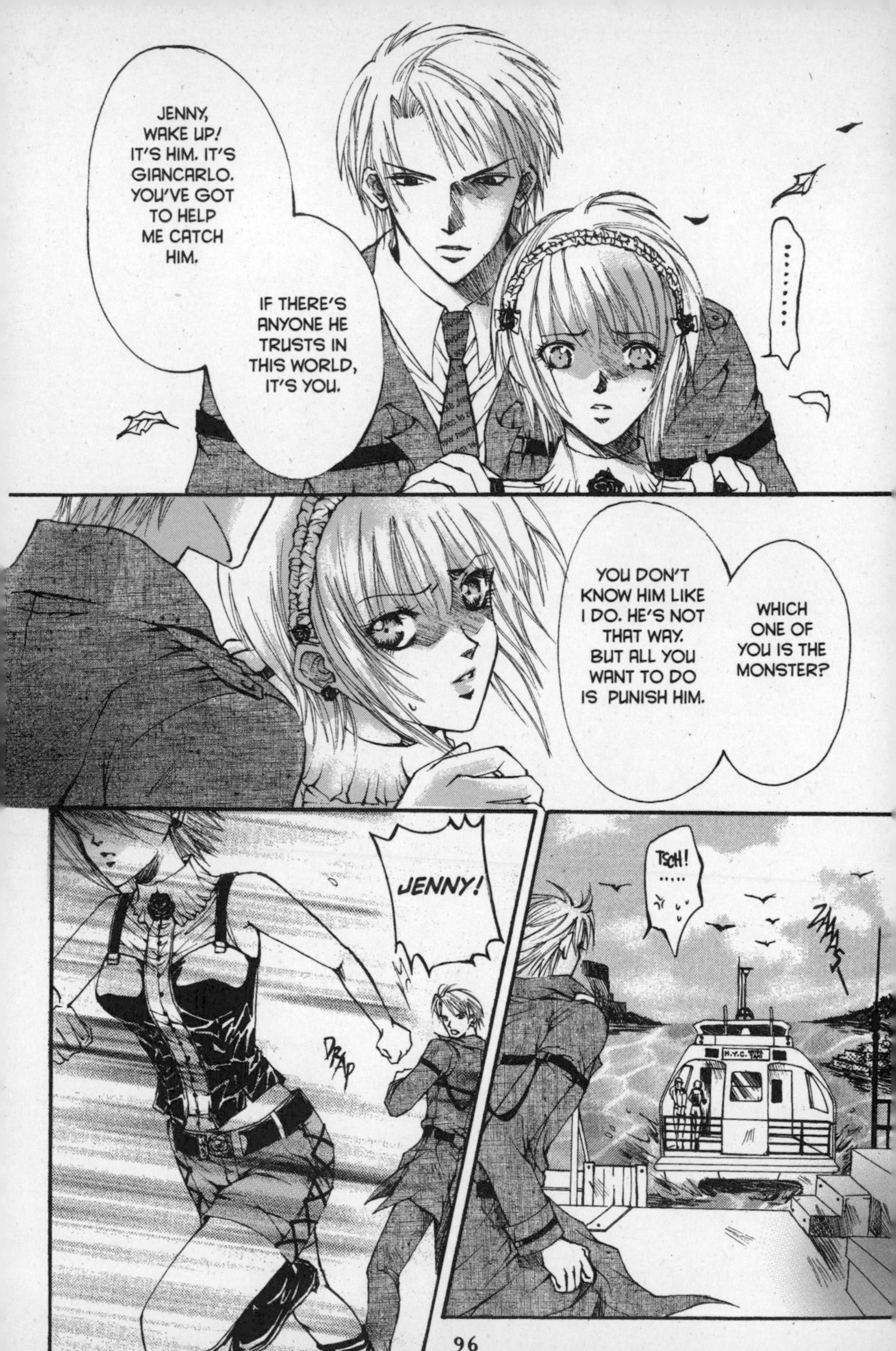

JENNY, WAKE UP! IT'S HIM. IT'S GIANCARLO. YOU'VE GOT TO HELP ME CATCH HIM.
IF THERE'S ANYONE HE TRUSTS IN THIS WORLD, IT'S YOU.
......
YOU DON'T KNOW HIM LIKE I DO. HE'S NOT THAT WAY. BUT ALL YOU WANT TO DO IS PUNISH HIM.
WHICH ONE OF YOU IS THE MONSTER?
JENNY!
DRAP
TSCH! .....

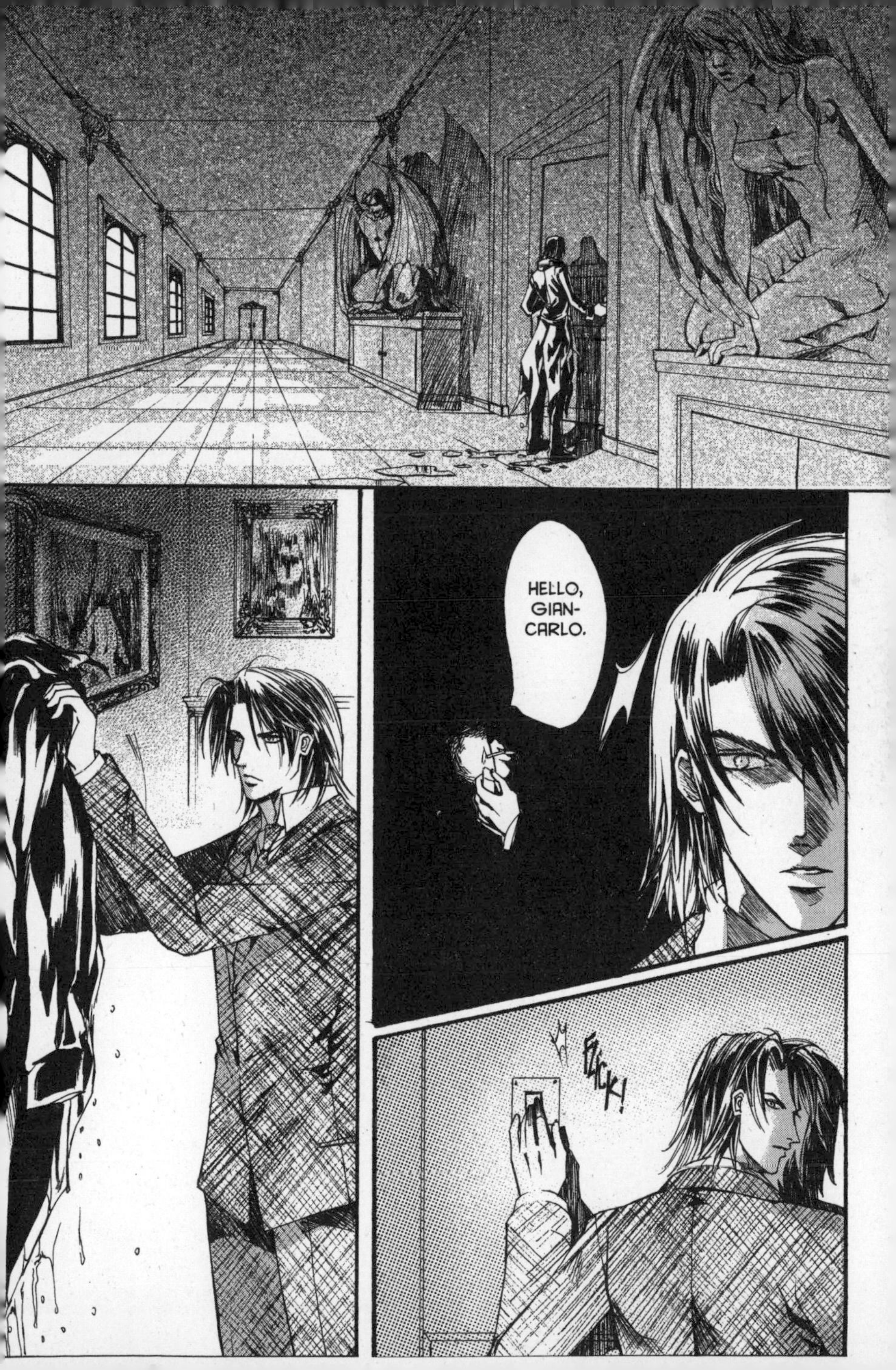
HELLO, GIAN-CARLO.
FLICK!

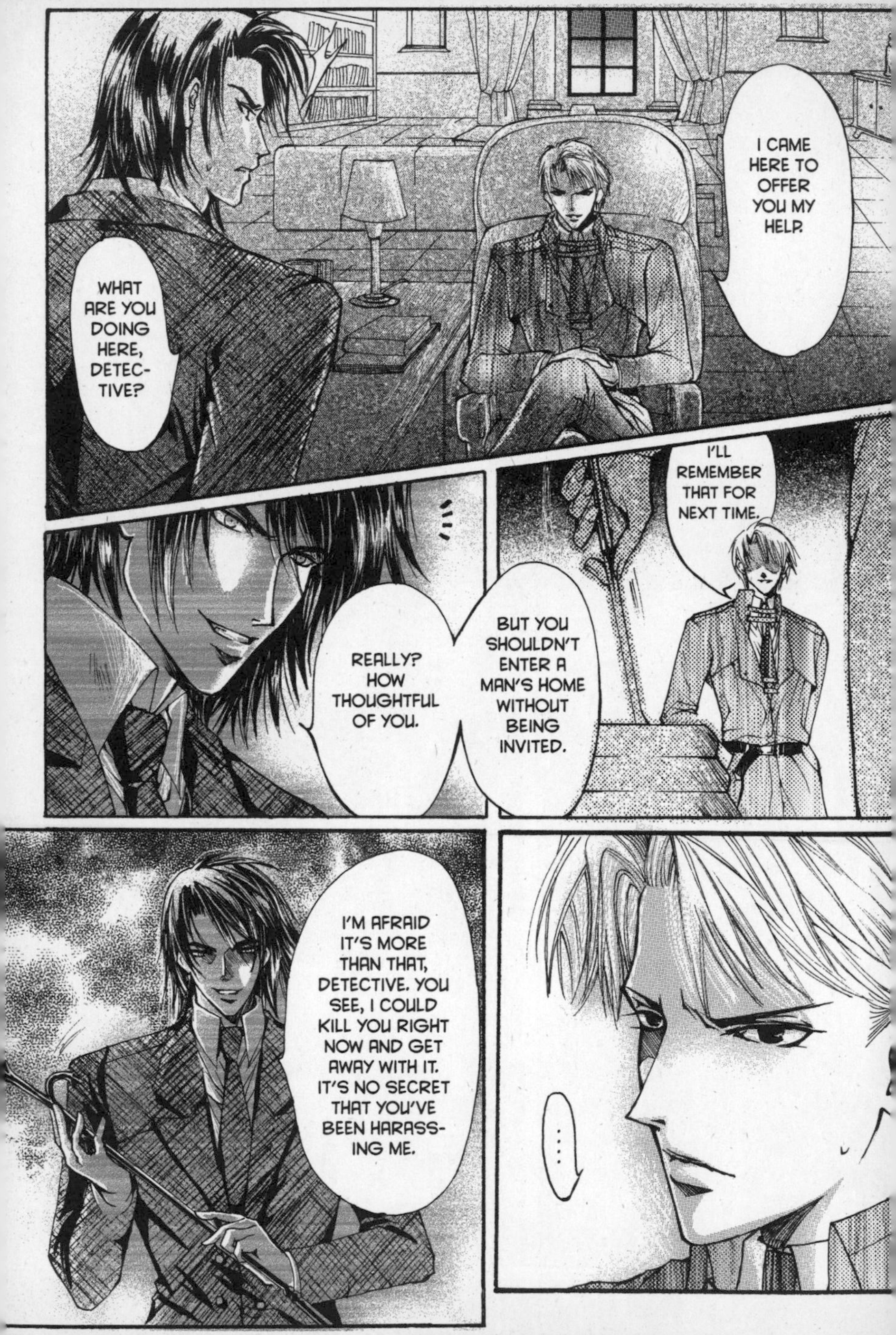
WHAT ARE YOU DOING HERE, DETECTIVE?
I CAME HERE TO OFFER YOU MY HELP.
REALLY? HOW THOUGHTFUL OF YOU.
BUT YOU SHOULDN'T ENTER A MAN'S HOME WITHOUT BEING INVITED.
I'LL REMEMBER THAT FOR NEXT TIME.
I'M AFRAID IT'S MORE THAN THAT, DETECTIVE. YOU SEE, I COULD KILL YOU RIGHT NOW AND GET AWAY WITH IT. IT'S NO SECRET THAT YOU'VE BEEN HARASS-ING ME.
....

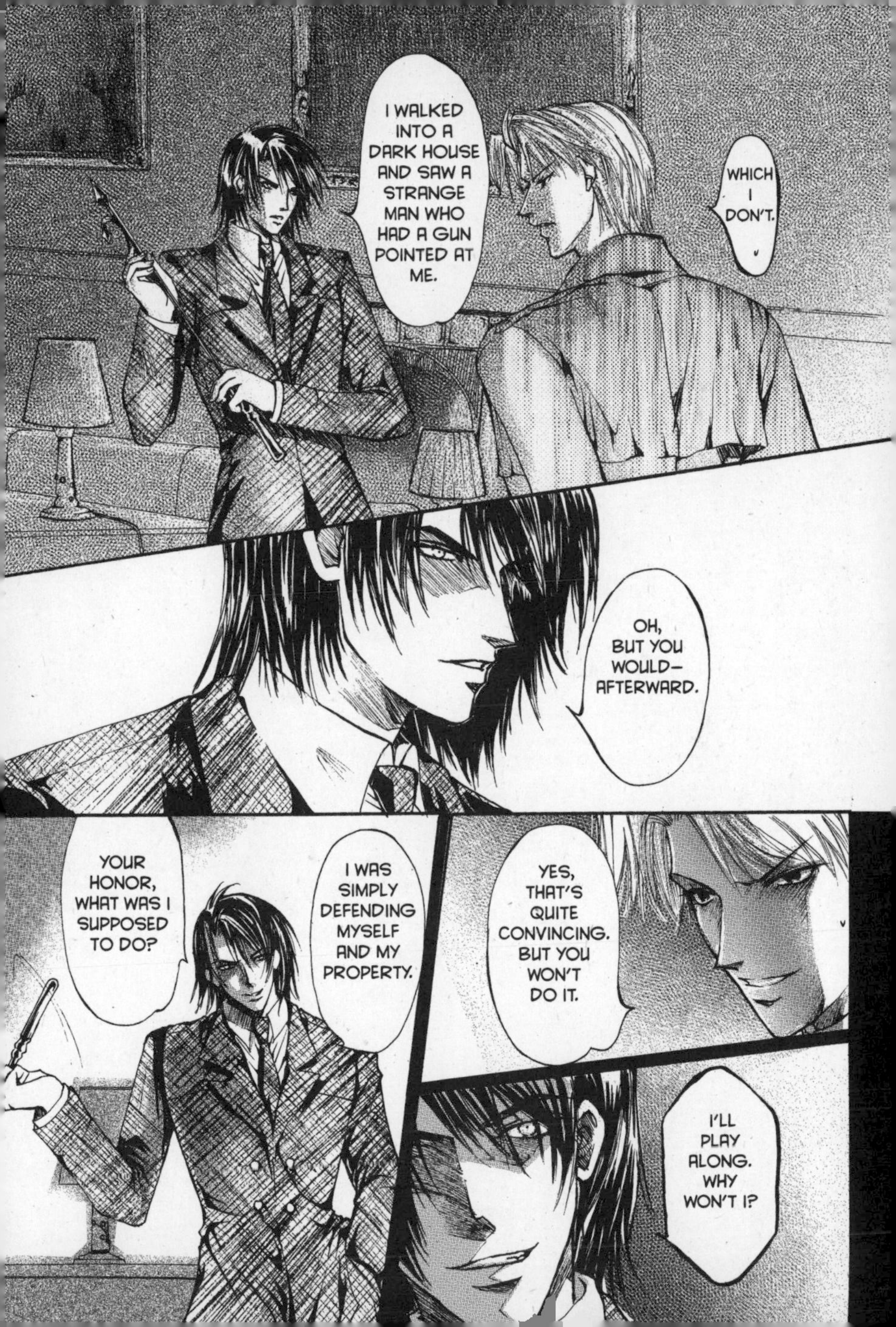
I WALKED INTO A DARK HOUSE AND SAW A STRANGE MAN WHO HAD A GUN POINTED AT ME.
WHICH I DON'T.
OH, BUT YOU WOULD— AFTERWARD.
YOUR HONOR, WHAT WAS I SUPPOSED TO DO?
I WAS SIMPLY DEFENDING MYSELF AND MY PROPERTY.
YES, THAT'S QUITE CONVINCING. BUT YOU WON'T DO IT.
I'LL PLAY ALONG. WHY WON'T I?

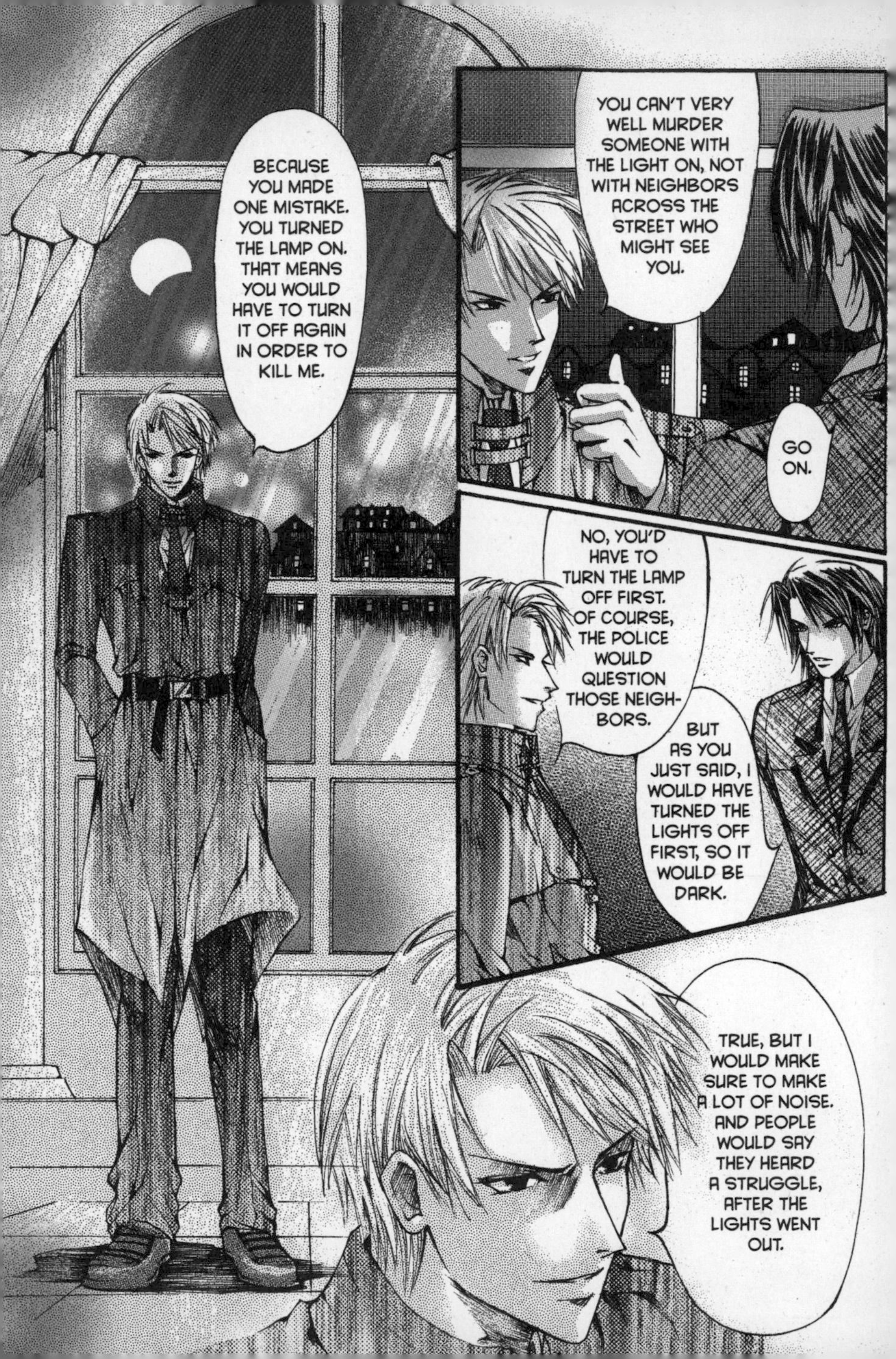
BECAUSE YOU MADE ONE MISTAKE. YOU TURNED THE LAMP ON. THAT MEANS YOU WOULD HAVE TO TURN IT OFF AGAIN IN ORDER TO KILL ME.
YOU CAN'T VERY WELL MURDER SOMEONE WITH THE LIGHT ON, NOT WITH NEIGHBORS ACROSS THE STREET WHO MIGHT SEE YOU.
GO ON.
NO, YOU'D HAVE TO TURN THE LAMP OFF FIRST. OF COURSE, THE POLICE WOULD QUESTION THOSE NEIGH-BORS.
BUT AS YOU JUST SAID, I WOULD HAVE TURNED THE LIGHTS OFF FIRST, SO IT WOULD BE DARK.
TRUE, BUT I WOULD MAKE SURE TO MAKE A LOT OF NOISE. AND PEOPLE WOULD SAY THEY HEARD A STRUGGLE, AFTER THE LIGHTS WENT OUT.

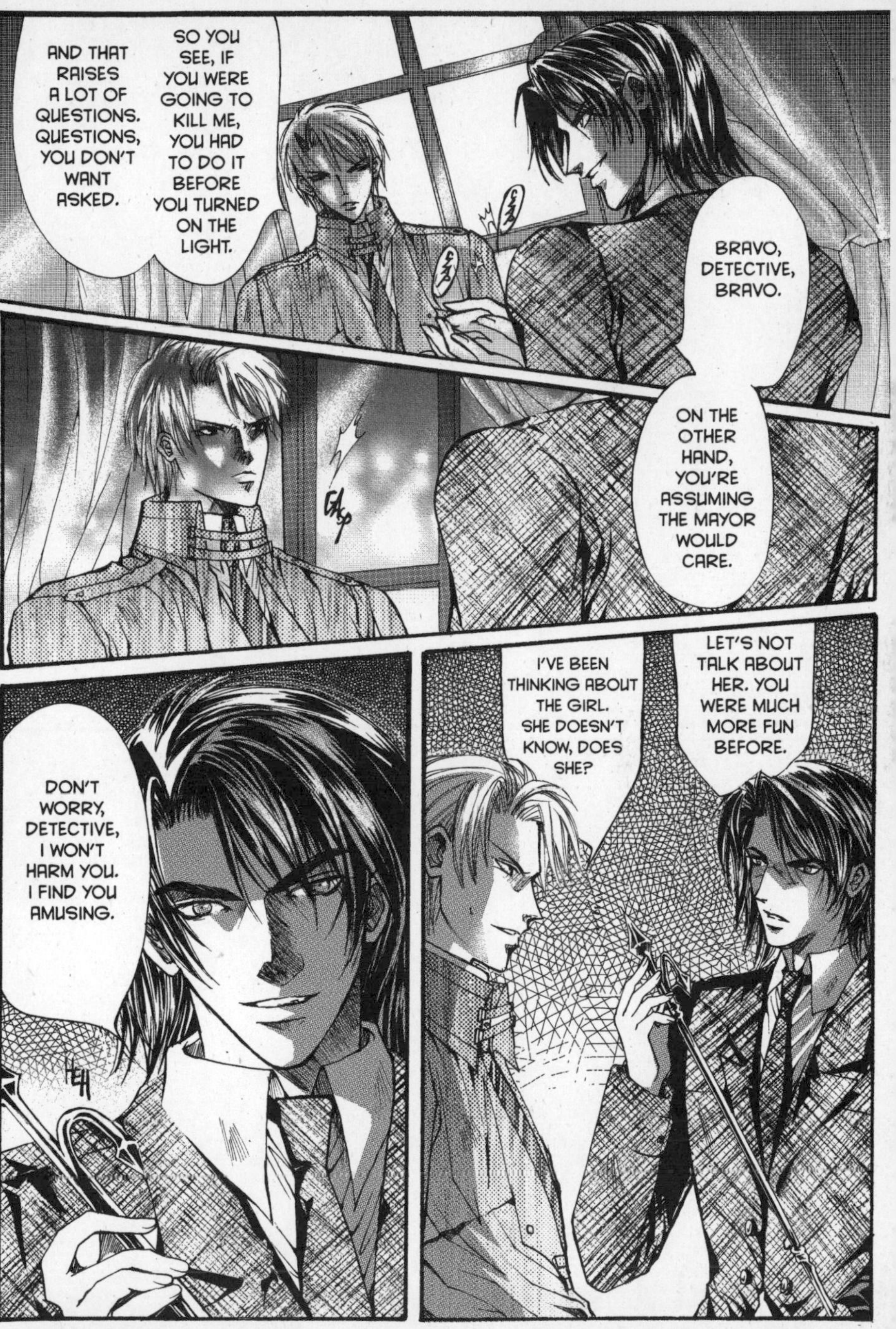

SO YOU SEE, IF YOU WERE GOING TO KILL ME, YOU HAD TO DO IT BEFORE YOU TURNED ON THE LIGHT.
AND THAT RAISES A LOT OF QUESTIONS. QUESTIONS, YOU DON'T WANT ASKED.
BRAVO, DETECTIVE, BRAVO.
GASP
ON THE OTHER HAND, YOU'RE ASSUMING THE MAYOR WOULD CARE.
DON'T WORRY, DETECTIVE, I WON'T HARM YOU. I FIND YOU AMUSING.
HEH
I'VE BEEN THINKING ABOUT THE GIRL. SHE DOESN'T KNOW, DOES SHE?
LET'S NOT TALK ABOUT HER. YOU WERE MUCH MORE FUN BEFORE.

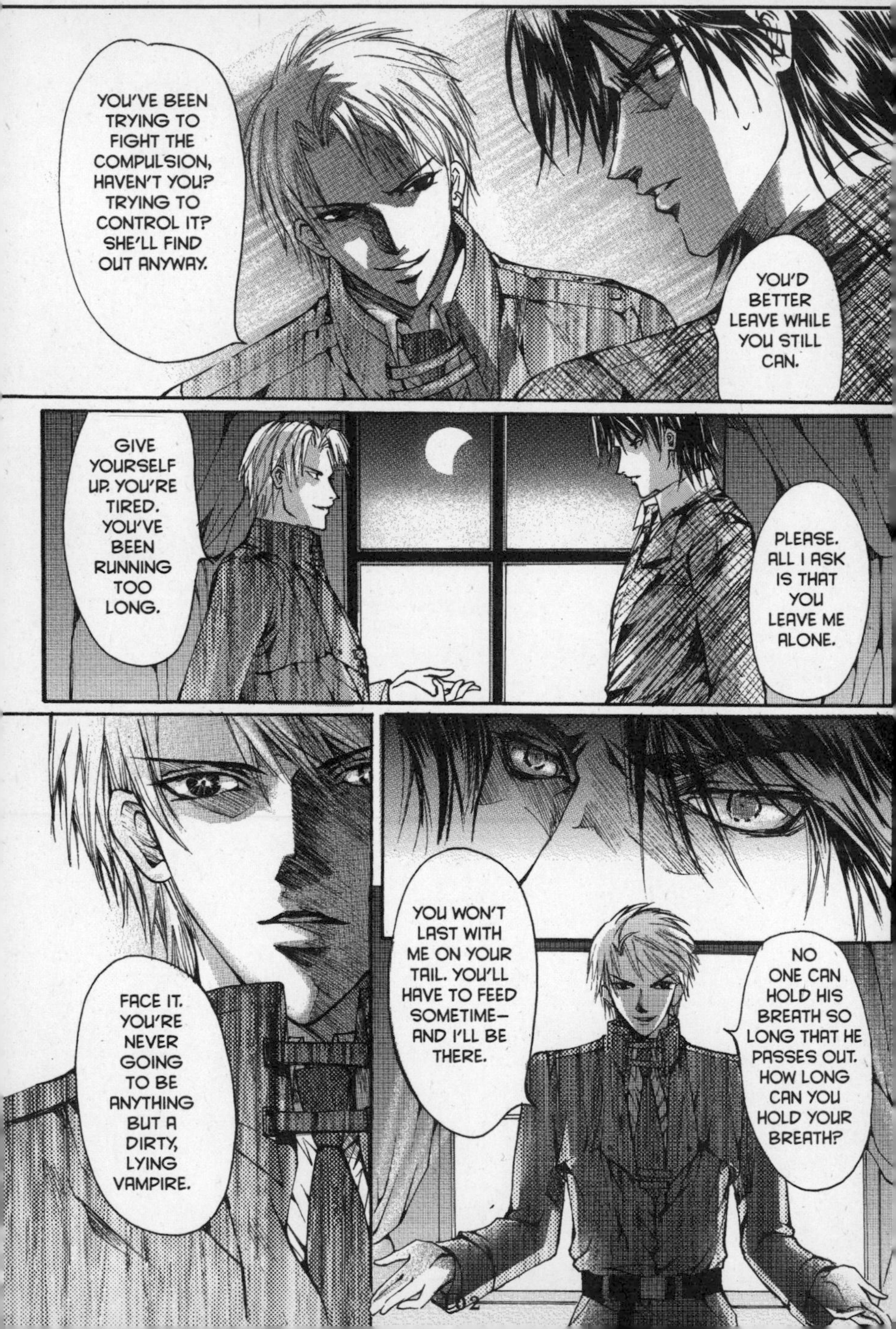
YOU'VE BEEN TRYING TO FIGHT THE COMPULSION, HAVEN'T YOU? TRYING TO CONTROL IT? SHE'LL FIND OUT ANYWAY.
YOU'D BETTER LEAVE WHILE YOU STILL CAN.
GIVE YOURSELF UP. YOU'RE TIRED. YOU'VE BEEN RUNNING TOO LONG.
PLEASE. ALL I ASK IS THAT YOU LEAVE ME ALONE.
FACE IT. YOU'RE NEVER GOING TO BE ANYTHING BUT A DIRTY, LYING VAMPIRE.
YOU WON'T LAST WITH ME ON YOUR TAIL. YOU'LL HAVE TO FEED SOMETIME— AND I'LL BE THERE.
NO ONE CAN HOLD HIS BREATH SO LONG THAT HE PASSES OUT. HOW LONG CAN YOU HOLD YOUR BREATH?

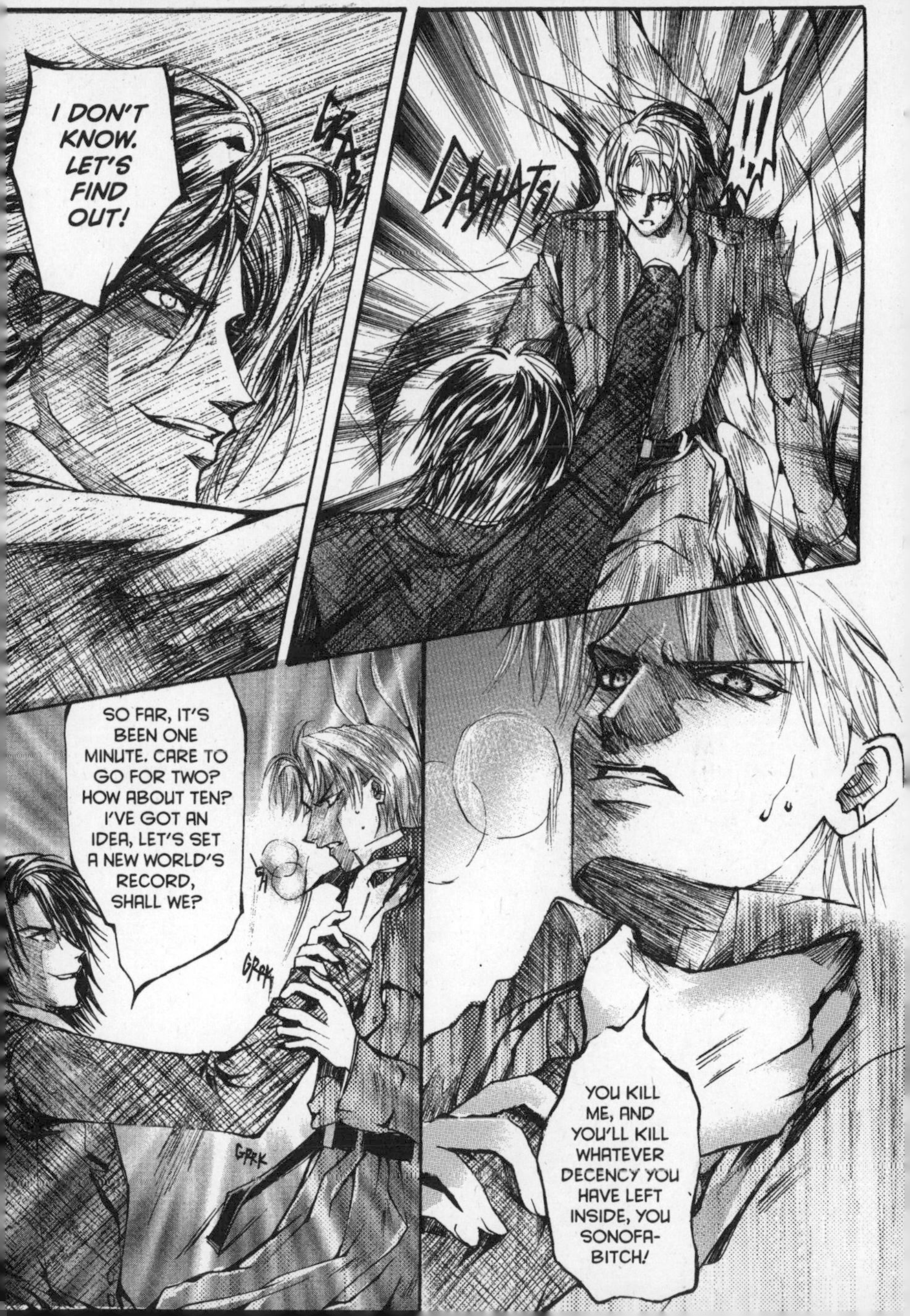
I DON'T KNOW. LET'S FIND OUT!
GRAB
GASHATS!
!!
SO FAR, IT'S BEEN ONE MINUTE. CARE TO GO FOR TWO? HOW ABOUT TEN? I'VE GOT AN IDEA, LET'S SET A NEW WORLD'S RECORD, SHALL WE?
GRAK
GRRK
YOU KILL ME, AND YOU'LL KILL WHATEVER DECENCY YOU HAVE LEFT INSIDE, YOU SONOFA-BITCH!

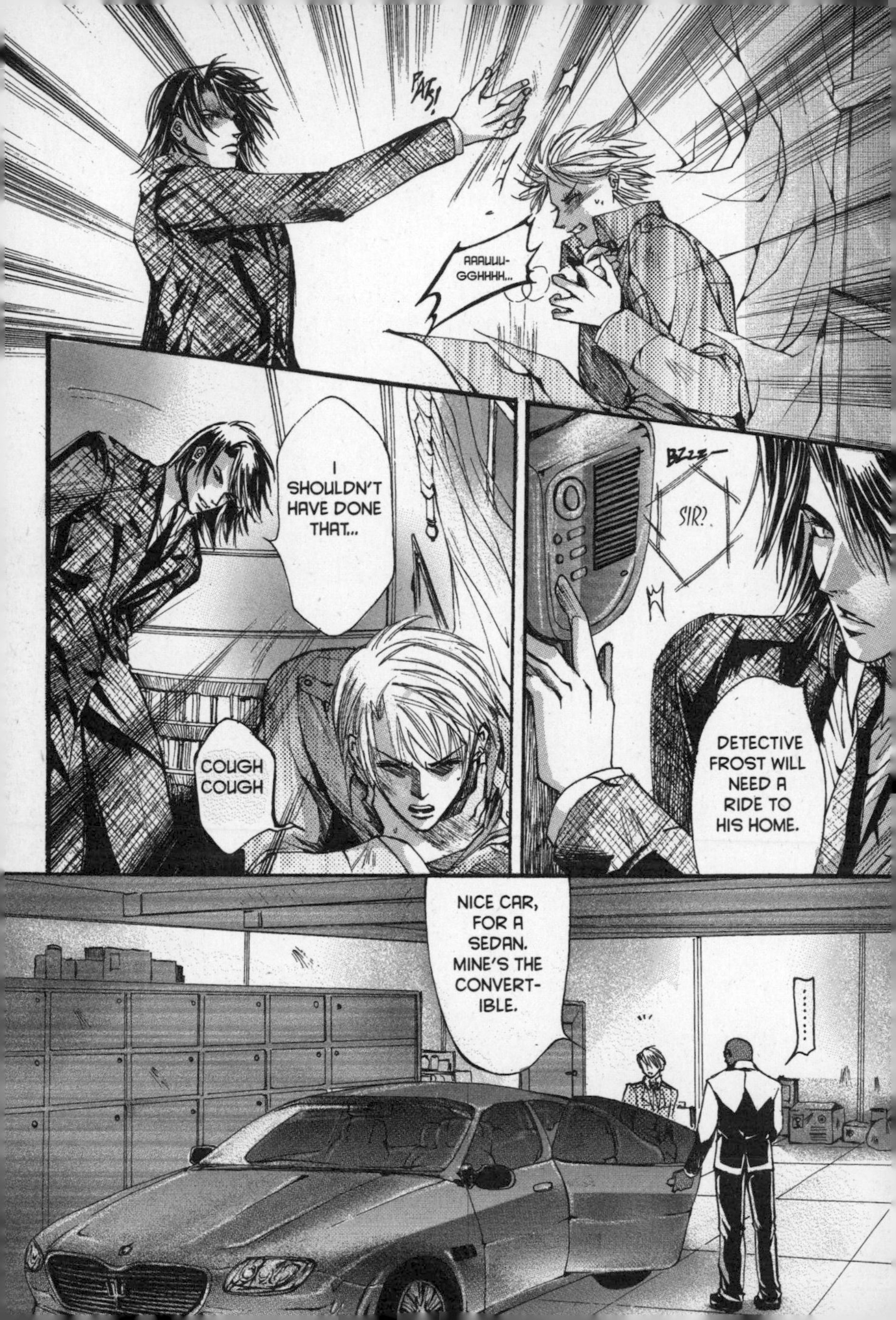
PAK!
AAAUUU-GGHHHH...
I SHOULDN'T HAVE DONE THAT...
COUGH COUGH
BZZZ
SIR?
DETECTIVE FROST WILL NEED A RIDE TO HIS HOME.
NICE CAR, FOR A SEDAN. MINE'S THE CONVERT-IBLE.
......

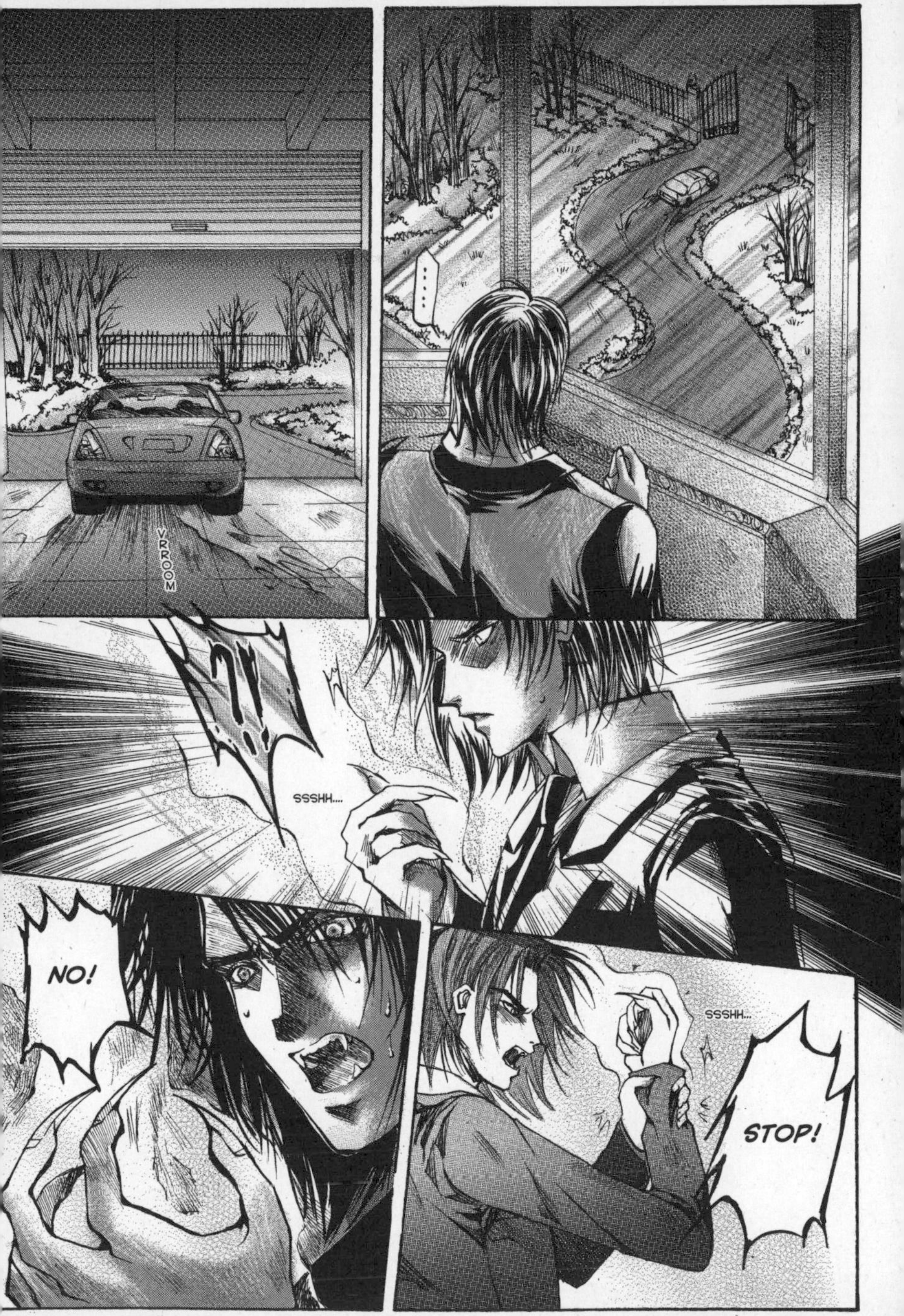
VRROOM
......
?!
SSSHH....
NO!
SSSHH...
STOP!

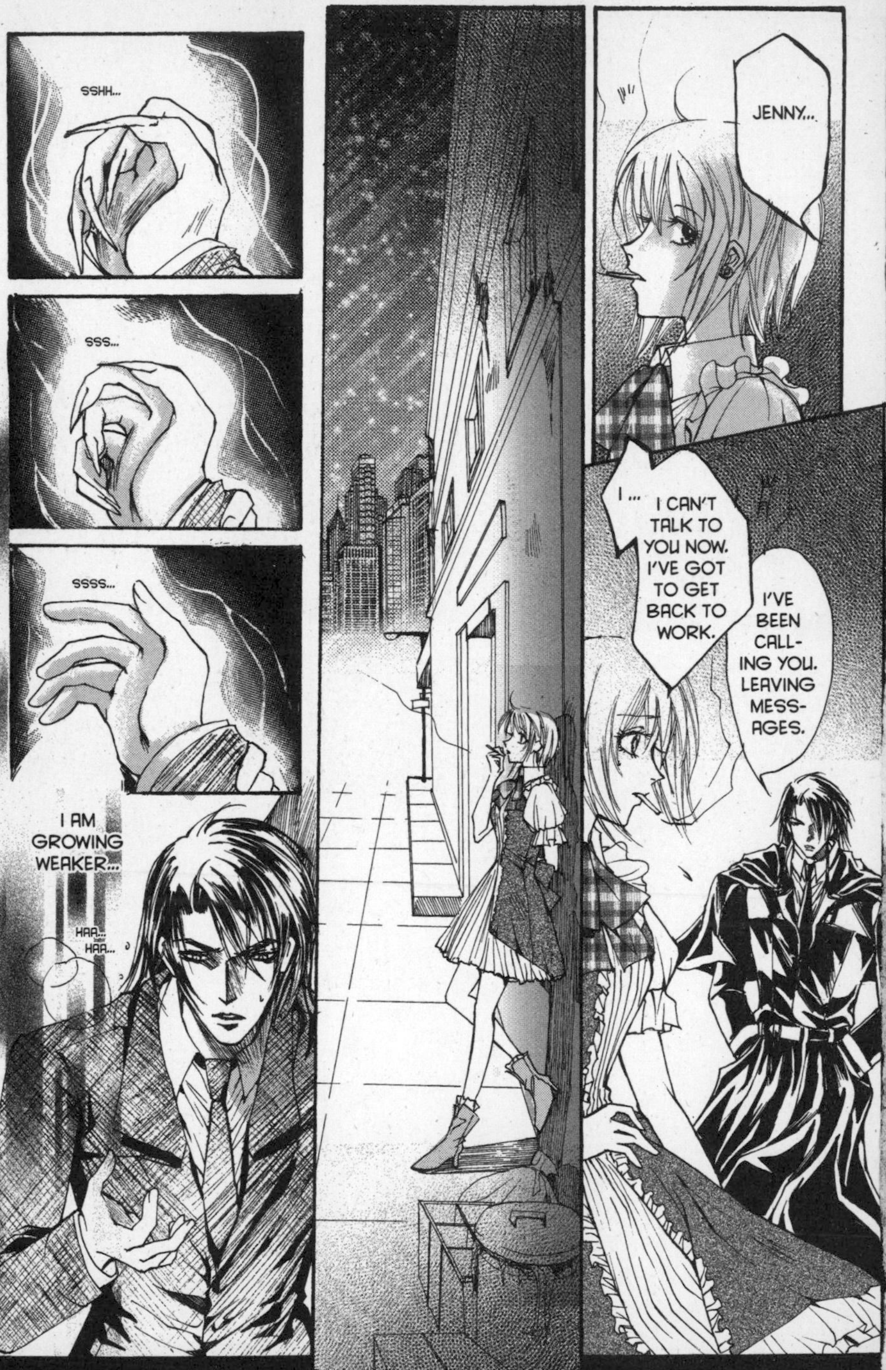
SSHH...
SSS...
SSSS...
I AM GROWING WEAKER...
HAA... HAA...
JENNY...
I ...
I CAN'T TALK TO YOU NOW. I'VE GOT TO GET BACK TO WORK.
I'VE BEEN CALL-ING YOU. LEAVING MESS-AGES.

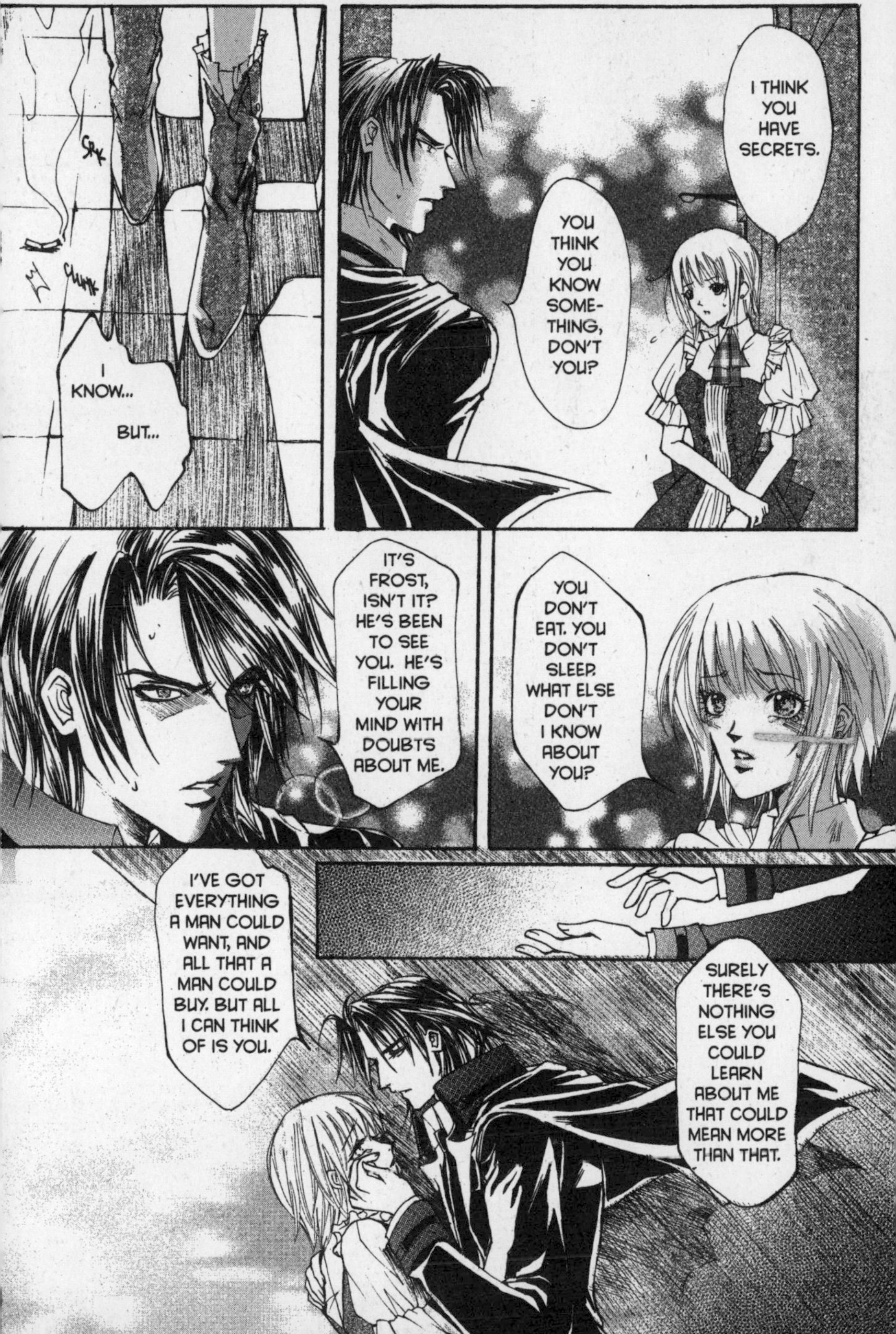
I KNOW...
BUT...
YOU THINK YOU KNOW SOMETHING, DON'T YOU?
I THINK YOU HAVE SECRETS.
IT'S FROST, ISN'T IT? HE'S BEEN TO SEE YOU. HE'S FILLING YOUR MIND WITH DOUBTS ABOUT ME.
YOU DON'T EAT. YOU DON'T SLEEP. WHAT ELSE DON'T I KNOW ABOUT YOU?
I'VE GOT EVERYTHING A MAN COULD WANT, AND ALL THAT A MAN COULD BUY. BUT ALL I CAN THINK OF IS YOU.
SURELY THERE'S NOTHING ELSE YOU COULD LEARN ABOUT ME THAT COULD MEAN MORE THAN THAT.

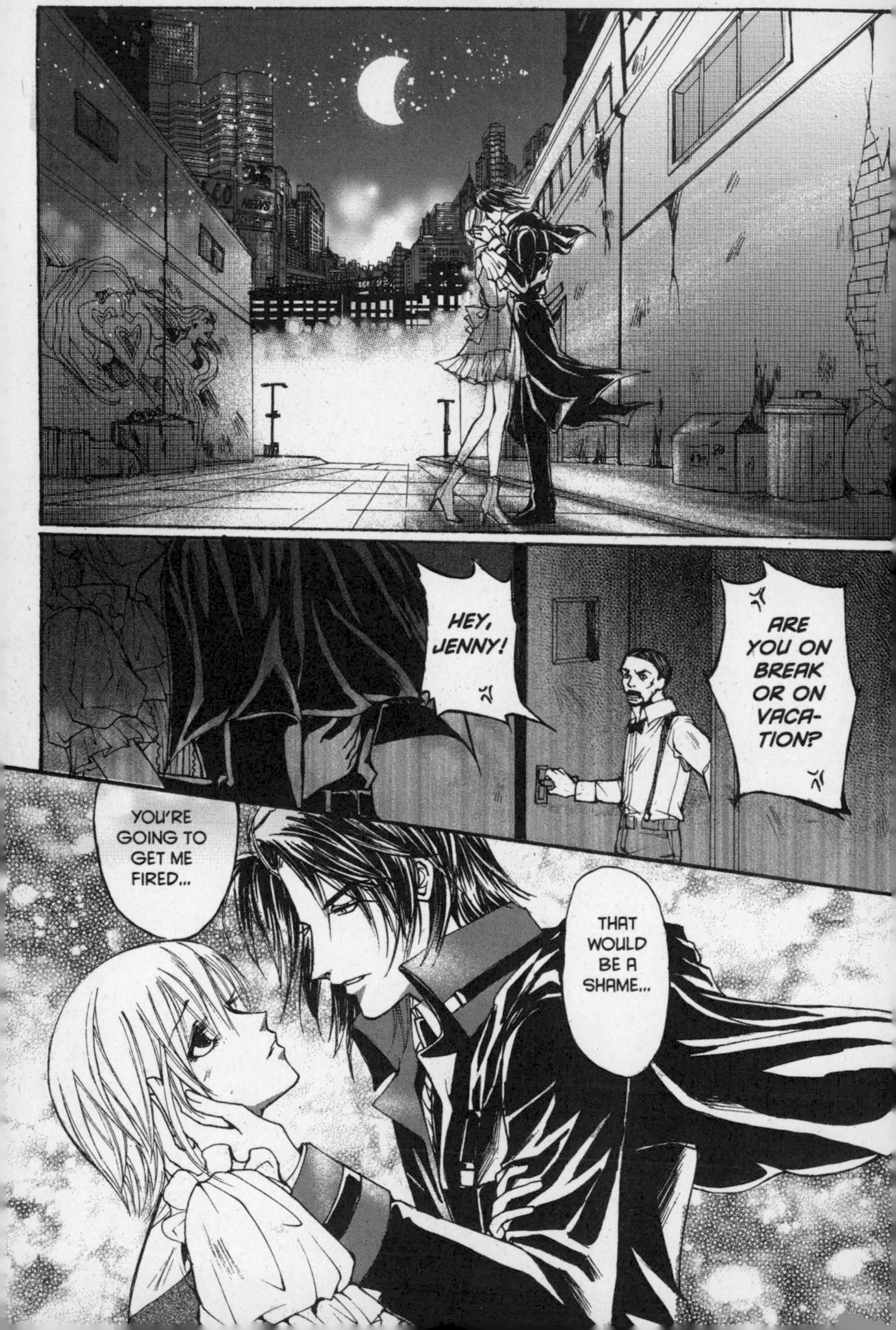
HEY, JENNY!
ARE YOU ON BREAK OR ON VACATION?
YOU'RE GOING TO GET ME FIRED...
THAT WOULD BE A SHAME...

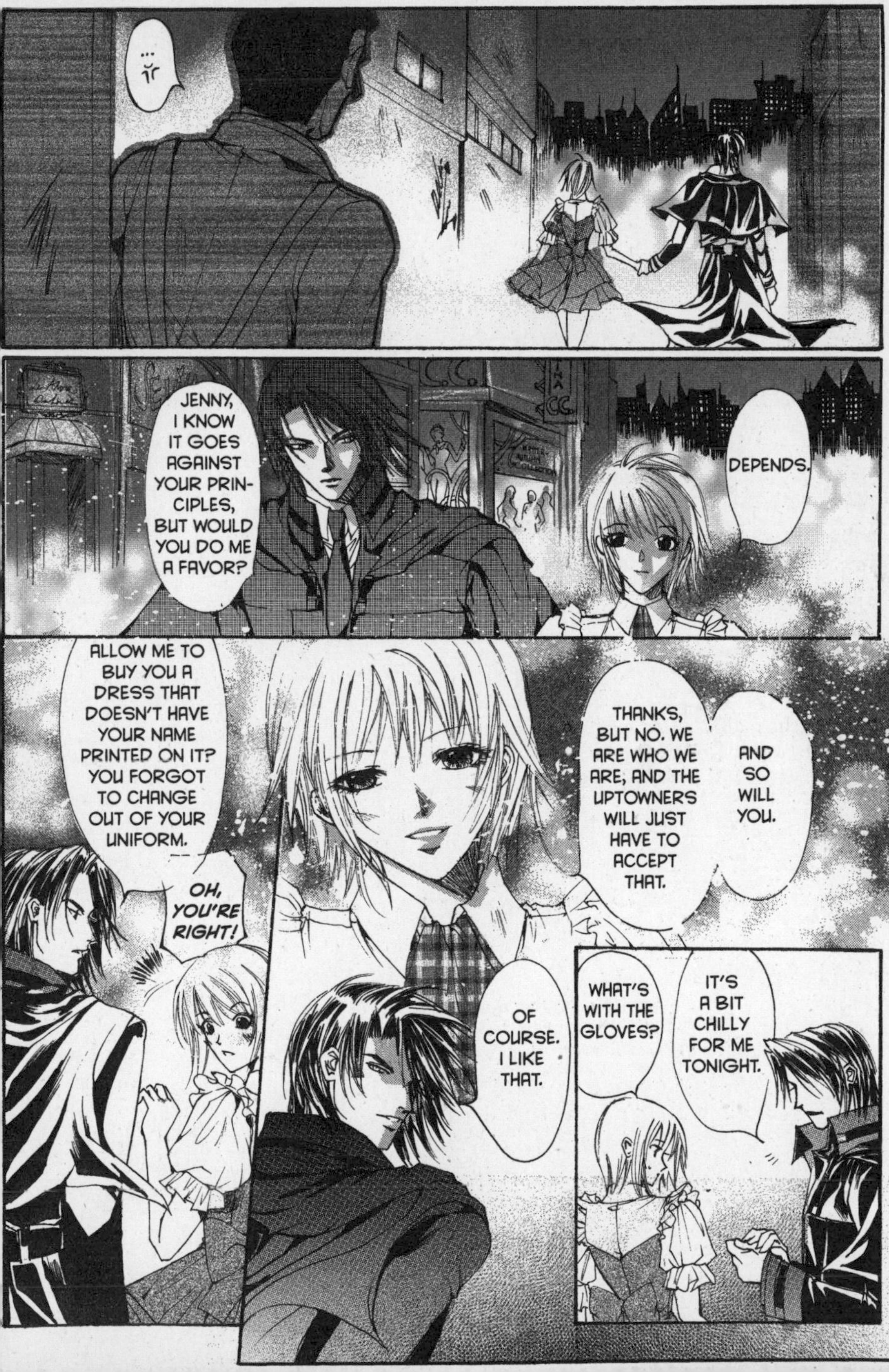
...
JENNY, I KNOW IT GOES AGAINST YOUR PRINCIPLES, BUT WOULD YOU DO ME A FAVOR?
DEPENDS.
ALLOW ME TO BUY YOU A DRESS THAT DOESN'T HAVE YOUR NAME PRINTED ON IT? YOU FORGOT TO CHANGE OUT OF YOUR UNIFORM.
OH, YOU'RE RIGHT!
THANKS, BUT NO. WE ARE WHO WE ARE, AND THE UPTOWNERS WILL JUST HAVE TO ACCEPT THAT.
AND SO WILL YOU.
OF COURSE. I LIKE THAT.
WHAT'S WITH THE GLOVES?
IT'S A BIT CHILLY FOR ME TONIGHT.

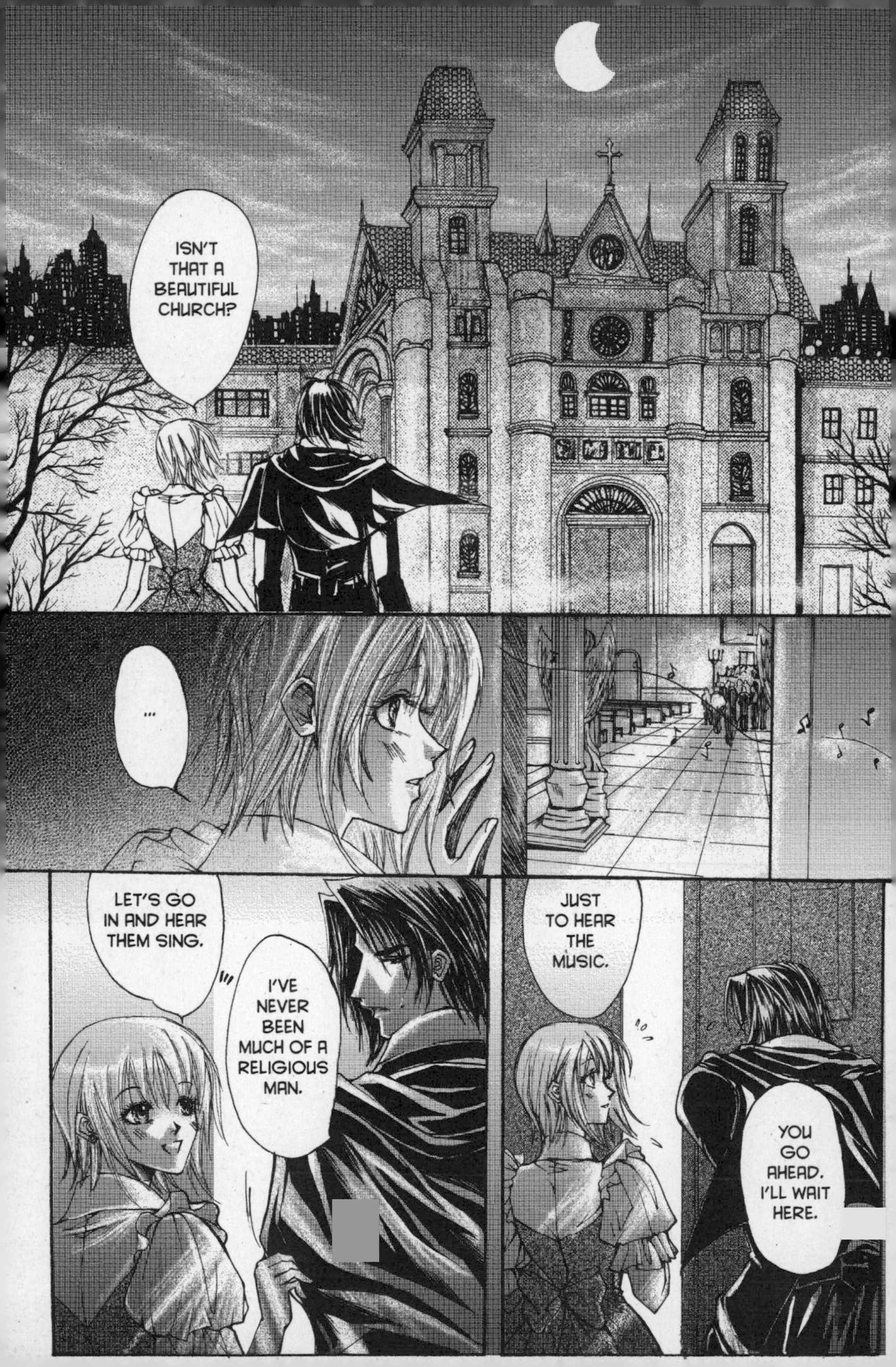
ISN'T THAT A BEAUTIFUL CHURCH?
...
LET'S GO IN AND HEAR THEM SING.
I'VE NEVER BEEN MUCH OF A RELIGIOUS MAN.
JUST TO HEAR THE MUSIC.
YOU GO AHEAD. I'LL WAIT HERE.

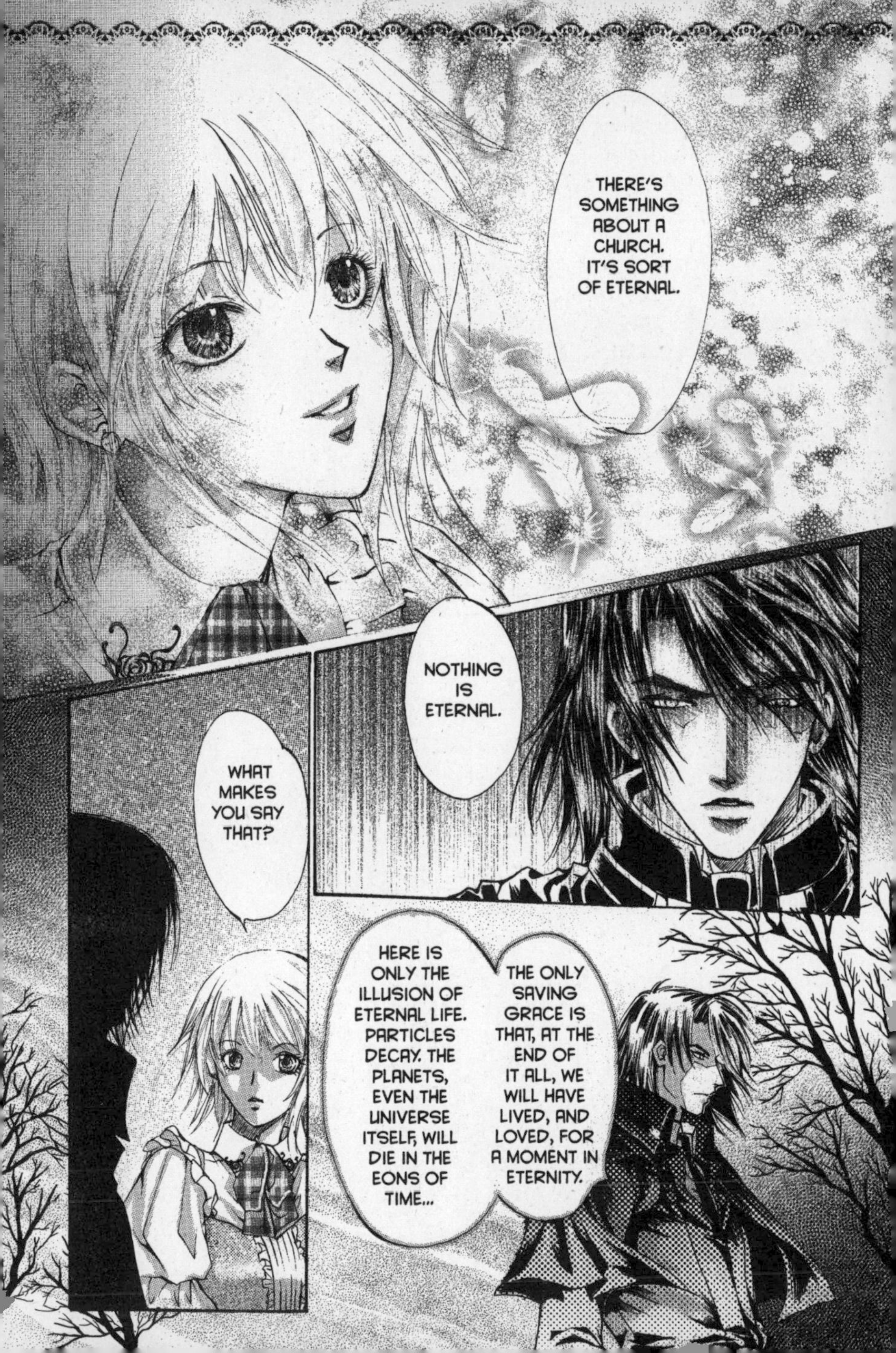
THERE'S SOMETHING ABOUT A CHURCH. IT'S SORT OF ETERNAL.
NOTHING IS ETERNAL.
WHAT MAKES YOU SAY THAT?
HERE IS ONLY THE ILLUSION OF ETERNAL LIFE. PARTICLES DECAY. THE PLANETS, EVEN THE UNIVERSE ITSELF, WILL DIE IN THE EONS OF TIME...
THE ONLY SAVING GRACE IS THAT, AT THE END OF IT ALL, WE WILL HAVE LIVED, AND LOVED, FOR A MOMENT IN ETERNITY.

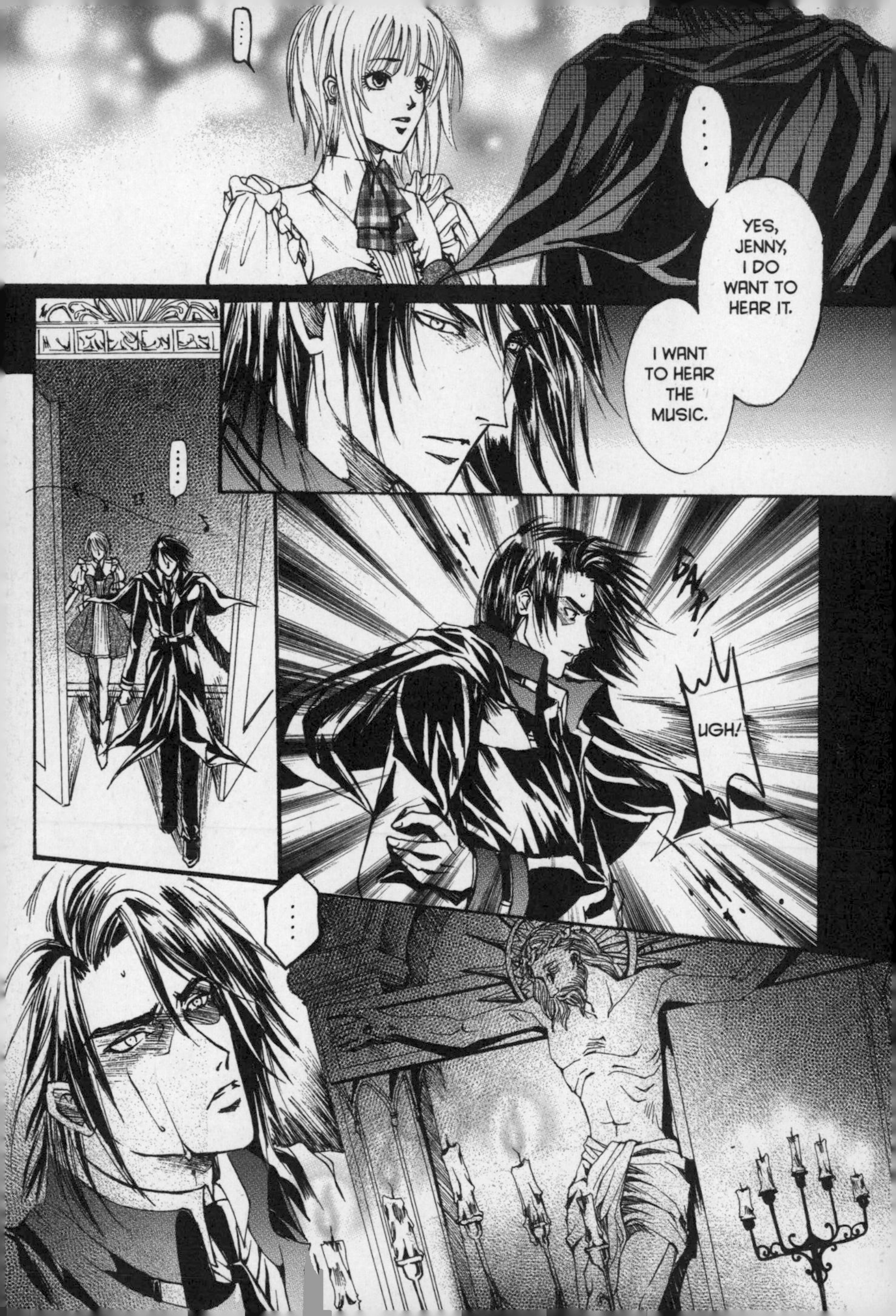
...
...
YES, JENNY, I DO WANT TO HEAR IT.
I WANT TO HEAR THE MUSIC.
...
UGH!
...

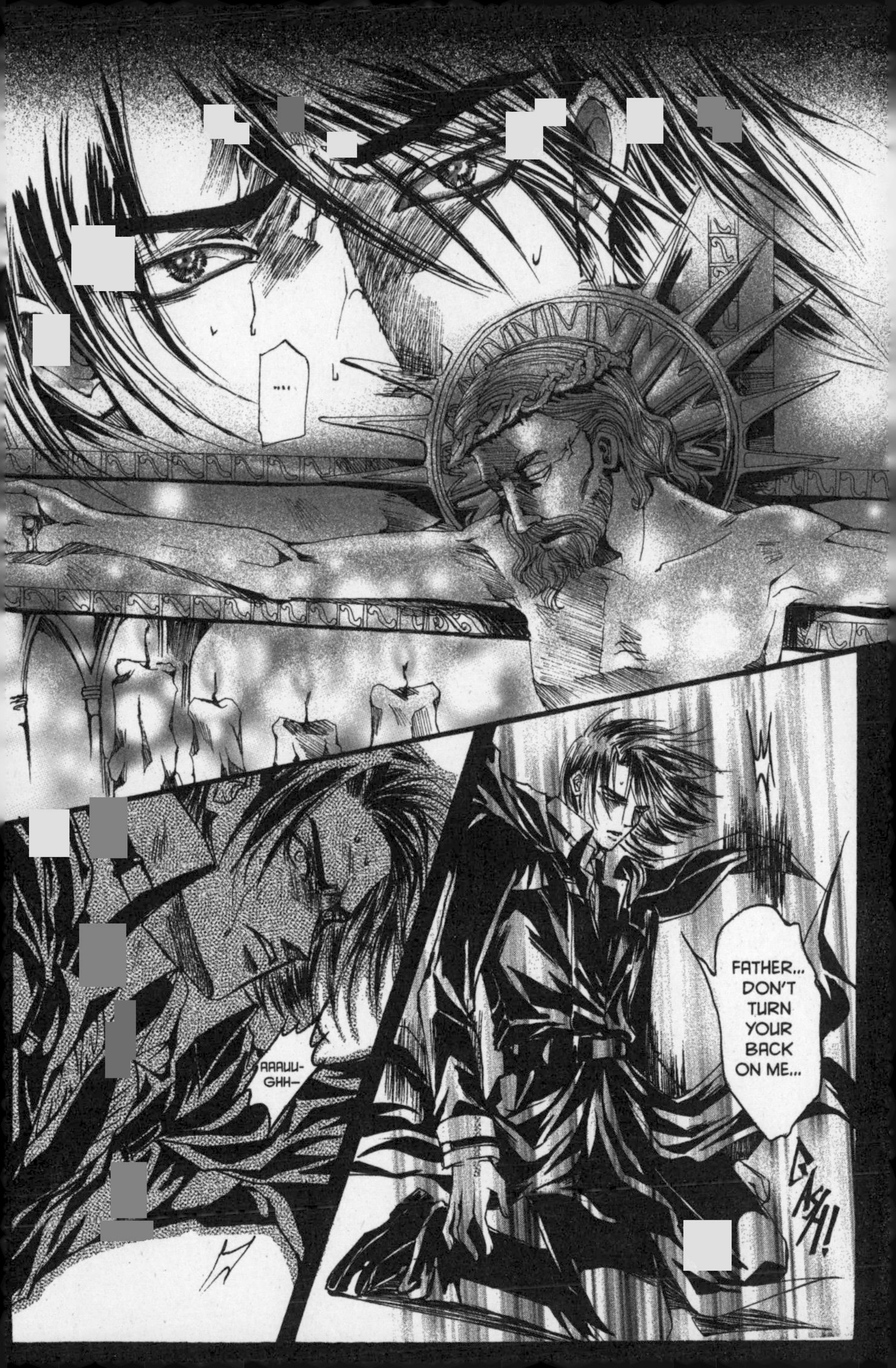
...
AAAUU-GHH-
FATHER... DON'T TURN YOUR BACK ON ME...
GASH!

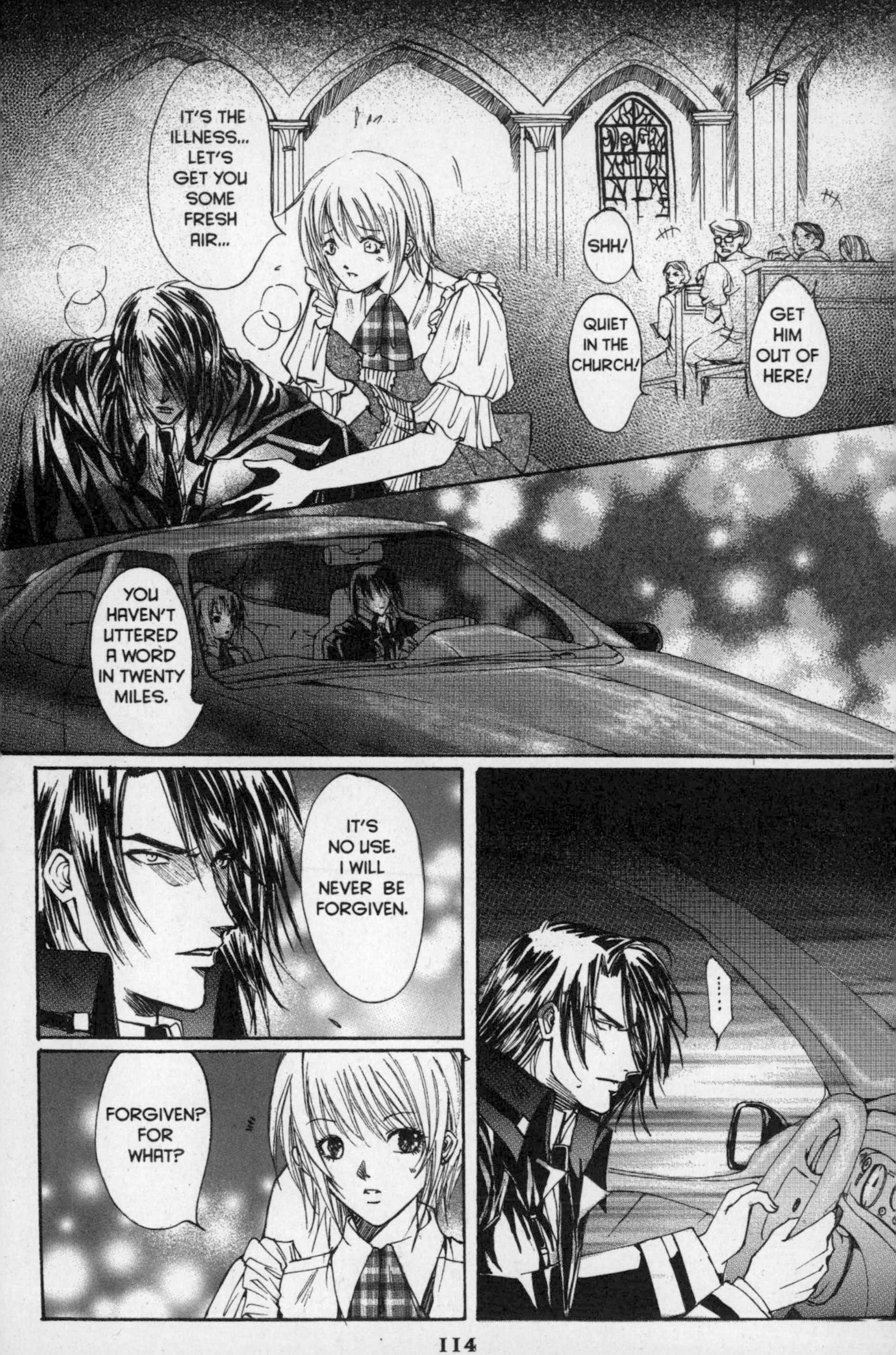
IT'S THE ILLNESS... LET'S GET YOU SOME FRESH AIR...
SHH!
QUIET IN THE CHURCH!
GET HIM OUT OF HERE!
YOU HAVEN'T UTTERED A WORD IN TWENTY MILES.
IT'S NO USE. I WILL NEVER BE FORGIVEN.
FORGIVEN? FOR WHAT?
......

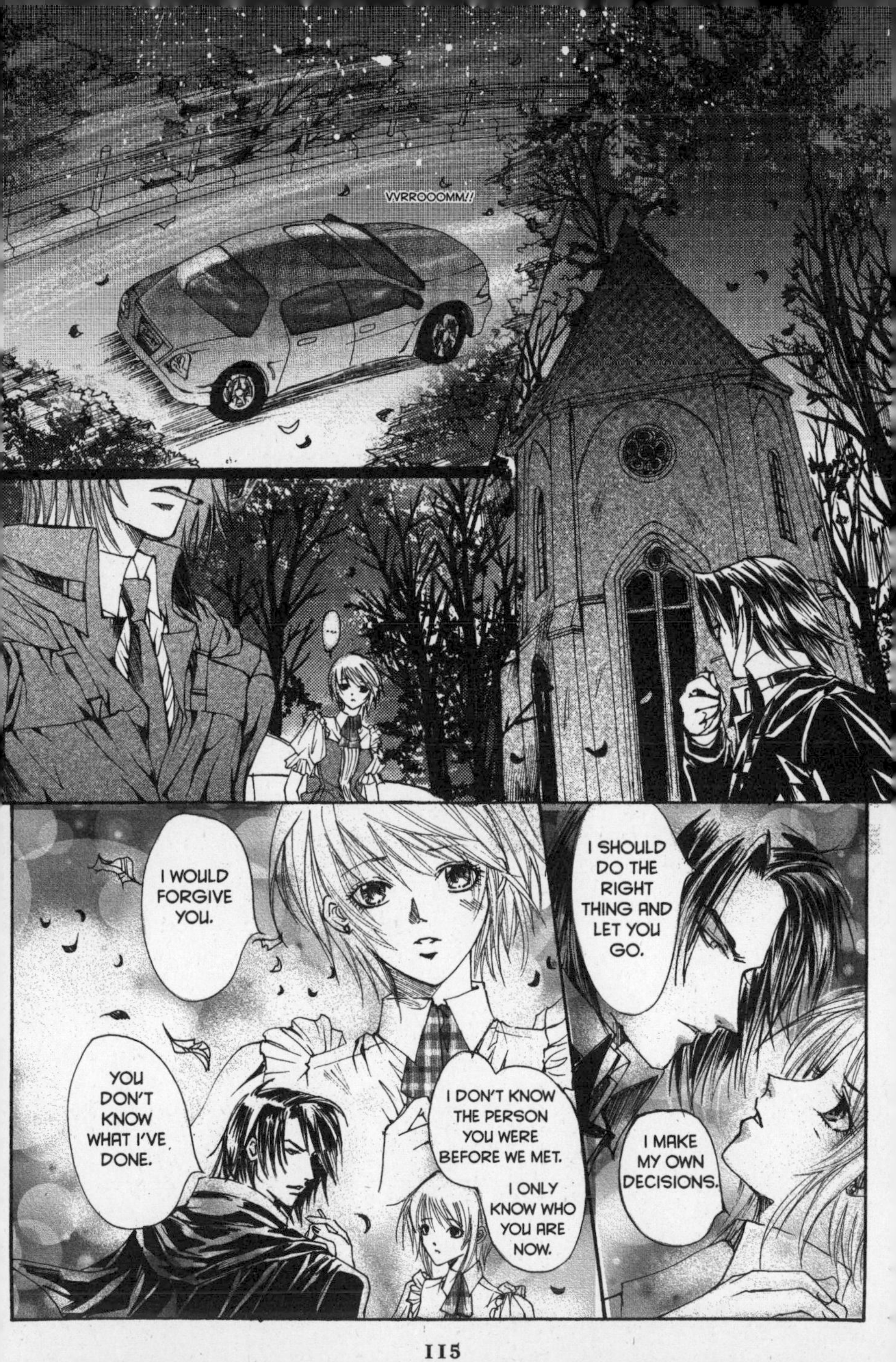
VVRROOOMM!!
I WOULD FORGIVE YOU.
YOU DON'T KNOW WHAT I'VE DONE.
I DON'T KNOW THE PERSON YOU WERE BEFORE WE MET.
I ONLY KNOW WHO YOU ARE NOW.
I SHOULD DO THE RIGHT THING AND LET YOU GO.
I MAKE MY OWN DECISIONS.

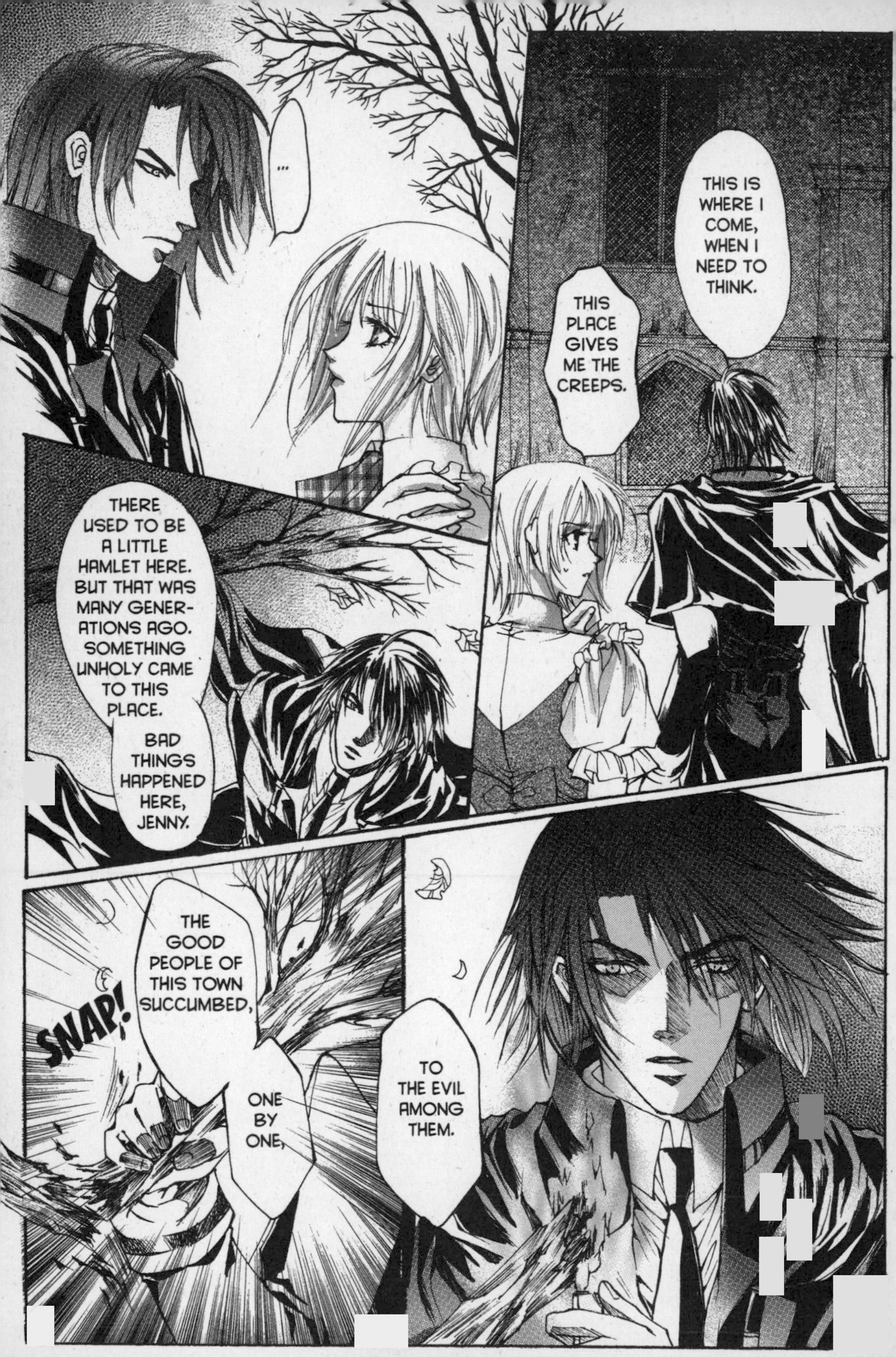
...
THERE USED TO BE A LITTLE HAMLET HERE. BUT THAT WAS MANY GENERATIONS AGO. SOMETHING UNHOLY CAME TO THIS PLACE.
BAD THINGS HAPPENED HERE, JENNY.
THIS IS WHERE I COME, WHEN I NEED TO THINK.
THIS PLACE GIVES ME THE CREEPS.
THE GOOD PEOPLE OF THIS TOWN SUCCUMBED,
SNAP!
ONE BY ONE,
TO THE EVIL AMONG THEM.

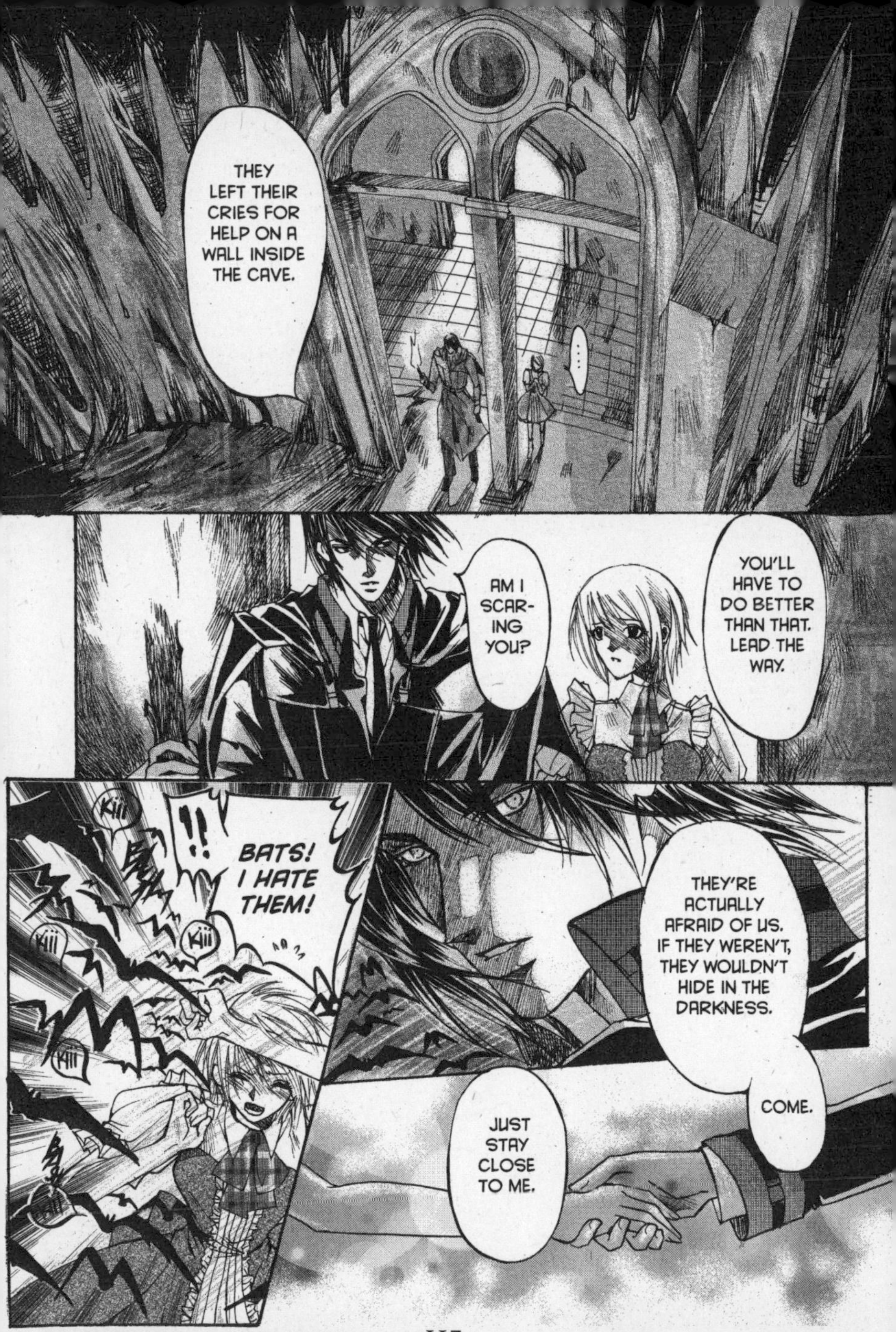
THEY LEFT THEIR CRIES FOR HELP ON A WALL INSIDE THE CAVE.
....
AM I SCAR-ING YOU?
YOU'LL HAVE TO DO BETTER THAN THAT. LEAD THE WAY.
Kiii
!!
BATS! I HATE THEM!
Kiii
Kiii
Kiii
THEY'RE ACTUALLY AFRAID OF US. IF THEY WEREN'T, THEY WOULDN'T HIDE IN THE DARKNESS.
COME.
JUST STAY CLOSE TO ME.

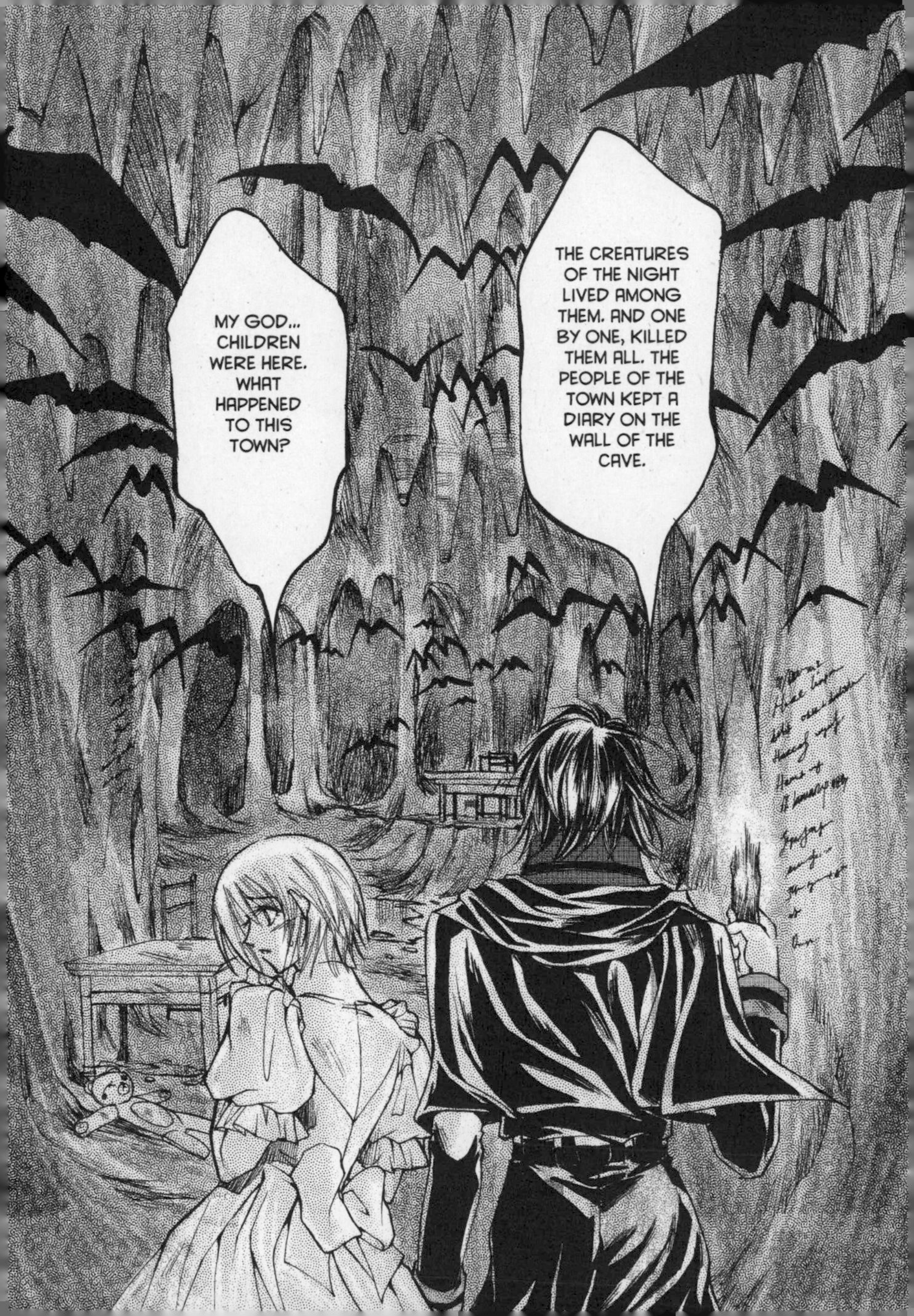
MY GOD... CHILDREN WERE HERE. WHAT HAPPENED TO THIS TOWN?
THE CREATURES OF THE NIGHT LIVED AMONG THEM. AND ONE BY ONE, KILLED THEM ALL. THE PEOPLE OF THE TOWN KEPT A DIARY ON THE WALL OF THE CAVE.

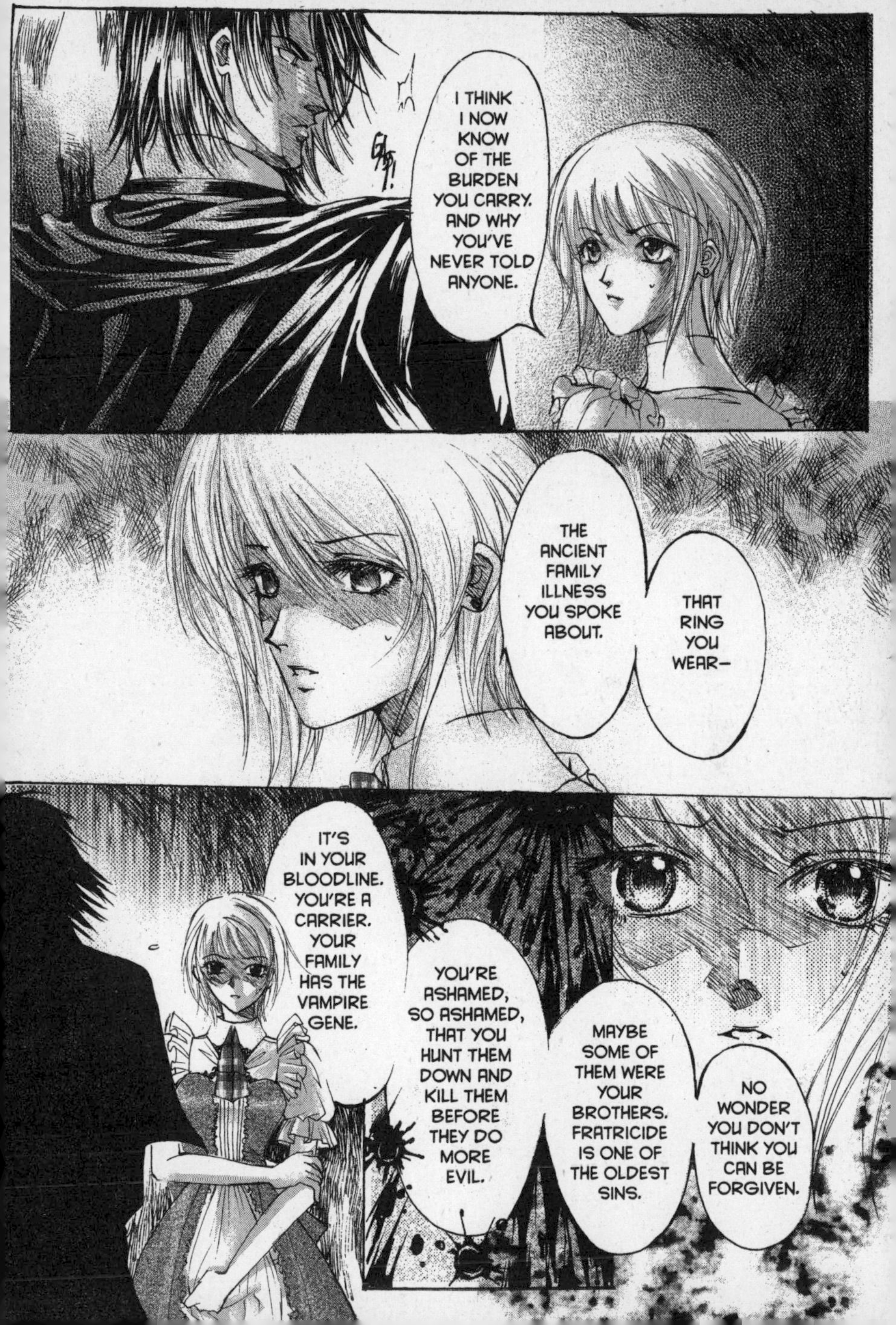
I THINK I NOW KNOW OF THE BURDEN YOU CARRY. AND WHY YOU'VE NEVER TOLD ANYONE.
THE ANCIENT FAMILY ILLNESS YOU SPOKE ABOUT.
THAT RING YOU WEAR–
IT'S IN YOUR BLOODLINE. YOU'RE A CARRIER. YOUR FAMILY HAS THE VAMPIRE GENE.
YOU'RE ASHAMED, SO ASHAMED, THAT YOU HUNT THEM DOWN AND KILL THEM BEFORE THEY DO MORE EVIL.
MAYBE SOME OF THEM WERE YOUR BROTHERS. FRATRICIDE IS ONE OF THE OLDEST SINS.
NO WONDER YOU DON'T THINK YOU CAN BE FORGIVEN.

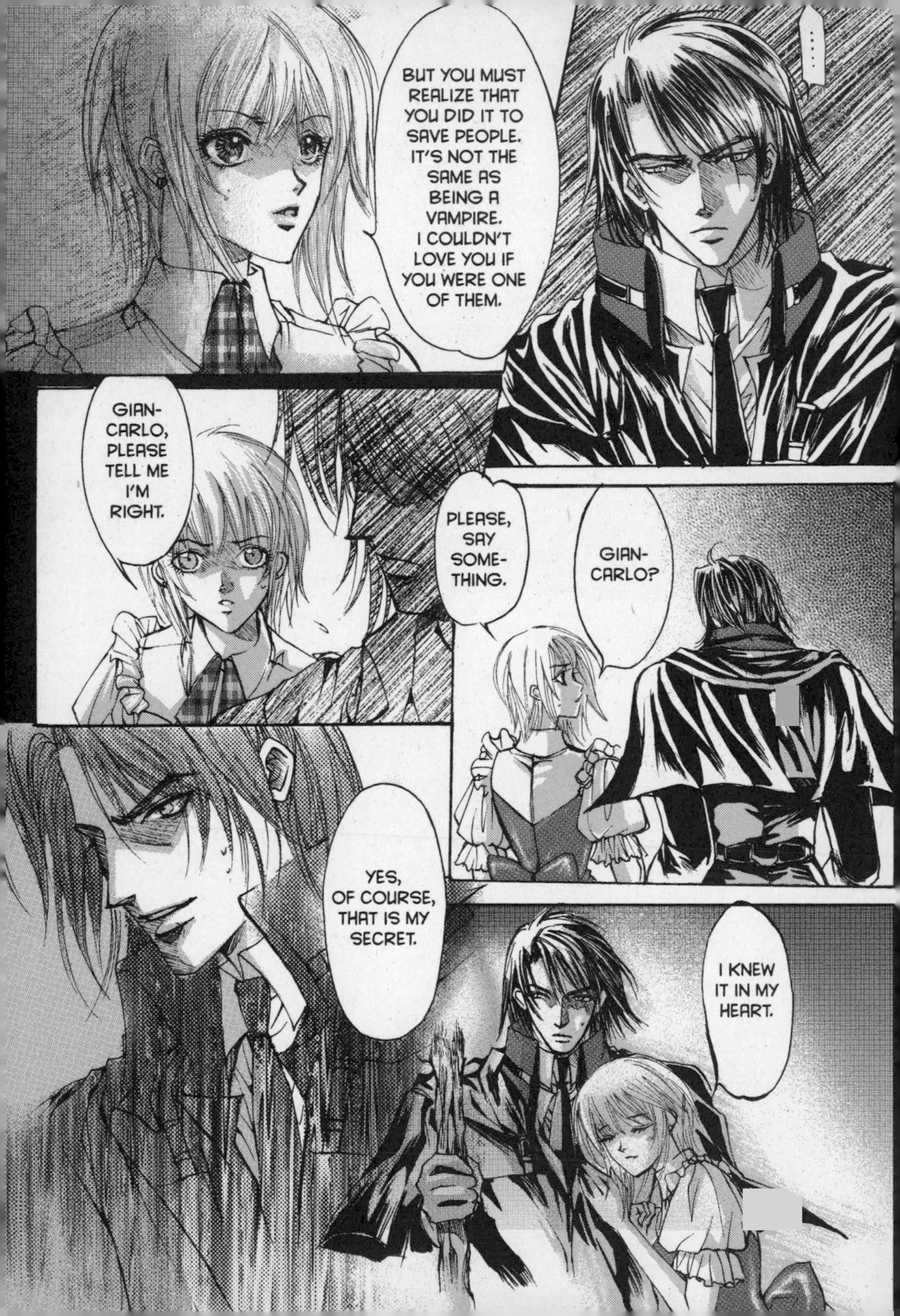
BUT YOU MUST REALIZE THAT YOU DID IT TO SAVE PEOPLE. IT'S NOT THE SAME AS BEING A VAMPIRE. I COULDN'T LOVE YOU IF YOU WERE ONE OF THEM.
......
GIAN-CARLO, PLEASE TELL ME I'M RIGHT.
PLEASE, SAY SOME-THING.
GIAN-CARLO?
YES, OF COURSE, THAT IS MY SECRET.
I KNEW IT IN MY HEART.

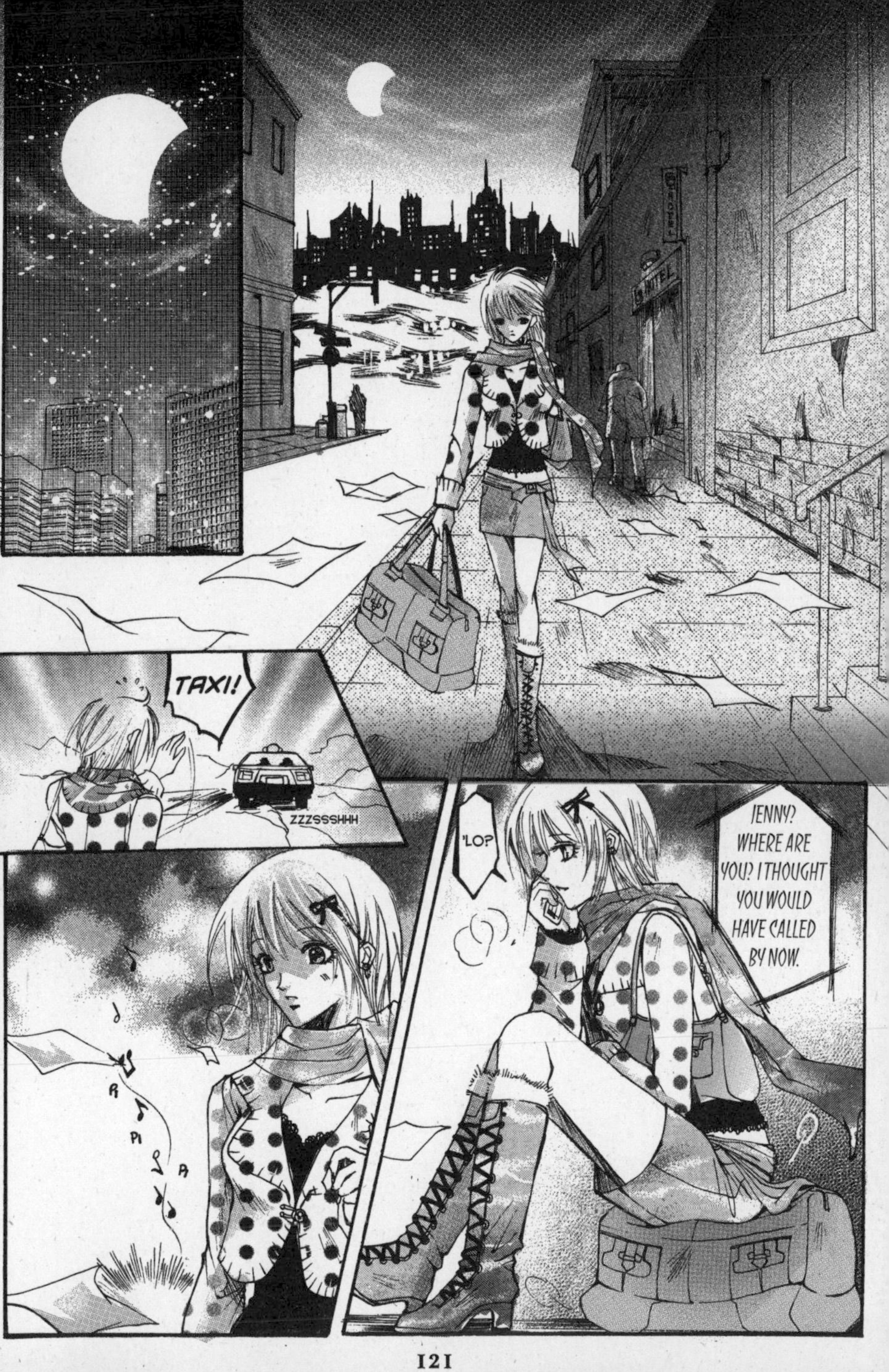
TAXI!
ZZZSSSHHH
Pi
Pi
Pi
'LO?
JENNY? WHERE ARE YOU? I THOUGHT YOU WOULD HAVE CALLED BY NOW.

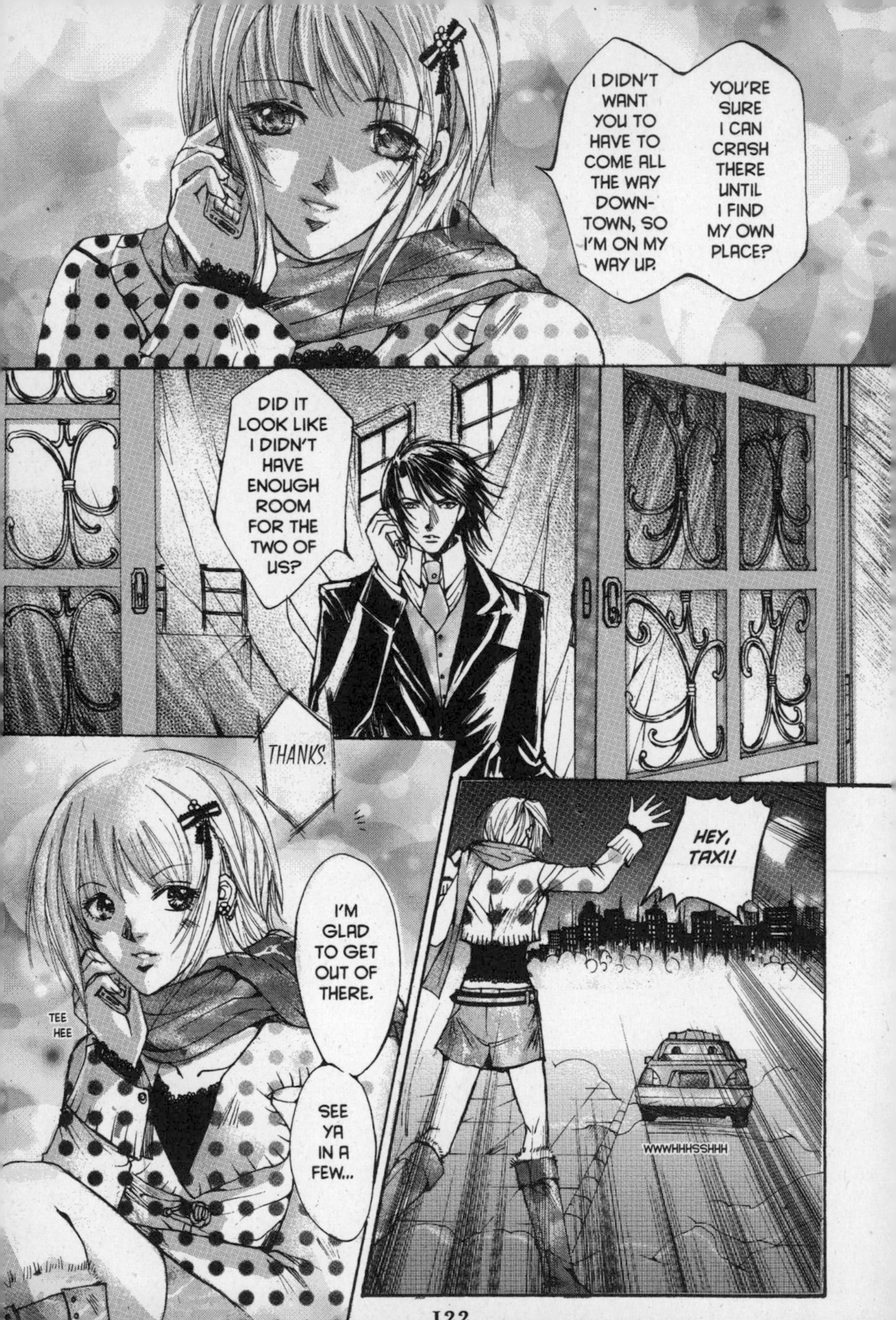
I DIDN'T WANT YOU TO HAVE TO COME ALL THE WAY DOWN-TOWN, SO I'M ON MY WAY UP.
YOU'RE SURE I CAN CRASH THERE UNTIL I FIND MY OWN PLACE?
DID IT LOOK LIKE I DIDN'T HAVE ENOUGH ROOM FOR THE TWO OF US?
THANKS.
TEE HEE
I'M GLAD TO GET OUT OF THERE.
SEE YA IN A FEW...
HEY, TAXI!
WWWHHHSSHHH

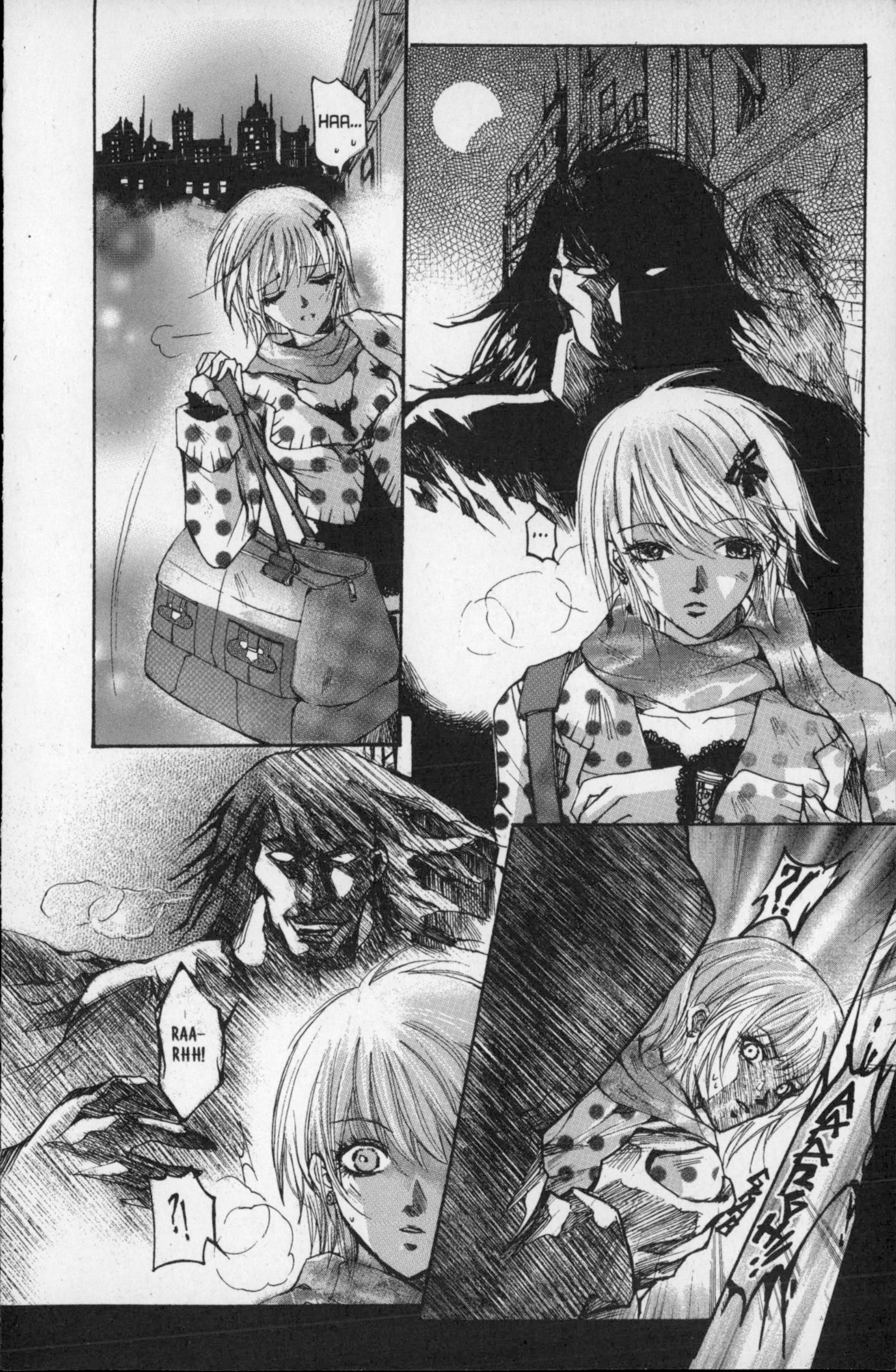
HAA...
...
RAA-RHH!
?!
?!
AAAAAH!!
GRAB

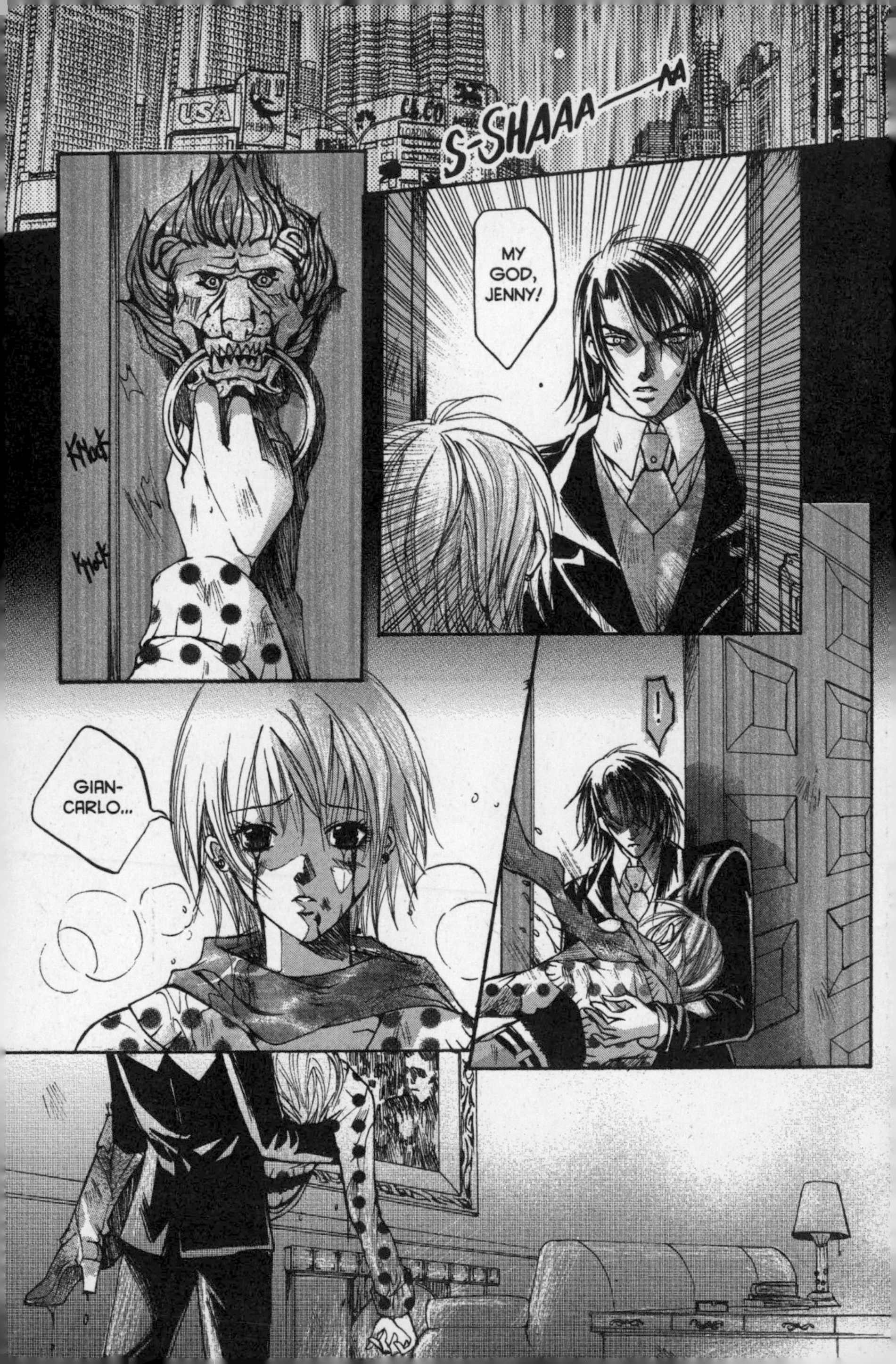
S-SHAAA——AA
KNOCK
KNOCK
MY GOD, JENNY!
GIAN-CARLO...
!

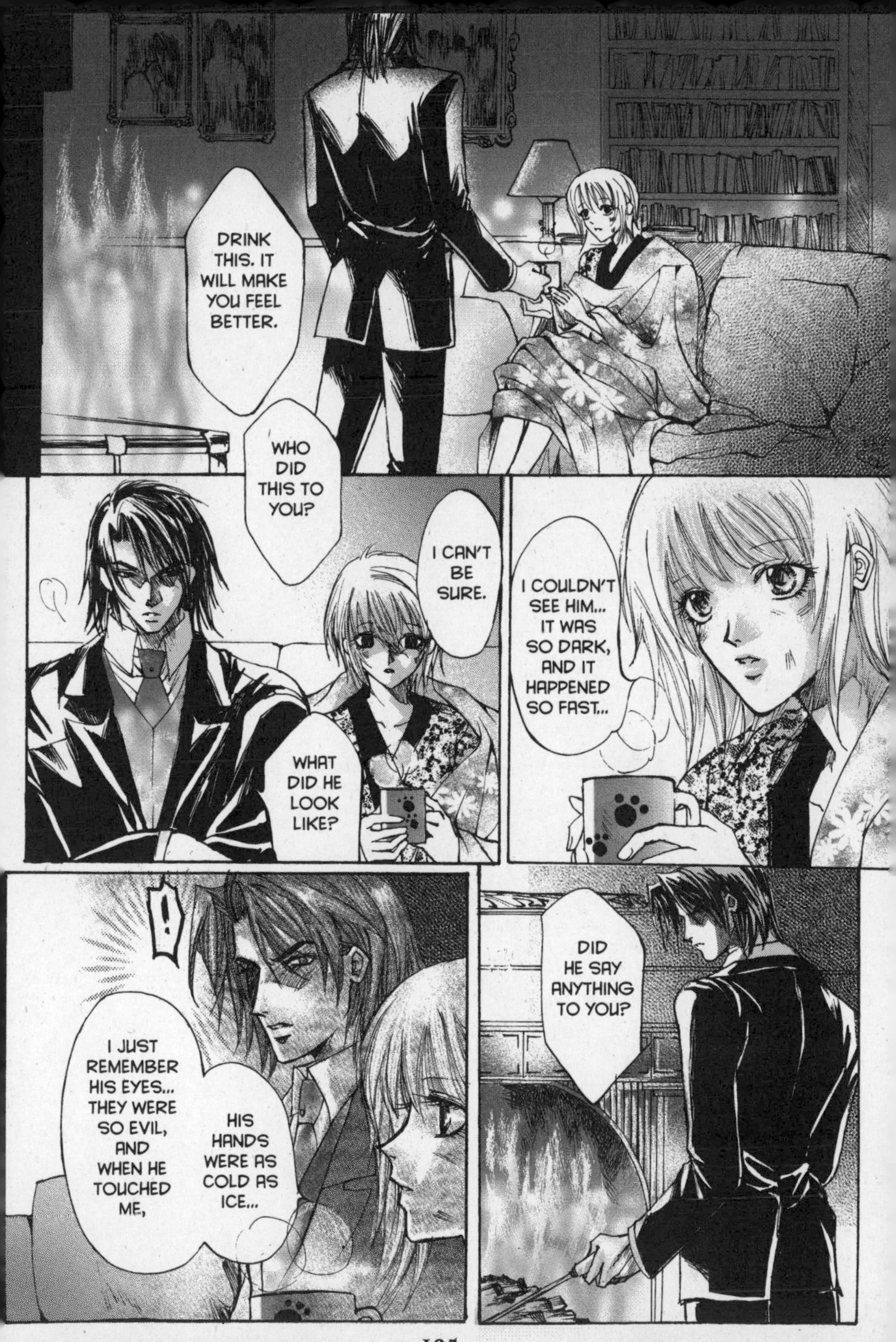
DRINK THIS. IT WILL MAKE YOU FEEL BETTER.
WHO DID THIS TO YOU?
I CAN'T BE SURE.
WHAT DID HE LOOK LIKE?
I COULDN'T SEE HIM... IT WAS SO DARK, AND IT HAPPENED SO FAST...
!
I JUST REMEMBER HIS EYES... THEY WERE SO EVIL, AND WHEN HE TOUCHED ME,
HIS HANDS WERE AS COLD AS ICE...
DID HE SAY ANYTHING TO YOU?

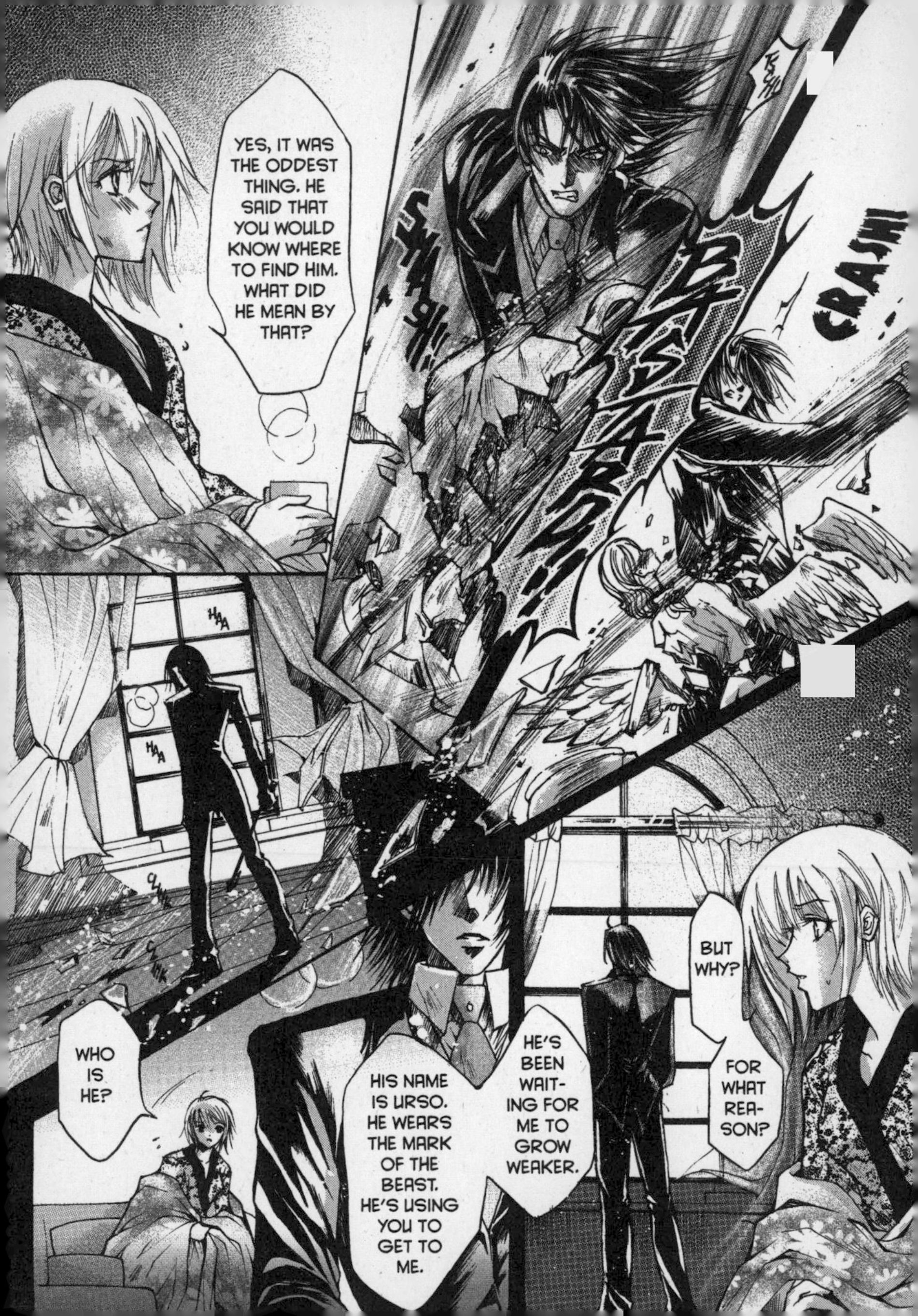

YES, IT WAS THE ODDEST THING. HE SAID THAT YOU WOULD KNOW WHERE TO FIND HIM. WHAT DID HE MEAN BY THAT?
CRASH!
HAA
HAA
CLANK
CLANK
WHO IS HE?
HIS NAME IS URSO. HE WEARS THE MARK OF THE BEAST. HE'S USING YOU TO GET TO ME.
HE'S BEEN WAIT-ING FOR ME TO GROW WEAKER.
BUT WHY?
FOR WHAT REA-SON?

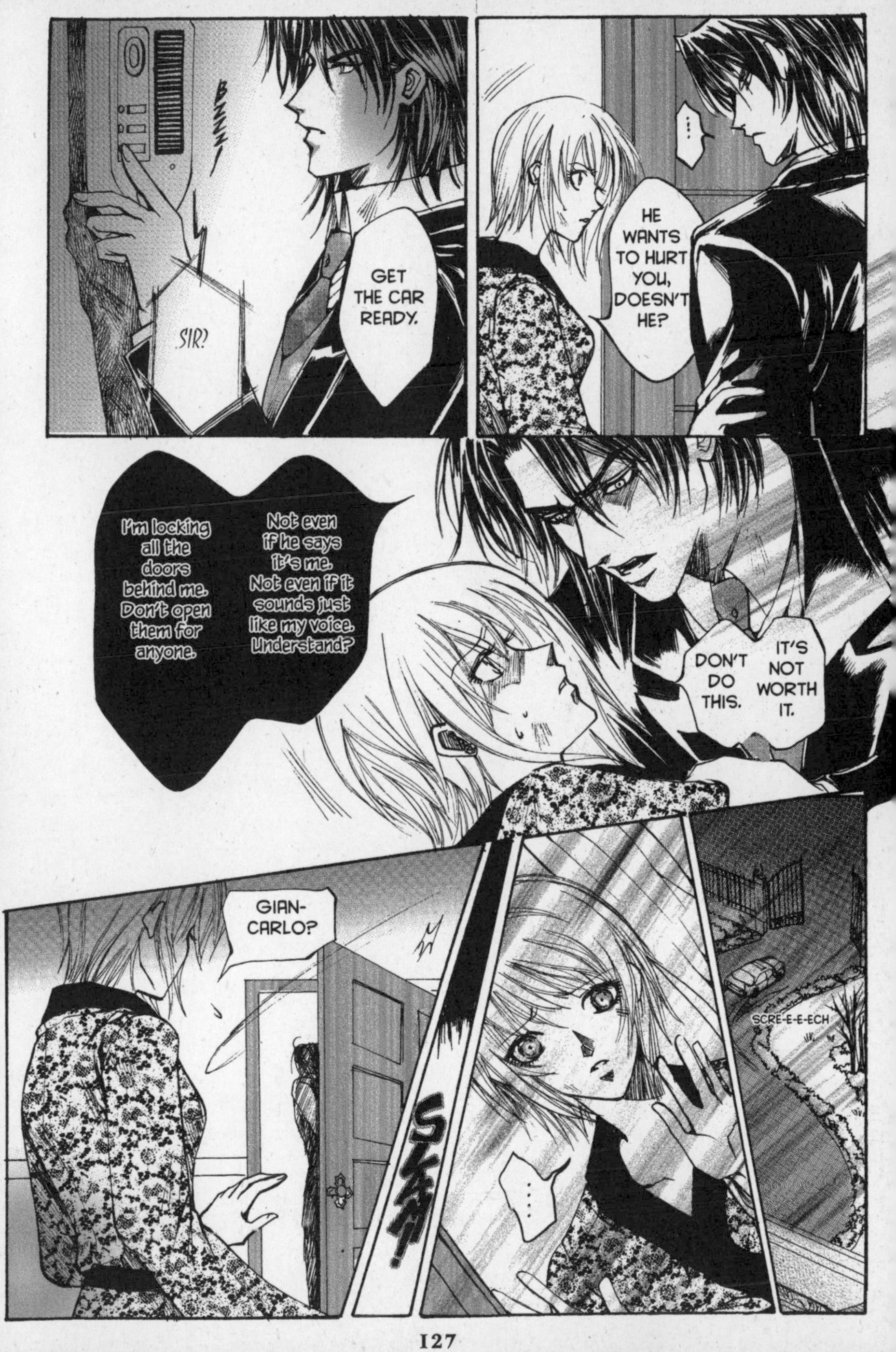
BZZZ!
SIR?
GET THE CAR READY.
...
HE WANTS TO HURT YOU, DOESN'T HE?
I'm locking all the doors behind me. Don't open them for anyone.
Not even if he says it's me. Not even if it sounds just like my voice. Understand?
DON'T DO THIS.
IT'S NOT WORTH IT.
GIAN-CARLO?
SLAM!
....
SCRE-E-E-ECH

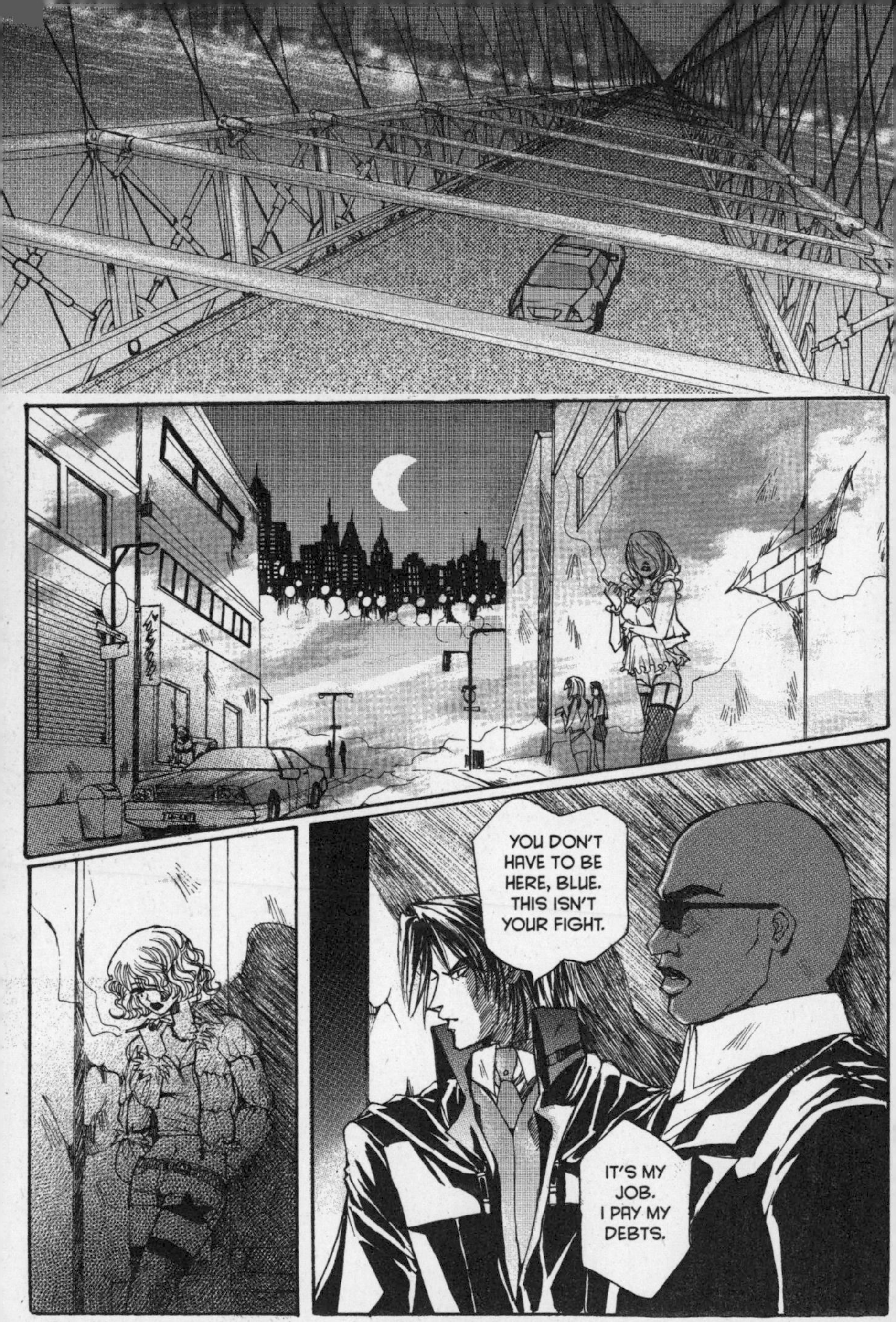
YOU DON'T HAVE TO BE HERE, BLUE. THIS ISN'T YOUR FIGHT.
IT'S MY JOB. I PAY MY DEBTS.

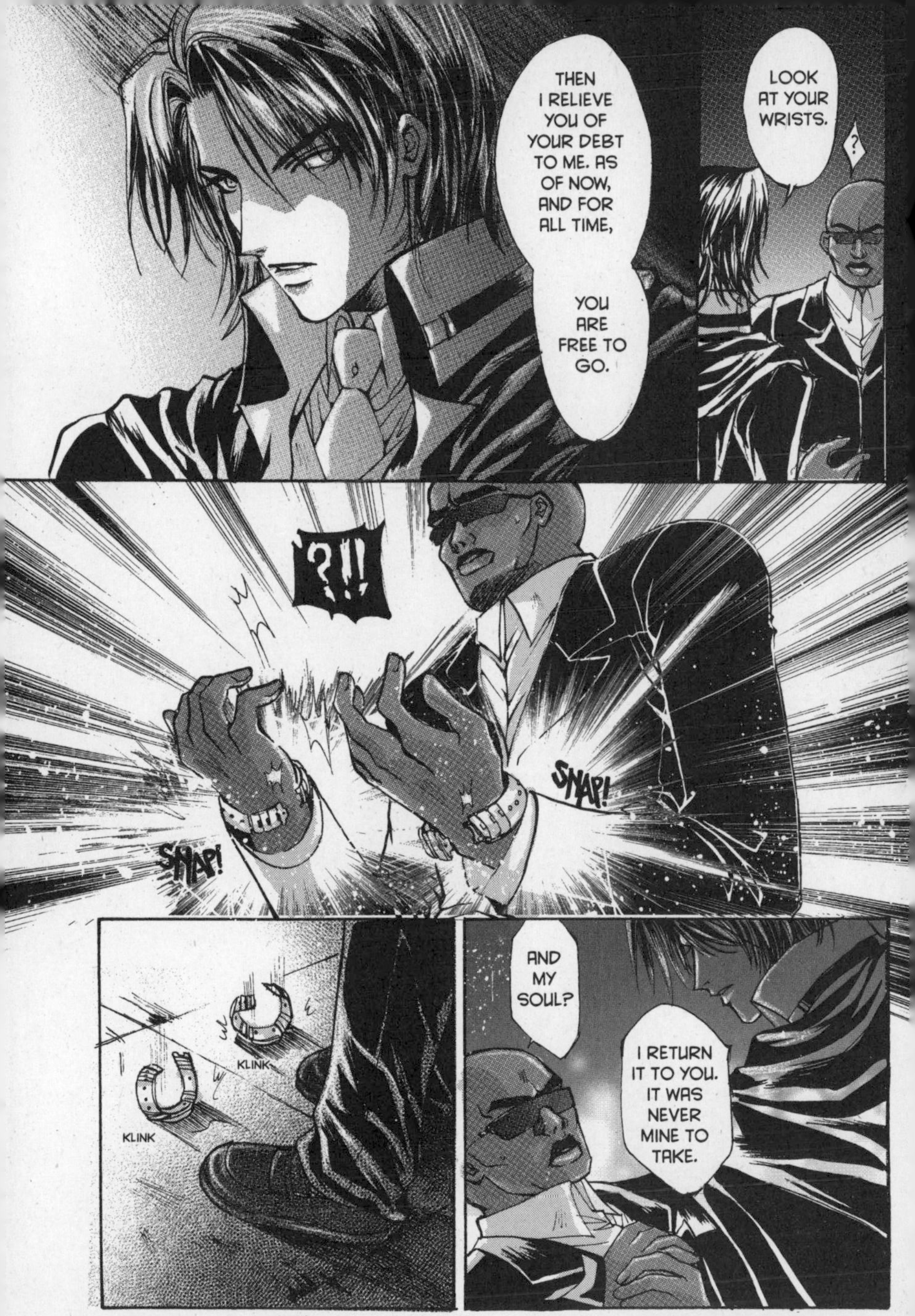
THEN I RELIEVE YOU OF YOUR DEBT TO ME. AS OF NOW, AND FOR ALL TIME,
YOU ARE FREE TO GO.
LOOK AT YOUR WRISTS.
?
?!!
SNAP!
SNAP!
KLINK
KLINK
AND MY SOUL?
I RETURN IT TO YOU. IT WAS NEVER MINE TO TAKE.

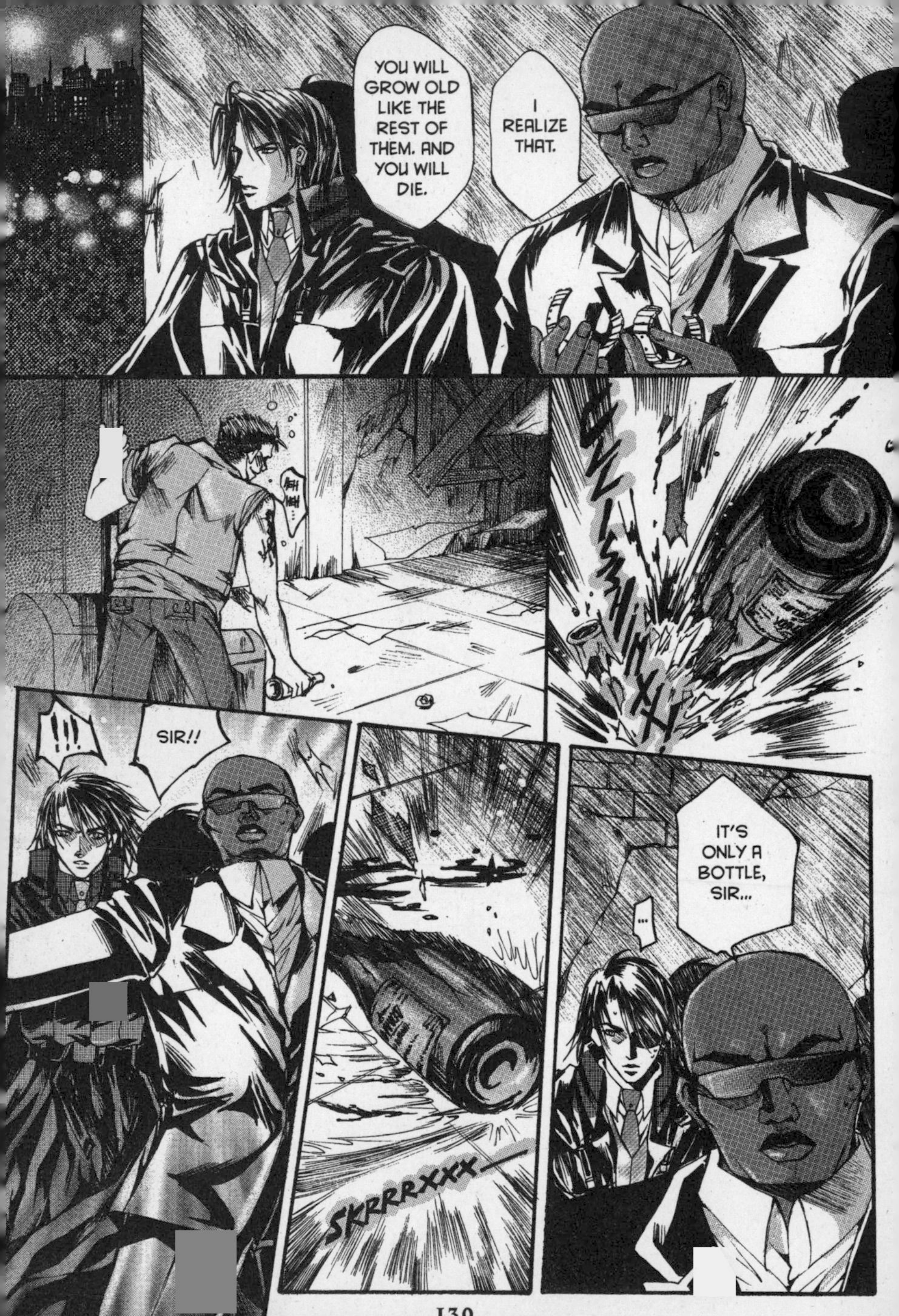

YOU WILL GROW OLD LIKE THE REST OF THEM. AND YOU WILL DIE.
I REALIZE THAT.
!!!
SIR!!
SKRRRXXX
...
IT'S ONLY A BOTTLE, SIR...

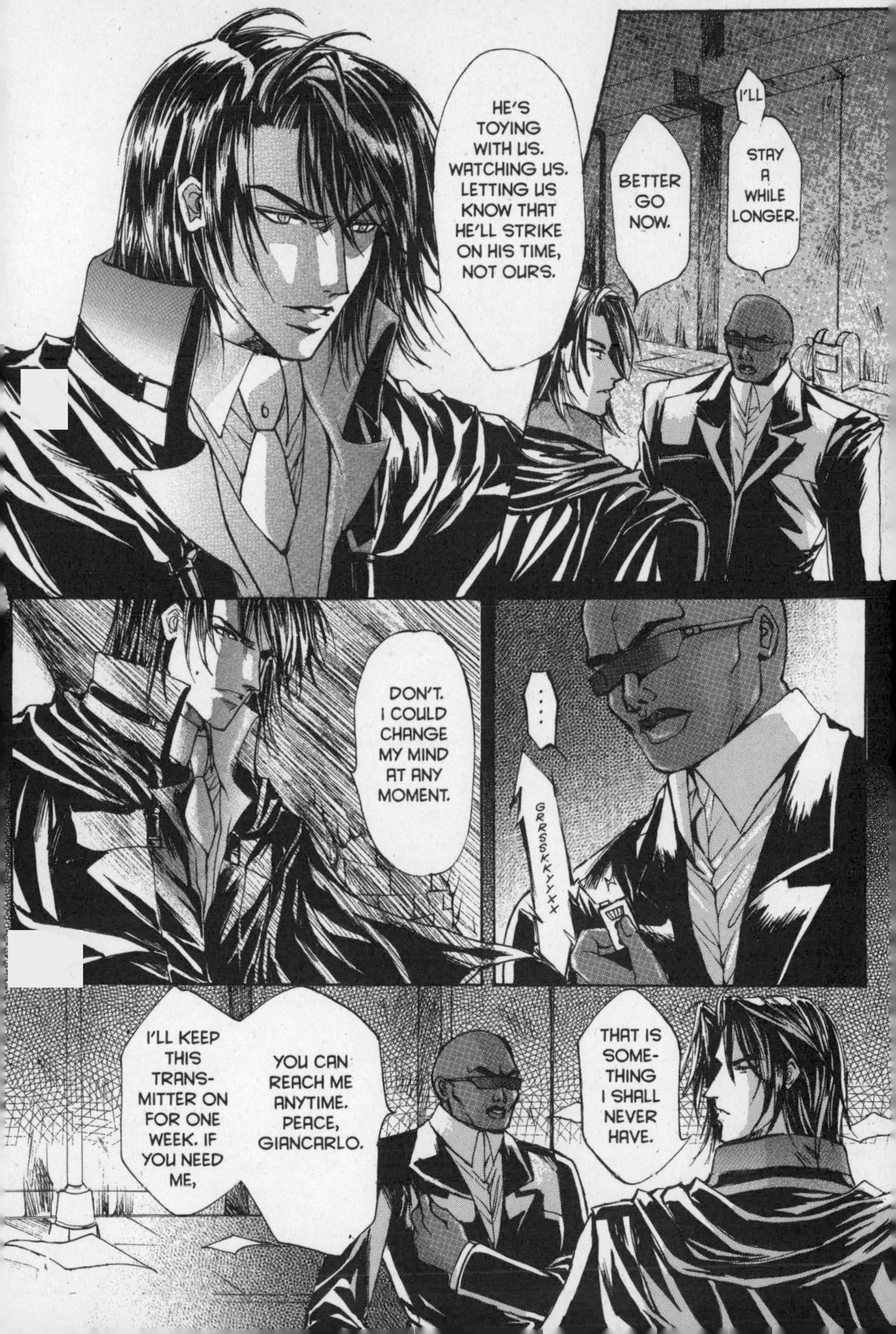
HE'S TOYING WITH US. WATCHING US. LETTING US KNOW THAT HE'LL STRIKE ON HIS TIME, NOT OURS.
BETTER GO NOW.
I'LL STAY A WHILE LONGER.
DON'T. I COULD CHANGE MY MIND AT ANY MOMENT.
....
GRRSSKKYYXX
I'LL KEEP THIS TRANS-MITTER ON FOR ONE WEEK. IF YOU NEED ME,
YOU CAN REACH ME ANYTIME. PEACE, GIANCARLO.
THAT IS SOME-THING I SHALL NEVER HAVE.

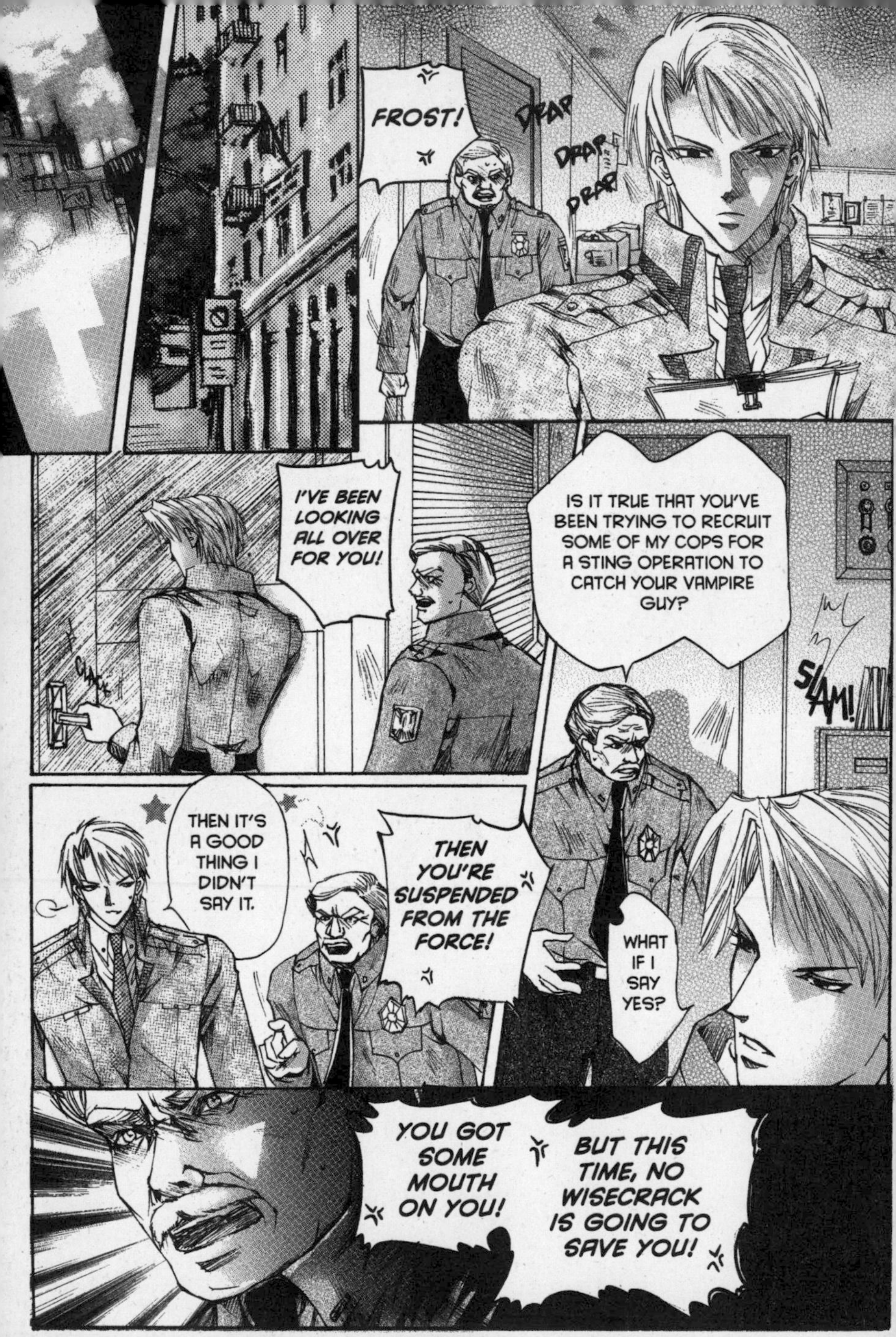

FROST!
DRAP
DRAP
DRAP
I'VE BEEN LOOKING ALL OVER FOR YOU!
CLACK
IS IT TRUE THAT YOU'VE BEEN TRYING TO RECRUIT SOME OF MY COPS FOR A STING OPERATION TO CATCH YOUR VAMPIRE GUY?
SLAM!
WHAT IF I SAY YES?
THEN IT'S A GOOD THING I DIDN'T SAY IT.
THEN YOU'RE SUSPENDED FROM THE FORCE!
YOU GOT SOME MOUTH ON YOU!
BUT THIS TIME, NO WISECRACK IS GOING TO SAVE YOU!

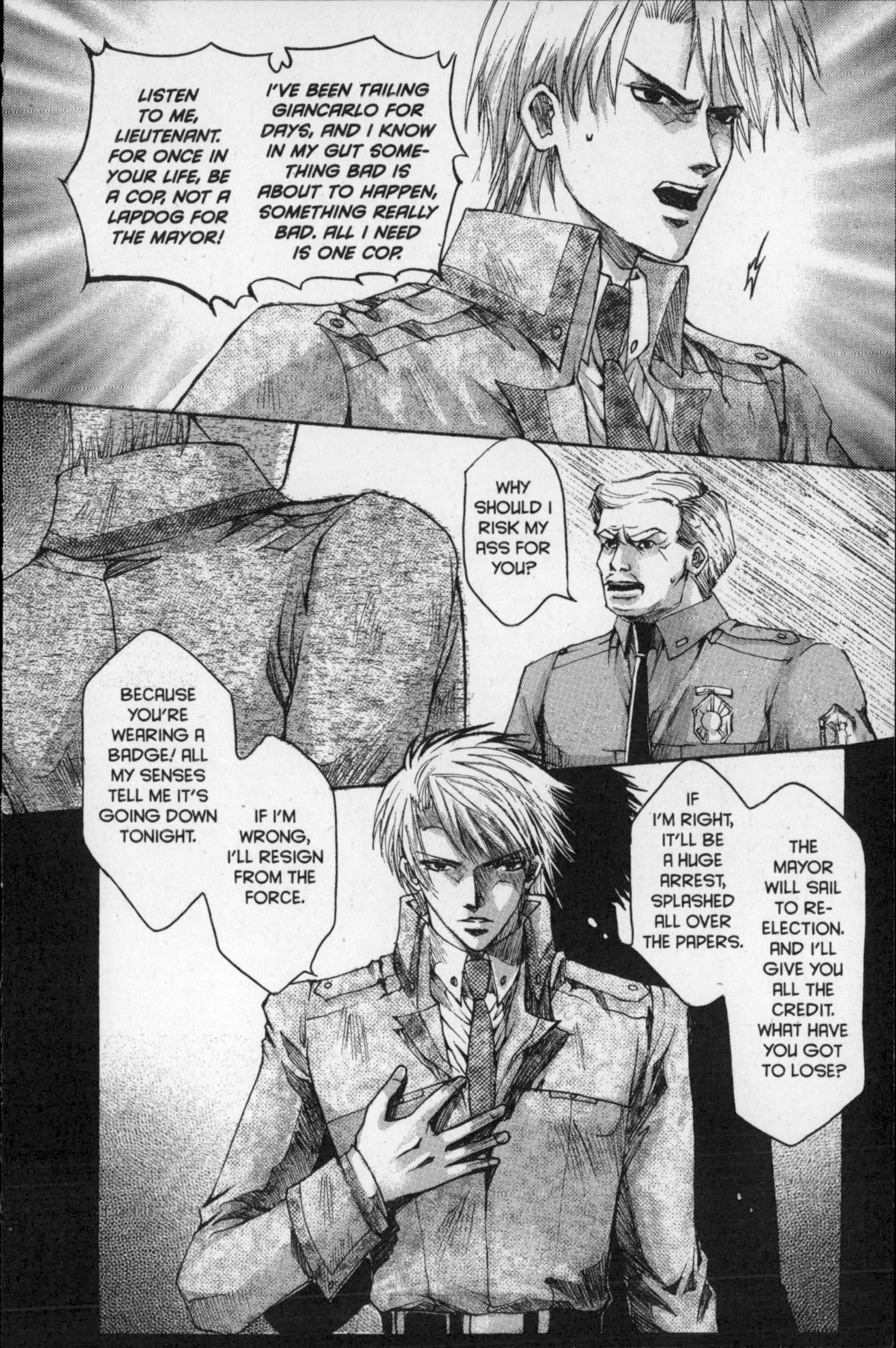
LISTEN TO ME, LIEUTENANT. FOR ONCE IN YOUR LIFE, BE A COP, NOT A LAPDOG FOR THE MAYOR!
I'VE BEEN TAILING GIANCARLO FOR DAYS, AND I KNOW IN MY GUT SOMETHING BAD IS ABOUT TO HAPPEN, SOMETHING REALLY BAD. ALL I NEED IS ONE COP.
WHY SHOULD I RISK MY ASS FOR YOU?
BECAUSE YOU'RE WEARING A BADGE! ALL MY SENSES TELL ME IT'S GOING DOWN TONIGHT.
IF I'M WRONG, I'LL RESIGN FROM THE FORCE.
IF I'M RIGHT, IT'LL BE A HUGE ARREST, SPLASHED ALL OVER THE PAPERS.
THE MAYOR WILL SAIL TO RE-ELECTION. AND I'LL GIVE YOU ALL THE CREDIT. WHAT HAVE YOU GOT TO LOSE?

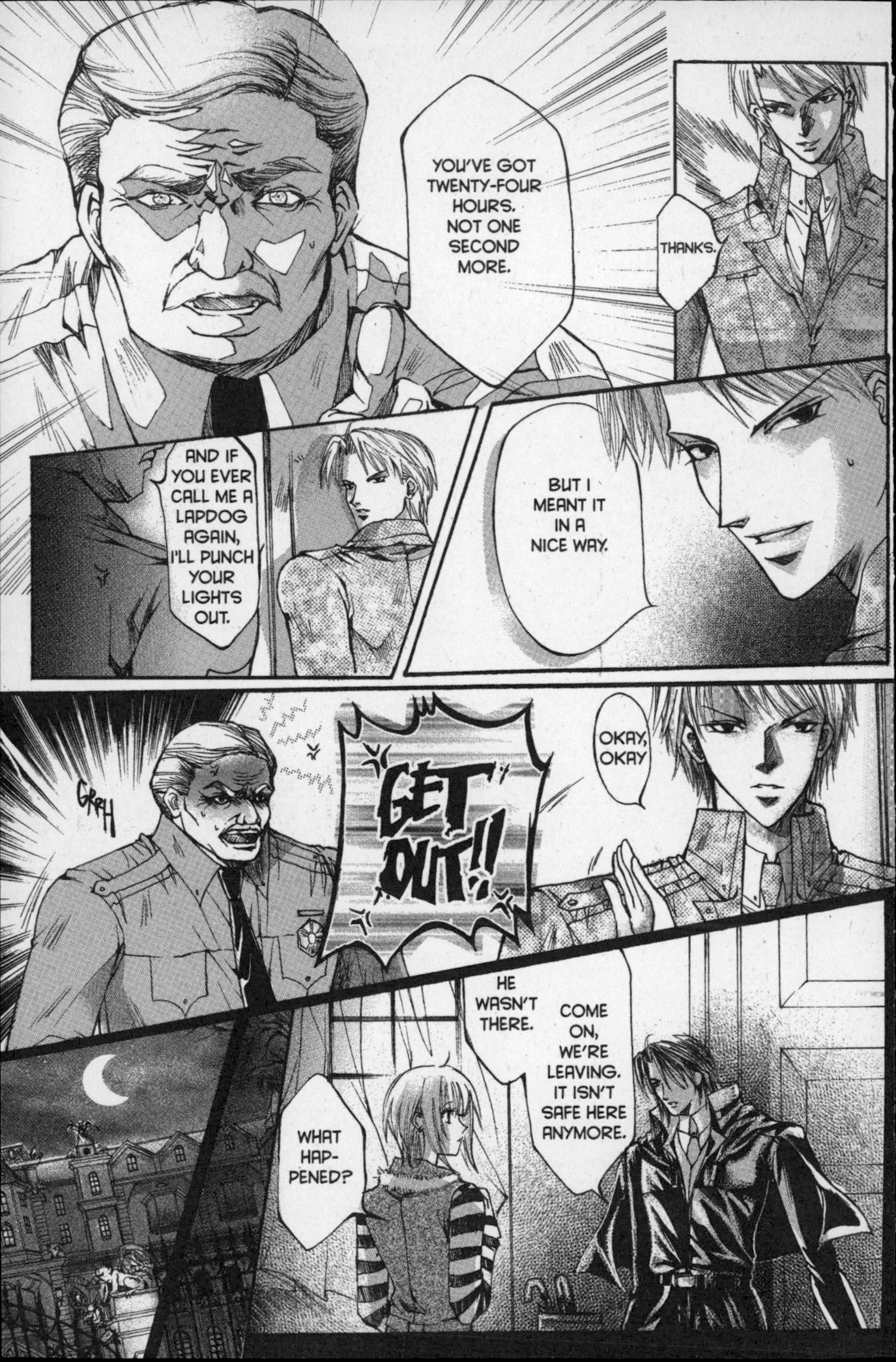
YOU'VE GOT TWENTY-FOUR HOURS. NOT ONE SECOND MORE.
THANKS.
AND IF YOU EVER CALL ME A LAPDOG AGAIN, I'LL PUNCH YOUR LIGHTS OUT.
BUT I MEANT IT IN A NICE WAY.
GRRH
GET OUT!!
OKAY, OKAY
WHAT HAP-PENED?
HE WASN'T THERE.
COME ON, WE'RE LEAVING. IT ISN'T SAFE HERE ANYMORE.

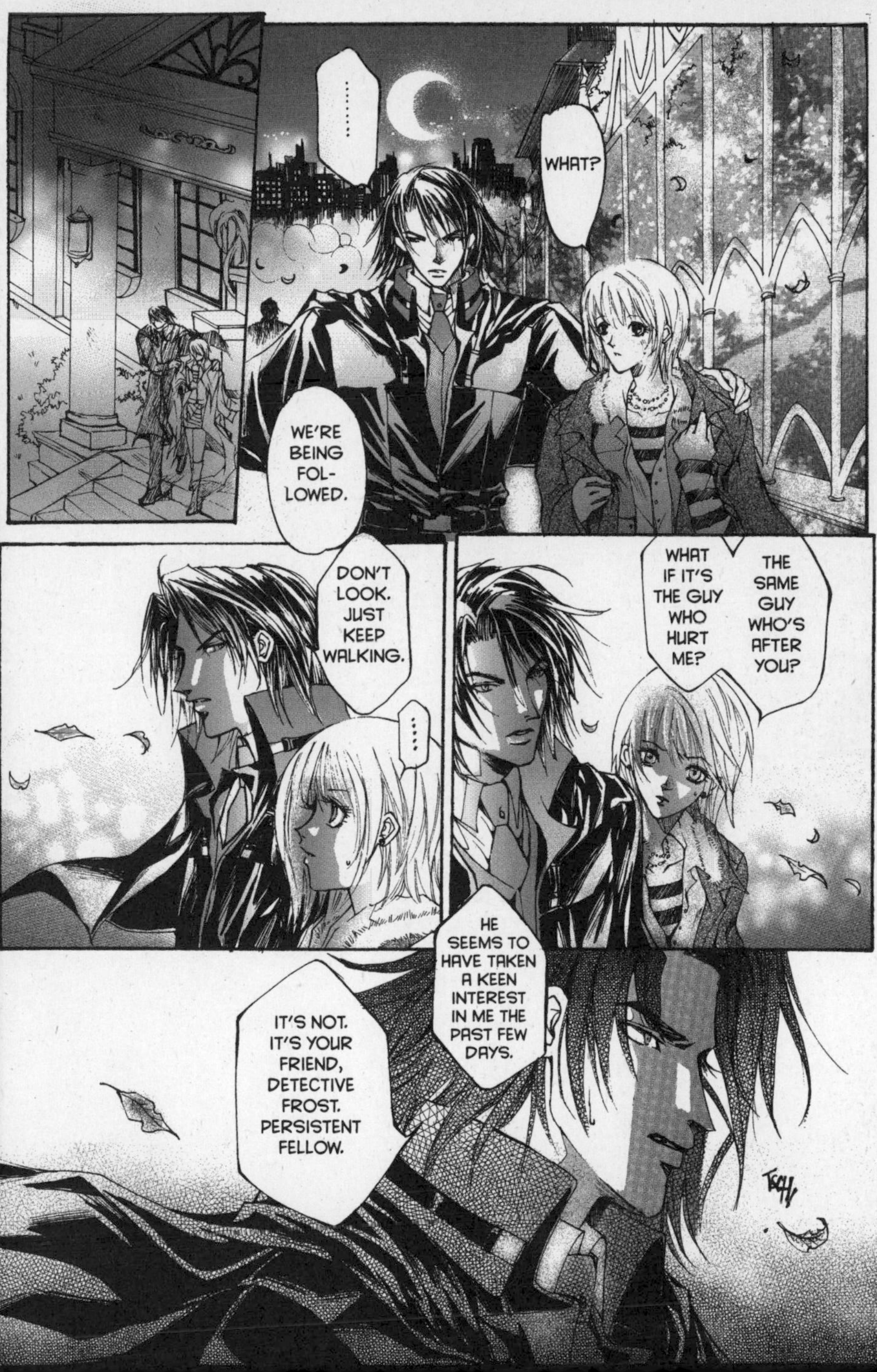
......
WHAT?
WE'RE BEING FOL-LOWED.
DON'T LOOK. JUST KEEP WALKING.
....
WHAT IF IT'S THE GUY WHO HURT ME?
THE SAME GUY WHO'S AFTER YOU?
IT'S NOT. IT'S YOUR FRIEND, DETECTIVE FROST. PERSISTENT FELLOW.
HE SEEMS TO HAVE TAKEN A KEEN INTEREST IN ME THE PAST FEW DAYS.

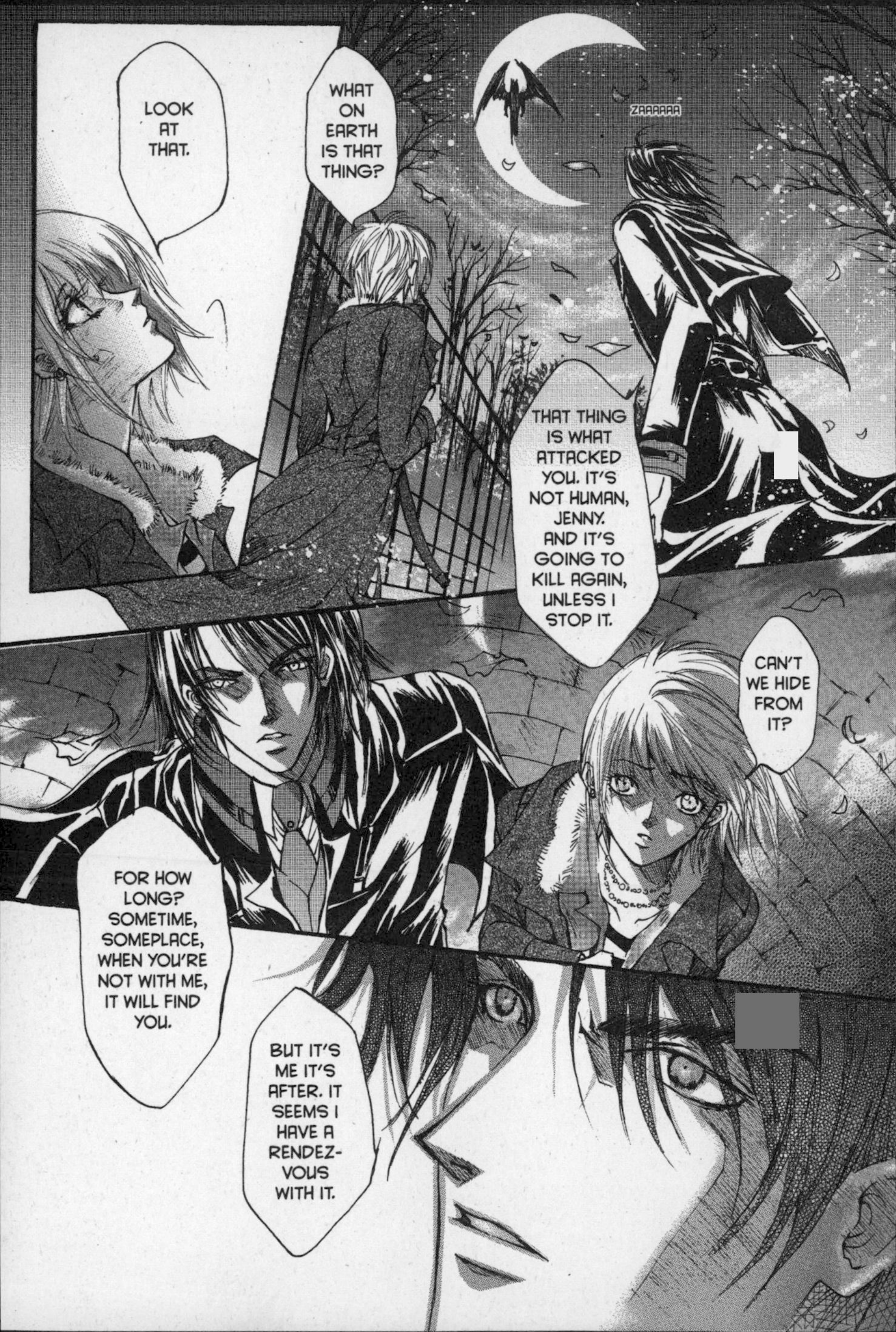
LOOK AT THAT.
WHAT ON EARTH IS THAT THING?
ZAAAAAA
THAT THING IS WHAT ATTACKED YOU. IT'S NOT HUMAN, JENNY. AND IT'S GOING TO KILL AGAIN, UNLESS I STOP IT.
CAN'T WE HIDE FROM IT?
FOR HOW LONG? SOMETIME, SOMEPLACE, WHEN YOU'RE NOT WITH ME, IT WILL FIND YOU.
BUT IT'S ME IT'S AFTER. IT SEEMS I HAVE A RENDEZ-VOUS WITH IT.

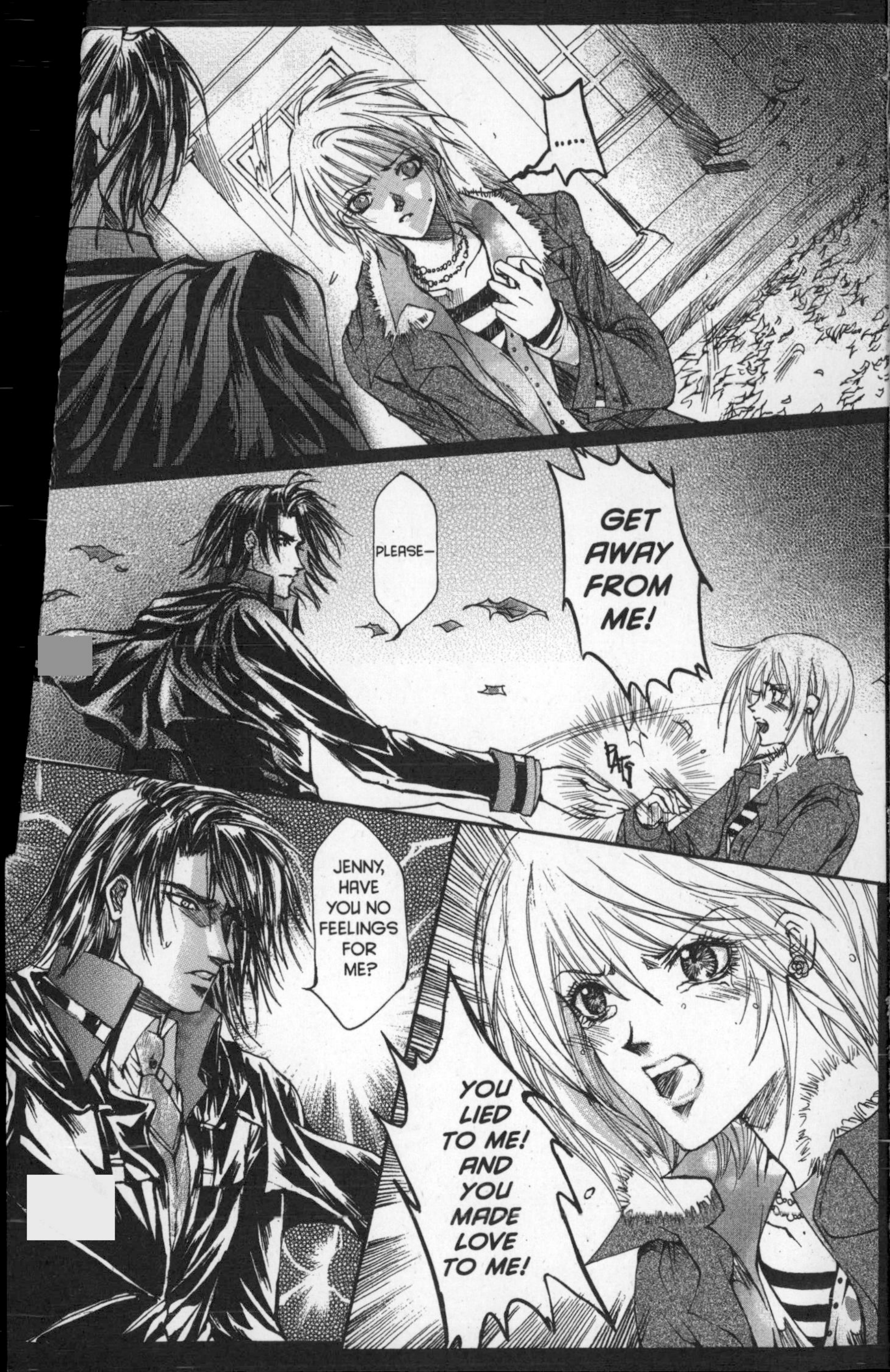
.....
PLEASE—
GET AWAY FROM ME!
JENNY, HAVE YOU NO FEELINGS FOR ME?
YOU LIED TO ME! AND YOU MADE LOVE TO ME!

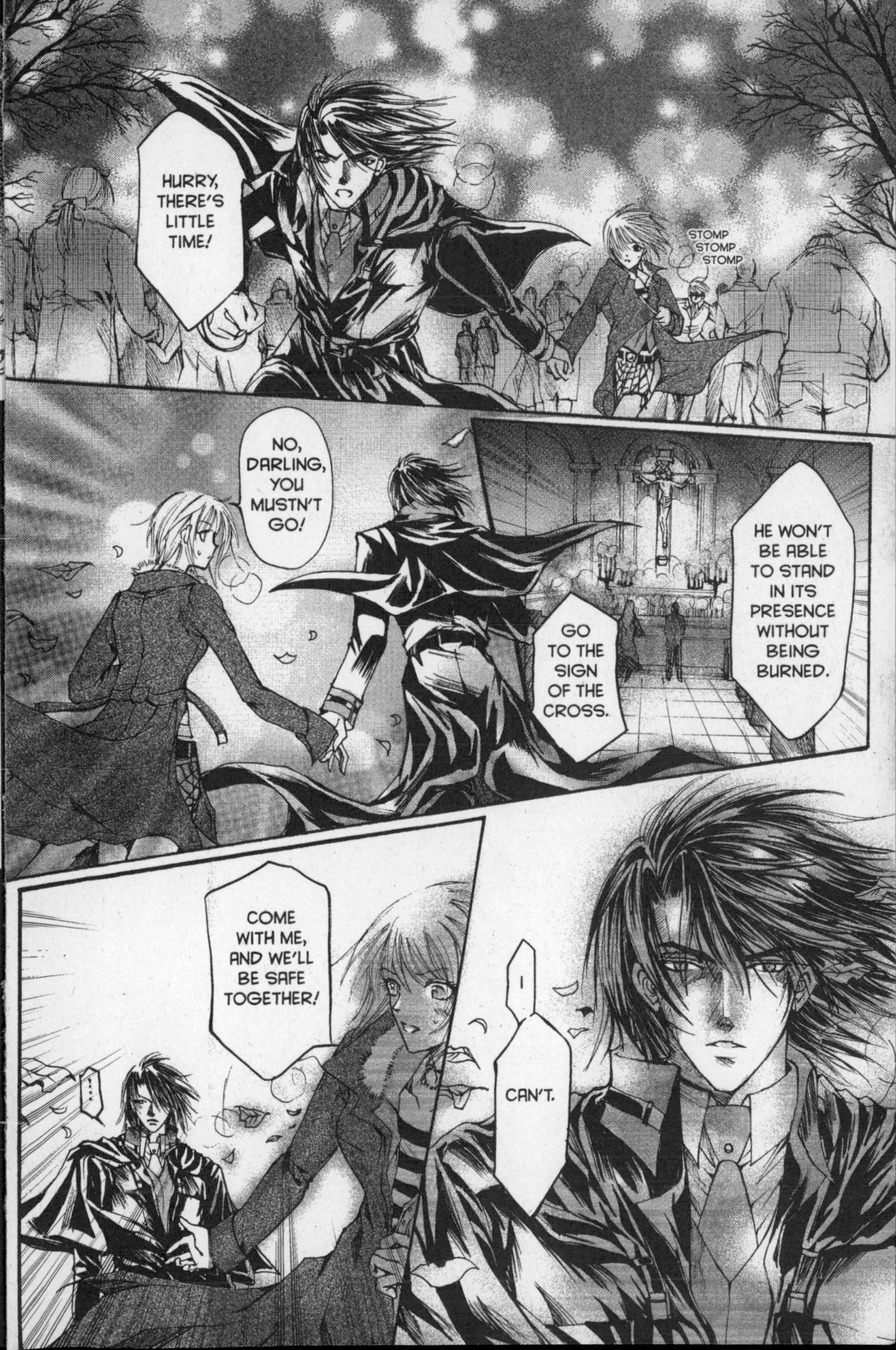
HURRY, THERE'S LITTLE TIME!
STOMP STOMP STOMP
NO, DARLING, YOU MUSTN'T GO!
GO TO THE SIGN OF THE CROSS.
HE WON'T BE ABLE TO STAND IN ITS PRESENCE WITHOUT BEING BURNED.
COME WITH ME, AND WE'LL BE SAFE TOGETHER!
...
I CAN'T.

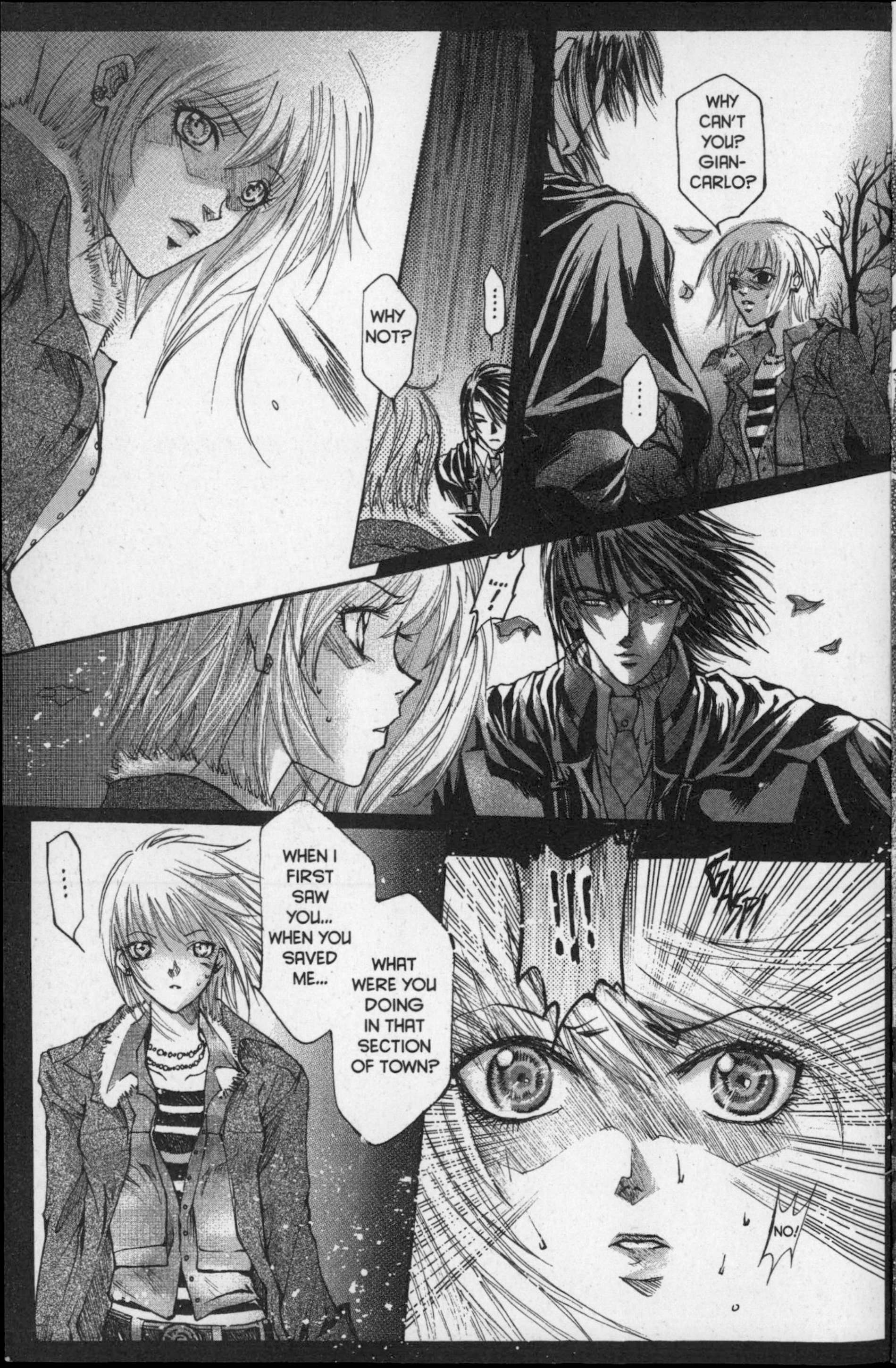
WHY NOT?
....
WHY CAN'T YOU? GIAN-CARLO?
....
....
WHEN I FIRST SAW YOU... WHEN YOU SAVED ME...
WHAT WERE YOU DOING IN THAT SECTION OF TOWN?
!!
GASP!
NO!
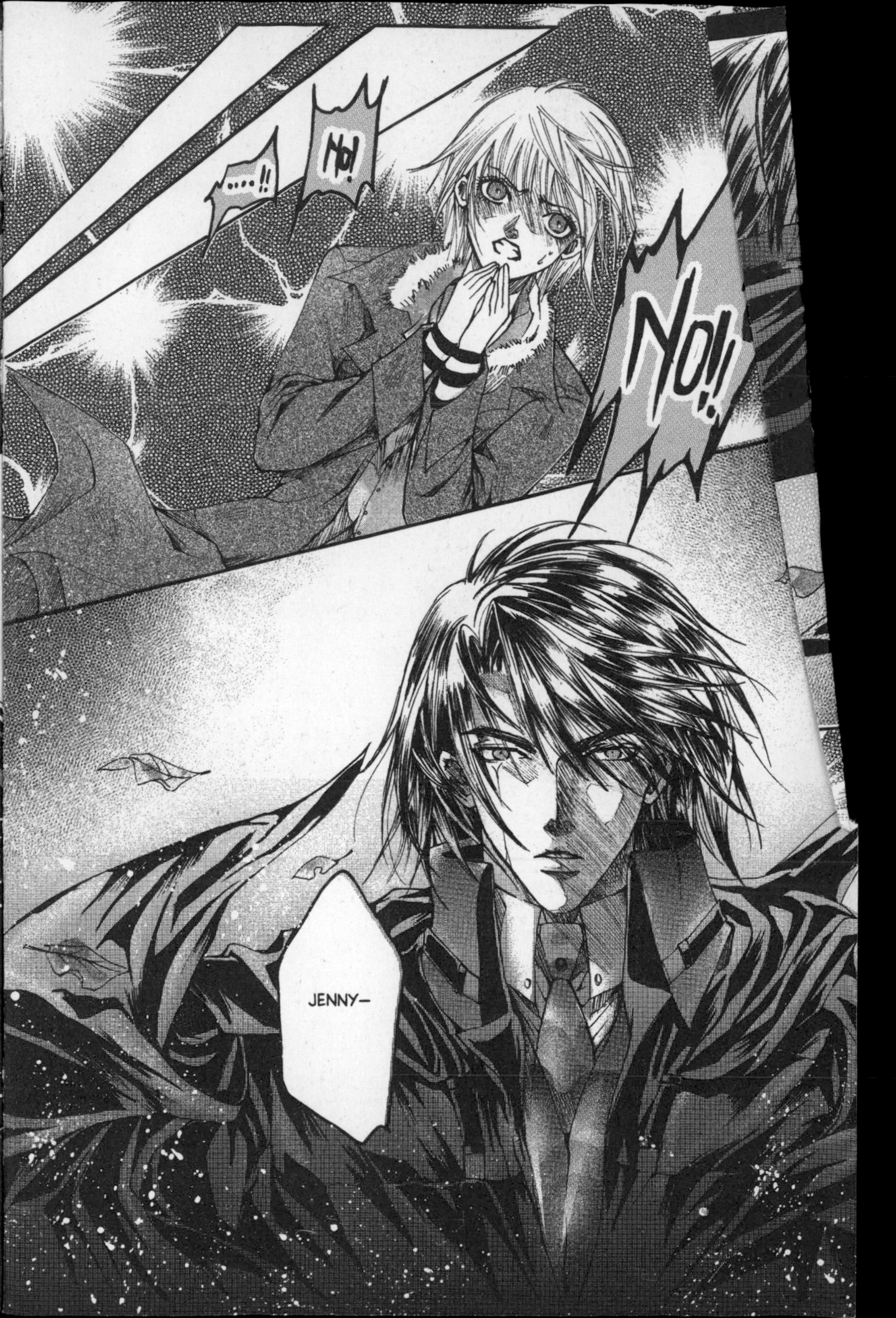
....!!
NO!
NO!!
JENNY—

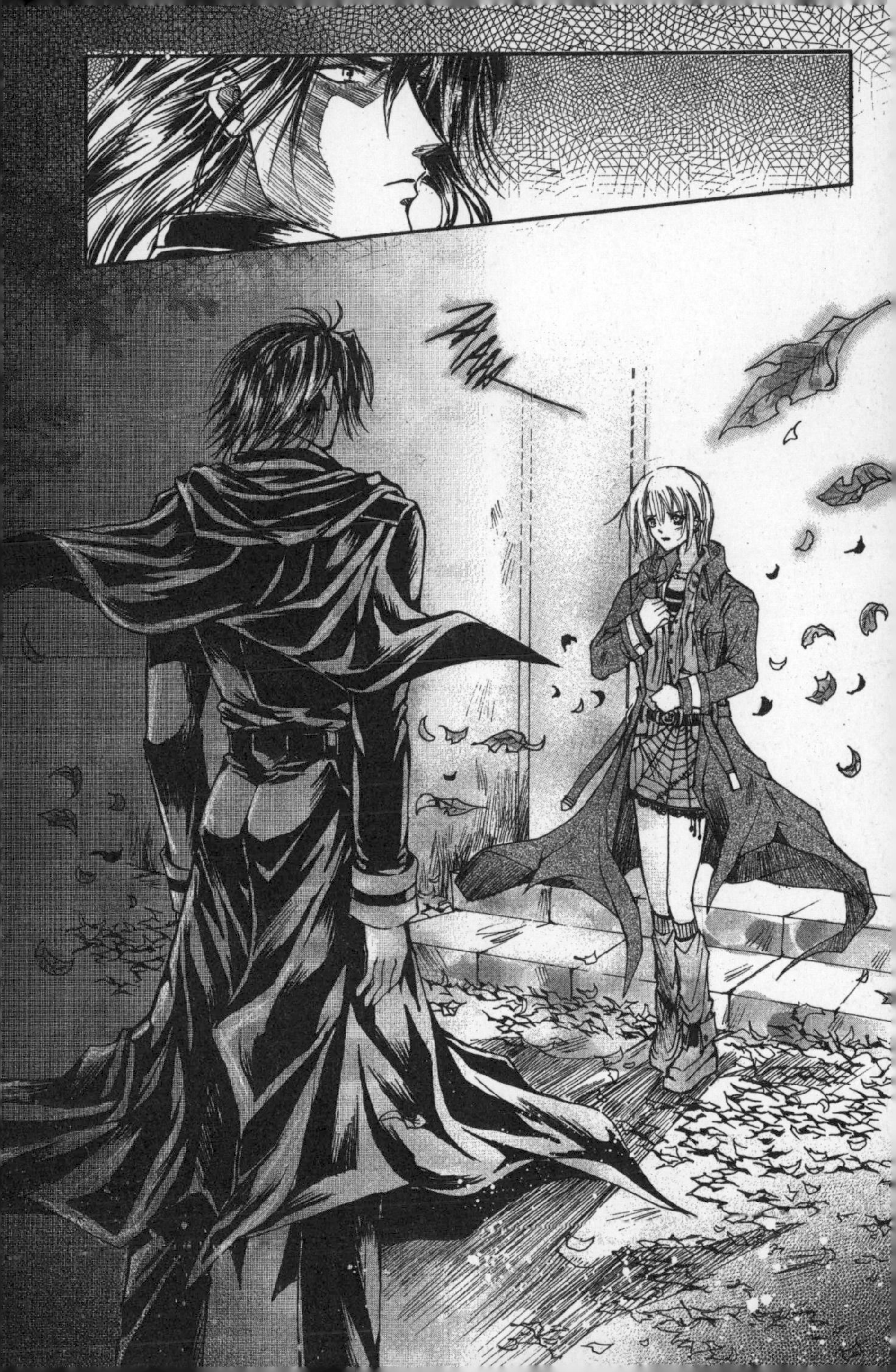

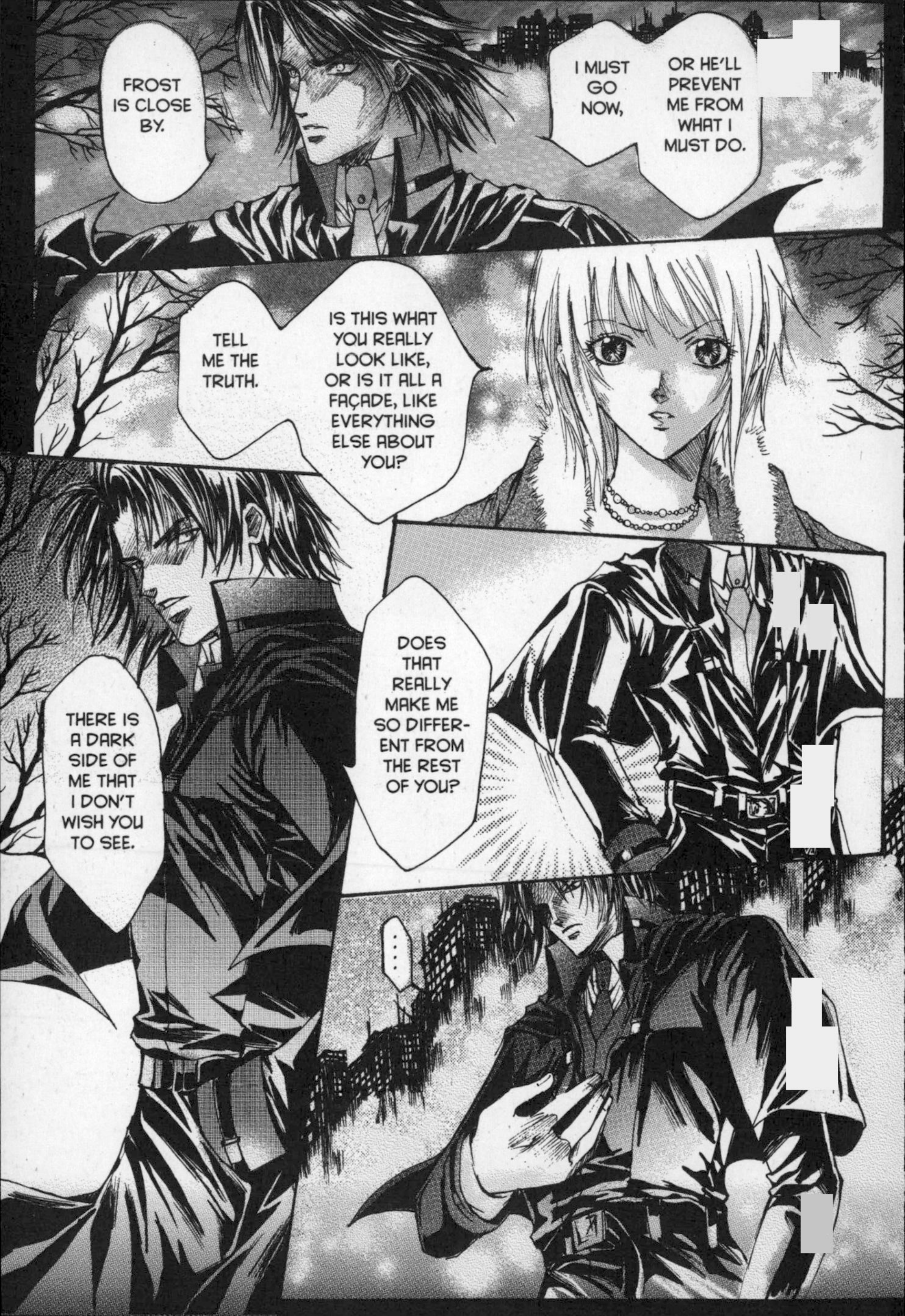
FROST IS CLOSE BY.
I MUST GO NOW,
OR HE'LL PREVENT ME FROM WHAT I MUST DO.
TELL ME THE TRUTH.
IS THIS WHAT YOU REALLY LOOK LIKE, OR IS IT ALL A FAÇADE, LIKE EVERYTHING ELSE ABOUT YOU?
THERE IS A DARK SIDE OF ME THAT I DON'T WISH YOU TO SEE.
DOES THAT REALLY MAKE ME SO DIFFER-ENT FROM THE REST OF YOU?
......

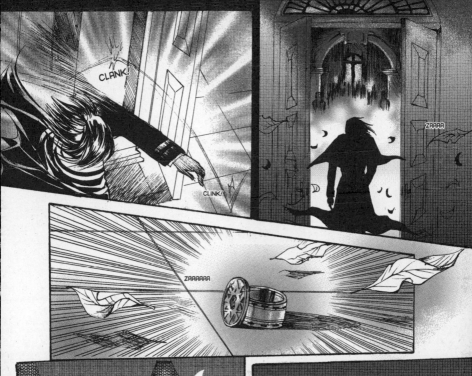

CLANK!

CLINK!

ZAAAA

ZAAAAAA

ZAAAA

143

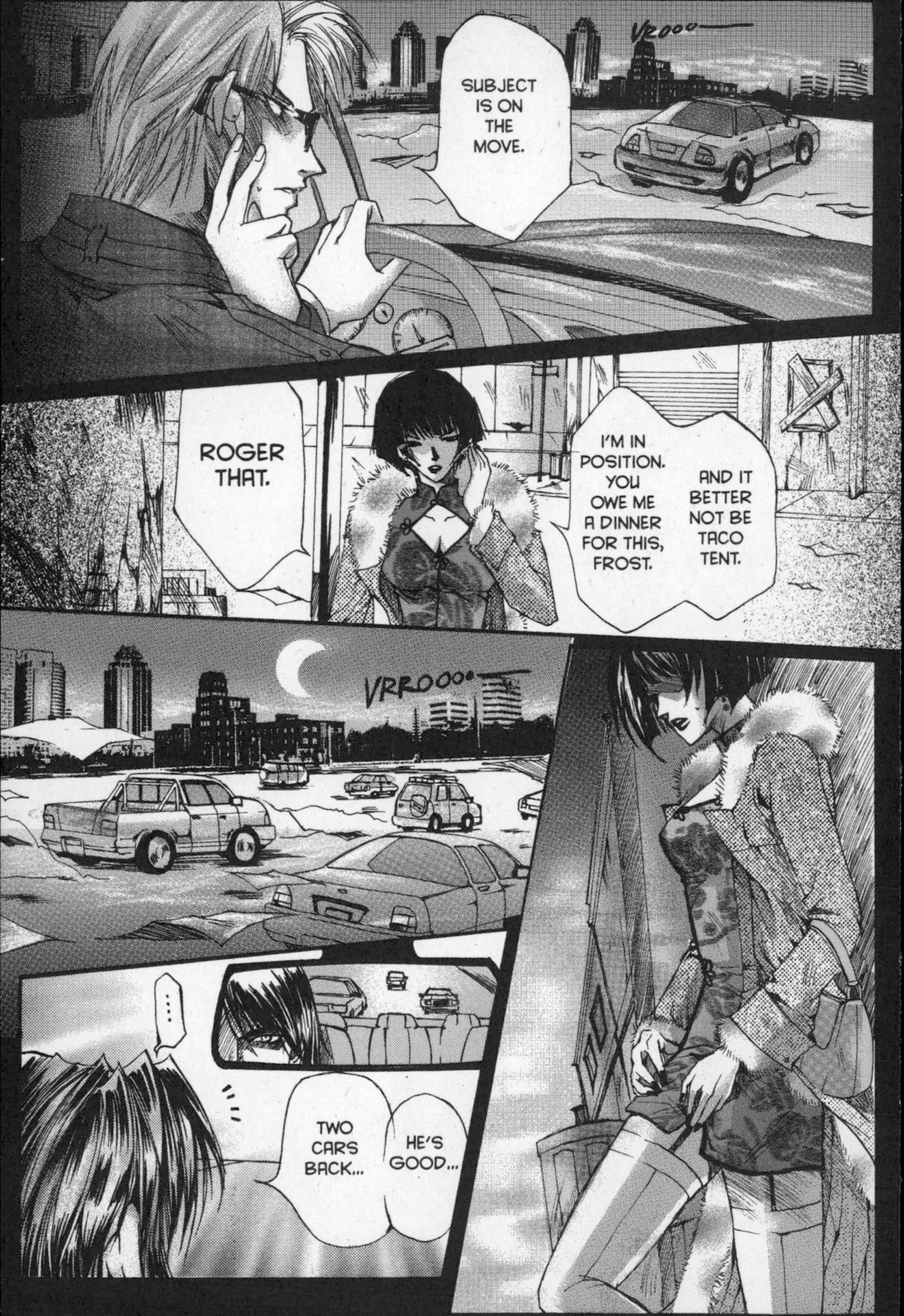
SUBJECT IS ON THE MOVE.
VROOO—
ROGER THAT.
I'M IN POSITION. YOU OWE ME A DINNER FOR THIS, FROST.
AND IT BETTER NOT BE TACO TENT.
VRROOO—
....
TWO CARS BACK...
HE'S GOOD...

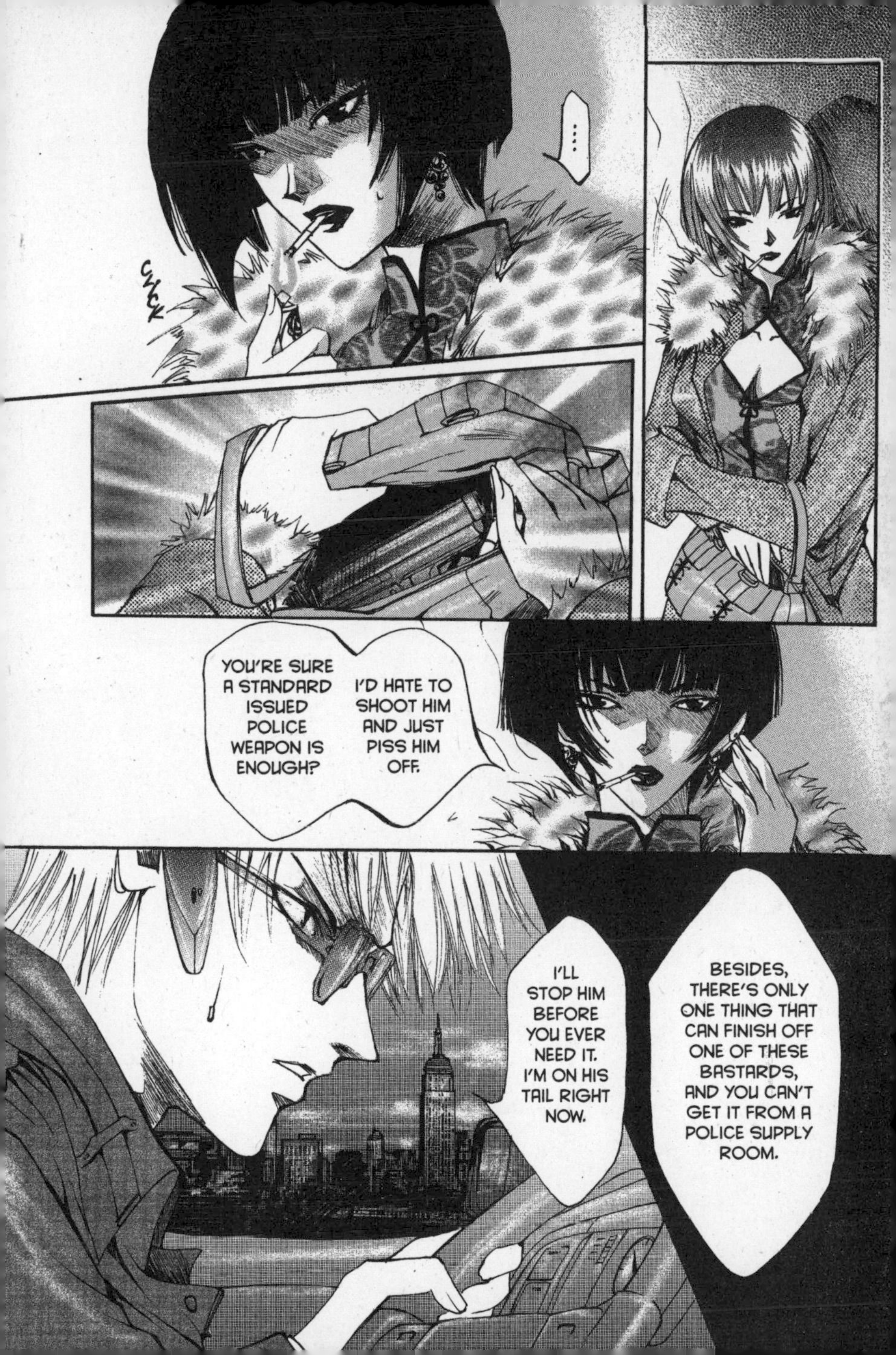

....
CLICK
YOU'RE SURE A STANDARD ISSUED POLICE WEAPON IS ENOUGH?
I'D HATE TO SHOOT HIM AND JUST PISS HIM OFF.
I'LL STOP HIM BEFORE YOU EVER NEED IT. I'M ON HIS TAIL RIGHT NOW.
BESIDES, THERE'S ONLY ONE THING THAT CAN FINISH OFF ONE OF THESE BASTARDS, AND YOU CAN'T GET IT FROM A POLICE SUPPLY ROOM.

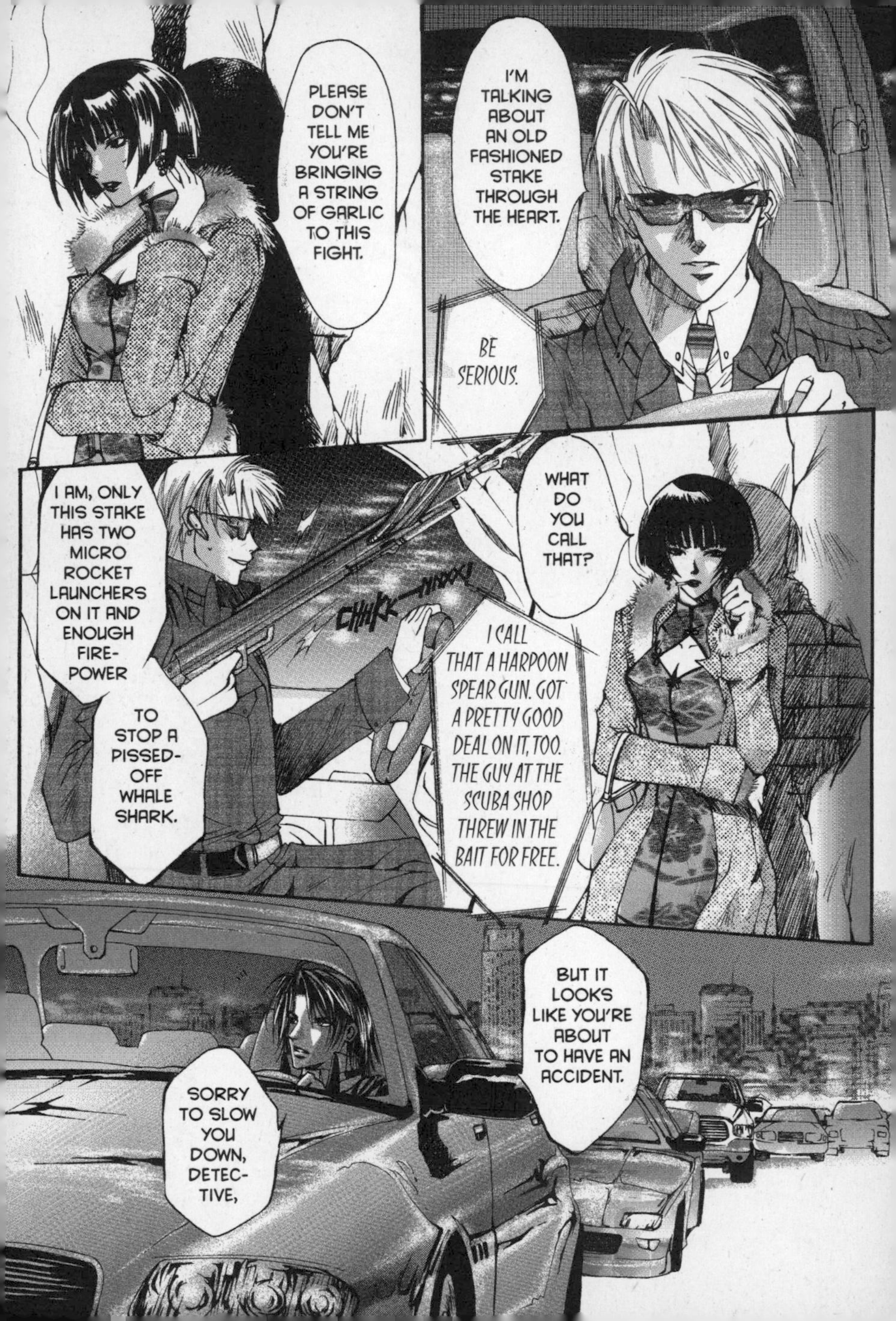
PLEASE DON'T TELL ME YOU'RE BRINGING A STRING OF GARLIC TO THIS FIGHT.
I'M TALKING ABOUT AN OLD FASHIONED STAKE THROUGH THE HEART.
BE SERIOUS.
I AM, ONLY THIS STAKE HAS TWO MICRO ROCKET LAUNCHERS ON IT AND ENOUGH FIRE-POWER
TO STOP A PISSED-OFF WHALE SHARK.
WHAT DO YOU CALL THAT?
I CALL THAT A HARPOON SPEAR GUN. GOT A PRETTY GOOD DEAL ON IT, TOO. THE GUY AT THE SCUBA SHOP THREW IN THE BAIT FOR FREE.
SORRY TO SLOW YOU DOWN, DETECTIVE,
BUT IT LOOKS LIKE YOU'RE ABOUT TO HAVE AN ACCIDENT.

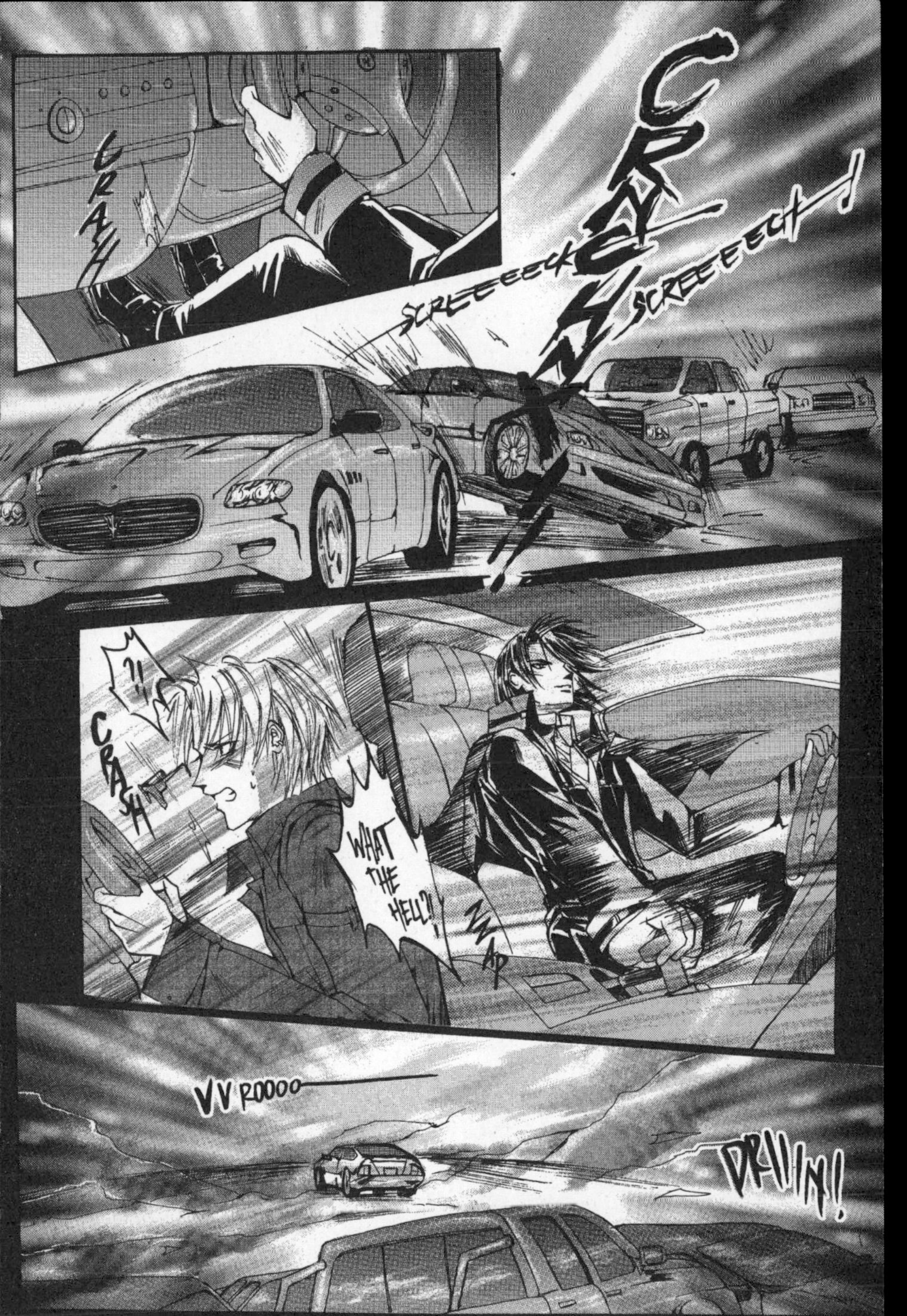

CRASH
CRASH!!
SCREEEEECK
SCREEEEECH
!!
CRASH
WHAT THE HELL?!
ZZAP
VVROOOO
DRIIIN!

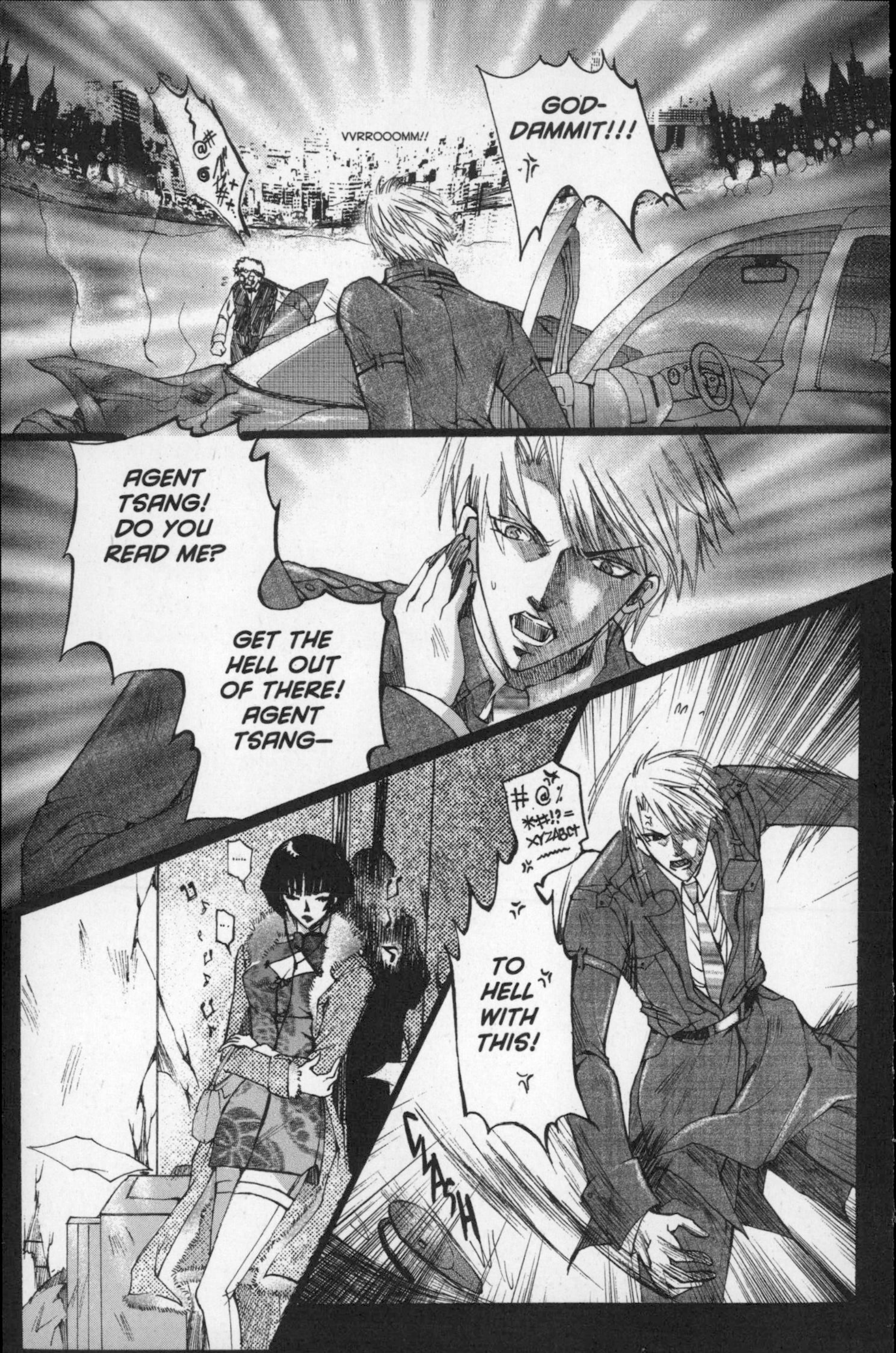

@#
@ ##+
VVRROOOMM!!
GOD-DAMMIT!!!
AGENT TSANG! DO YOU READ ME?
GET THE HELL OUT OF THERE! AGENT TSANG—
...
#.@%
*#!?=
XYZABC+
TO HELL WITH THIS!
CRASH

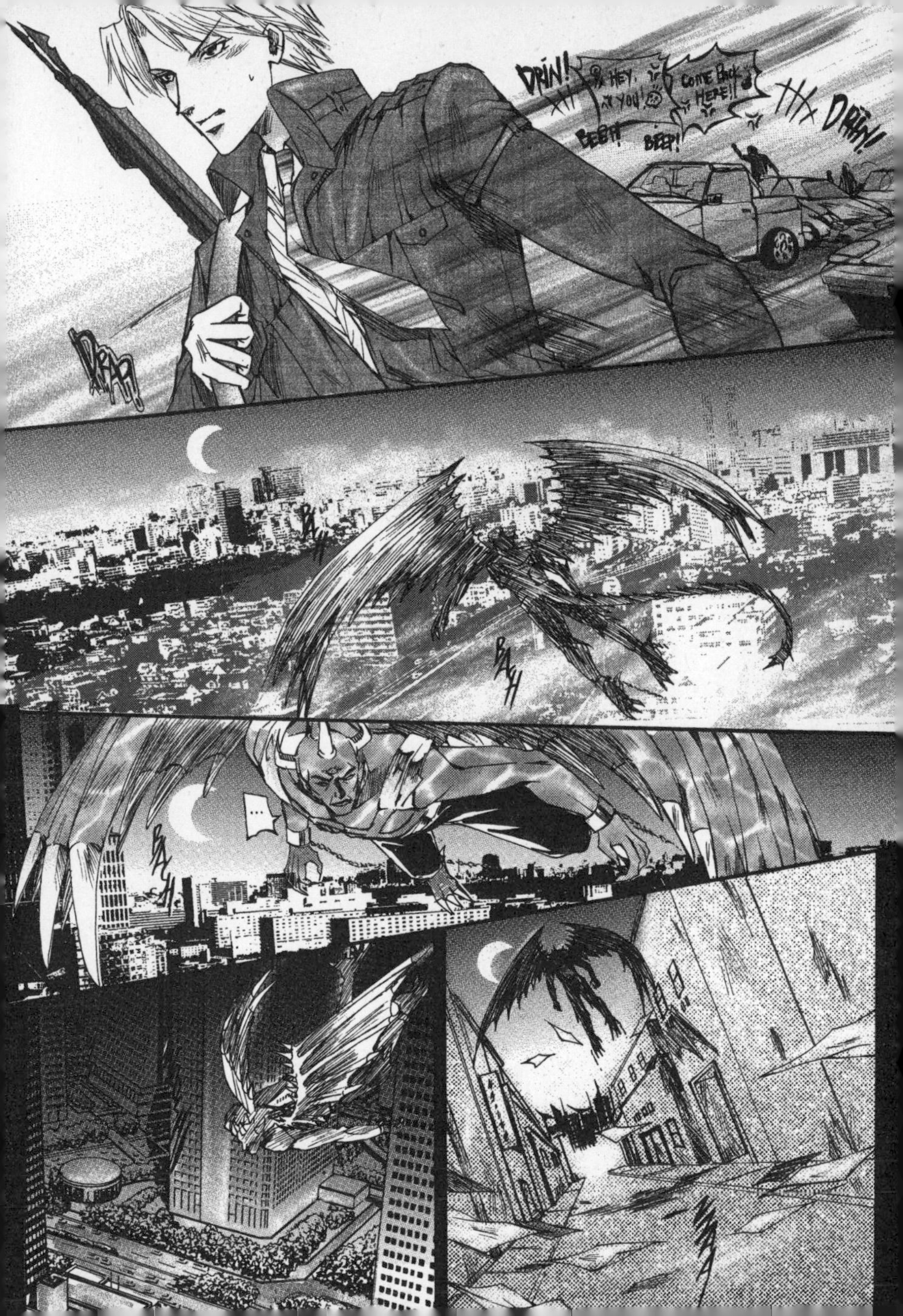
DRIN!
HEY, YOU!
COME BACK HERE!!
BEEP!
BEEP!
DRIN!
DRAP!
BACH
BACH
...
BACH

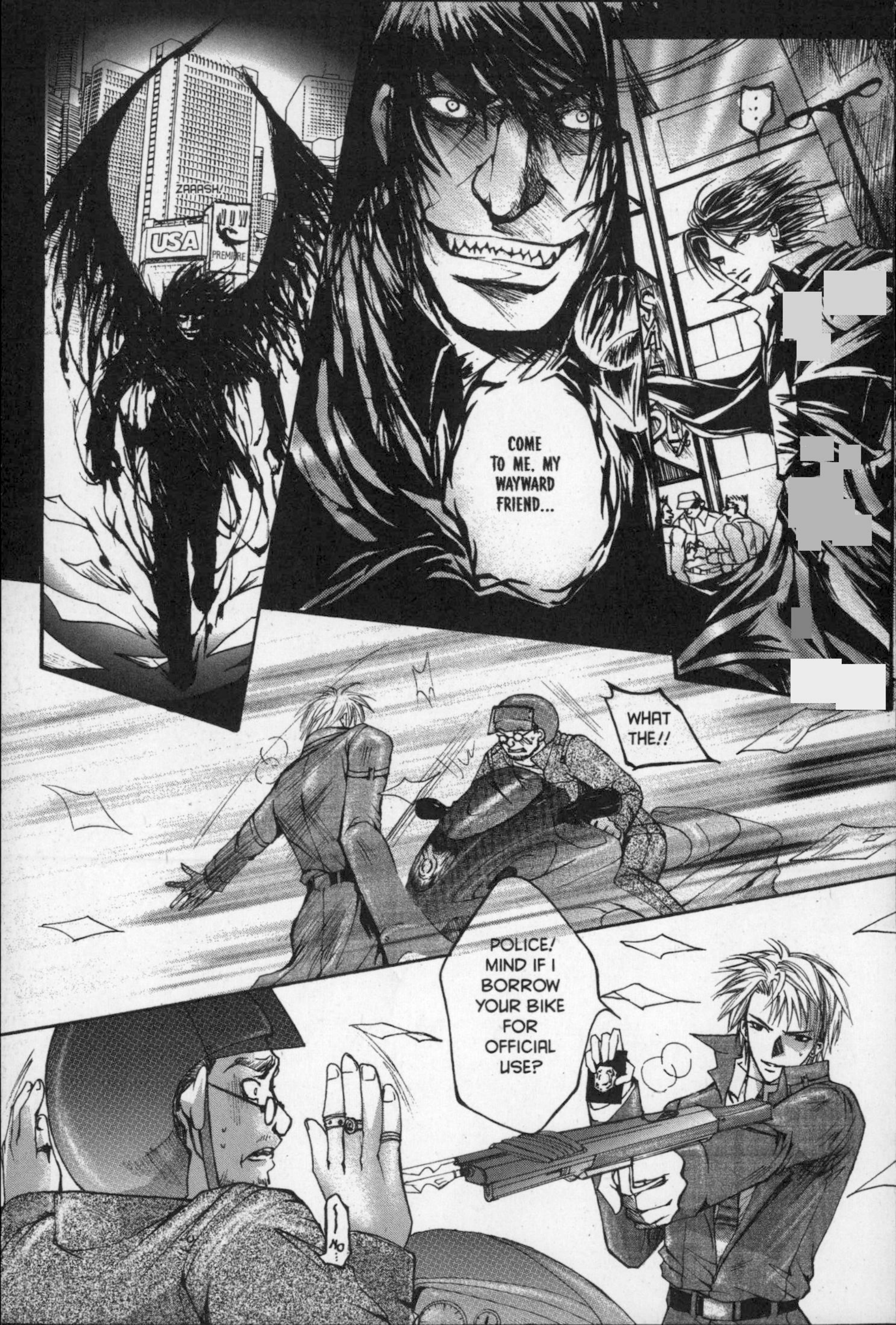
ZAAASH!
USA
NOW
PREMIERE
COME TO ME, MY WAYWARD FRIEND...
WHAT THE!!
POLICE! MIND IF I BORROW YOUR BIKE FOR OFFICIAL USE?

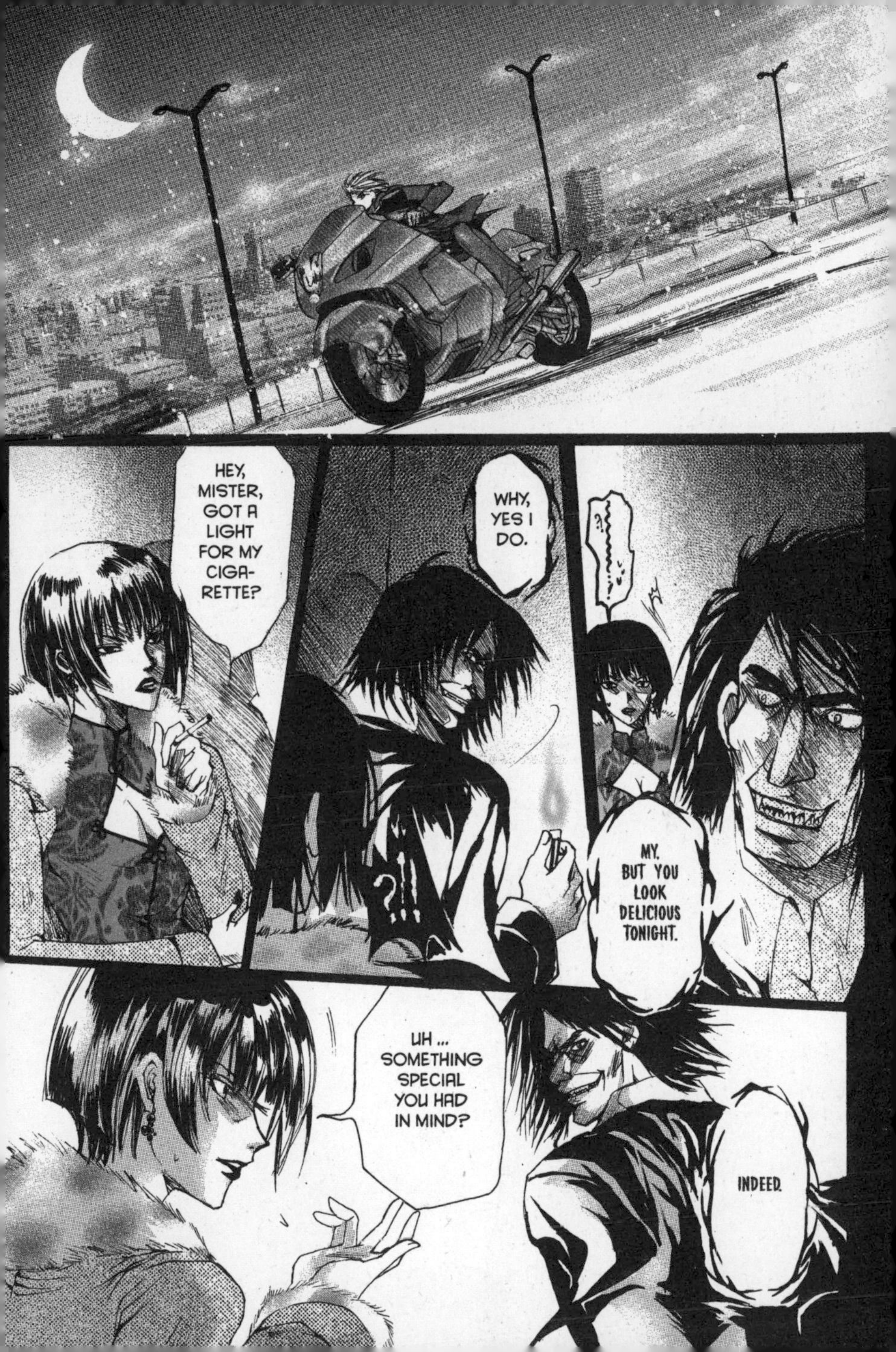
HEY, MISTER, GOT A LIGHT FOR MY CIGA-RETTE?
WHY, YES I DO.
...!?
MY. BUT YOU LOOK DELICIOUS TONIGHT.
UH ... SOMETHING SPECIAL YOU HAD IN MIND?
INDEED.

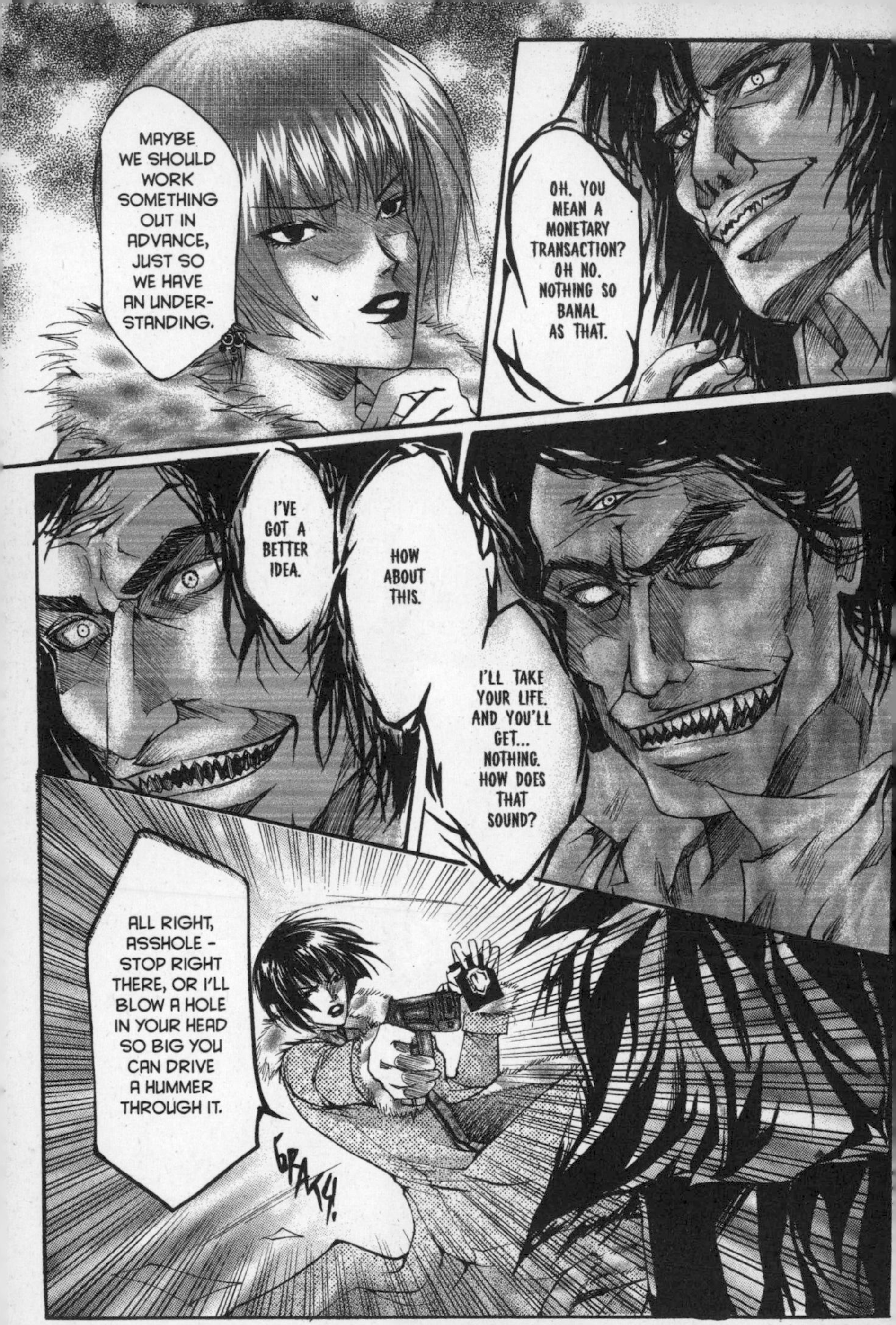
MAYBE WE SHOULD WORK SOMETHING OUT IN ADVANCE, JUST SO WE HAVE AN UNDER-STANDING.
OH. YOU MEAN A MONETARY TRANSACTION? OH NO. NOTHING SO BANAL AS THAT.
I'VE GOT A BETTER IDEA.
HOW ABOUT THIS.
I'LL TAKE YOUR LIFE. AND YOU'LL GET... NOTHING. HOW DOES THAT SOUND?
ALL RIGHT, ASSHOLE – STOP RIGHT THERE, OR I'LL BLOW A HOLE IN YOUR HEAD SO BIG YOU CAN DRIVE A HUMMER THROUGH IT.

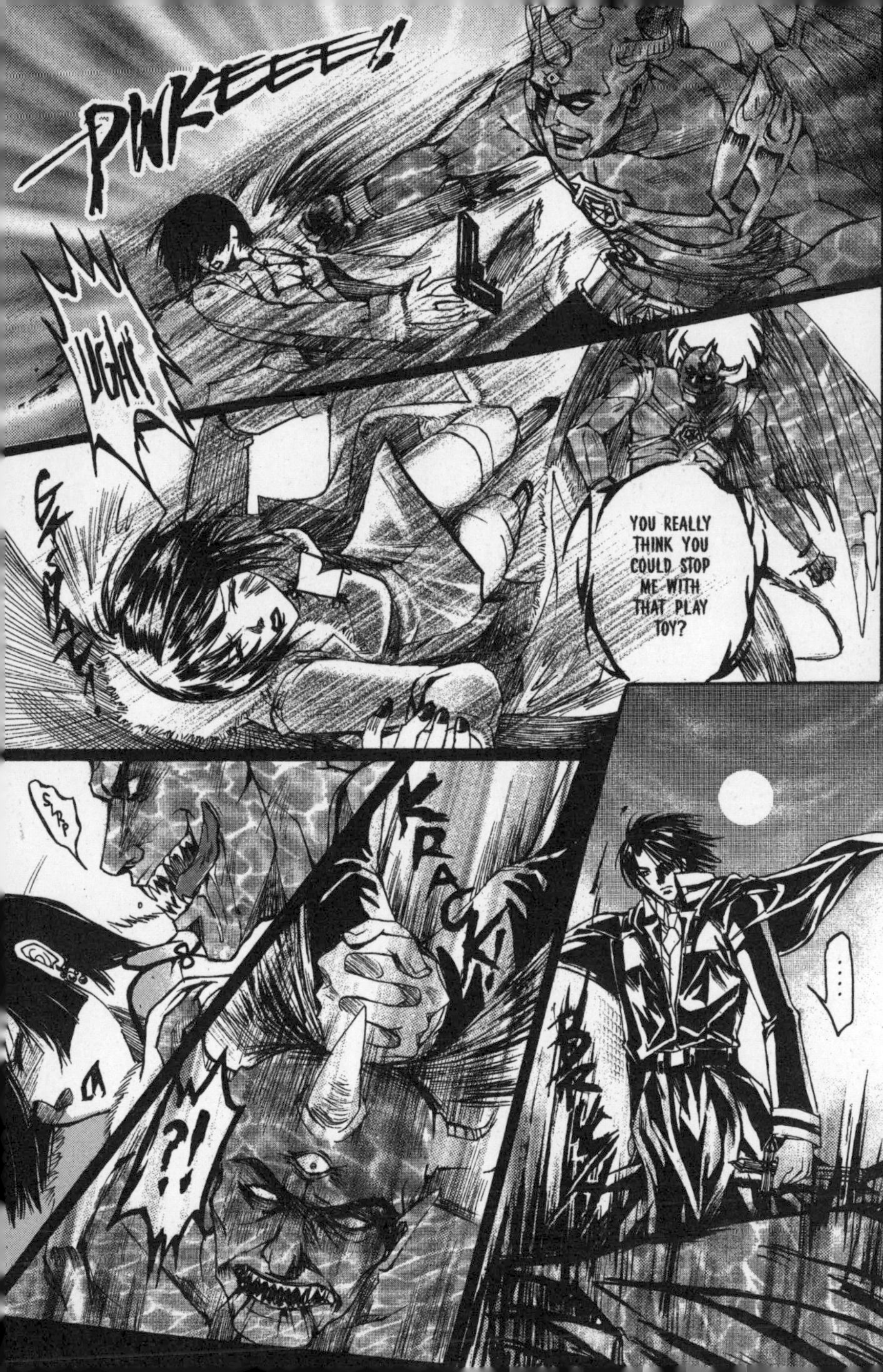
PWKEEEE!!
UGH!
YOU REALLY THINK YOU COULD STOP ME WITH THAT PLAY TOY?
SLRP
KRACK!
?!
...

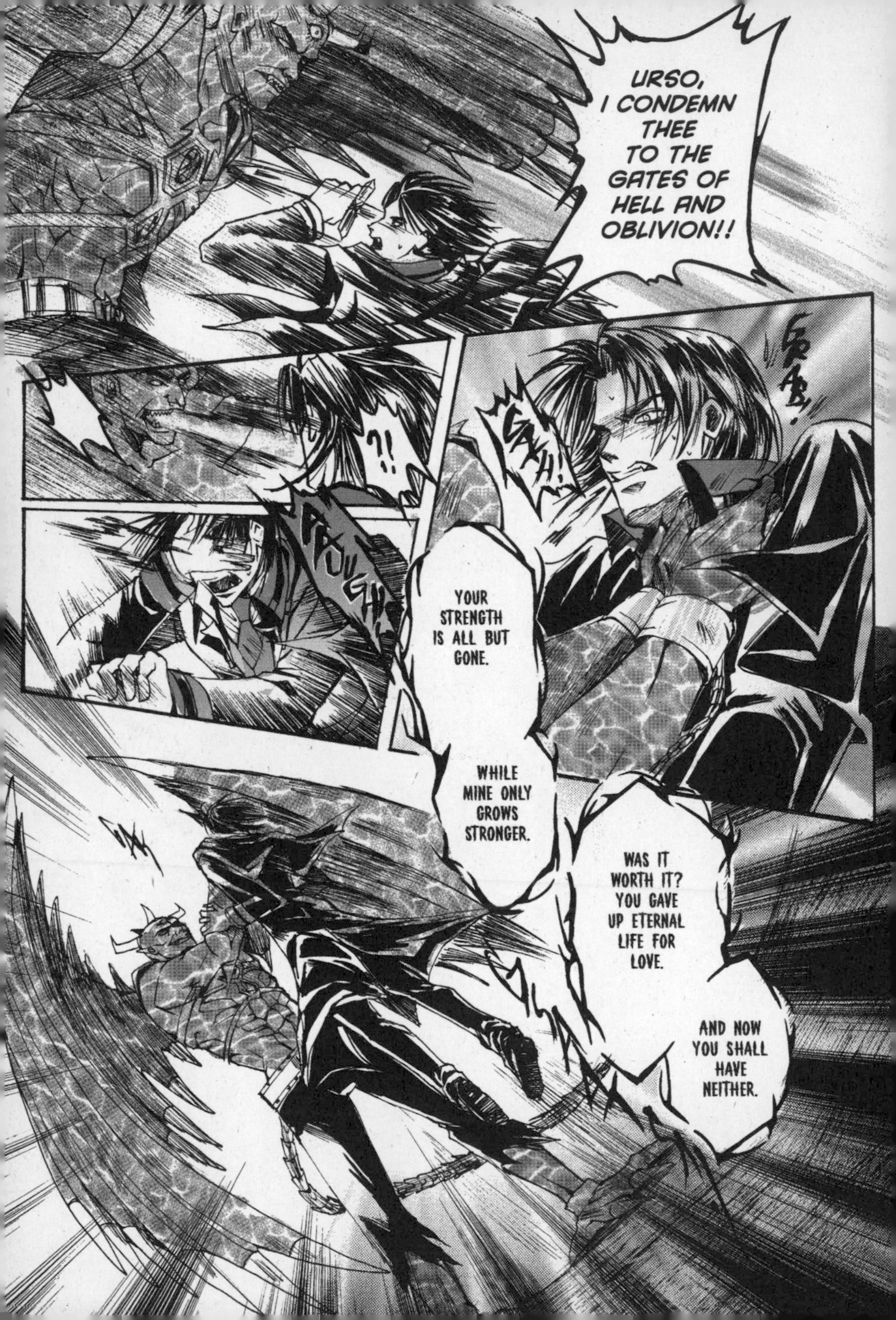
URSO, I CONDEMN THEE TO THE GATES OF HELL AND OBLIVION!!
?!!
PFOUGH!
GAAH!
GRAB!
YOUR STRENGTH IS ALL BUT GONE.
WHILE MINE ONLY GROWS STRONGER.
WAS IT WORTH IT? YOU GAVE UP ETERNAL LIFE FOR LOVE.
AND NOW YOU SHALL HAVE NEITHER.

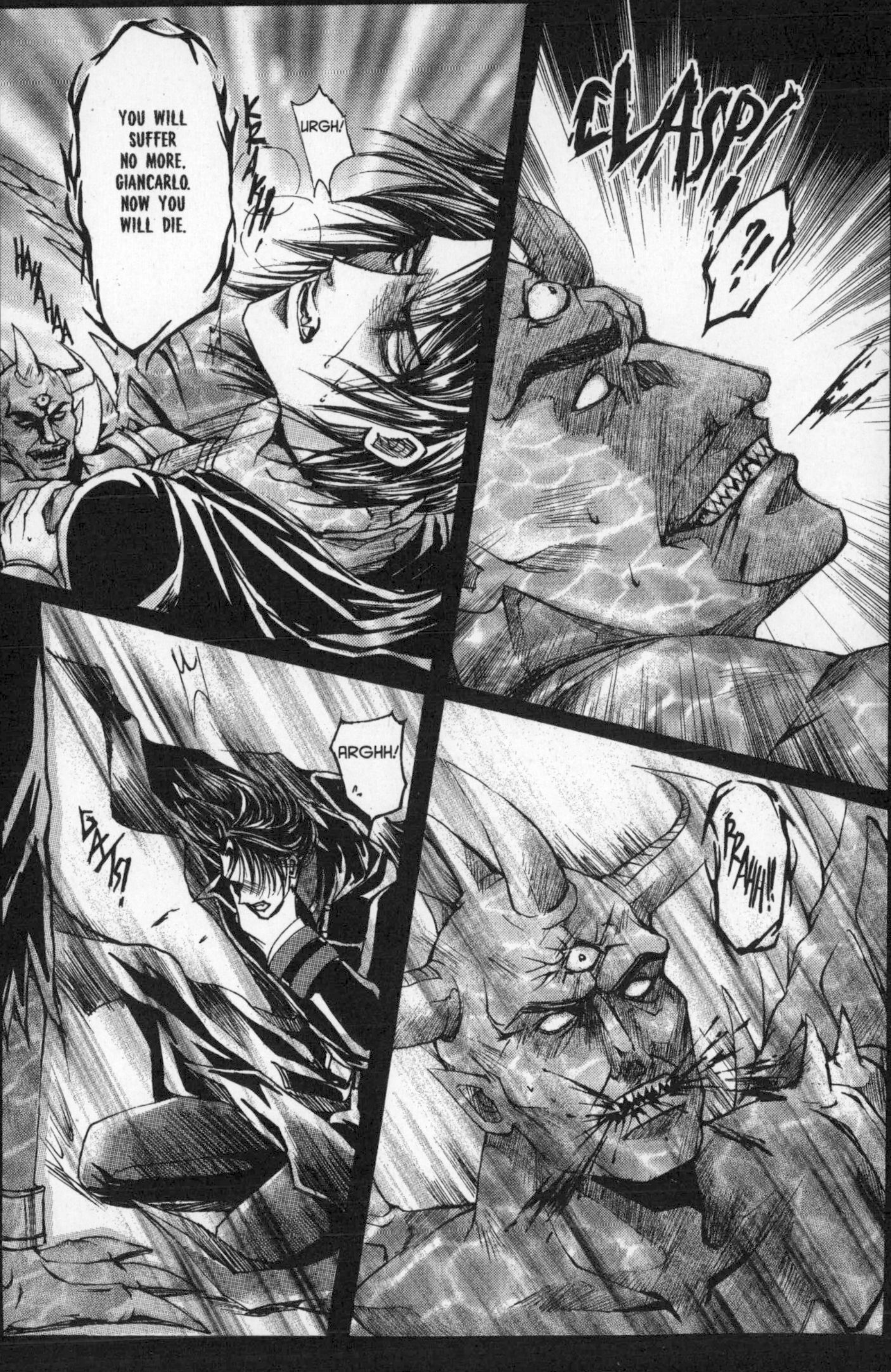
YOU WILL SUFFER NO MORE, GIANCARLO. NOW YOU WILL DIE.
HAHAHAHAA
KRAKH!
URGH!
CLASP!
?!
ARGHH!
GASH!
RRAHH!!

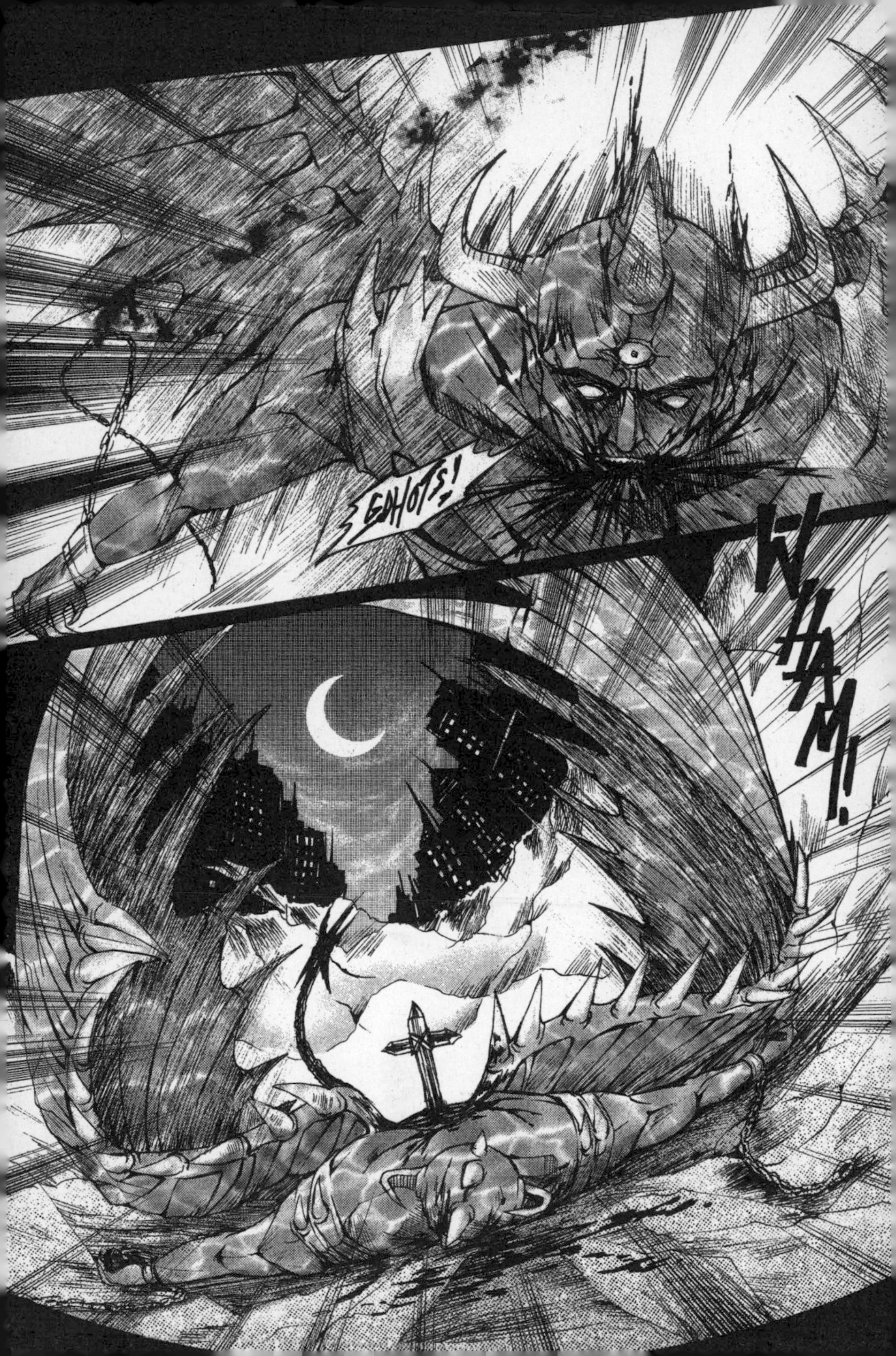
GAHOTS!
WHAM!

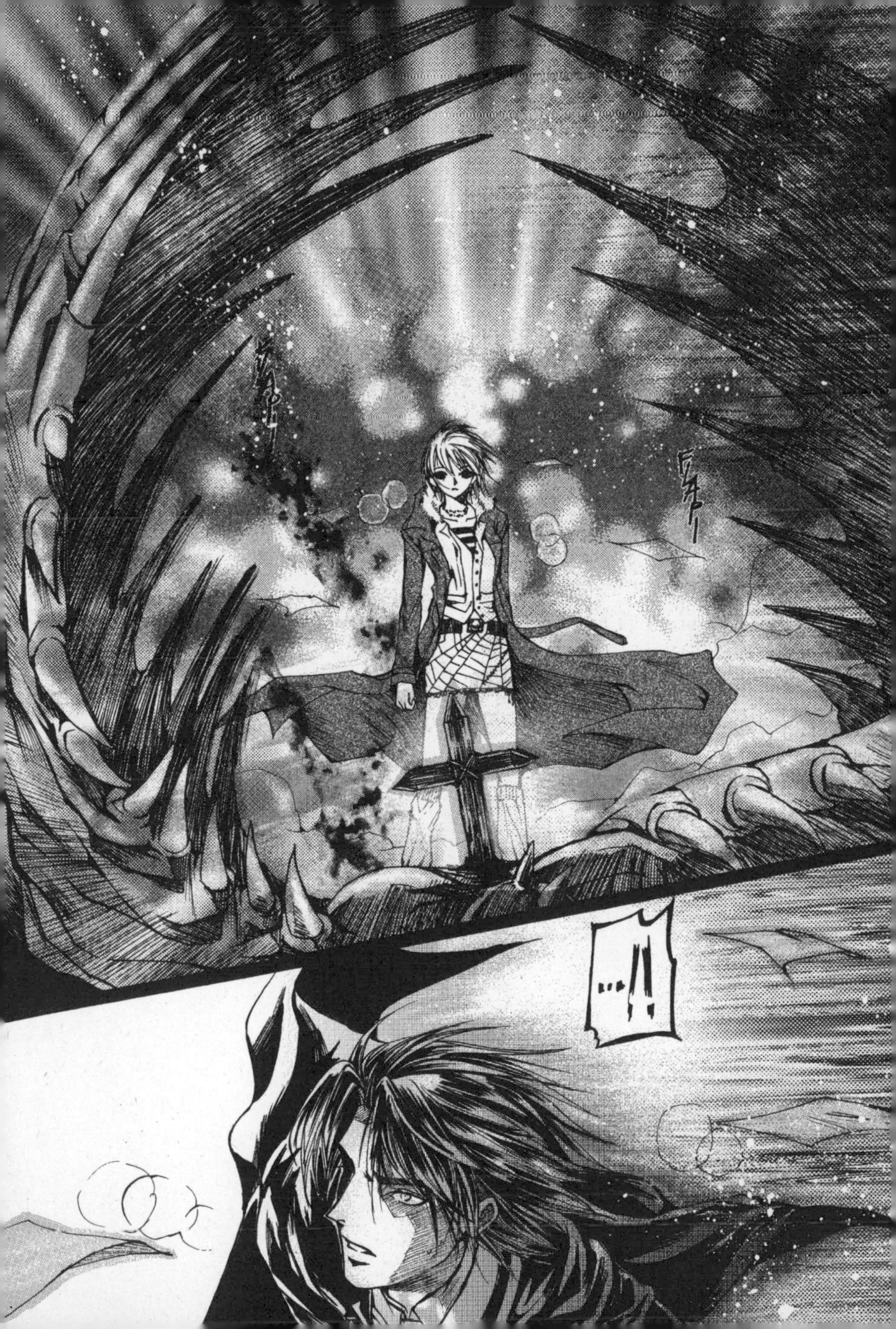
…!!

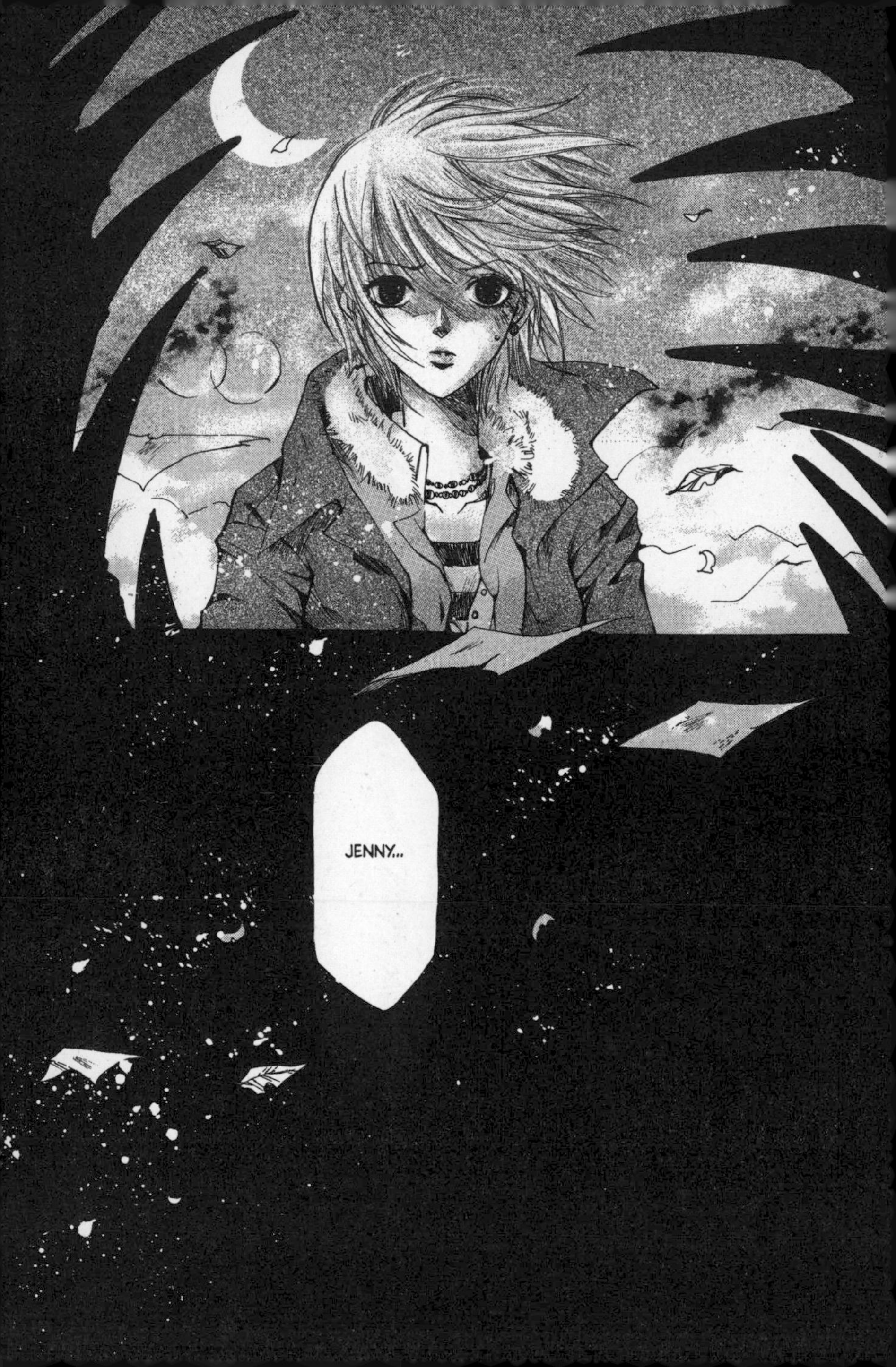
JENNY...

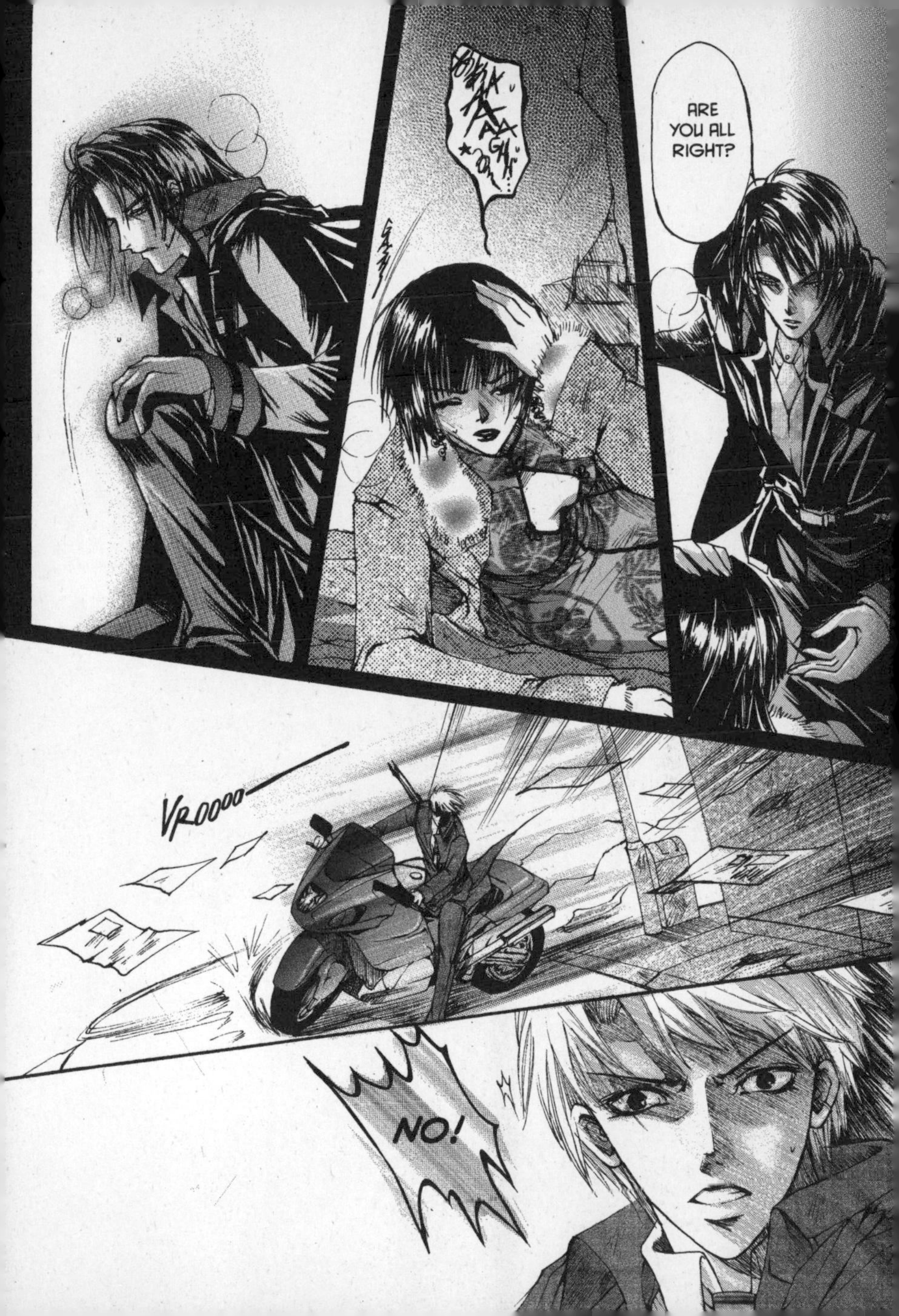
ARE YOU ALL RIGHT?
VROOOO
NO!

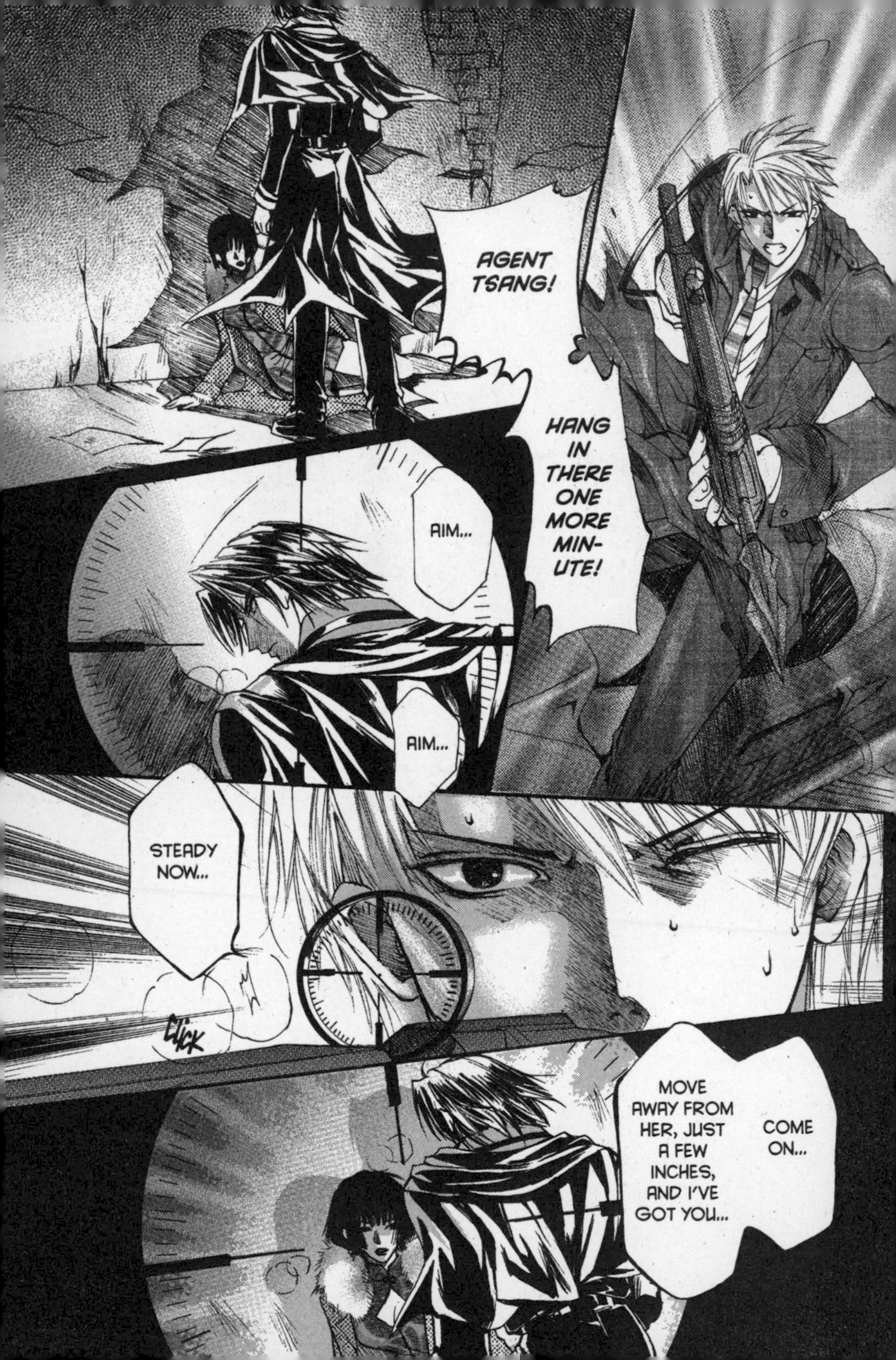
AIM...
AIM...
AGENT TSANG!
HANG IN THERE ONE MORE MIN-UTE!
STEADY NOW...
CLICK
MOVE AWAY FROM HER, JUST A FEW INCHES, AND I'VE GOT YOU...
COME ON...

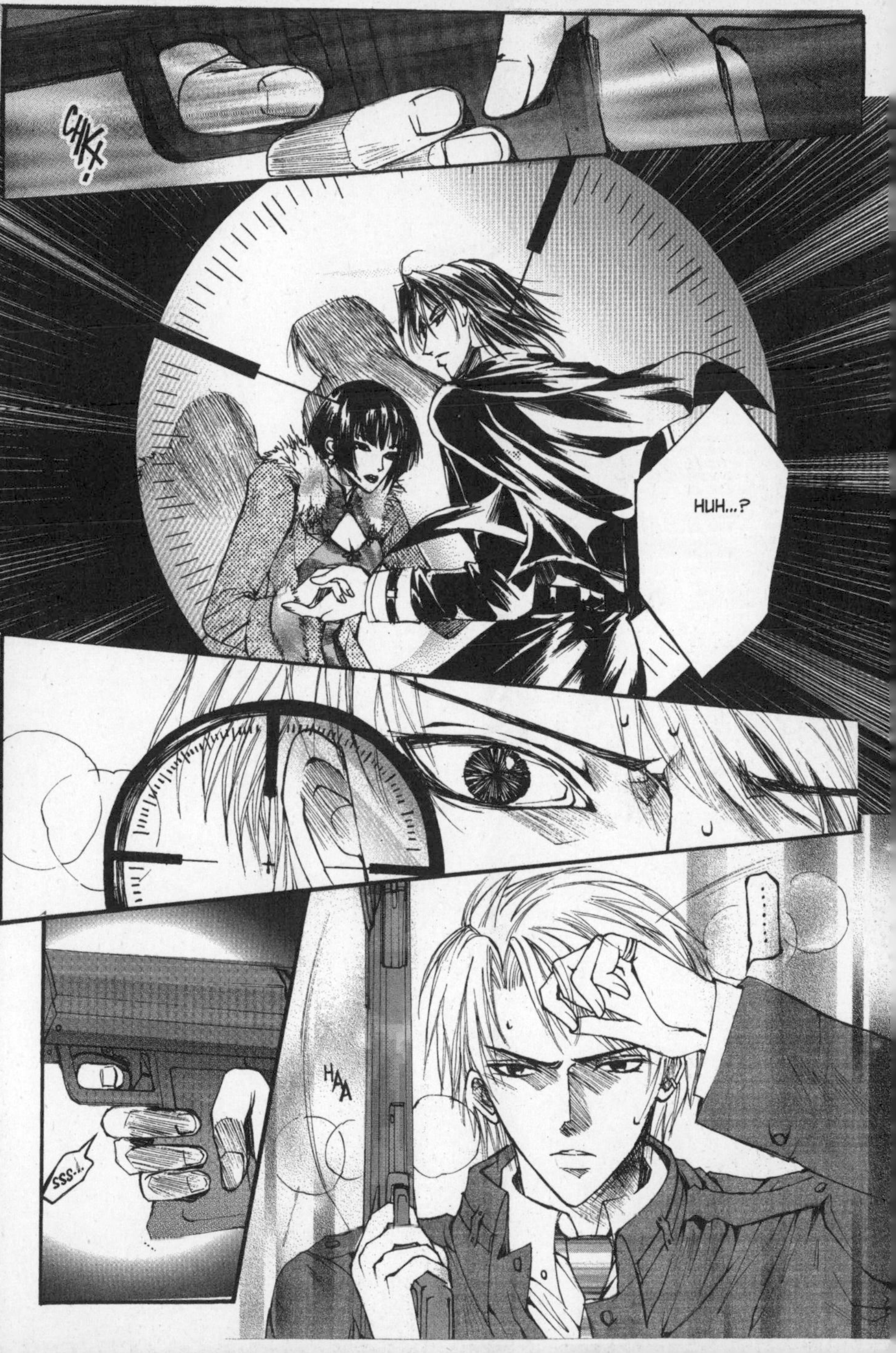
CHK!
HUH...?
SSS..!
HAA
......

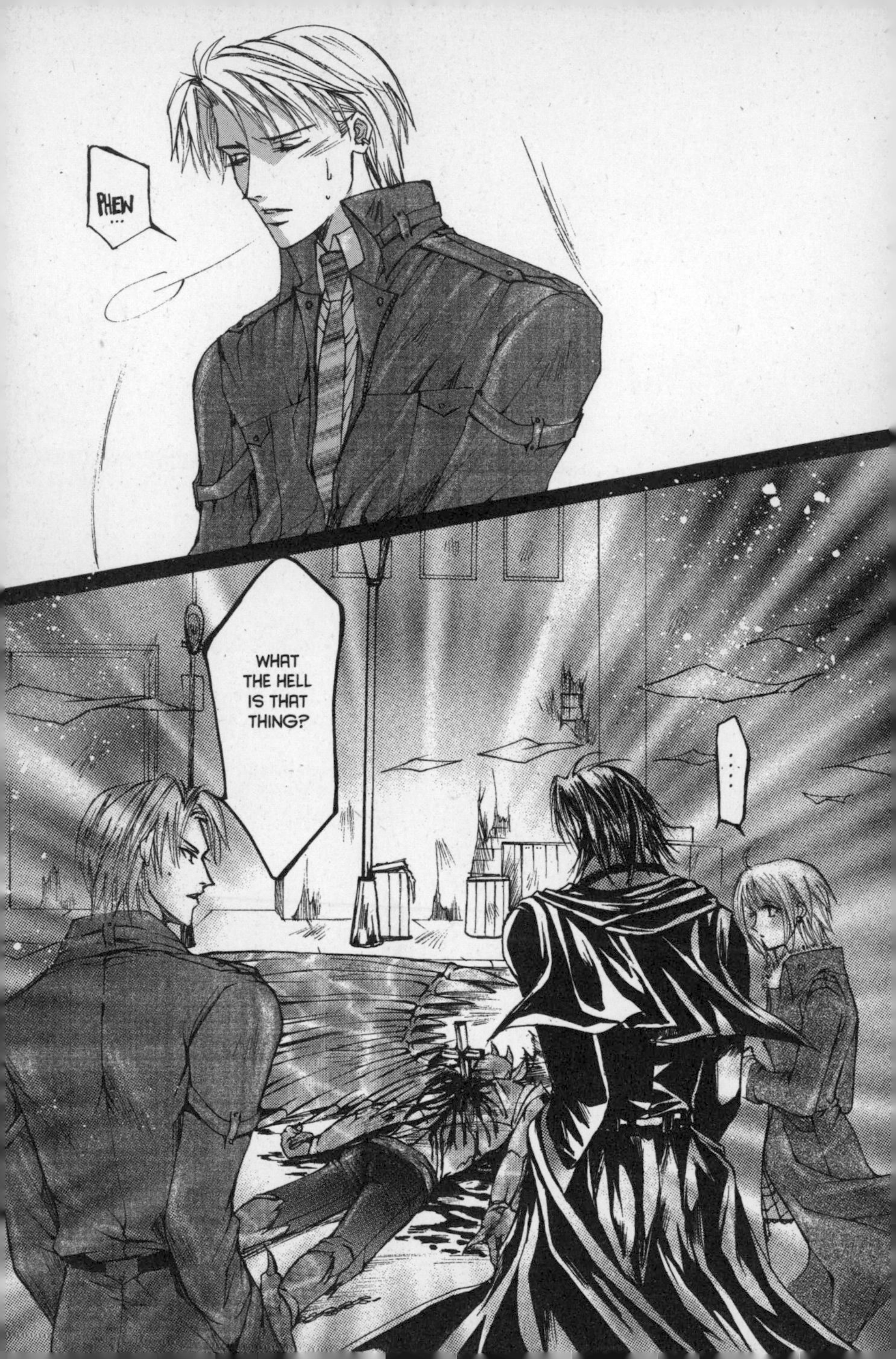
PHEW
...
WHAT THE HELL IS THAT THING?
......

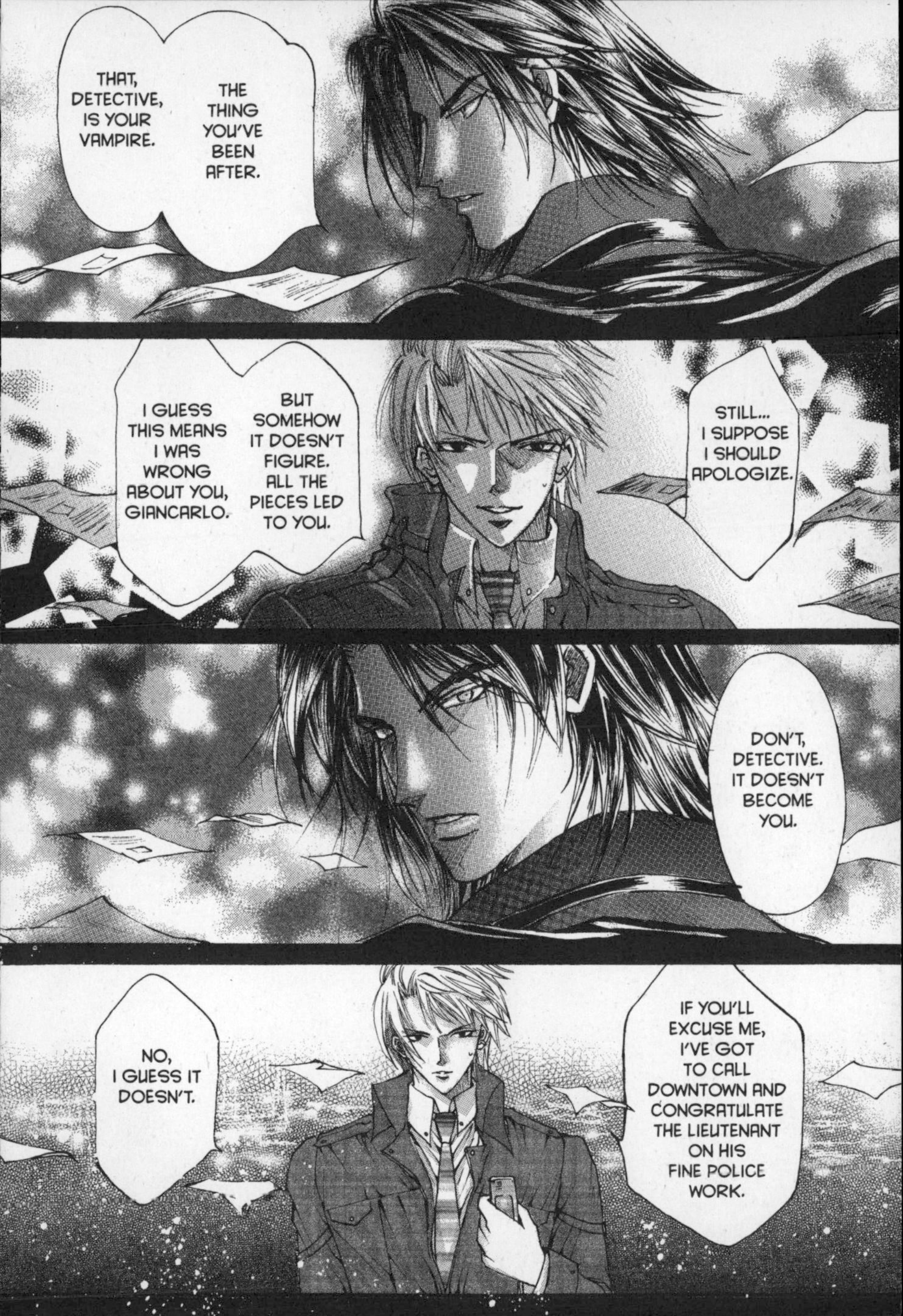
THAT, DETECTIVE, IS YOUR VAMPIRE.
THE THING YOU'VE BEEN AFTER.
I GUESS THIS MEANS I WAS WRONG ABOUT YOU, GIANCARLO.
BUT SOMEHOW IT DOESN'T FIGURE. ALL THE PIECES LED TO YOU.
STILL... I SUPPOSE I SHOULD APOLOGIZE.
DON'T, DETECTIVE. IT DOESN'T BECOME YOU.
NO, I GUESS IT DOESN'T.
IF YOU'LL EXCUSE ME, I'VE GOT TO CALL DOWNTOWN AND CONGRATULATE THE LIEUTENANT ON HIS FINE POLICE WORK.

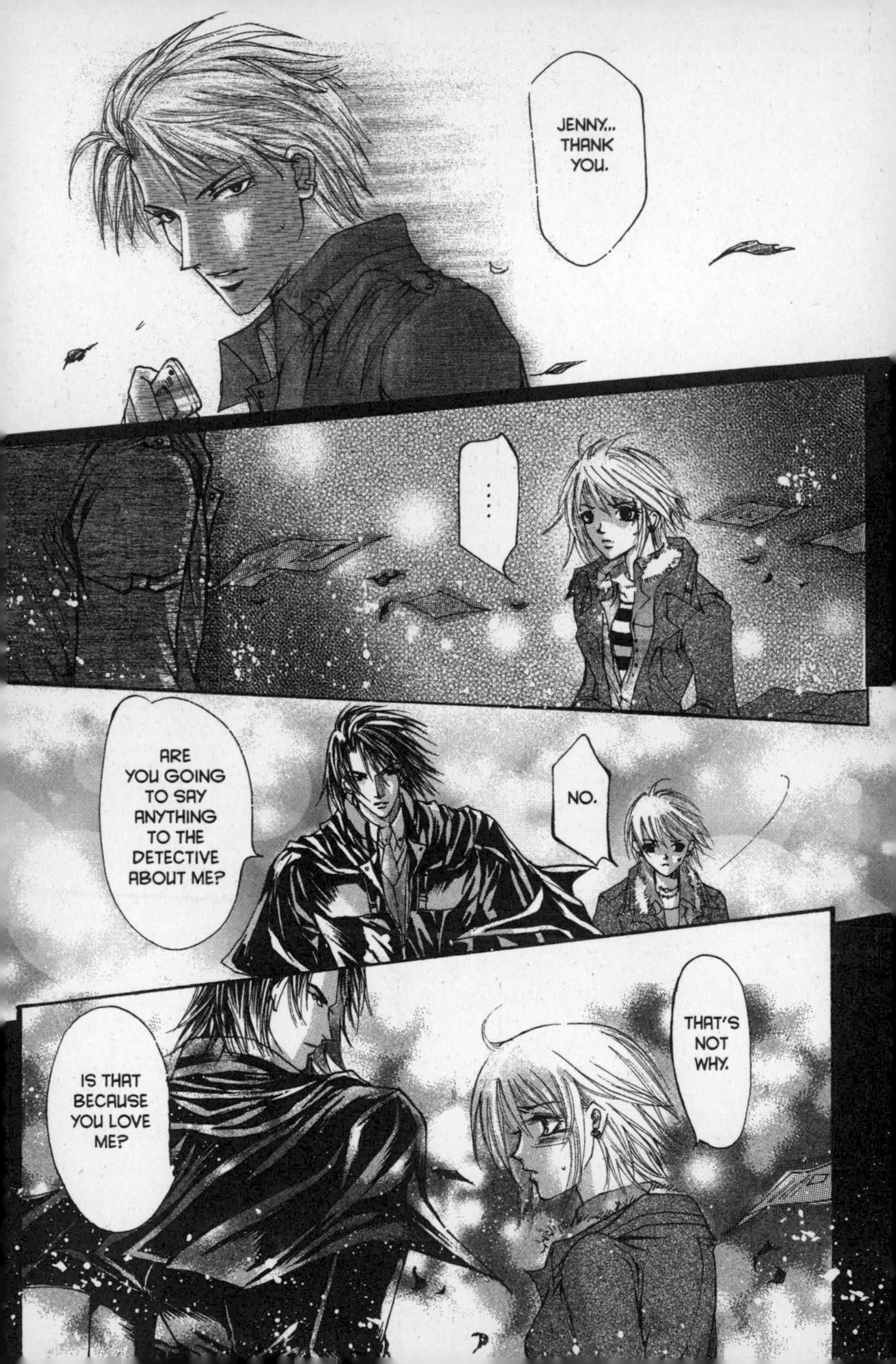
JENNY... THANK YOU.
....
ARE YOU GOING TO SAY ANYTHING TO THE DETECTIVE ABOUT ME?
NO.
IS THAT BECAUSE YOU LOVE ME?
THAT'S NOT WHY.

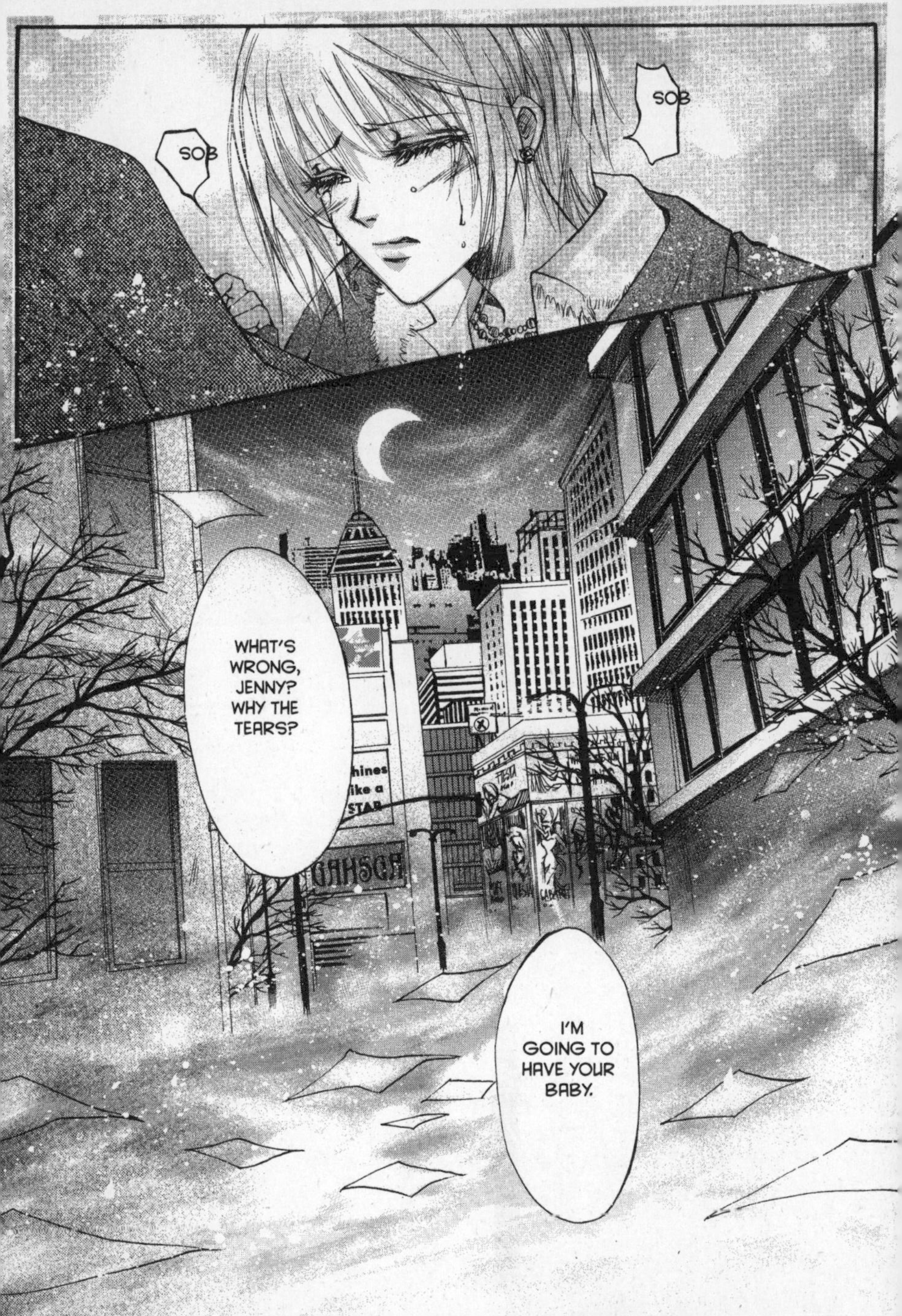
SOB
SOB
WHAT'S WRONG, JENNY? WHY THE TEARS?
I'M GOING TO HAVE YOUR BABY.

AFTERWORD

Christopher Hart

WWW.CHRISHARTBOOKS.COM

I was driving to a bookstore with my wife, Maria, to get some manga, and suddenly an idea breezed past my brain just long enough for me to notice it: What if a vampire had a conscience?

That's one of those ideas that might sound small but has huge and dramatic ramifications.

The idea intrigued me...

I don't remember whether we ever made it to the bookstore, because, by then, I was thinking only about the story brewing inside my head.

It has always struck me that horror stories are metaphors for the human condition: obsession, compulsion, love, and death. And in this case, it's the vampire's desperate compulsion that drives him to do the terrible things he does. Can he be forgiven for that which he cannot control? What if he tried to change? Could he be forgiven then? Should he be forgiven?

But what could possibly make a vampire want to give up his ways, which result in eternal life, albeit the darkest existence?

It had to be a women. What if a vampire were to fall in love with the woman he had planned to kill? He has never experienced love before. It would undo him. Confuse him. And what of his evil brethren? Would other vampires allow him to leave the Brotherhood of Darkness?

I pitched a short version of the idea to Anzu, to see if she wanted to illustrate it. She liked it right away and wanted to hear more. It must have been frustrating for her, because I wouldn't say another word about the story until I had the entire thing completely crystallized in my mind—and on paper. I didn't want to tell her ideas she might fall in love with that I might decide to cut later. Weeks went by, and I kept e-mailing her notes saying that I was busy working on it. She probably thought I was playing video poker on the computer. But finally, I sent her a complete outline, with everything in it, including passages of dialogue.

Instantly, she began drawing the characters. Anzu lives in Singapore, and I'm in the USA, so we never communicate in real time. Everything is delayed about twelve hours. This means that she would sometimes wake up to find a zillion e-mails from me when I had a burst of inspiration. Pity the poor woman.

My work schedule is pretty stable: I start around 6:30 a.m. and finish at about 5:30 in the evening. After dinner, when my kids do their homework, I usually go back into my studio and get a little more work done.

Anzu's favorite character in the book is Detective Frost. I enjoyed writing Frost's dialogue. But if I had to choose, I'd say my favorites are Giancarlo and Jenny. Whenever they were in a scene together, I felt the tension of the moment rising as I tapped out the action on the keyboard. Sometimes, I forgot I was the writer—I wanted to find out what was going to happen next, just like the reader! At least, that's how I hope you'll feel about the story.

The Reformed fuses two popular genres: horror and crime noir. The result is horror-noir, a rugged and dark world of passion, betrayal, honor, and death. I like adding grit to the horror genre instead of just gore. I think it adds to the mood and mystery. I'm a huge film noir fan, and I like to read noir pulp classics. There is something compelling about the darkly gleaming world in which noir characters live. These characters are on a quiet search for their own humanity in a world of bleakness. Maybe this time, one of them might find it.

AFTERWORD BY ANZU

Come visit me on the Web at:
WWW.ANZU-ART.COM
HTTP://ANZU-MANGA.DEVIANTART.COM
HTTP://THIRST.THEWEBCOMIC.COM

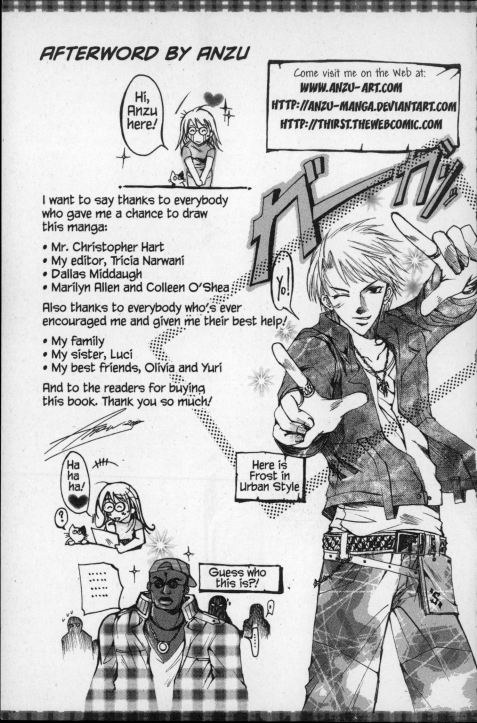

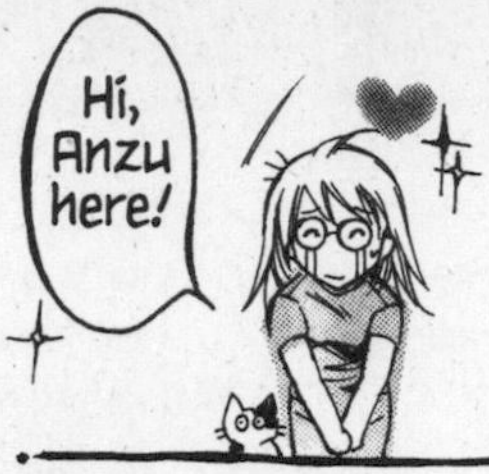
Hi, Anzu here!

I want to say thanks to everybody who gave me a chance to draw this manga:

- Mr. Christopher Hart
- My editor, Tricia Narwani
- Dallas Middaugh
- Marilyn Allen and Colleen O'Shea

Also thanks to everybody who's ever encouraged me and given me their best help!

- My family
- My sister, Luci
- My best friends, Olivia and Yuri

And to the readers for buying this book. Thank you so much!

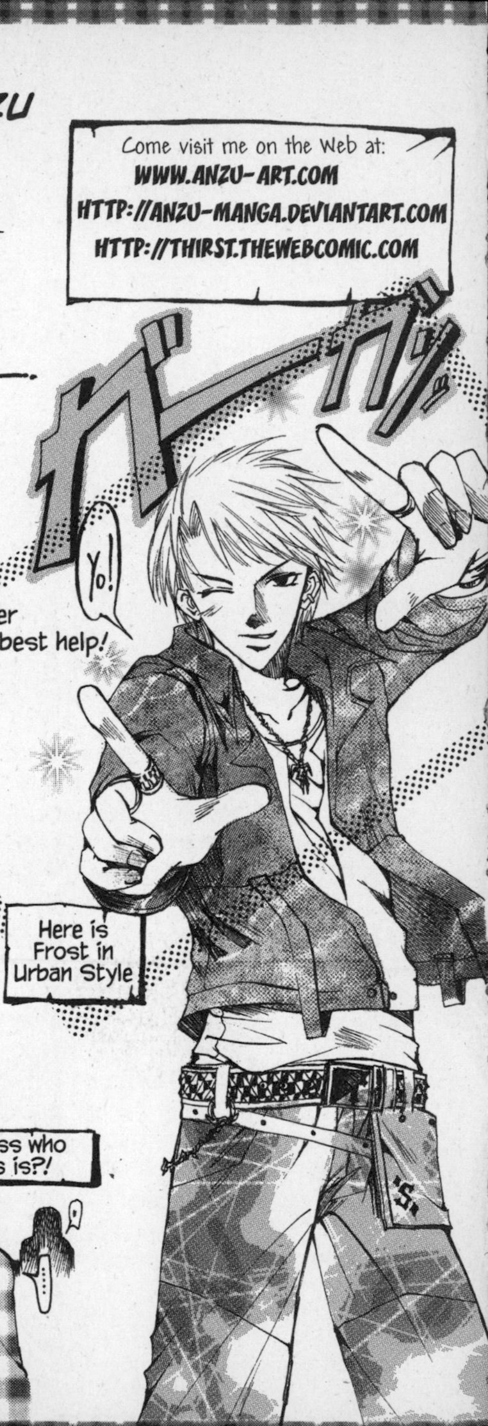
Yo!
Here is Frost in Urban Style

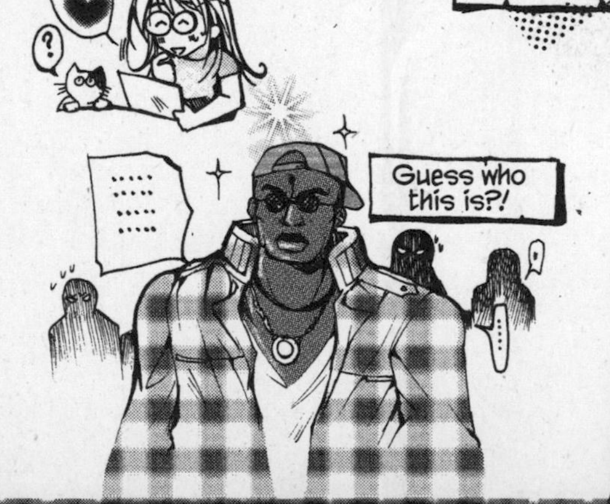
Ha ha ha!
?
Guess who this is?!

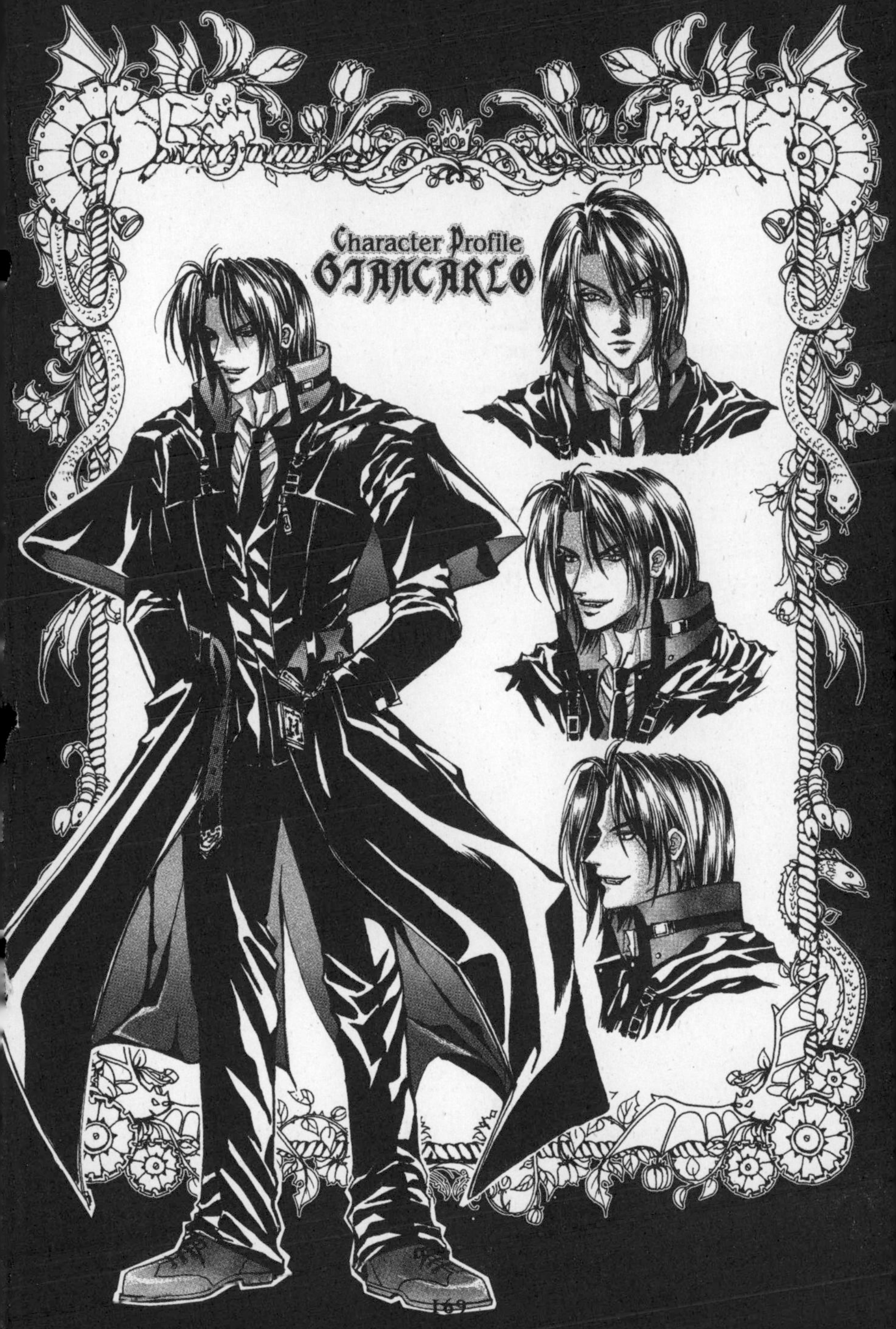
Character Profile
GIANCARLO

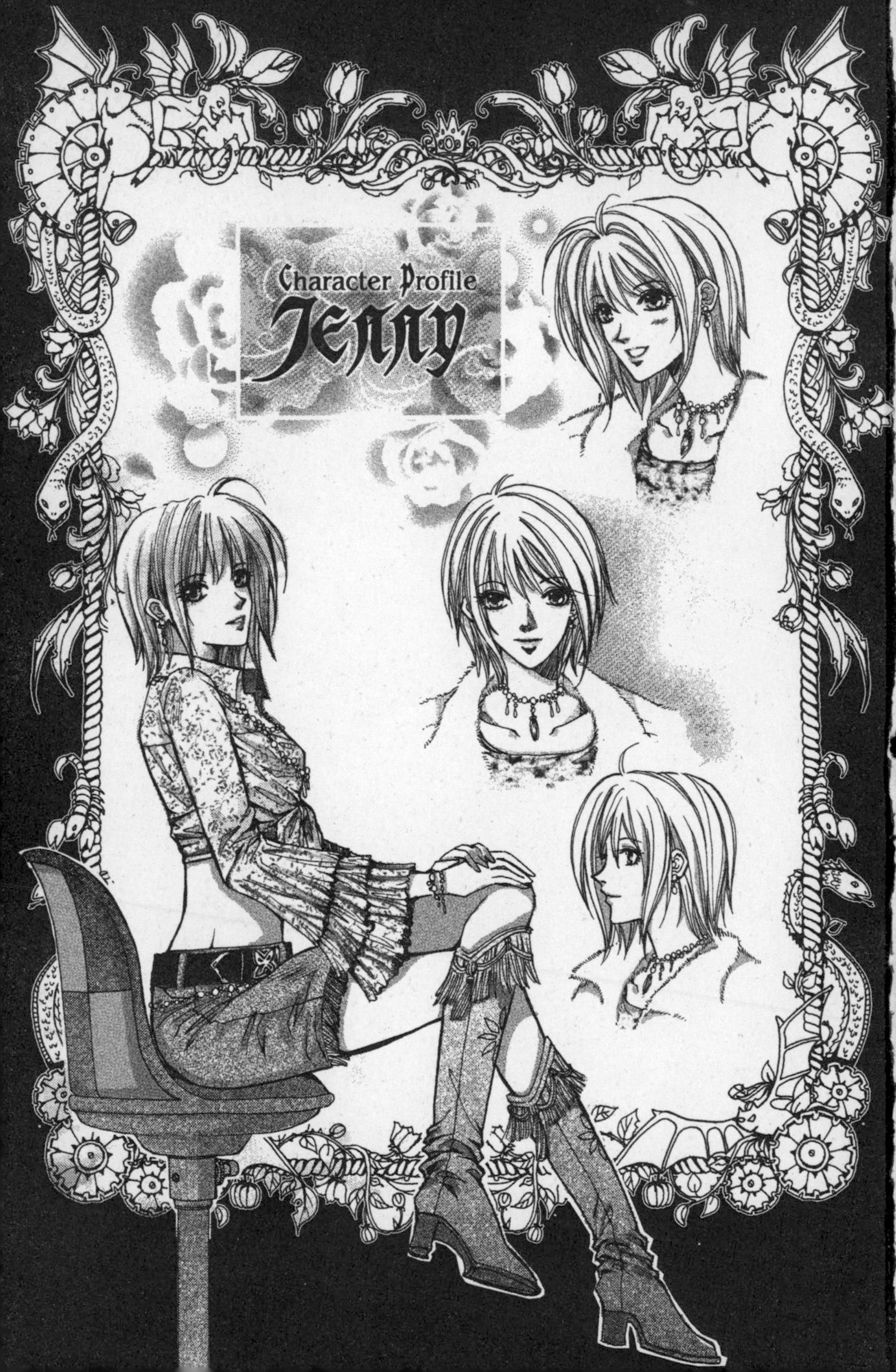
Character Profile
Jenny